Acknowledgements

In writing this book I have had the advice and assistance of a great many individuals who let me impose on their interest or their good nature. I am especially indebted to the following:

To McGeorge Bundy for many stimulating conversations and for criticizing part of the manuscript.

To Carl J. Friedrich for encouraging me in my effort to combine a study of history with that of politics.

To Klaus Epstein for reading almost the entire manuscript and moderating some of my generalizations with his extraordinary historical knowledge.

To Stephen Graubard for reading part of the manuscript and for the stimulus of many an evening's conversation.

To John Conway for his civilized interpretation of the nature of conservatism.

Corrine Lyman has proof-read the entire manuscript and made many exceedingly helpful suggestions. Nancy Jarvi typed the manuscript.

Without my wife's patience and her assistance this book would never have been completed.

I have dedicated the book to Professor William Y. Elliott, to whom I owe more, both intellectually and humanly, than I can ever repay.

Needless to say, the shortcomings of this book are my own.

H.K.

A World Restored

A World Restored

METTERNICH, CASTLEREAGH AND THE PROBLEMS OF PEACE 1812-22

Henry A. Kissinger

HOUGHTON MIFFLIN
COMPANY BOSTON

1973

To

WILLIAM Y. ELLIOTT

FIRST SENTRY PRINTING C

ISBN: 0-395-17229-2 SENTRY

Printed in the United States of America

Contents

I

Introduction

I

It is not surprising that an age faced with the threat of thermonuclear extinction should look nostalgically to periods when diplomacy carried with it less drastic penalties, when wars were limited and catastrophe almost inconceivable. Nor is it strange in such circumstances that the attainment of peace should become the overriding concern or that the need for peace should be thought to provide the impetus for its attainment.

But the attainment of peace is not as easy as the desire for it. Not for nothing is history associated with the figure of Nemesis, which defeats man by fulfilling his wishes in a different form or by answering his prayers too completely. Those ages which in retrospect seem most peaceful were least in search of peace. Those whose quest for it seems unending appear least able to achieve tranquillity. Whenever peace—conceived as the avoidance of war—has been the primary objective of a power or a group of powers, the international system has been at the mercy of the most ruthless member of the international community. Whenever the international order has acknowledged that certain principles could not be compromised even for the sake of peace, stability based on an equilibrium of forces was at least conceivable.

Stability, then, has commonly resulted not from a quest for peace but from a generally accepted legitimacy. "Legitimacy" as here used should not be confused with justice. It means no more than an international agreement about the nature of workable arrangements and about the permissible aims and methods of foreign policy. It implies the acceptance of the framework of the international order by all major powers, at least to the extent that no state is so dissatisfied that, like Germany after the Treaty of Versailles, it expresses its dissatisfaction in a revolutionary foreign policy. A legitimate order does not make conflicts impossible, but it limits their scope. Wars may occur, but they will be fought *in the name of* the existing structure and the peace which follows will be justified as a better expression of the "legitimate", general consensus. Diplomacy in the classic sense, the adjustment of differences through negotiation, is possible only in "legitimate" international orders.

Whenever there exists a power which considers the international order or the manner of legitimizing it oppressive, relations between it and other powers will be revolutionary. In such cases, it is not the adjustment of differences within a given system which will be at issue, but the system itself. Adjustments are possible, but they will be conceived as tactical manœuvres to consolidate positions for the inevitable showdown, or as tools to undermine the morale of the antagonist. To be sure, the motivation of the revolutionary power may well be defensive; it may well be sincere in its protestations of feeling threatened. But the distinguishing feature of a revolutionary power is not that it feels threatened—such feeling is inherent in the nature of international relations based on sovereign states—*but that nothing can reassure it*. Only absolute security—the neutralization of the opponent—is considered a sufficient guarantee, and thus the desire of one power for absolute security means absolute insecurity for all the others.

Diplomacy, the art of restraining the exercise of power, cannot function in such an environment. It is a mistake to assume that diplomacy can always settle international disputes if there is "good faith" and "willingness to come to an agreement". For in a revolutionary international order, each power will seem to its opponent to lack precisely these qualities. Diplomats can still meet but they cannot persuade, for they have ceased to speak the same language. In the absence of an agreement on what constitutes a reasonable demand, diplomatic conferences are occupied with sterile repetitions of basic positions and accusations of bad faith, or allegations of "unreasonableness" and "subversion". They become elaborate stage plays which attempt to attach as yet uncommitted powers to one of the opposing systems.

For powers long accustomed to tranquillity and without experience with disaster, this is a hard lesson to come by. Lulled by a period of stability which had seemed permanent, they find it nearly impossible to take at face value the assertion of the revolutionary power that it means to smash the existing framework. The defenders of the status quo therefore tend to begin by treating the revolutionary power as if its protestations were merely tactical; as if it really accepted the existing legitimacy but overstated its case for bargaining purposes; as if it were motivated by specific grievances to be assuaged by limited concessions. Those who warn against the danger in time are considered alarmists; those who counsel adaptation to circumstance are considered balanced and sane, for they have all the good "reasons" on their side: the arguments accepted as valid in the existing framework. "Appeasement", where it is not a device to gain time, is the result of an inability to come to grips with a policy of unlimited objectives.

But it is the essence of a revolutionary power that it possesses the courage of its convictions, that it is willing, indeed eager, to push its principles to their ultimate conclusion. Whatever else a revolutionary power may achieve therefore, it tends to erode, if not the legitimacy of the international order, at least the restraint with which such an order operates. The characteristic of a stable order is its spontaneity; the essence of a revolutionary situation is its self-consciousness. Principles of obligation in a period of legitimacy are taken so much for granted that they are never talked about, and such periods therefore appear to posterity as shallow and self-righteous. Principles in a revolutionary situation are so central that they are constantly talked about. The very sterility of the effort soon drains them of all meaning, and it is not unusual to find both sides invoking their version of the "true" nature of legitimacy in identical terms. And because in revolutionary situations the contending systems are less concerned with the adjustment of differences than with the subversion of loyalties, diplomacy is replaced either by war or by an armaments race.

II

This work will deal with a decade which throws these problems into sharp relief: the conclusion and the aftermath of the wars of the French Revolution. Few periods illustrate so well the dilemma posed by the appearance of a revolutionary power, the tendency of terms to change their meaning and of even the most familiar relationships to alter their significance. A new philosophy boldly claimed that it would recast the existing structure of obligations, and Revolutionary France set about to give this claim effect. "What can make authority legitimate?" had been defined by Rousseau as the key question of politics and, however they might try, his opponents could not eliminate the question. Henceforth, disputes no longer concerned the adjustment of differences within an accepted framework, but the validity of the framework itself; the political contest had become doctrinal: the balance of power which had operated so intricately throughout the eighteenth century suddenly lost its flexibility and the European equilibrium came to seem an insufficient protection to powers faced by a France which proclaimed the incompatibility of its political maxims with those of the other states. But the half-hearted effort of Prussia and Austria to restore the legitimate ruler of France to his former position only accelerated the revolutionary *élan*. A French army based on conscription, inconceivable to even the most absolutist ruler by the grace of God, defeated the invading armies and overran the Low Countries. And then there appeared a conqueror who sought to translate the moral claims of the French Revolution into reality. Under the impact of Napoleon, there disintegrated not only the system of legitimacy of the eighteenth century, but with it the physical safeguards which, to contemporaries at least, seemed the prerequisite of stability.

The Napoleonic Empire for all its extent demonstrated however the tenuousness of a conquest not accepted by the subjugated peoples. Although Napoleon had succeeded in overthrowing the existing concept of legitimacy, he could not replace it with an alternative. Europe was unified from the Niemen to the Bay of Biscay, but force had replaced obligation, the material achievements of the French Revolution had outrun their moral base. Europe was united, but only negatively, in its opposition to a power felt as foreign (which is the surest indication of the absence of legitimacy), in a consciousness of "otherness" which was soon endowed with moral claims and became the basis of nationalism.

When Napoleon was defeated in Russia, the problem of constructing a legitimate order confronted Europe in its most concrete form. For opposition can create a wide consensus, perhaps even the widest attainable one, but its components, united by what they do not like, may be greatly at odds about what should replace it. It is for this reason that the year 1812 is the starting point of our discussion. However one conceives it—and it has been given a variety of interpretations ranging from the moral vindication of national self-determination to the tragic destiny of the Hero—this year marked the moment when it became evident that Europe was not to be organized by force. But the alternative was not nearly so apparent. It was clear that there were new forces loose in the world clamouring for popular participation in government. But it seemed equally evident that these forces had been responsible for a quarter-century of turmoil. The French Revolution had dealt a perhaps mortal blow to the divine right of kings; yet the representatives of this very doctrine were called upon to end the generation of bloodshed. In these circumstances what is surprising is not how imperfect was the settlement that emerged, but how sane; not how "reactionary" according to the self-righteous doctrines of nineteenth-century historiography, but how balanced. It may not have fulfilled all the hopes of an idealistic generation, but it gave this generation something perhaps more precious: a period of stability which permitted their hopes to be realized without a major war or a permanent revolution. And our account will end in 1822, when the international order which emerged out of the revolutionary conflict assumed the form it was to retain for over a generation. The period of stability which ensued was the best proof that a "legitimate" order had been constructed, an order accepted by all the major powers, so that henceforth they sought adjustment within its framework rather than in its overthrow.

That Europe rescued stability from seeming chaos was primarily the result of the work of two great men: of Castlereagh, the British Foreign Secretary, who negotiated the international settlement, and of Austria's minister, Metternich, who legitimized it. This is not to say that an international order emerged from personal intuition. Every statesman must attempt to reconcile what is considered just with what is considered possible. What is considered just depends on the domestic structure of his state; what is possible depends on its resources, geographic position and determination, and on the resources, determination and domestic structure of other states. Thus Castlereagh, secure in the knowledge of England's insular safety, tended to oppose only *overt* aggression. But Metternich, the statesman of a power situated in the centre of the Continent, sought above all to *forestall* upheavals. Convinced of the unassailability of its domestic institutions, the insular power developed a doctrine of "non-interference" in the domestic affairs of other states. Oppressed by the vulnerability of its domestic structure in an age of nationalism, the polyglot Austro-Hungarian empire insisted on a generalized right of interference to defeat social unrest wherever it occurred. Because Britain was threatened only if Europe fell under the domination of a single power, Castlereagh was primarily concerned with constructing a balance of forces. Because the balance of power only limits the scope of aggression but does not prevent it, Metternich sought to buttress the equilibrium by developing a doctrine of legitimacy and establishing himself as its custodian.

Each failed as he succeeded: Castlereagh in making Britain a permanent part of the concert of Europe; Metternich in preserving the principle of legitimacy he had striven so hard to establish. But their achievements were not inconsiderable: a period of peace lasting almost a hundred years, a stability so pervasive that it may have contributed to disaster. For in the long interval of peace the sense of the tragic was lost; it was forgotten that states could die, that upheavals could be irretrievable, that fear could become the means of social cohesion. The hysteria of joy which swept over Europe at the outbreak of the First World War was the symptom of a fatuous age, but also of a secure one. It revealed a millennial faith; a hope for a world which had all the blessings of the Edwardian age made all the more agreeable by the absence of armament races and of the fear of war. What minister who declared war in August 1914, would not have recoiled with horror had he known the shape of the world in 1918, not to speak of the present?[1]

That such a world was inconceivable in 1914 is a testimony to the work of the statesmen with whom this book deals.

[1] One who had such an intuition and did so recoil was, of course, the British Foreign Secretary, Lord Grey.

II

The Continental Statesman

I

IN the task of constructing a new international order which Napoleon's defeat in Russia so unexpectedly thrust on Europe, the problems of Austria took on an almost symbolic quality, both for geographic and historical reasons. Situated in the centre of Europe, amidst potentially hostile powers, with no natural frontiers and a polyglot composition of Germans, Slavs, Magyars and Italians, Austria was the seismograph of Europe. It was certain to be the first victim of any major upheaval because war could only increase the centrifugal elements of a state whose sole bond of union was the common crown. And because Austria's need for stability was so great and because law is the expression of the status quo, Austria stood for the sense of limit and the importance of the equilibrium, for the necessity of law and the sanctity of treaties: "Austria," said Talleyrand, "is the Chamber of Peers of Europe."

But even more than its geographic location, its domestic structure symbolized the dilemmas of Europe. Until the end of the eighteenth century, the Austrian Empire had been among the most vigorous of the European states. As late as 1795 the Prussian patriot, Stein, could still favourably compare the cohesiveness and prosperity of the Austrian monarchy with that of Prussia. But now with Russian armies sweeping westward, came the first rumblings that were to transform the Austrian Empire into the "prison of nations". Not that its system of government grew more oppressive, only that its legitimacy came increasingly to be questioned. For a prison is not only a physical but also a psychological state. It would have occurred to no one in the eighteenth century that the Habsburg Emperor was a "foreigner" merely because he represented a German dynasty. Because in the nineteenth century this was emerging as a truism and because the defensive makes adaptation difficult, Austria's policy was destined to become increasingly inflexible. The Austrian

Empire had not changed, but history was beginning to pass it by.

The tattered remnants of the Grande Armée which appeared in Central Europe in the winter of 1812 therefore represented to Austria an augury both of success and of danger: of success, for with the collapse of Napoleon's army, Austria for the first time in three years would be able to conduct a truly independent policy, a policy not limited by the consciousness that survival depended on the will of one man; and of danger, for it was still not clear what would emerge out of the chaos of the disintegrating French power. The new doctrines of nationalism and rationalized administration could not but be dissolving for so intricate, indeed so subtle, a structure as this last survivor of the feudal period. Nor was it yet certain whether the pressure from the West was not about to be replaced by a similar threat from the East. How to avoid both impotence and dissolution? How to achieve both peace and proportion, both victory and legitimacy?

When the fate of empires is at stake, the convictions of their statesmen are the medium for survival. And success depends on the correspondence of these convictions with the special requirements of the state. It was Austria's destiny that in its years of crisis it was guided by a man who epitomized its very essence; it was its destiny and not its good fortune, for as in Greek tragedy, the success of Clemens von Metternich made inevitable the ultimate collapse of the state he had fought so long to preserve.

Like the state he represented, Metternich was a product of an age in the process of being transcended. He was born in the eighteenth century of which Talleyrand was to say that nobody who lived after the French Revolution would ever know how sweet and gentle life could be. And the certitude of the time of his youth never left Metternich. Contemporaries might sneer at his invocation of the maxims of sound reason, at his facile philosophizing and polished epigrams. They did not understand that it was an accident of history which projected Metternich into a revolutionary struggle so foreign to his temperament. For like the century that formed him, his style was adapted better to the manipulation of factors treated as given than to a contest of will, better to achievement through proportion than through scale. He was a Rococo figure, complex, finely carved, all surface, like an intricately cut prism. His face was delicate but without depth, his conversation brilliant but without ultimate seriousness. Equally at home in the salon and in the Cabinet, graceful and facile, he was the *beau-ideal* of the eighteenth-century aristocracy which justified itself not by its truth but by its existence. And if he never came to terms with the new age it was not because he failed to understand its seriousness but because he disdained it. Therein too his fate was the fate of Austria.

It was this man who for over a generation ruled Austria, and often Europe, with the same methods of almost nonchalant manipulation he had learned in his youth. But no amount of deviousness could obscure the fact that he was engaged in a revolutionary contest and this imparted an unintended tenseness to Metternich's most subtle manœuvres. He might achieve victory but not comprehension and for this reason he came to use the proudest claim of the Enlightenment, the belief in the universality of the maxims of reason, with increasing self-consciousness as a weapon in the revolutionary struggle. Had Metternich been born fifty years earlier, he would still have been a conservative, but there would have been no need to write pedantic disquisitions about the nature of conservatism. He would have moved through the drawing-rooms of the fashionable world with his undeniable charm and grace, subtly and aloofly conducting his diplomacy with the circuitousness which is a symbol of certainty, of a world in which everybody understands intangibles in the same manner. He would still have played at philosophy, for this was the vogue of the eighteenth century, but he would not have considered it a tool of policy. But, in a century of seemingly permanent revolution, philosophy was the only means of rescuing universality from contingent claims. It was for this reason that Metternich fought so insistently against the identification of his name with his period, an attitude seemingly so inconsistent with his vanity. If there was a "Metternich system", his achievements would be personal, his battle meaningless. "To individualize an idea," he insisted, "leads to dangerous conclusions, as if an individual could be a cause; a wrong conception for when it does apply it indicates that a cause does not exist but is dissimulated."[1] It is the dilemma of conservatism that it must fight revolution anonymously, by what it *is*, not by what it *says*.

So it came about that Metternich in his never-ending battle against revolution went back to the doctrines of the age in which he had been

[1] Metternich, Clemens, *Aus Metternich's Nachgelassenen Papieren*, 8 Vols. Edited by Alfons von Klinkowström. (Vienna, 1880). Vol. VIII, p. 186. Henceforward referred to as N.P.

brought up, but interpreted them with an inflexibility which had been unnecessary when they were still taken for granted and which distorted their essence in application. He was still of the generation to whom the "great clockwork" or the "golden age" was more than an idle dream. There was a fitness in the universe which corresponded to man's noblest aspirations; a well-ordered mechanism the understanding of which insured success and whose laws could not be violated with impunity: "States, just as human beings, often transgress laws, the only difference is the severity of their penalty."[1] "Society has its laws just as nature and man. It is with old institutions as with old men, they can never be young again. . . . This is the way of the social order and it cannot be different because it is the law of nature . . . the moral world has its storms just like the material one."[2] "One can not cover the world with ruins without crushing man beneath them."[3] Metternich used these truisms of eighteenth-century philosophy to oppose revolution and liberalism, not because they were wicked, but because they were unnatural, not only because he did not wish to live in the world his opponents attempted to create, but because that world was doomed to failure. Revolution was an assertion of will and of power, but the essence of existence was proportion, its expression was law, and its mechanism an equilibrium.

For these reasons the conservative statesman was the supreme realist and his opponents the "visionaries". "I am a man of prose," Metternich insisted in his political testament, "and not of poetry."[4] "My point of departure is the quiet contemplation of the affairs of this world, not those of the other of which I know nothing and which are the object of faith which is in strict opposition to knowledge. . . . In the social world . . . one must act cold-bloodedly based on observation and without hatred or prejudice. . . . I was born to make history not to write novels and if I *guess* correctly this is because I *know*. Invention is the enemy of history which knows only discoveries, and only that which exists can be discovered."[5] This was the myth of the philosopher-king, the ideal eighteenth-century ruler, who stood above the plane where personal feelings reign, cool, composed, superior. Statesmanship was the science of the interests of

[1] N.P., I, p. 35.
[2] N.P. III, p. 322.
[3] N.P. VIII, p. 184.
[4] N.P. VII, p. 635.
[5] N.P. VIII, p. 184.

states,[1] and subject to laws entirely analogous to the laws of the physical world. The statesman was a philosopher who understood these maxims, who performed his tasks but reluctantly, for they deflected him from the source of the only real enjoyment, the contemplation of truth;[2] he was responsible only to his conscience and to history—to the former because it contained his vision of truth, to the latter because it provided the only test of its validity.

The reaction against Metternich's smug self-satisfaction and rigid conservatism has tended for over a century now to take the form of denying the reality of his accomplishments. But a man who came to dominate every coalition in which he participated, who was considered by two foreign monarchs as more trustworthy than their own ministers, who for three years was in effect Prime Minister of Europe, such a man could not be of mean consequence. To be sure, the successes he liked to ascribe to the moral superiority of his maxims were more often due to the extraordinary skill of his diplomacy. His genius was instrumental, not creative; he excelled at manipulation, not construction. Trained in the school of eighteenth-century cabinet diplomacy, he preferred the subtle manœuvre to the frontal attack, while his rationalism frequently made him mistake a well-phrased manifesto for an accomplished action. Napoleon said of him that he confused policy with intrigue, and Hardenberg, the envoy of Hanover at Vienna, wrote the following analysis of Metternich's diplomatic methods at the height of the crisis of 1812: "Endowed with a high opinion of the superiority of his ability . . . he loves finesse in politics and considers it essential. Since he does not have sufficient energy to mobilize the resources of his country . . . he attempts to substitute cunning for strength and character. . . . It would suit him best if a fortunate accident—the death of Napoleon or great successes of Russia—were to create a situation where he could let Austria play an important role."[3] Friedrich von Gentz, for long Metternich's closest associate, has left probably the best capsule description of Metternich's methods and personality: "Not a man of

[1] N.P. I, p. 33.

[2] See N.P. III, p. 342, or N.P. III, p. 357, among many examples. For a full discussion of Metternich's political thought see Chapter XI.

[3] Oncken, Wilhelm, *Oesterreich und Preussen im Befreiungskriege*, 2 Vols. (Berlin, 1880). Vol. II, p. 88. This report, written to the Prince Regent of Great Britain (who was, of course, also Elector of Hanover and eager to align Austria against Napoleon), is perhaps as significant for the light it throws on the frustration which Metternich's careful machinations inspired in some of his contemporaries as for its comment on Metternich's methods.

strong passions and of bold measures; not a genius but a great talent; cool, calm, imperturbable and calculator *par excellence*."[1]

This, then, was the statesman to whom Austria's fate was entrusted in 1812: doctrinaire, but in the universalist manner of the eighteenth century; devious, because the very certainty of his convictions made him extremely flexible in his choice of means; matter-of-fact and aloof; coldly pursuing the art of statecraft. His characteristic quality was tact, the sensibility to nuance. Such a man might have dominated the eighteenth century, but he was formidable in any age. A mediocre strategist but a great tactician, he was a master of the set battle in periods when the framework was given or the objectives imposed from the outside. Such a period was the year 1812, and the issue for Metternich was not so much the liberation of Europe as the restoration of the equilibrium both moral and physical.

II

Metternich, the most Austrian statesman, did not see Austria until his thirteenth year and did not live there until his seventeenth. Born in the Rhineland, educated in Strasburg and Mainz, and raised in Brussels where his father was Governor-General of the Low Countries, Metternich had the typical upbringing of the eighteenth-century aristocrat. Cosmopolitan and rationalist, he was always more at home in the French language than in the German. But however typical Metternich was of the eighteenth-century aristocracy, he did not follow their wishful evaluation of the French Revolution. The wars of Napoleon did not seem to him like the wars of the eighteenth century, set battles with finite objectives which left the basic structure of obligations unaffected. Nor did he believe it possible to satisfy the conqueror by compromise, to moderate him by concession or to obligate him by alliance. "All nations have made the mistake," he wrote in 1807, "to attach to a treaty with France the value of a peace, without immediately preparing again for war. No peace is possible with a revolutionary system, whether with a Robespierre who declares war on chateaux or a Napoleon who declares war on Powers."[2] And this belief was reinforced by his conviction that the principle of solidarity of states superseded that of revolution:

[1] Srbik, Heinrich von, *Metternich der Staatsmann und der Mensch*, 2 Vols. (Munich, 1925). Vol. I, p. 144.

[2] N.P. III, p. 147.

"Isolated states exist only as the abstractions of so-called philosophers. In the society of states each state has interests . . . which connect it with the others. The great axioms of political science derive from the recognition of the true interests of *all* states; it is in the general interests that the guarantee of existence is to be found, while particular interests—the cultivation of which is considered political wisdom by restless and short-sighted men—have only a secondary importance. . . . Modern history demonstrates the application of the principle of solidarity and equilibrium . . . and of the united efforts of states against the supremacy of one power in order to force a return to the common law. . . . What then becomes of egotistical policy, of the policy of fantasy and of miserable gain?"[1]

But in 1801, when Metternich began his diplomatic career, the solidarity of states seemed unattainable, for "nothing is more difficult to harmonize than eternal and incontestable principles and a system of conduct adopted in direct opposition to them".[2] There remained only the task of creating a balance of power not, to be sure, in order to guarantee universal peace but to achieve a tolerable armistice. Metternich's first diplomatic reports, when, at the age of twenty-eight, he was appointed Austrian envoy in Saxony, reveal the conception of this equilibrium which was to guide his policy throughout his life: the power of France must be reduced; Austria and Prussia must forget their recent past, the wars fought for the possession of Silesia. Not competition but co-operation was their natural policy. An equilibrium was possible only through a strong central Europe backed by England, for the interests of a power exclusively commercial and of a power entirely continental could never lead to rivalry.[3]

But an equilibrium based on considerations of power is the most difficult of all to establish, particularly in a revolutionary period following a long peace. Lulled by the memory of stability, states tend to seek security in inactivity and to mistake impotence for lack of provocation. The conqueror is to be tamed by reason and perhaps by collaboration; by policies, in short, which cannot conceive mortal threats or total destruction. Coalitions against revolutions have usually come about only at the end of a long series of betrayals and upheavals, for the powers which represent legitimacy and the status

[1] N.P. I, p. 34.
[2] N.P. II, p. 236.
[3] N.P. II, p. 4f.

quo cannot "know" that their antagonist is not amenable to "reason" until he has demonstrated it. And he will not have demonstrated it until the international system is already overturned.

Metternich was to experience this when he was sent in 1804 to negotiate an alliance with Prussia. He found a court which saw in the preparation for self-defence the most certain provocation for war and in concerted action the seed of universal doom. Almost alone among his contemporaries, Metternich understood the weakness of Prussia, still surrounded by the nimbus of Frederick the Great, but demoralized by a long period of peace. "There exists," he wrote in his whimsical fashion, "a conspiracy of mediocrities . . . united by the common terror of any decisive action. . . . There is nobody to remind the king that his army might perhaps be utilized to greater advantage on the field of battle than on the plains of Berlin and Potsdam. The Prussian monarchy which has tripled in size since the death of Frederick II (The Great) has declined in real strength. Frederick William III will certainly not use a language from the centre of his vast dominions which was not foreign to Frederick II from the walls of a capital which never ceased being an armed camp."[1]

The construction of the equilibrium therefore depended not merely on strength but on the resolution to use it. If the fear of France prevented joint action, perhaps the fear of Russia could create it. "We shall conquer Prussia only in Russia," Metternich said, and began a diplomatic campaign which brought Russian troops to the Prussian borders with an ultimatum of alliance or war. But the King of Prussia refused to accept so patent an infraction of the "normal relations" of states and threatened to resist by force of arms. War was averted only by the precipitation of Napoleon, who marched troops through a section of Prussian territory and thereby brought on himself the wrath of Frederick William's outraged probity which he had never been able to earn as a conqueror bent on dominating Europe. Everything seemed won. A Prussian negotiator was sent to Vienna to make final arrangements for a treaty of alliance; the Prussian army moved towards the flanks of the French forces invading Bohemia, Russian troops were traversing Poland. A decisive defeat for Napoleon seemed in the making.

But timid men are more likely to be moved to trepidation than to daring in the face of great opportunities. The traditions of a century

[1] Oncken, II, p. 68f.

of uninterrupted expansion, the "rules" of Cabinet diplomacy according to which the maximum bargain had to be struck in the hour of greatest need, combined to cause Prussia to delay its final commitment. It is the essence of mediocrity that it prefers the tangible advantage to the intangible gain in position. Thus Prussia chose this precise moment to haggle over a military frontier along the Weser and to advance a proposal of armed mediation on "reasonable" terms to obtain one more proof of Napoleon's perfidy.[1] In vain did Metternich preach his lesson of the equilibrium, of security based on the relations of states and not on territorial extent; in vain did he inquire how a power could mediate on its own behalf.[2] This was not a problem of logic. While Prussia hesitated, the French army wheeled south and defeated the Austrians and Russians at Austerlitz.

Again a point was reached where the theory of limited wars counselled peace, while the reality of revolutionary conflict indicated perseverance. Metternich's struggle was now with his own government. He insisted that Napoleon's seeming omnipotence was but the reflection of the disunity of his opponents, that the combined Allied armies still far outnumbered Napoleon's. He urged that the defeat be frankly avowed, but that it serve as the moral basis for a renewed effort.[3] But if Prussia used the crisis to clinch her gains, Austria saw in it an opportunity to trim her losses and negotiated a separate peace. Meanwhile, Napoleon's army deployed against Prussia, not yet to destroy her, but to intimidate her into becoming an accomplice by incorporating Hanover and thus isolating herself from Great Britain. And the Russian armies returned to Poland. "One hundred thousand men have defeated five times their number," Metternich exclaimed. "Where is manna? When will God appear from the wings?" And he added that he was in a state of conditional despair, but that only death, which destroyed all hopes, could make his despair unconditional.[4] Little wonder that henceforth Metternich sought to delay the Austrian commitment until after that of all of its potential allies; that he distrusted protestations of loyalty based on promises of future fulfilment; that he constructed alliances only after a period of a deliberation that seemed maddening to those eager for

[1] It is interesting to note that armed mediation was precisely Metternich's policy in 1813. See Chapters IV and V. Prussian historians have argued that armed mediation was designed to give Prussia an opportunity to mobilize her army.

[2] N.P. II, p. 64.

[3] N.P. II, p. 92f.

[4] Srbik, *Metternich* I, p. 111.

Austrian co-operation, but which was essential to test the moral strength of the coalition.

III

It is the nature of statesmen conducting a policy of petty advantage to seek in vacillation a substitute for action. A policy which lets itself be influenced by events—which in the formal phrase "awaits developments"—is likely to seek the remedy against a decision recognized as erroneous in adopting its extreme opposite, without considering the possibility of intermediary solutions. So Prussia, whose hesitations had largely caused the disaster of 1806, suddenly awakened to the realization that, despite the incorporation of Hanover, its relative position had been weakened and foolhardily plunged into the war with France it had so desperately attempted to avoid during the previous year. But Napoleon was not to be defeated in single combat. Prussia suffered at Jena and Auerstädt the fate of Austria at Austerlitz. Once more promised Russian support proved illusory. After a Russian defeat at Friedland, Napoleon and Alexander met on a raft in the river Niemen at Tilsit, there to complete the division of the world.

But the final overthrow of the existing structure paradoxically seemed to restore Metternich's confidence in eventual triumph. For now the incommensurability between Napoleon's material and moral base was apparent, the intermediary powers had been eliminated, the time of unlimited victories gained by limited wars was over. Victory henceforth would depend on domestic strength, and Napoleon, having failed to establish a principle of obligation to maintain his conquests, would find his power sapped by the constant need for the application of force. Metternich had in the meantime become ambassador to Paris, from where he sent a flood of advice, deferential and subtle, respectful but unremitting, for domestic reorganization, for continuing military reform, for evading Napoleon's suggestions of disarmament, for strengthening national cohesion. "Public opinion," wrote Metternich in 1808, "is one of the most powerful weapons, which like religion penetrates the most hidden corners where administrative measures lose their influence; to despise public opinion is like despising moral principles. . . . [Public opinion] requires a cult all its own. . . . Posterity will hardly believe that we regarded silence as an effective weapon in this, the century of words."[1] And he summed up his goals in an eloquent dispatch written soon after the news of Tilsit in 1807: "A day will arrive through the wisdom of our government, when three hundred thousand men will play the first role in a Europe of universal anarchy; at one of those moments which always follow great usurpations. Nobody can predict the date save that nothing delays it except the life of a single individual who has not taken any steps to prevent the inevitable chaos."[2] Force might conquer the world but it could not legitimize itself. It was Austria's task to preserve her integrity as the repository of all that remained of the old principles and the old forms, and this in the course of time was bound to bring Austria powerful allies.[3]

Napoleon's war in Spain seemed to confirm Metternich's expectations. For the first time, Napoleon was confronted by an enemy which did not surrender after a lost battle and the resources of which did not augment those of France. The early reverses of Napoleon's replacement army shattered the myth of his invincibility. "We have learned a great secret," Metternich wrote in 1808, "Napoleon has but one army, the Grande Armée and French recruits are no better than those of other nations." He took it for granted that Spain would be defeated militarily, but that it would not be pacified. Since Napoleon's character would not let him think of withdrawing, Spain would remain a drain on French resources of men and material. Even more important was the moral gain. Austerlitz had demonstrated that it was risky to be Napoleon's enemy; Jena, that it was disastrous to remain neutral; but Spain proved beyond doubt that it was fatal to be Napoleon's friend.

What, then, were the alternatives? To be oneself, Metternich argued, and not to lose a moment in repairing past losses.[4] There was no doubt that Napoleon aimed at Austria's destruction for, both by its extent and the principles it represented, its existence was incompatible with his universal domination.[5] But there was a limit to usurpations as Spain had demonstrated. A resolute opponent, moreover, would now find allies even within France, in all the individuals satiated by glory and eager to enjoy its rewards undisturbed; above

[1] N.P. II, p. 192. Compare this with Metternich's later utterances, for example N.P. III, p. 440, or N.P. VIII, p. 238.

[2] N.P. II, p. 122f.

[3] Srbik, *Metternich*, I, p. 129.

[4] N.P. II, 248f.

[5] N.P. II, 178f.

all, in Talleyrand and Fouché, whom Metternich described as being like sailors eager to mutiny against a daring pilot, but not until the ship has struck some rocks.[1] Any war outside the natural limits of the Rhine, the Alps, and the Pyrenees was no longer the war of France but the war of Napoleon, Metternich quoted Talleyrand as saying.

But Metternich did not look to allies merely within France. Once more he resurrected his plan of an Austro-Russian understanding. He proposed that the Tsar be approached directly with a frank explanation of Austria's determination and difficulties, coupled with a specific proposal of military co-operation.[2] He explained to the Russian Foreign Minister, Roumazoff, then in Paris, how unnatural the alliance of Russia and France was and how impossible a durable peace in a Europe without a strong centre.[3] The homilies on the nature of the equilibrium proved unavailing, however. In 1809, as in 1805 and 1806, Russia stood by passively while the conqueror advanced to its borders.

So Austria found itself engaged in 1809 in a war for survival, a war fought, for the first and last time in Metternich's period, in the name of national identity and by an army based on conscription. Even Metternich was swept along by the national enthusiasm, so foreign to his cosmopolitan outlook. "[Napoleon] bases his hopes for success," he wrote to his chief, Stadion, "on the slowness of our movements, on the repose which we will take after our first success, or the discouragement . . . and the paralysis which will follow our first defeat. . . . Let us therefore adopt his principles. Let us not consider ourselves victorious until the day *after* the battle, nor defeated until four days later. . . . Let us always carry the sword in one hand and the olive branch in the other, always ready to negotiate but negotiating only while advancing. . . . A man cannot run the same risks as an ancient Empire. . . . We are, for the first time *strong in ourselves*, let us act it . . . let us never forget that the year 1809 is either the end of an old era or the beginning of a new one."[4]

But it was to be neither. There may be a fitness of things in the universe, but it does not operate in a finite time and certainly not in a brief one. The finest army ever created by Austria was defeated and

[1] N.P. II, 268f.
[2] See, for example, N.P. II, 171f., 286f.
[3] N.P. II, 270f.
[4] N.P. II, 295f.

the Emperor, unwilling to risk everything, sued for peace. Never again, under Metternich, was Austria to attempt solitary efforts or to stake its fate on the moral disposition of its people. The war of 1809 was thus neither the end nor the beginning of an era, but rather a turning-point and a continuation. It was a turning-point, for it confirmed the already powerful hesitation of the Emperor to build further on the support of the polyglot nationalities composing his Empire. Henceforth, he was to seek security in stability, in the least possible change of existing institutions. And it was the continuation of a mode of government which had lost its *élan* and its self-confidence, which knew its limits but hardly its goals, particularly in domestic matters, and which hedged its risks by the careful involvement of the largest possible number of allies. The foundations of the "Metternich system" were laid in 1809.

This was the year, too, when Emperor Franz asked Metternich to become his Foreign Minister, a post he was not to relinquish for thirty-nine years. It was symbolic of the lessons Austria drew from the war, that the man who more than any other had urged it now became the architect of peace, who would repair by cunning, patience, and manipulation what had been lost by total commitment.

IV

A state defeated in war and menaced by dissolution has two broad choices: open opposition or persuasion. If it treats the defeat as a reflection on its national resolution but not on its strength, it will attempt to make up for its deficiency on the battlefield by a greater mobilization of its resources, a higher development of its morale, until another and more favourable opportunity permits it to try again the contest in arms. This was the attitude of Austria after 1805. Or it may become convinced of its physical impotence and strive to save its national substance by adaptation to the victor. This is not necessarily a heroic policy, although in certain circumstances it may be the most heroic of all. To co-operate, without losing one's soul, to assist without sacrificing one's identity, to work for deliverance in the guise of bondage and under enforced silence, what harder test of moral toughness exists?

This was, in any case, the policy of Austria after 1809, imposed, at least in part, by its physical impotence. For the peace deprived Austria of one-third of its territories, its defensive bastions and its outlet to the sea. Along the Adriatic coast the new French province of Illyria foreshadowed later designs on Hungary while the Duchy of Warsaw to the north represented a mortgage on Austria's good behaviour. And the Empire was financially so ruined that Napoleon did not even limit its army, well aware that Austria did not possess sufficient resources to maintain a substantial force. "If after 1805," Metternich told the Emperor in his first statement of policy, "Austria was still strong enough to work for the general deliverance . . . it will now be forced to seek its security in adaptation to the French system. I need hardly repeat how little we fit into this system so contrary to all principles of a rightly conceived policy. . . . But never again can we think of resistance without Russian help. That vacillating court may awaken more quickly when it can no longer earn an exclusive merit through its miserable policy. . . . Only one escape is left to us: to conserve our strength for better days, to work for our preservation with gentler means—and not to look back."[1]

All the elements of Metternich's policy are united here: the conviction of the incompatibility of a system of conquest with an organized international community, the distrust of Russia, the failure of alliances, the flexibility of tactics for the achievement of a goal which, because it reflected universal laws, was none the less inevitable for seeming so remote. Metternich was proposing a policy which today we would call "collaboration". It is a policy which can only be carried out by a state certain of its moral strength or overwhelmed by the consciousness of moral impotence. It is a policy which places a peculiar strain on the domestic principles of obligation for it can never be legitimized by its real motives. Its success depends on its appearance of sincerity, on the ability, as Metternich once said, of seeming the dupe without being it. To show one's purpose is to court disaster; to succeed too completely is to invite disintegration. In such periods the knave and the hero, the traitor and the statesman are distinguished, not by their acts, but by their motives. At what stage collaboration damages the national substance, at what point it becomes an excuse for the easy way out, these are questions that can be resolved only by people who have lived through the ordeal, not by abstract speculation. Collaboration can be carried out successfully only by a social organism of great cohesiveness and high morale, because it presupposes a degree of confidence in the leadership which makes treason seem inconceivable. The moral strength of Austria,

[1] N.P. II, p. 311f.

on which Metternich counted to achieve victory in war, failed in this objective; but it saved Austria in a period of humiliating peace.

This, then, was Metternich's policy: to keep all options open, to retain a maximum freedom of action, but to limit all commitments by the need to win French confidence. Austria joined the Continental System against England, but it never broke relations with it. Metternich remained in close touch with Hardenberg, the envoy of Hanover and thus indirectly of the Prince Regent of Great Britain. He went so far as to express the hope—through Hardenberg—that relations between Austria and Britain would not only remain friendly but extend to mutual advice.[1] Correct relations were maintained with Russia, but it was made clear that French forbearance, not Russian assistance, was considered the basis of Austrian policy. The condition of Austrian survival was a relaxation of French pressure. But pressure would not be relaxed and negotiations would be meaningless without a framework of confidence. And confidence presupposed a principle to which Napoleon found it possible to agree, which identified the interests of Austria and France, at least to a certain extent. How to reconcile the claims of universal domination with those of equilibrium, of the state to which every limit was a challenge, and of the Empire for which limitation was the condition of survival?

There was one weak point in the Napoleonic structure, however, which Metternich had never tired of pointing out: that legitimacy depends on acceptance, not imposition; that for all its conquests the fate of the French Empire depended on the life of one man. Metternich, therefore, appealed to the sense of insecurity of the parvenu to create the only bond which Napoleon would recognize as a "claim". He bartered legitimacy for time, a hope for permanence against a promise of survival. He arranged for the marriage of the daughter of Emperor Franz, the Apostolic Majesty and the last Holy Roman Emperor, whose house had ruled for five hundred years, with Napoleon, the Corsican, who had ruled for ten. "Whenever Napoleon destroys something," Metternich wrote to the Emperor in 1810, "he speaks of guarantees. This expression in its usual sense is hardly compatible with his actions. A guarantee commonly rests on the state of political relationships. . . . But Napoleon does not appreciate the political aspect of guarantees; he aims at *reality*, at a surety. Thus

[1] Oncken, II, p. 52. See also Luckwaldt, *Oesterreich und Die Anfaenge Des Befreiungskrieges*, (Berlin, 1898), p. 31.

each usurpation becomes for him a guarantee *of his strength* and of his existence. . . . In this sense he motivates each overthrow of a throne . . . by the semblance of self-defence. . . . In the marriage with the daughter of Your Majesty Napoleon found a guarantee which he had sought in vain . . . in the overthrow of the Austrian throne."[1] Thus, Metternich transcended the chasm between opposing legitimacies which characterizes revolutionary situations, by boldly using Napoleon's concept of legitimacy—the only one he recognized—against him. And just as Napoleon's conquests were due to the fact that his opponents could not conceive a policy of unlimited objectives, so Napoleon's final overthrow was caused by his own inability to comprehend the instability of dynastic relations.

Metternich did not wait long to take advantage of his new position. He visited Paris in order to help the new Empress acclimatize herself—and to divine Napoleon's next move. He obtained very few concessions: a slight reduction in the Austrian indemnity, the permission to float a loan in Belgium and to mediate between the Pope and Napoleon. But he left with an invaluable conviction: that a French attack on Russia was inevitable, that it would probably occur in the summer of 1812, and that Austria would have a respite for this reason, if no other. Although Austria used the interval to restore its finances, the imminence of war posed a new dilemma, for now the Russian alliance so long and so desperately sought seemed available for the asking, the continental equilibrium was again within reach. Even Prussia, since Tilsit reduced to a power of the second rank, extended feelers for an alliance. But Metternich was well aware that the defeat of 1809 had left the Austrian Empire without any margin for error. He knew that another lost war or even a protracted one would lead to its disintegration and he trusted neither the physical strength of Prussia nor the moral stamina of Russia. On the other hand, argued Metternich in a memorandum to the Emperor, an alliance with France was out of the question, for it would undermine the source of Austrian strength, its claim to moral superiority, while neutrality would incur the hostility of Russia without obtaining the friendship of France. It would exclude Austria from any voice in the future peace settlement and condemn her to the role of a second-class power.[2]

A series of paradoxes may be intriguing for the philosopher but

[1] N.P. II, p. 411.
[2] See Metternich's long analysis for the Emperor, N.P. II, 410f.

they are a nightmare for the statesman, for the latter must not only contemplate but resolve them. An alliance with Russia might lead to the defeat of Napoleon, but it might also cause the brunt of the war to fall on Austria and end with another Russian betrayal. An alliance with France would undermine Austria's moral position, while armed neutrality would exhaust her material resources. Austria had thus reached precisely the point where collaboration begins to pay diminishing returns, the borderline between passive struggle and loss of will. Metternich attempted to escape this dilemma by limiting his commitment, while the other powers extended theirs. He hoped to restore to Austria a measure of freedom of action, while utilizing the crisis to develop her strength. The means he chose was a further step on the road of adaptation to France, but hedged in a manner which testified to Metternich's inward reserve. An alliance was negotiated with France providing for an Austrian auxiliary corps of thirty thousand men to operate under the direct command of Napoleon and to utilize French supplies. In return, Napoleon guaranteed the integrity of the Austrian Empire and promised Austria not only territorial compensations in proportion to her exertions, but a "memorial", an additional and presumably "disproportionate" territorial accretion to symbolize the lasting harmony of France and Austria.[1] Whatever one may think of the morality of this step, there is no doubt that it achieved Metternich's objectives. Austria could arm, not only without the opposition, but with the encouragement of France. It had been assured of a voice in the peace settlement and obtained a symbolic expression of a preferential status in the French system. The territorial accretion was contingent on French victory—in which case it would serve as a counterweight to France—and meaningless in case of French defeat. Not without justice could Metternich describe the Austrian war effort as neither a war of conquest, nor a defensive war, but a war of conservation.[2] It was an alliance *infiniment limité*.[3]

It now remained to make clear the limitation of the Austrian commitment. Metternich told Hardenberg that Austria had had no alternative, that she would never cease considering herself the core of resistance to Napoleon. But he added, that open resistance was foolhardy until Austria was more powerful and he urged Britain to

[1] Oncken, II, p. 85.
[2] N.P. II, p. 440.
[3] Oncken, II, p. 47.

increase its diversion in Spain.[1] At the same time he assured Russia that Austria had no aggressive intent and made the startling proposal that Austria and Russia agree on the conduct of the war to preserve the Austrian auxiliary corps and to keep it from serious participation in the main operation. He suggested that Russia concentrate troops in Galicia to justify Austrian inaction and to furnish a pretext for the creation of yet another army corps.[2] But he evaded Russian requests that he reduce these offers to writing. Determined not to risk Austria's existence in the first battle, Metternich strove by the dexterity of his manœuvres to achieve the isolation which an insular location furnished more favoured powers, until he had gauged the constellation of forces and could let Austria play its real and traditional role: the organization of the coalition and the legitimization of the peace.

V

This, then, was Metternich's position when the first news of the French disaster in Russia reached him. The war of 1805 had taught him the tenuousness of alliances and that of 1809 their necessity. The events of 1805 had convinced him that imminent danger might justify isolation as well as coalition, that continental policy could not be conducted *ad hoc*. The disaster of 1809 had led him to believe that national *élan* was no substitute for a material base. Throughout this period Russia's conduct had been ambiguous. She had helped destroy the powers which could act as a barrier against France and, until her own territories were threatened, had recoiled from combat after the first defeat. Now, as Russian troops swept westward, Metternich feared their success as much as their irresolution. He had not fought nearly a decade for the equilibrium in order to replace the supremacy of the West by a dominance from the East. And he had not nursed Austria back to a modicum of strength to risk it in a fit of enthusiasm. When Russia pointed out that the moment for a change of sides had arrived, Metternich replied that Austria's present position was not of its own choosing, that a power whose very existence depended on the recognition of the sanctity of treaty relations could not simply break an alliance, and that Austrian policy was based not on sentiment but on cold calculation.[3]

[1] Oncken, II, p. 824.
[2] Oncken, II, p. 93. See also Luckwaldt, p. 39.
[3] Oncken, I, p. 47.

The moment had indeed arrived when, as Metternich had predicted, three hundred thousand men could play the first role in a Europe of universal anarchy. But Austria had barely one-fifth that number and half of them were in Russia with Napoleon. Even more important, Austria had to test, not only Russian resolution, but the kind of war it would wage. For Austria was interested not in the freedom of nations, but in the liberty of historical states. A people's war might involve the dissolution of the polyglot Empire, a national crusade might lead to the overthrow of the dynasties on which Austria's German position was based. "How hard is the fall of a great man," exclaimed Metternich. ("*Que la chute d'un grand homme est lourde.*") ". . . All the plans of the poor central powers must be directed towards not being ground to powder (*zermalmt*)."[1] Everything depended, therefore, not only on the defeat of Napoleon but on the manner in which it was achieved, not only on the creation of a coalition but also on the principle in the name of which it was to fight.

"If a great state is forced to act in a situation of great peril," Metternich said during the Crimean War, in a situation which he never ceased to consider analogous to that of 1813, "it must at least secure for itself the position of supreme leadership."[2] This was all the more important for the great Central Empire situated in the middle of contending states whose rear was protected by the sea or by the steppes: "Before Austria enters a war it must secure not only its military but its moral position."[3] But it was clear what Austria's moral position required: a war of states, not of nations, a coalition legitimized by a doctrine of conservatism and stability, and brought about, if possible, in the name of existing treaties rather than by their rupture.

In addition, considerations of power inspired Metternich with caution. For Napoleon, although defeated in Russia, was still the master of the Low Countries, of Italy, and of Illyria. The secondary German powers of the Confederation of the Rhine were still his satellites; Prussia his ally. And Metternich was confirmed in his deliberate policy by his conviction that the time had come to put his familiarity with Napoleon's character to good use. "Napoleon and I spent years together," he wrote in 1820, "as if at a game of

[1] Luckwaldt, p. 41.
[2] N.P. VIII, p. 371.
[3] N.P. VIII, p. 364f.

chess, carefully watching each other; I to checkmate him, he to crush me together with the chess figures."[1] This was the symbolization of the issue of the period: the man of will and the man of reason, the principle of universality and the sense of limit, the assertion of power and the claim of legitimacy. But whatever else the events of 1812 had proved, they had demonstrated that the game could no longer be won by pulverizing either the antagonist or the pieces; that it had to be played according to its own rules which placed a premium on subtlety and not on brute strength. The longer Napoleon hesitated in recognizing this truth, the more certain his ultimate defeat. Universal claims, if backed by substantial force or opposed by insufficient resolution, can, through their very enormity, disintegrate the structure of international relations. But when the means are limited and the antagonist determined, the memory of great successes may cause the delusion which is a prelude to disaster.

The kind of game Metternich decided to play was, moreover, not one of the bold manœuvre, which risked everything on a quick checkmate. Rather it was deliberate and cunning, a game where the advantage lay in a gradual transformation of the position, in which the opponent's moves were utilized first to paralyse and then to destroy him, while the player marshalled his resources. It was a game whose daring resided in the loneliness in which it had to be played, in the face of non-comprehension and abuse by both friend and foe; whose courage lay in its imperturbability when one wrong move might mean disaster and loss of confidence might spell isolation; whose greatness derived from the skill of its moves and not from the inspiration of its conception. It was a game at the end of which Austria had attained the Supreme Command of the Alliance, had deflected the war from its territories, had based the Coalition on the Cabinets and not on the peoples and thereby had assured a peace, the legitimization of which was consistent with her continued existence. It was not heroic, but it saved an empire.

Metternich's opening gambit was a dispatch to the Austrian *chargé d'affaires* at the French Headquarters in Vilna, sent on 9 December, when it was known that Napoleon had failed, but not how seriously he had been defeated. Subtle and sarcastic, at the same time conciliatory and threatening, it set the tone of the sub-

[1] N.P. III, p. 332.

sequent efforts and determined the kind of game this was to be. Its significance resided less in its content, which was only the first step in an intricate manœuvre, the full implications of which were not to become apparent for seven months, than in its tone, in its assertion of the independence which Metternich considered the equivalent of health in the individual.[1] It began with an ironical summary of the existing situation: "Austria has too much respect to permit itself an opinion about the military dispositions of the greatest commander of the century. It was a novel problem, the Cabinet of St Petersburg had given so many proofs of its inconstancy that *even* [my italics] the soberest calculation permitted the assumption that an enterprise so much against all probability as the conquest of Moscow . . . would induce Alexander to negotiate. But this hope had been disappointed; Russia had found it easy to surrender the interests of its allies; it could not be induced to surrender its own."

This paragraph was preliminary to a long analysis of the military and psychological possibilities, which resolved itself into the proposition that all the victories of the Grande Armée had achieved nothing, that the conquest of Russia was impossible, the motive for a separate peace non-existent. What then was the solution? Austria's good offices, Metternich replied, for the negotiation of a general peace. Only Austria, he maintained, could approach the other nations without offending their dignity, while it was united to France by bonds of family. The state which kept fifty million people in the centre of Europe in check had the duty to speak of peace even towards France, if only to maintain appearances. This threatening affirmation of Austria's good faith was followed by another ambiguity: "The Emperor of the French seems to have foreseen what is happening today when he told me so frequently that the marriage [to Marie Louise] had transformed the face of Europe. The moment is near, it may have already arrived, when Napoleon will draw the *real* advantage from this fortunate alliance." And Metternich concluded with a phrase he not only underlined but stressed, of subtle obtuseness and devious daring: "When our exalted master learned of the evacuation of Moscow, he summed up the essence of his attitude in these few words: 'The moment has come when I can show the Emperor of the French who I am.' I will confine myself to repeating these words of His Majesty, so simple and at the same time so energetic, and I empower you to communicate them to the Duke of

[1] Text, Oncken, I, p. 17.

Bassano [French Foreign Minister]. Any commentary will only detract from their force."[1]

Thus Metternich opened the campaign which was to lead to a Coalition against Napoleon by offering his antagonist peace. In this manner, he took the first step in obtaining French approval for transforming the alliance into neutrality, the neutrality into mediation, and the mediation into war, all accomplished in the name of existing treaties and initially motivated by concern for the great ally. It may be asked why Metternich had to choose a procedure so indirect, a method so intricate and so difficult to legitimize. Why not attempt to adapt the Austrian domestic structure to the national *élan* sweeping across Europe? But a statesman must work with the material at hand and the domestic structure of Austria was rigid, much more rigid, paradoxically, than the international one. But before we examine the impact of the Austrian domestic structure on Metternich's foreign policy, we must turn to another statesman, the Foreign Minister of the power which had fought Napoleon most persistently. He, too, attempted to animate a coalition and he, too, appeared on the scene by advancing a plan for peace.

[1] The dispatch is printed in Oncken, I, p. 36f.

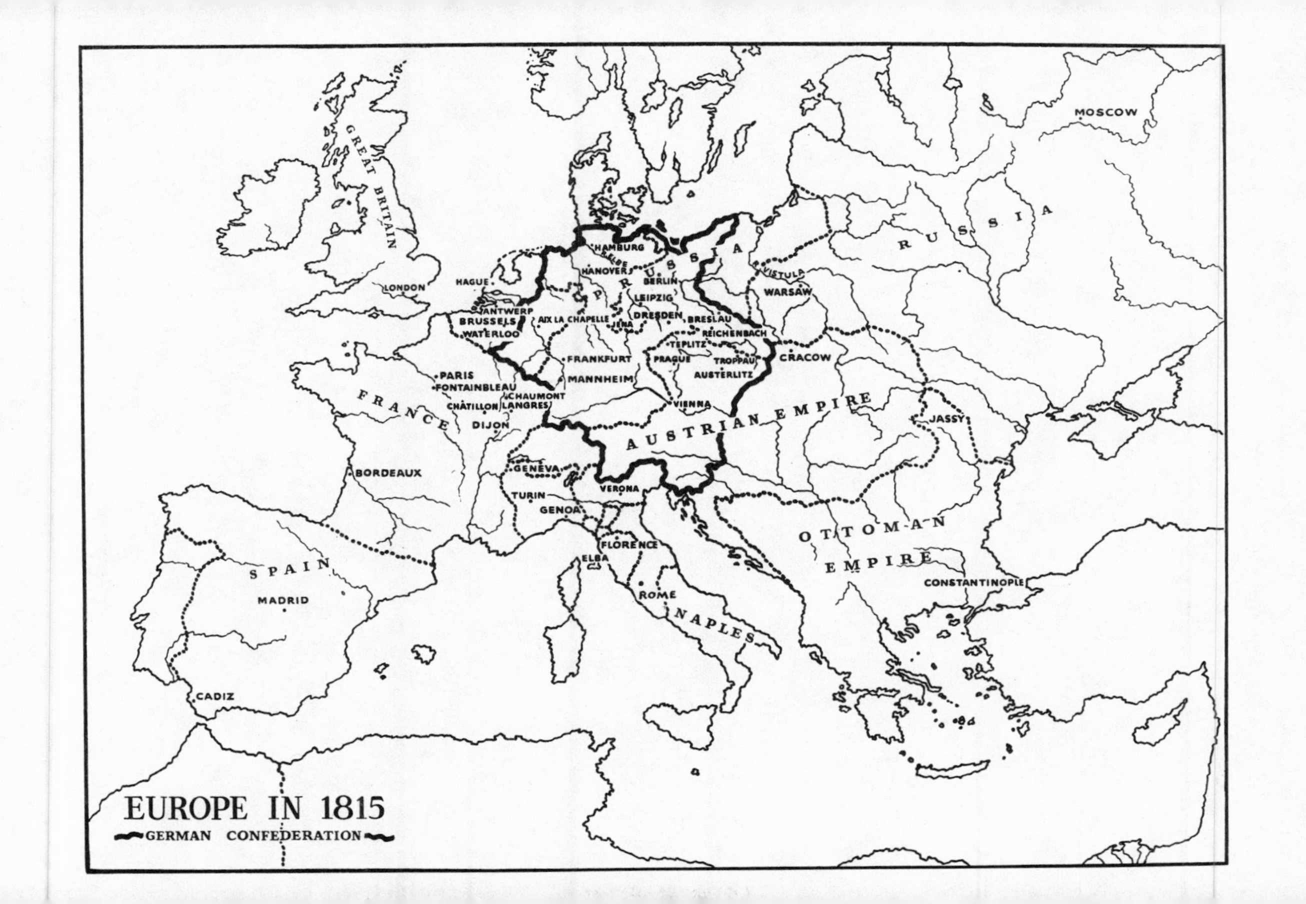
EUROPE IN 1815
GERMAN CONFEDERATION
MOSCOW
RUSSIA
GREAT BRITAIN
LONDON
HAGUE
ANTWERP
BRUSSELS
WATERLOO
AIX LA CHAPELLE
HAMBURG
ELBE
HANOVER
PRUSSIA
BERLIN
LEIPZIG
DRESDEN
JENA
BRESLAU
REICHENBACH
TEPLITZ
PRAGUE
TROPPAU
AUSTERLITZ
VISTULA
WARSAW
CRACOW
FRANKFURT
MANNHEIM
VIENNA
PARIS
FONTAINBLEAU
CHAUMONT
CHÂTILLON
LANGRES
DIJON
FRANCE
AUSTRIAN EMPIRE
JASSY
BORDEAUX
GENEVA
TURIN
VERONA
GENOA
FLORENCE
ELBA
ROME
NAPLES
OTTOMAN EMPIRE
CONSTANTINOPLE
SPAIN
MADRID
CADIZ

III

The Insular Statesman

I

THE memory of states is the test of truth of their policy. The more elementary the experience, the more profound its impact on a nation's interpretation of the present in the light of the past. It is even possible for a nation to undergo an experience so shattering that it becomes the prisoner of its past. Such was not the case with the Britain of 1812, however. It had had its shock and it had survived. But although its moral structure remained unimpaired, it emerged from the ordeal of nearly a decade of isolation with the resolve never to stand alone again.

If one were free to draw a prescription for a man to give effect to this resolution, there are few one would be less likely to select than Lord Castlereagh, who became British Foreign Secretary at the very moment that the Grande Armée was assembling at the Niemen. Born in Ireland, of an old, if undistinguished, family, he had undergone the typical education of the British landed aristocracy at a time when contacts with the Continent were tenuous and foreign affairs confined to makeshift coalitions against the revolutionary tide. His career had been solid but unspectacular. His first public acts were connected with putting down the Irish Rebellion and abolishing the Irish Parliament, acts which helped to establish his reputation as an ogre to liberalism. He had served as Secretary of War under Pitt, and this association was to lay the foundation of his later policy. For the greater part of this period he was overshadowed by the more brilliant Canning. In 1809, after an unfortunate duel, both men had to retire from public office. Castlereagh returned in 1812, as Foreign Secretary and leader of the House of Commons, in the Cabinet of Lord Liverpool which was not expected to last more than a few months. So well established was Canning's "expertise" in foreign affairs that Castlereagh offered to relinquish to him the Foreign Office provided he could retain his position as leader of the House of Commons. But so dismal seemed the prospects of the Liverpool Cabinet that Canning refused, not to attain his goal for another decade. Castlereagh's place in history thus came about almost as an afterthought, as unobtrusively as his personality.

Yet it was this man, more than any other, who forged again a European connection for Britain, who maintained the Coalition, and negotiated the settlement which in its main outlines was to last for over fifty years. Psychologists may well ponder how it came about that this Irish peer, whose career had given no indication of profound conceptions, should become the most European of British statesmen. No man more different from his great protagonist, Metternich, could be imagined. Metternich was elegant, facile, rationalist; Castlereagh, solid, ponderous, pragmatic; the former was witty and eloquent, if somewhat pedantic; the latter cumbersome in expression, although effective in debate; Metternich was doctrinaire and devious; Castlereagh, matter-of-fact and direct. Few individuals have left behind them such a paucity of personal reminiscences. Icy and reserved, Castlereagh walked his solitary path, as humanly unapproachable as his policy came to be incomprehensible to the majority of his countrymen. It was said of him that he was like a splendid summit of polished frost, icy, beautiful, aloof, of a stature that nobody could reach and few would care to. It was not until his tragic death that the world was to learn the price of solitude.

Yet as a symbol of the British experience Castlereagh could hardly have been more appropriate. For the war had not been fought by Britain against a revolutionary doctrine, much less in the name of an alternative one, but against a universal claim; not for freedom but for independence; not for a social order but for an equilibrium. This was to be a constant source of misunderstanding with the Continental nations, particularly Austria. To the Continental nations it was a war not only for independence, but for *their* independence in terms of their historical experience; for Great Britain it was for a Europe in which universal dominion would be impossible. For Austria it was a war for the survival of a social order; for Great Britain, a war for the creation of the "great masses" necessary to contain France.[1] In 1821, while Metternich was constructing a doctrine for universal interference to combat what he conceived as the danger of world

[1] Castlereagh, Viscount, *Correspondence, Dispatches and Other Papers*, 12 Vols. Edited by the Marquess of Londonderry. (London, 1848–52). Vol. VIII, p. 355. Henceforward referred to as C.C.

revolution, Castlereagh reminded him that the Napoleonic wars had been fought by Great Britain on the basis of material considerations in which British interests were obviously involved, not because of vague enunciations of principle.[1]

British objectives are for this reason easier to state in negative than in positive terms. They reflected the policy of an island power to which the Continent, if unified under a single rule, represented a mortal threat; of a social structure conscious of such uniqueness—and the consciousness is more important than the fact of uniqueness—that it felt threatened by domestic transformations in foreign countries only if they involved a *forcible* extension abroad. It was a defensive conception of foreign policy which saw Britain in the role of balancer in a Europe of equilibrium. And, since the equilibrium was conceived in political rather than in social terms, it was thought to depend on a balance among states of approximately equal power, not on a principle of legitimacy. Britain, which had combated the *outward projection* of the French Revolution, fought for a Europe whose structure would prohibit conquest. Austria, and the other Continental states, which had been brought to the brink of dissolution by the *fact* of the French Revolution and the impossibility, both geographical and psychological, of isolation, fought for a Europe whose "legitimacy" made universal conquest inconceivable. Because a balancer cannot perform his function unless the differences among the other powers are greater than their collective differences with the balancer, the British nightmare was a continental peace which excluded Britain. Because a society cannot function if constantly on the defensive against forces attacking its myth, the European nightmare was permanent revolution.[2]

This is not to say that British statesmen did not prefer some domestic structures to others. But their preference was based on the greater likelihood that these governments would maintain the European equilibrium. The Liverpool Cabinet was an infinitely more uncompromising opponent of Napoleon's continued rule than even the Austrian government. But this opposition had nothing to do with the "legitimacy" of the Bourbons; it stemmed from a conviction that no peace with Napoleon could be permanent. "Who will say," Castlereagh said after Napoleon's escape from Elba, "if [Napoleon]

[1] Webster, Sir Charles, *The Foreign Policy of Castlereagh*, 2 Vols. (London, 1931 and 1925). Vol. II, p. 554 (Appendix).

[2] See Chapters XI and XIV for fuller discussion.

again rules the destinies of France that Europe can be tranquil, secure or independent. I consider that in the question now at issue in France is involved the more vital question whether Europe can return to that moral system by which . . . the interests of mankind are to be upheld or whether we shall remain, as we have been during the last twenty years, under the necessity of maintaining a system of military policy; whether Europe shall in the future present the spectacle of an assemblage of free or of armed nations."[1]

When Castlereagh opposed revolution, it was not, as with Metternich, because it was "unnatural" but because it was unsettling. The opprobrium heaped upon Castlereagh by liberals mistakes his intentions. Whenever he felt he could safely do so, he advocated moderate and conciliating measures, if never "liberal" ones.[2] But the repose of Europe was paramount; doctrines of government had to be subordinated to international tranquillity. "It is not insurrection we want in Italy but disciplined force under sovereigns we can trust,"[3] he wrote in 1818 to Lord William Bentinck who was engaged on a scheme to confer the blessings of the British constitution on the reluctant Sicilians. And he added the following doctrine of the primacy of foreign over domestic policy; of the equilibrium of power over the equilibrium of social structure: ". . . I cannot bring myself to wish that the too extensive experiment in the science of government, already in operation throughout Europe, should be at once augmented by similar creations in Italy. It is impossible not to perceive a great moral change coming on in Europe, and the principles of freedom are in full operation. The danger is that the transition may be too sudden . . . to make the world better or happier. We have new constitutions launched in France, Spain, Holland and Sicily. Let us see the result before we encourage further attempts. . . . In Italy it is all the more necessary to abstain if we wish to act in concert with Austria and Sardinia. . . ." This expressed the British Tory's distrust of sudden or doctrinaire change and the British statesman's belief in the controlling nature of the Coalition.

It was to the Coalition born of war that Castlereagh looked as a permanent expression of the equilibrium. Since he saw in the war a defence against hegemony, it was only natural that he should con-

[1] Hansard (Commons), 20 March, 1815.

[2] See, for example, his advice to the French King, Webster II, p. 504 (Appendix) or to the Spanish King, C.C. X, p. 26.

[3] C.C. IX, p. 434.

sider the alliance as a protection against future aggression. Since the Revolutionary wars had assumed such scope because the universality of Napoleon's claims had undermined all confidence, the restoration of good faith to international relations was the prerequisite of permanent peace. "If jealousies are not repressed," he wrote in 1814 to his problem child, Lord William Bentinck, ". . . it is not for military concert but for war amongst ourselves we should prepare; and unless the parties can place themselves not only in friendly but in confidential relations, they will create the evil they desire to avoid."[1] In short, Britain, as the power whose sole Continental interest was stability, should function as the mediator of rivalry. Relatively indifferent to the parochial claims of the Continental states, it could advocate the solutions that made for general tranquillity. But Britain could do this only if it were not suspected of selfish motives. For this reason, Castlereagh never ceased insisting on moderation, on a peace of equilibrium not of preponderance; on a goal of harmony, not of vengeance. While travelling to the headquarters of the Allied Sovereigns at Basle, he told his companion, Ripon, "that one of the difficulties he expected to encounter in the approaching negotiations would arise from the want of confidential intercourse between the great powers *as a body*; and that many pretensions might be modified by bringing the respective parties into unrestricted communications embracing in confidential discussions all the great outstanding issues."[2] And while he was engaged in one of his periodic disputes with a Cabinet always distrustful of Continental involvements, he wrote: "Our reputation on the Continent as a feature of our strength, power and confidence is of more real moment than any acquisition."[3]

There was only one point on which an island nation could not yield, that of maritime rights. Because command of the seas had enabled Britain to survive ten years of isolation, maritime rights acquired a significance out of proportion to their real importance. But who is to quarrel with a people's interpretation of its past? It is its only means of facing the future, and what "really" happened is often less important than what is thought to have happened. Blockade and the right to search neutral vessels were considered the major factors in ending Napoleon's domination, and Castlereagh was only stating a truism of British policy when he wrote to Cathcart,

[1] C.C. IX, p. 431, 3 April, 1814.
[2] C.C. I, p. 128.
[3] C.C. IX, p. 474, 19 April, 1814.

the British envoy to the Tsar: "Great Britain may be driven out of a Congress but not out of her maritime rights and if the Continental nations know their own interest they will not hazard this."[1]

Up to this point Castlereagh's views on foreign relations were in harmony with those of the country or at least could be made palatable to it. But when Castlereagh began to transform the Alliance against Napoleon into an international organization to preserve the peace, he was to separate himself not only from the country and the Cabinet but also from his allies. For co-operation, based on a commitment in effect confined to French aggression, proved too little for the Continental nations and too much for the British domestic structure. The Continental nations could not be satisfied with an alliance so limited because their margin of safety was too narrow. It was very well for Castlereagh to warn Metternich against conducting foreign policy on precautionary grounds.[2] Metternich did not have an English Channel behind which to assess developing events and across which to interfere at the moment of maximum advantage. His security depended on the first battle, not on the last; precaution was his *only* policy. And European government, however limited in commitment, was too much for the British domestic structure. Canning, not Castlereagh, spoke for the nation when he warned that a commitment to attend European congresses regularly would involve Britain in a new and very questionable policy: "It will involve [Britain] deeply in all the politics of the Continent, whereas our true policy has always been not to interfere except in great emergencies and then with a commanding force."[3]

This was the doctrine of non-interference, the reverse side of the belief in the uniqueness of British institutions. It expressed the conviction that transformations of foreign governments could not affect British institutions, that threats to British security were political, not social in nature. Who possessed the mouth of the Scheldt was important to Britain, because on it depended unchallenged control of the Narrows. It was not important who possessed the throne of Naples—at least after Murat's overthrow. The corollary of this was a translation into international terms of the political beliefs of British society. The right of each nation to its own

[1] C.C. IX, p. 39, 14 July, 1813.
[2] Webster, II, p. 106.
[3] C.C. XII, p. 56, 20 October, 1818.

form of government was an axiom acknowledged by both sides of the House of Commons. Foreign intervention in the domestic affairs of other states might be justified on the grounds of overriding necessity, although never approved; it might be tolerated, but never admitted as a universal right. And it was Parliament and public opinion which provided the limiting condition of Castlereagh's foreign policy: "We act from the necessity imposed upon us of always keeping our case in a shape which, if produced in Parliament would justify our vigilance."[1] Castlereagh spoke for Parliament, if not for himself, when he replied to a proposal by the Tsar for European intervention against the revolution in Spain: "When the territorial balance of Europe is disturbed, [Britain] can interfere with effect, but she is the last government in Europe which can be expected or can venture to commit herself on any question of an absolute character. . . . We shall be found in our place when *actual danger* [my italics] menaces the system of Europe: but this country cannot and will not act upon abstract principles of precaution. The Alliance which exists had no such purpose in its original formation. It was never so explained to Parliament; if it had, most assuredly the sanction of Parliament would never have been given to it."[2]

All the elements of Castlereagh's policy are united in this dispatch: The equilibrium of Europe is political in nature and Britain will fight against any attempt to upset it. But the threat must be overt, not speculative; and the action must be defensive, not precautionary. Revolutions, although undesirable, are not an actual danger. "The Emperor's policy," Castlereagh told Lieven, the Russian ambassador, in reply to an attempt to use the Alliance to repress a revolution in Naples, "is a vain hope, a beautiful phantom which England above all cannot pursue. . . . It is proposed now to overcome the *revolution*; but so long as this revolution does not appear in more distinct shape . . . England is not ready to combat it. Upon any other question purely political she would always deliberate and act in the same way as all the other Cabinets."[3]

"Upon any *other* question *purely* political"—this was the foreign policy doctrine of an insular power convinced of the unassailability of its domestic institutions. This distinction between the political and

[1] C.C. XII, p. 90, 7 December, 1813.
[2] Webster, II, p. 240.
[3] Webster, II, p. 283.

the social element was to remain inadmissible for Metternich, the Continental statesman. But the difference was not yet apparent in 1812. The threat to the equilibrium was clear; the need for a coalition obvious. The revolution in the guise of a military dictatorship had to be suppressed whether in the name of the social or the territorial equilibrium. It was therefore only natural that Metternich began his campaign by offering peace in order to create a moral framework, while Castlereagh advanced a territorial settlement in order to achieve a physical equilibrium.

II

Castlereagh was at his best when the objectives were determinate, when there was a Coalition to be maintained, a settlement to be negotiated, a dispute to be resolved. This was the situation in 1813, and his objective was the liberation of Europe and the restoration of the balance of power. But Europe was not to be liberated without the defeat of Napoleon. To Castlereagh this was so obvious that Metternich's subtleties seemed like subterfuges and evasions. The statesman of "plain dealing", contemplating Europe from the safety of the Channel and the relative isolation of a decade, could hardly be expected to be sympathetic to a policy that talked peace while it prepared for war, all the less so when the success of this policy depended on its seeming sincerity. He therefore returned a very sharp reply to Metternich's overtures, which, in its legalistic phrasing, testified to a conception of foreign relations where appearances are the only reality. It exhibited abruptly the very ambiguity on the glossing over of which depended the success of Metternich's policy: Austria, it argued, was an auxiliary of France. It could have entered the war against Russia only on the plea of necessity or of justice. If the former, Austria was bound, upon being relieved of the pressure of necessity, to put an end to its engagement and to consult its own good. If, however, Austria considered Napoleon's war just, it was in effect asking Great Britain to concur with the Continental system. Britain could therefore not co-operate with Austrian peace efforts until Austria had shown a disposition for independence.[1]

But Castlereagh feared a Continental peace which excluded Great Britain even more than Austria's efforts to force Britain to negotiate

[1] C.C. VIII, p. 276f. This is a draft by Cooke, but it undoubtedly reflected Castlereagh's arguments.

prematurely. Any settlement, however unsatisfactory, was preferable to the continued exclusion of the balancer from the balance of power. It was only appropriate, therefore, that Castlereagh should attempt to animate the Continental powers by giving British objectives their most inclusive formulation and that he should go back to his great mentor, Pitt, for inspiration. Pitt, in 1804, had confronted a situation not dissimilar to Castlereagh's in 1813. Then, as in 1813, Europe was striving to restore its equilibrium against attempted universal domination, although the nature of the threat was not yet generally understood and the illusion of the possibility of separate accommodation persisted. At the same time that Metternich was attempting to convince a wavering Prussia of the impossibility of peaceful co-existence with a Napoleonic France, the young Tsar of Russia, Alexander, had sent an agent to Britain to negotiate a coalition and to arrange for British subsidies. Still in his liberal phase, the Tsar was not content with an alliance to reduce or overthrow Napoleon's Empire. The coalition was to be a crusade, its goal universal peace.

Well might the sober Pitt wonder at the scheme which the Russian envoy unfolded. The old Europe, argued Alexander, was gone for ever and a new one had to be created; nothing less than the overthrow of the last vestiges of feudalism and the reform of nations by endowing them with liberal constitutions could restore stability. Not even the Ottoman Empire was considered beyond salvation. And lest any power disturb the harmony of constitutional states, Alexander added a number of safeguards: States were to be required to submit their disputes to mediation by third parties; any state that defied the new Europe should bring upon itself an immediate coalition of all the other powers; Great Britain and Russia, by virtue of their geographic position, were to guarantee the settlement.[1] There were some references to territorial arrangements, particularly with respect to Sardinia and a vague plan for the organization of Germany, but they did not really interest Alexander. Peace was to be assured by social harmony; war avoided by making it inconceivable.

But Pitt was not prepared to embark on a crusade for constitutional liberty. Nor was he willing to consider the surrender of British maritime rights, which the Tsar had suggested should be the British contribution to international good will. On the other hand, he did not wish the Coalition to founder over a dispute in political philosophy. In order to escape this dilemma, and to induce the Tsar to defer his

[1] Webster, I, p. 54f.

proposals for social amelioration until the peace conference, Pitt attempted to give the primary British objective, the reduction of French power, concrete expression. Thus came about the Pitt peace plan, stillborn in 1805, but resurrected in 1813 to form the basis of the post-war settlement.

Pitt's plan began by reducing the Russian suggestions to three basic objectives with which he concurred: "(a) To rescue from the dominion of France those countries which it has subjugated since the beginning of the Revolution and to reduce France within its former limits as they stood before that time, (b) to make such arrangements with respect to the territories recovered from France as may provide for their serenity and happiness and may at the same time constitute a more effective barrier in the future against encroachments on the part of France, (c) to form, at the restoration of peace, a general agreement and guarantee for the mutual protection and security of different Powers and for re-establishing a general system of public law in Europe."[1]

These propositions were merely abstract formulations of desirable goals. Pitt therefore proceeded to sketch the structure that would give them reality. Since Great Britain and Russia, he argued, were both without territorial ambitions and capable of taking a general view, it was for them to agree on the nature of the European equilibrium and to secure its acceptance by the other powers. And since French hegemony had been brought about by reducing the secondary powers to satellites, the new balance of power should be based on the controlling influence of the Great Powers. To be sure, the restoration of national independence was to be the primary goal of the alliance, but there existed several states which had demonstrated, either by their rapid collapse or by their subservience to France, their unfitness for self-government. Their territories were to be used to induce the Great Powers to join the Coalition and to create the "great masses" to contain France. The states marked for extinction included Genoa, the Ecclesiastical possessions on the left bank of the Rhine and the Spanish possessions in Northern Italy. Austria and Prussia were to be the chief beneficiaries, Austria in Italy and Prussia in Germany. By inducing Austria to become a major Italian power, Pitt hoped to eliminate the rivalry between Austria and Prussia in Germany which had provided so many pretexts for French intervention.

[1] Text in Webster, Sir Charles, *British Diplomacy*, 1813–15, (London, 1921), p. 389f. Henceforward referred to as B.D.

Europe was thus to be organized into a society of five major powers: Britain, France, Russia, Austria, and Prussia. France was to be surrounded by a ring of secondary powers, each with a barrier of fortresses to absorb the first French onslaught and a major power in reserve. Holland, supported by Prussia, was to guard the North; Sardinia, backed by Austria, the South; the Austro-Prussian alliance was to protect the Centre. The whole arrangement was to be safeguarded by a general treaty between all the major powers guaranteeing the territorial settlement and by a separate treaty between Russia and Great Britain in effect guaranteeing the guarantee.

There in a few sparse pages, in uninspired language, was symbolized the nature of the British commitment. It was to be a war for security not for doctrine, against universal conquest not against revolution. Its goal was a stable balance of power brought about by the reduction of France and the augmentation of the Central Powers. It was to be protected by a *territorial* guarantee as the expression of the equilibrium and by a special guarantee of the "unselfish" powers as a symbol of international good faith. Only on two points was Great Britain to prove adamant: maritime rights, about which Pitt's plan was significantly silent, and a Holland free from the control of a major power.

The pragmatism of this plan was its strength and its weakness. It led to a single-mindedness of purpose which enabled Britain to secure its major goals before any other power. But it also involved a mechanical conception of international relations which made no allowance for changing relationships among the powers. The equilibrium aimed at was based on a defensive conception: the threat of an aggressive France. As long as this threat was universally recognized, it sufficed to legitimize the balance of power. When new problems arose, however, and different threats appeared, the nature of the equilibrium had to be defined anew. In this new definition, the old unanimity could hardly be recaptured, for only in revolutionary periods do threats assume universal scope; only then are defensive coalitions to be generalized. The very stability of the peace will tend to disintegrate a wartime alliance if nothing holds it together save the memory of common danger.

But this was still in the distance. With the Grande Armée defeated and British isolation seemingly at an end, Castlereagh resurrected the Pitt plan by sending it to Cathcart with the following letter: "The political arrangement of Europe is perhaps more difficult at this early moment to decide on. . . . The main features we are agreed upon that to keep France we need great masses, that Prussia, Russia and Austria are to be . . . as powerful as ever, and that the inferior states must be summoned to assist or pay the forfeit of resistance. . . . As an outline to reason from I send you . . . a dispatch on which the confederacy in 1805 was founded; the Emperor of Russia probably does not have this interesting document at Headquarters (. . . I well remember having more than one conversation with Mr. Pitt on its details, *before he wrote it* [Castlereagh's italics]). Some of the suggestions may now be inapplicable, but it is so masterly an outline for the restoration of Europe that I should be glad if your lordship would reduce it to distinct propositions and learn the bearing of his Imperial Majesty's mind upon its contents."[1] In this manner, the Pitt plan became the blueprint of Castlereagh's policy. So successful was he to be in achieving its goals that in 1815 he could lay the Pitt Plan before the House of Commons as the justification of the Vienna settlement.

But, in April, 1813, it was still premature. For it was not yet certain whether there was to be peace or war, and if war, what kind of war. The coalition was still to be formed; Napoleon's new army yet to be tested. Austria was still engaged on its intricate measures and spoke of mediation, while Castlereagh could hardly restrain his impatience. The great guardian of the Coalition could not operate until the Coalition had been constructed. In this task Metternich was engaged, and until he had finished all else had to wait.

[1] C.C. VIII, p. 356, 8 April, 1813.

IV

Metternich and the Definition of the Political Equilibrium

I

"[POLICY] is like a play in many acts," Metternich wrote once, "which unfolds inevitably once the curtain is raised. To declare then that the performance will not take place is an absurdity. The play will go on, either by means of the actors . . . or by means of the spectators who mount the stage. . . . Intelligent people never consider this the essence of the problem, however. For them it lies in the decision whether the curtain is to be raised at all, whether the spectators are to be assembled and in the intrinsic quality of the play. . . ."[1] By the end of 1812 the curtain had been raised, but it revealed a stage in disarray on which a careful designer was imperceptibly moving the pieces until he had created a pattern to his liking. And since the designer was not willing immediately to reveal the nature of the arrangement he was aiming at, he resisted, sometimes testily, all outside pressures to hasten his work.

When Metternich had offered Napoleon his good offices for a *general* peace, he had embarked on a policy from which he knew there was no return. Had Metternich wished merely to be released from the burdensome French alliance, he could have offered his assistance for a separate peace with Russia and withdrawn into neutrality had he failed. But by aiming at a *general* peace he involved the interests of the Austrian Empire in the most direct fashion. Should Napoleon fail to accept the terms Metternich was in the process of developing, no option would remain but to appear in the ranks of his foes. For the conditions would be, by definition, the outline of the only Europe which Austria could find compatible with its safety. Metternich, who prided himself on his knowledge of Napoleon's character, could have had few expectations that Napoleon would

[1] N.P. VIII, p. 190.

accept, not because the conditions would be ungenerous, but because they were conditions.

It was therefore with no doubt about the gravity of the step that Metternich launched a diplomatic campaign in the name of the French alliance, at the end of which Austria's moral and military leadership of the anti-French coalition was a fact which required no further negotiation. Because the success of this campaign depended on the illusion of sincerity, any action which might put Austrian motives into doubt had to be avoided. Russian pleas for a declaration of policy were evaded or went unanswered, and when Lord Cathcart sent an emissary to hasten Austria's entry into the war, Metternich returned the reply that he knew no Lord Cathcart and that, when ready, he would deal with Britain in London. And because the Austrian bargaining position depended on the illusion of independence, freedom of action became Metternich's primary goal: "The first of all interests is independence," Metternich wrote early in January, 1813. "Great successes of either contender without the exhaustion of their military forces was a prospect which could only create new discomfitures for Austria. . . . [But] at the beginning of 1813 Austria is strong through the exhaustion of the two other Imperial Courts. . . . It is for this reason that we have impressed on all our steps towards France that feeling of independence whose sentiment will become increasingly positive with each passing day."[1]

But it was an independence of a paradoxical nature evidenced by the indirectness of its measures, the tone of its language, and the hesitancy of compliance with Napoleon's wishes; an independence which proved all the more effective for being accomplished in the name of bondage. Its first expression was in the form of instructions for the Austrian emissary Bubna, sent to Napoleon ostensibly to adapt the alliance to new circumstances but in reality to divine Napoleon's intentions and to anticipate any embarrassing French overtures.[2] The instructions, meant to be repeated to Napoleon, raised once more the issue of Austrian mediation and tied it to the disposition of the Austrian auxiliary corps which represented the nucleus of Austrian power. They began with the usual ambiguous reference to Napoleon's defeat: despite an endless series of mistakes, despite the absence of a single military talent, Russia had emerged victorious. It was a victory of incalculable consequence. "The people of Europe," Metternich

[1] Oncken, I, p. 80f., 3 January, 1813.
[2] Luckwaldt, p. 62.

argued ambiguously, "have learned during the past twenty years to judge military strength. They cannot be deceived regarding the probable consequences of recent events." The only solution was peace, mediated by Austria, which owed a great obligation to Napoleon, but an even greater one to its own people. But should the war continue, Metternich insisted, it was evident that the *common cause* [my italics] would be served best by a retreat of the Austrian auxiliary corps to Galicia, there to be joined by the corps of observation, for the creation of which Metternich had obtained permission in 1812 by arranging for a Russian "threat".[1] Thus Metternich, while creating the moral climate for independence, was careful to assemble the resources to make it effective. Napoleon was to learn that a too ardent embrace can crush.

There ensued a contest as stylized as a Japanese play and with rules as intricate. For both sides were eager to obscure the real nature of the issue, to preserve appearances and to keep their options open: Napoleon in order to recreate his army, to sweep Austria along and to cajole or intimidate her to step into the breach left by the collapse of the Grande Armée; Metternich in order to gain time to test the resolution of his would-be allies, to cover his retreat should they be found wanting and to build the power which could defy Napoleon without exposing Austria to the first onslaught. It was a test of endurance in which blows had to be struck with high decorum and accepted as if there could be no discrepancy between appearance and reality. It was a test of patience in which pinpricks had to be noted with smiling grace and ambiguity ignored as if life could be no different. A man who has been used to command finds it almost impossible to learn to negotiate, because negotiation is an admission of finite power. But a nation situated in the centre of Europe cannot find security save in a world in which negotiation is the normal pattern of relation. For Napoleon, everything depended on exhibiting his continuing omnipotence; for Metternich, on demonstrating the limitations of French power.

This led to a strange and inconclusive dialogue, for both sides were reluctant to press the full implications of their position. Napoleon, in his first interview with Bubna on 31 December, stressed the superiority of French resources, his resolution to invade Russia again and demanded the doubling of the Austrian auxiliary corps. Metternich, who had been approached with similar proposals by the

[1] Text. Oncken, I, p. 390f., 20 December, 1812.

French ambassador in Vienna, replied on 3 January that a continuation of so "unpolitical" a war would represent a moral weakening of the monarchy. He added ominously that too much had depended for Austria on the correct estimate of French resources to be mistaken about their *real* state and that Austria knew how to distinguish between recruits and an army.[1] The French Foreign Minister, Count de Bassano, argued that Metternich was mistaken regarding the real French strength and that an experienced Austrian observer in Paris would soon enlighten him about Napoleon's vast power. The threat in Metternich's dispatch of 9 December[2] of fifty million kept in check by Austrian goodwill had not gone unnoticed, but Bassano warned that war between Austria and France would be a war for survival and not a political war.[3] Metternich, who knew this only too well, was not interested in recriminations, however, and even less in a test of strength. How could Austria, he replied soothingly, be accused of comparing its resources with those of France when it was merely attempting to protect its territory, that of a French ally, against the Russian flood? Austria, which kept fifty million people in check, Metternich concluded with an oblique persistence tantamount to an assertion of power, deserved French moral support, instead of French distrust.[4] In the meantime, on 7 January, Napoleon had written a bombastic letter to the Austrian Emperor again cataloguing his resources and demanding the doubling of the Austrian auxiliary corps and the right of transit of French troops through Austrian territory in return for French subsidies.

Everything now depended on the fate of the Austrian auxiliary corps, purposely staffed by cadres and the key to any mobilization of strength. The first goal of Austrian policy—political mobility—had been achieved. For Napoleon, on the occasion of the interview with Bubna on 31 December, had affirmed his readiness to accept the Austrian peace effort but he had urged that it be backed by increasing the auxiliary corps.[5] Napoleon, in this manner, exhibited the extent of his misunderstanding. He ascribed Austria's hesitations to cowardice, and he sought to overcome what he took to be Austria's fears by giving it a consciousness of its power; but Metternich was seeking strength in order to be able to defy Napoleon if necessary. Napoleon

[1] Oncken, I, p. 69f.
[2] See Chapter II, p. 26f.
[3] Luckwaldt, p. 72.
[4] Text, Oncken, I, 400f.
[5] Oncken, I, p. 66.

saw in the auxiliary corps the shield behind which to recreate his army, Metternich considered it the nucleus of Austrian independence. Because the parvenu from Corsica identified obligation with personal relations, he could not conceive that a father might make war on the husband of his daughter. Because the House of Habsburg had learned in its reign of five hundred years that history transcends the individual, it consulted only the considerations which might insure its permanence.

Schwarzenberg, the commander of the auxiliary corps, was authorized to negotiate directly with his Russian opposite number, and he utilized this permission to arrange a "theoretical" battle whose intricacy might have done a Chinese general proud. He urged the Russian commander to transfer his operations from the south to the north of the Austrian corps, and he suggested a flanking movement which would leave no option but a withdrawal to Galicia.[1] Metternich approved this manœuvre and finally ordered the auxiliary corps to withdraw towards Cracow. On 30 January, Schwarzenberg was empowered to sign an armistice of indefinite duration.[2]

In this manner the auxiliary corps was saved, and Austria regained her freedom of action through an almost overly subtle manœuvre of Cabinet diplomacy. Two letters were dispatched to Napoleon, in the name of Emperor Franz but drafted by Metternich, the first a reply to Napoleon's demands of 7 January, the second announcing Schwarzenberg's withdrawal from the Vistula. The first letter, dated 23 January, began once more with the, by now almost obligatory, protestation of Austrian friendship, coupled with a recital of French reverses and therefore by implication of Austria's relative strength: ". . . I have noticed with a feeling of pain that Your Majesty does not extend to me the confidence . . . to which I feel entitled after so repeated signs of my friendly care. . . . I do not deceive myself, that is to say, I do not ascribe to the military merit of the enemy misfortunes which are the result of circumstances beyond all human power. . . . I am far from doubting the military means of France. On the contrary I base on them . . . the hope for peace."[3] With this ironic phrase Metternich noted the catalogue of French power and drew from it a conclusion precisely opposed to Napoleon's intentions, that it constituted one more argument for peace.

[1] Oncken, I, p. 99. Also Luckwaldt, p. 68.
[2] For details and implications of the armistice, see Luckwaldt, p. 83f.
[3] Text, Oncken, I, p. 405f.

In fact, the letter continued, Austria had exceeded Napoleon's wishes. Not sixty but a hundred thousand men would be mobilized: "Ranged on the flanks of the enemy, they are designed to intimidate Russia and to inspire even England with caution." But even these grandiloquent words added up to still another argument for peace, because only the hope for peace could induce the peoples of Austria to make the requisite sacrifices for the creation of this force. The letter was thus an evasion and a snare. It rejected all of Napoleon's requests in the name of a common effort, and it made this evasion a means to commit Napoleon more deeply to Austrian mediation. The corollary that the newly created Austrian strength would have to be used, by definition as it were, against the power which in the eyes of the Austrian Cabinet prevented a settlement, was left by Metternich for the future.

The second letter, dated 24 January, contained the crux of the Austrian position. For it made plain that the hundred thousand men, which were so generously being created, were to be concentrated for the defence of Austria, not on behalf of France. However submissive the tone, nothing could obscure the fact that the road across Poland was now open. With a cynicism which testifies to Metternich's increasing confidence that on the level of cabinet diplomacy *he* was the master, the letter explained that the withdrawal of the Headquarters of the Grande Armée—that so-called army as Metternich described it maliciously in an accompanying letter—had interrupted communications with Schwarzenberg. "In an emergency of such scope, that Your Majesty's deputy has left his headquarters I was forced to see to the welfare of my auxiliary corps by direct measures. . . . I do not doubt that my orders meet the intentions of Your Majesty."[1] When Bubna read this passage to Napoleon, the latter exhibited signs of profound emotion, not of rage, Bubna reported, but of consternation at an unexpected turn of events, the full seriousness of which Napoleon fully appreciated.[2] The withdrawal of the Austrian corps and the insolence of Metternich's communications were more than an act of independence; they were a demonstration of Napoleon's impotence. For the first time Napoleon could do no more than accept measures to which in any other situation he would have replied with a declaration of war.

The difference between the defection of Prussia and the defection

[1] Text, Oncken, I, p. 407.
[2] Oncken, I, p. 107; Luckwaldt, p. 86.

of Austria is symptomatic for the issues of the period. The armistice which Yorck, the commander of the Prussian auxiliary corps, concluded at Tauroggen became a symbol of national independence and freedom from foreign bondage. It was promptly disavowed by the Prussian King who remembered Napoleon as the victor of Jena and Auerstädt. The withdrawal of the Austrian corps was accomplished as an act of state and so communicated to Napoleon. Prussia broke with Napoleon in violation of existing treaties; Austria regained her freedom of action in their name. A policy of patriotic *élan* or cabinet diplomacy, of a war of peoples or a war of states, these were the alternatives of 1813. Metternich had no doubt which alternative Austria was to choose and to create its framework was his next goal.

II

Had Castlereagh known the full extent of Metternich's activities, he would hardly have been so concerned about the possibility of a separate arrangement with France. Having regained his freedom of action, all of Metternich's efforts were directed to keeping the situation fluid, drawing the other powers on and paralysing Napoleon. For Metternich realized that his actions had made it impossible for Austria to permit another total French victory. A Napoleon of limited power might accept Austrian self-will because he had no other choice. But a conquering Napoleon was not likely to forgive this friendship which paralysed, this mediation which isolated.

The withdrawal of the Austrian corps had in fact served a double purpose. It had concentrated the forces of the Empire and, by opening the way across Poland, had furnished a test of Russian resolution. Metternich well knew that important leaders of the Russian army, including their commander, Kutusoff, were in favour of stopping the pursuit of the Grande Armée at the Russian border. Now, as Russian troops began to cross the Vistula, this danger had been banished, but the scope of the Russian operations depended in part on Prussian support. For, after its losses of the previous year, Russia did not have the power to continue its advance into Central Europe unaided. Metternich strove to bring Prussia into the war and to commit Russia to a campaign beyond its borders.

Metternich thus used his newly-won "mobility" to deflect the course of events from Austria's boundaries and to remain aloof until Russia had more firmly defined its objectives. For Metternich had reason to fear Russian success almost as much as Russian irresolution. A document drawn up by the Polish patriot, Czartorisky, had come into his possession through "extraordinary circumstances"—presumably through an attack of "street robbers" which was the preferred method of operation of the Austrian secret police. It called for the reunion of all Polish provinces in a Kingdom of Poland, connected with Russia only through the person of the monarch.[1] But Metternich, who had fought Napoleon's establishment of the Duchy of Warsaw as a symbol of Polish nationalism, was not prepared to have that nationalism satisfied as a consequence of Napoleon's defeat. He chose a method for dealing with this problem as illustrative of the deviousness of his tactics as of his resourcefulness: he transmitted the captured documents to Napoleon. In thus furnishing a proof of his loyalty on an issue which it was safer to see aired in the French than in the Austrian press, he at the same time demonstrated to Napoleon the futility of any hopes for a separate peace with Russia.[2] For Russia could hardly aspire to overthrow the Duchy of Warsaw, Napoleon's personal creation, without having achieved a crushing victory. Thus began the contest over Poland, which was not to end for two years and which nearly embroiled Europe in another war.

An argument over the disposition of Poland was still premature, however. Prussia had not yet declared herself, and Russia was unable to advance much further unaided. At this moment Prussia sent a negotiator, Knesebeck, to Vienna to offer an alliance and to obtain advice.

Prussia was in a desperate dilemma. The defeat of 1806 had reduced it to the status of a second-class power and to a territorial extent of only a third of its former size. And its role in the war against Russia had emphasized its position as Napoleon's vassal. It had served as the base of supply of the Grande Armée; its corps had fought under the command of a French marshal. Now, with Russian armies sweeping westward, the fate of Poland seemed in store for Prussia which Frederick the Great had elevated to the rank of a major power by an act of will. The Prussian Cabinet, contem-

[1] Text, Oncken, I, p. 219f.

[2] And lest any doubt remain in Napoleon's mind of his isolation and therefore of Austria's importance, Metternich induced the Russian Ambassador in Vienna, Stackelberg, to sign a joint note to Napoleon which spoke of the impossibility of a separate peace between Russia and France. Luckwaldt, p. 133.

plating events from the perspective of past impotence, was paralysed by the risks inherent in all contingencies: a renewed French advance, great Russian victories, popular passions, or Austrian neutrality. It knew the object of its fears but neither the nature of its goals nor the extent of its power. The Russian advance only added to its problems. Russian emissaries were pressing for a declaration against Napoleon by threatening to retain East Prussia in case of victory, while a wave of national enthusiasm swept across the rump state, and Stein, the former Prussian minister, assembled the East Prussian Estates in defiance of the King. A war of annihilation or national disintegration seemed Prussia's only alternatives. The mission of Knesebeck was a plea not to leave Prussia alone in Europe with the two great peripheral powers, Russia and France.

This placed Metternich into a difficult position. In contrast to the more parochial statesmen of the "Austrian School", he never ceased regarding a strong Prussia as a prerequisite of Austrian security and the European equilibrium. But, in January, 1813, Prussia could become strong only at the expense of France, not through an alliance with Austria. An alliance, besides ending Austrian mediation before it had fairly begun, would have strengthened the "peace party" at the Prussian court which envisioned a neutral centre separating the great contenders, as if neutrality depended on an act of volition and not on a level of strength to make it effective.[1] But the refusal of the alliance might throw Prussia inexorably into the arms of Russia and extend Russian influence deep into Central Europe. How to embark Prussia on war and still leave open the possibility of later co-operation? How to commit Russia and avoid her preponderance?

Metternich escaped this dilemma by treating the identity of Austrian-Prussian interests as so self-evident that no explicit arrangement was required. Copies of all dispatches to Paris had been forwarded all along to the Prussian ministry to demonstrate the increasing independence of the Austrian tone. Now Metternich went one step further. At his first interview with Knesebeck he insisted that Austria, far from fearing a Prussian alliance with Russia, actually welcomed it as a test of Russian determination.[2] He followed this up with a dispatch to his ambassador in Berlin, suggesting that Prussia reconstitute its army in Silesia under the pretext of defending the Oder and, he added sardonically, far from the pernicious

[1] For the Prussian peace party, see Luckwaldt, p. 97.
[2] Oncken, I, p. 132, Knesebeck report.

example of General Yorck.[1] In thus demonstrating to Prussia that both Central Powers could play the Austrian game, Metternich identified Austrian interests with the Prussian cause. He was not yet committed to assist Prussia in obtaining her objectives, but he could not now permit Prussia to suffer the full consequences of Napoleon's wrath.

But if Metternich desired a Prussian change of front to draw Russia into Central Europe, he at the same time wanted Prussia to limit its commitment to leave open the possibility of future co-operation, particularly on the Polish question. Prussia, backed by Austria, was to serve as an obstacle to Russian ambitions, not as an extension of Russian policy. He therefore had to demonstrate that Austrian reserve was both temporary and tactical, designed more surely to attain the common objectives. The method he chose was characteristically indirect: an analysis of Austrian intentions, drafted by Knesebeck on 14 January, which Metternich corrected and sent to Berlin with a covering letter of disavowal to protect himself should the dispatch fall into French hands.[2] The memorandum began with a comparison of the Prussian and Austrian positions: Prussia, which in signing its treaty of alliance with France had so obviously yielded to force, was entitled to break its bonds as soon as foreign pressure was removed. But Austria, united to France by marriage and by a treaty signed with the appearance of freedom, could not simply change sides without offending the dignity of its ruler. Austria's task must be to regain its freedom with the consent of Napoleon, to *be released from its bonds by France itself.* This goal had been achieved. From the moment that Napoleon had accepted Austrian mediation, Austria's situation had been completely transformed.

But although Austria had now regained its freedom of action, it would go no further, warned the Knesebeck memorandum, until Russia had made its intentions clearer. Until Russia had avowed its goals, Austria would confine itself to the following steps: to move its auxiliary corps slowly towards Silesia; to arm, in direct proportion to the Russian advance, each province as it came in contact with Russian forces; to paralyse France's allies by demonstrating through example that French demands for help could and should be refused. Austria's passive activity was thus designed to force Russia to pursue

[1] Oncken, I, p. 135.
[2] Text, Oncken, I, p. 138f.

its advantages and to encourage Germany to work for its own deliverance without relying on a solitary, heroic effort by Austria.

This demonstrated how well Metternich had learned the lessons of 1805. The coalition was to have the widest possible base and Austria was not to engage itself until its risks had been minimized. And the next paragraph revealed that the experience of 1809 had no more been forgotten. It defined the ultimate Austrian objective "as a great, *voluntary* . . . alliance in the centre of Europe, based on the *independence of states* and the security of property which would found a system of justice to replace the existing system of *forced* coalitions . . . and to oppose any designs for aggrandisement, *from whatever quarter*." Every word was chosen for maximum effect in this enunciation of the legitimizing principle, in the name of which Austria proposed to fight Napoleon. A *voluntary* alliance of states implied Metternich's determination to prevent a unification of Germany on the basis of national self-determination. A system of justice was to replace Napoleon's system of force, but it was to be based on the security of property and designed to forestall the sweeping reforms envisioned by the national enthusiasm of the North. Above all, Austria was not fighting against Napoleon as an individual but against French hegemony, and it was not prepared to replace one universal rule by another.

With this warning against Russian designs in Poland and Prussian ambitions in Germany, Metternich made clear the nature of the Austrian commitment: Austria based its hopes for success not on the ideals of an impatient generation, but on the wisdom of historical experience, not on popular enthusiasm but on the evaluation of the conqueror's psychology. "The whole policy of Austria," wrote Metternich in one of his marginalia, "is founded on Napoleon's character and it must be judged in the light of Austria's experience with this character and with foreign cabinets, particularly those of Southern Germany."[1] In this manner, Metternich channelled the moralistic fervour of Russia and the national impetuosity of Prussia into a concert of precise measures which imperceptibly transformed the moral basis of their effort. It was a policy whose seeming opportunism made possible the attainment by stages of an objective which might have been indignantly rejected had it been exhibited to full view immediately; it disdained the dramatic gesture and thereby made its achievements all the more secure through the semblance

[1] Oncken 1, p. 141.

of disinterest. So well, even insidiously, had Metternich implanted the legitimacy of his objectives, that almost every Austrian objective came to be offered to it by another power. If one compares the Knesebeck memorandum with the course of events as it finally took shape, one finds hardly any deviation. That many great dreams went unfulfilled thereby and many energies unharnessed is another matter.

Although Knesebeck's mission failed in obtaining an Austrian alliance, it gave Prussia the reassurance it required. The Austrian Emperor told the Prussian envoy that *nothing*—and therefore not even a Prussian betrayal of his son-in-law—could undermine Austria's intimate relations with Prussia.[1] And Metternich had made Austrian intentions quite clear. On 6 February, the Prussian King called for the formation of volunteer battalions. On 8 February, Knesebeck was sent on another mission, this time to the Tsar, to negotiate the treaty which came to be known as the treaty of Kalish, which ranged Prussia on the side of Russia and committed Russia to fight in the centre of Europe.

III

When Metternich encouraged Prussia to make its alliance with Russia, he had committed Austria not to permit a complete French victory. It was now time to create, under the guise of negotiations of peace, the coalition which would assure French defeat. On 8 February, the same day that Knesebeck was sent on his mission to the Tsar, Metternich prepared instructions for two emissaries. Baron Wessenberg was to go to London and Baron Lebzeltern to the Headquarters of the Tsar to attempt to persuade these two powers to accept Austrian mediation. It was a task of peculiar difficulty. Britain had to be made to appreciate the problems of a Continental power, that the *fact* of a coalition against Napoleon was no more important than the *mode* of its accomplishment, that victories are won not only by battles but by the choice of the battlefield. And Alexander had to be convinced that vast dreams were not a substitute for the balance of power. The formation of the Coalition would depend on whether Britain could be brought to understand the importance of the legitimizatoin of the equilibrium and Russia to accept a definition of limits.

The introductory passage was identical in both instructions. It

[1] Text, Oncken, I, p. 154. See also Luckwaldt, p. 105.

began with a logical quibble: Austria, it maintained, was not a mediator but an intermediary. It was the role of a mediator to dictate terms of peace; it was the function of an intermediary to *carry* conditions of peace from one camp to the other. Great Britain and Russia, if they knew their real interests, would therefore attempt to transform Austria from an intermediary into a mediator. But before the conditions of peace could be defined there would have to be agreement on the general axioms from which they might be derived.

The import of these remarks was unmistakable. Austria had appeared to France as a mediator and thereby implied a commitment to fight for the conditions of peace it was about to propose, although the fact that commitment would be directed against France —as the only power in a position to make the requisite sacrifices— had eluded Napoleon. But Great Britain and Russia were asked *to make mediation worth while*; to define, not the conditions of peace, but the general framework which might justify Austrian action. The Central Empire was demanding legitimacy as the price for its participation in the war.

At this point the two dispatches diverged. The part destined for Britain was an appeal for understanding and an exposition of the relations between a Continental and an insular power: "Those who prefer precipitation to coolly calculated measures, the dreamers who, unacquainted with our resources and our relations to other powers, burn with desire to throw themselves into the fray, are incapable of appreciating our political system. . . . The greatest consideration in the present crisis is the necessity in which we find ourselves of preventing with all our means the transfer of the war into the interior of our states. . . . The transformation of the war of the North into a war of the South . . . would relieve Napoleon from the embarrassment of continuing the war in an exhausted territory and would make him once more the master of the situation. . . . If England consults the interests which connect it with the Continent, if it appreciates the value . . . of a European equilibrium, it will wish to preserve the *one* power which can contain the ambition both of Russia and of France. . . . It must not see in Austria the power which must exhaust itself at a moment when nothing guarantees complete success and failure would involve the most dire consequences. . . . We should have lost all advantages of our central position . . . had we adopted any other measures than the present system."[1]

[1] Text, Oncken, I, p. 416f.

If the dispatch to London amounted to a request for understanding, the instructions for the emissary to the Tsar exhibited the distrust induced by a decade of Russian ambiguity.[1] The difference between Russia and Great Britain, Metternich argued, lay in the greater reliability of the island power. As for Russia, its recent successes, as unexpected as their effect was profound, might only magnify the tendency towards exaltation which the Russian court had always exhibited. To be sure, skilful diplomacy could exploit Russian instability. But it could not overlook the dangers posed by the Russian appetite for conquest, its use of revolutionary movements and the possibility that it might withdraw after the first reverse into arrogant isolation. For all these reasons, the journey of Lebzeltern had been delayed in order to give events an opportunity to mature. But now, concluded Metternich with the pride of a master adding the finishing touches to his work, the decisive moment had arrived: "Prussia's change of policy has probably been decided upon; in a few days the Russian armies will have reached the Oder; our mobile armies are situated on their flanks and even in their rear; their future operations are dependent on our good will; we can promote or arrest them; the moment to negotiate has therefore arrived." With these sparse phrases, matter-of-fact and prosaic as if the enthusiasm of Northern Europe had not even been heard of, Metternich announced the end of the first phase of his policy. The protagonists had been engaged, their options taken away. Austria emerged free through the constraint of the other powers, powerful through their need for her. This was indeed the moment to negotiate.

When, after various "illnesses" along the way, Lebzeltern arrived, on 5 March, at the Russian headquarters at Kalish in Poland, he found a situation which bore out Metternich's diagnosis. The Treaty of Alliance with Prussia had been signed a few days previously. It had guaranteed Prussia the territorial extent of before 1806, but it had said nothing about the location of these territories. The very vagueness of the wording, the stipulation that territories conquered in North Germany be used to augment Prussia, could leave no other conclusion than that the Tsar meant to use Prussia's Polish possessions to realize his Polish plans. But although Metternich had known about the Tsar's Polish plans, he had ordered Lebzeltern to delay his arrival as long as possible to avoid the very concerted action the Prussian negotiator sought so desperately. His main

[1] Text, Oncken, I, 421f.

object was to commit Russia. He was confident of his ability to outmanœuvre Alexander on the question of Poland later on. Lebzeltern arrived at a moment of general rejoicing at the decisive turn in events, while the monarchs were protesting their eternal friendship and patriots were drafting proclamations to the German people. It seemed impossible for Austria to stand apart from the national enthusiasm.

But enthusiasm can be dangerous when negotiating alliances, for it deprives the negotiator of the pretence of freedom of choice which is his most effective bargaining weapon. The Prussian plenipotentiary had arrived in Kalish in fact committed by the transports of patriotism of his people; and, when he hesitated on the Polish question, the Tsar concluded the alliance by appealing directly to the Prussian King with protestations of his good faith. Prussia's choice was limited by the fervour of its commitment, but Austria was not to be put off by invocations of generalities, much less by revolutionary threats. "With phrases which on close examination dissolve into thin air, such as the defence of civilization, nothing tangible can be defined,"[1] Metternich said once. It was Lebzeltern's task to see to it that the Tsar spoke tangibly.

He had brought with him, in addition to his instructions, two letters from his Emperor to the Tsar, whose friendly tone could not hide their avoidance of any concrete proposal,[2] and which left no doubt that Austria was not to be carried along by vague promises of moral crusades. The same reserve was shown by Lebzeltern who had been instructed by Metternich that his only task was to *receive* overtures.[3] When the Tsar, on 8 March, asked in exasperation what Austria *really* wanted, Lebzeltern replied coolly that it was up to the Tsar to formulate some general proposition as the basis of negotiation. It was then that the Tsar defined war aims, which included the return to Austria of all its former possessions; the independence of Prussia and its augmentation; the liberation of Germany from the French yoke; and the resumption by Austria of the Imperial Crown.[4]

Thus Austria obtained as a Russian offer what Prussia had been unable to achieve as a demand. It was guaranteed not only its old extent but its ancient territories. A limitation was put on the Tsar's

[1] N.P. VIII, p. 365.
[2] Text, Oncken, I, p. 448.
[3] Luckwaldt, p. 135.
[4] Oncken, I, p. 354.

Polish plans, for the Tsar, by his reply, had deprived himself of the Austrian third of Poland. Only the resumption of the Imperial Crown did not interest Metternich. He told Hardenberg, the envoy of Hanover, that having tasted full independence, the German sovereigns would submit to Austria but to undermine her position.[1] Napoleon had kept his Confederation of the Rhine together by an aura of invincibility and the threat of force. But Austria, already hardly a match for France, could not expose itself to future wars with a France reinforced by disgruntled German princes. A Germany composed of independent states, united by treaty or by law, was much more preferable. He did not add, although he might have, that this arrangement would assure Austrian predominance in Germany. Impotent independence would prove a more powerful bond than jealous vassalage. The fear of Prussian hegemony, of French invasion and of domestic upheaval, would represent a more effective device for Austrian supremacy than a relic of the Holy Roman Empire.

On 29 March, the Tsar not only reiterated his previous offer to Lebzeltern but added to it a proposal that Austria define its own boundaries. He gave Austria a free hand in Southern Germany and promised to support whatever overture Metternich chose to make to these courts.[2] Thus Metternich, by the end of March, 1813, had achieved his primary objectives. Russian armies stood in the centre of Europe embarked on a mortal struggle with France. Prussia had joined the common enemy. Only Austria stood not finally committed. Its major aims had been recognized by the Allies while Napoleon had accepted its mediation. It was gaining strength daily, not, to be sure, through the enthusiasm of its people, but through its discipline and through the tenacity of its leadership. The object of the struggle had been defined as a war for an equilibrium, for a society of states and not of nations, for a Germany of many sovereignties and for a conservative Europe. Only now that Austria's legitimizing principle had been recognized was Metternich ready to define what he understood by the European equilibrium. It is a tribute to his skill and patient preparation that what might have been considered a declaration of Austrian self-interest came to be seen as the expression of simple justice.

[1] C.C. IX, p. 60. See also Luckwaldt, p. 112f.
[2] Oncken, I, p. 359.

IV

The occasion was one of those almost imperceptible steps away from the French alliance, one of those moves which bared a little bit more of Central Europe to the Russian Army, accomplished as usual in the name of existing treaties. After the Austrian auxiliary corps had withdrawn from the Vistula, the defence of the next river line, that of the Oder, depended on its disposition. If it withdrew towards Silesia, the remnants of the Grande Armée, concentrated at the centre of the Oder, might have a chance to arrest the Russian advance until the arrival of Napoleon's new army in the spring. If it withdrew southward, the Oder line would be outflanked and the scene of the battle transferred another one hundred and fifty miles deeper into Central Europe to the Elbe. Metternich ordered Schwarzenberg to withdraw to the South in the direction of Cracow.

He announced this decision in a dispatch to Count Bubna, written as if an alternative were not even conceivable and under the pretext of announcing a happy occasion: Prince Schwarzenberg, the former Ambassador to Paris, who had negotiated the Treaty of Alliance and who had left his post to command the auxiliary corps, was returning to Paris where he was no doubt sorely needed. He would enlighten Napoleon as to the real relationship of forces in Central Europe. The possibility of defending river lines in Poland was an illusion fostered by Polish émigrés who, Metternich added sarcastically, were akin to the French émigrés; they did not hesitate to expend the resources of others in their cause, for they had everything to gain, nothing to lose and therefore nothing to defend. There followed an imposing estimate of Russian forces in Poland—which was none the less precise and detailed for having no relation to reality—an assertion that Schwarzenberg's corps had in fact delayed this impressive army for over four weeks, in short, that Austrian measures were precisely calculated to conserve the strength of the Alliance.[1]

But Schwarzenberg did not leave for Paris immediately. Over four weeks were to elapse before his departure; and, when Metternich drew up his instructions for Schwarzenberg on 18 March, Prussia had already changed sides, and the Tsar had guaranteed the Austrian objectives. Even then Schwarzenberg did not go directly to Paris. He stopped at the capitals of the South German states, still connected to France by treaties of alliance, and urged them to evade French

[1] Text. Oncken, I, p. 306f. (German), p. 430f. (French), 18 February.

demands for military assistance. Schwarzenberg was not to have his first interview with Napoleon until 9 April, and by that time Poland was well in the rear of the Russian armies.

Schwarzenberg's mission gave Metternich an opportunity, however, to elaborate his conception of the equilibrium. His instructions to Schwarzenberg began with a historical summary designed to throw into relief the need for a balance of power:[1] A series of wars had upset all previous ideas about the nature of the equilibrium. After 1807 only three major powers, France, Russia, and Austria, had remained on the Continent, and two of these were, in effect, allied against the third. But the war of 1809, however disastrous materially, had strengthened Austria morally. It had led to the establishment of close relations between France and Austria, and this in turn had sown the seeds of discord between Russia and France. Metternich continued with a summary of other causes of Russo-French tension, an account of the outbreak of the war and Austrian efforts to avert it, all of which culminated in this proposition: the defeat of France had overthrown all calculations, a new equilibrium had to be constructed. Austria had offered its mediation precisely because no power could be more interested in the restoration of the equilibrium than the state whose geographic position condemned it to devastation in any war of two powers which could come into contact only at its expense.

But at the very moment when Austria had transmitted its offer of mediation to Napoleon, Metternich explained innocently, an event had occurred as unexpected as its consequences were serious, the alliance of Prussia with Russia. Far from condemning the Prussian measure, however, Metternich called it a logical result of Prussia's suffering since 1806. And, lest Napoleon attempt to restore his fortunes by crushing his erstwhile ally, Metternich identified the fate of Prussia with that of Austria: "The attitude of the [European] powers differs as their geographical situation. France and Russia have but a single frontier and this hardly vulnerable. The Rhine with its triple line of fortresses assures the repose of . . . France; a frightful climate, . . . makes the Niemen a no less safe frontier for Russia. Austria and Prussia find themselves exposed on all sides to attack by their neighbouring powers. Continuously menaced by the preponderance of these two powers, Austria and Prussia can find tranquillity only in a wise and measured policy, in relations of good

[1] Text, Oncken, I, 439f.

will among each other and with their neighbours; their independence . . . can in the long run only be assured by their own strength. Each weakening of one of the Central Powers represents the most direct blow at the existence of the other. . . ."

The dispatch, despite its calm tone, thus represented a challenge and a definition of limit. If Metternich's analysis was correct, the war Napoleon was preparing would have no object. If Prussia was to be preserved and, if possible, strengthened, the phrase about the French frontier on the Rhine was not idle rhetoric, but represented the definition of the extent of French power which Metternich considered compatible with the peace of Europe. And the instructions to Schwarzenberg were a warning to Napoleon to have no illusions. Austrian adherence to the French alliance could not be bought by the prospect of territorial aggrandisement. The Central Empire was not interested in victory, but in repose. Not territorial extent, but the relative strength of powers, not scale but proportion, were the guarantees of Austrian security: "The Emperor . . . will never seek an illusory gain in the destruction of a friendly state. . . . Austria, by assisting in the destruction of the other intermediary power, would sign its own death warrant." By means of the Schwarzenberg instructions Metternich announced that the period of revolutionary conquest was over; that Napoleon, the man of will, could have peace only by a recognition of limits; that France, which had sought security in dominion, could achieve it only by renunciation. Austria was committed to the restoration of the equilibrium, *against* Napoleon if necessary.[1]

Within the space of a few days Castlereagh and Metternich had defined the nature of the Europe they sought to establish. They agreed that the equilibrium depended on a strong Central Europe, which, in turn, presupposed a powerful Austria and Prussia. They agreed that the power of France would have to be reduced, although Metternich was much vaguer about the nature of these limits than Castlereagh. This was by no means accidental. Castlereagh was constructing a coalition *against* France. The memory of the ordeal barely survived caused the statesman of the island power to attempt to

[1] Metternich did not exclude a Continental peace without Great Britain. But in that case Napoleon would have to demonstrate that a continuation of the war served only British interests; in short, he would have to consent to so drastic a limitation of French power that Europe could feel secure even without British support. The offer of a Continental peace was a mirage, a demonstration of its futility.

neutralize the *cause* of the war, the disturber of the peace. But for Metternich the defeat of Napoleon was not the end of a problem but the occasion to define a continuing relationship. He was, therefore, less concerned with the containment of France than with the distribution of power; less with barrier fortresses than with the relative strength of states. To Castlereagh the reduction of France was the guarantee of European repose; to Metternich the limits of France depended on the extent of Russia. Castlereagh advanced the Pitt plan as one of his first measures after relations with the Continent were re-established. Metternich did not advance his notion of the equilibrium until *after* a tortuous and deliberate diplomacy had established the moral framework of the alliance. To Castlereagh the *fact* of Napoleon's predominance was a sufficient impetus for the creation of the coalition and all that remained to be settled was the essentially technical question of how best to restrain the aggressor. To Metternich the *nature* of the peace was the primary issue and he was therefore concerned with the essentially moral question of how to legitimize the settlement.

V

As Metternich contemplated the situation at the end of March, 1813, he might well be satisfied. Austria had transformed itself from a French auxiliary to the pivotal power of Europe and it had obtained its peace terms as an unconditional offer from its allies-to-be. It had spoken so insistently to both sides of the impossibility of a separate peace, that the fact that all negotiations had to go through Austria came to be accepted as an elementary fact. By thus keeping the threads of events in his hands, Metternich could co-ordinate his measures with the growth of Austrian strength. In December he had disposed of barely fifty thousand men; in January the Emperor spoke to Napoleon of one hundred thousand and, at his first interview with Napoleon, Schwarzenberg was to indicate the prospect of twice that number. The danger of catastrophe, in case of a sudden attack, was diminishing. All this was achieved, if not with the blessing, at least with the toleration of Napoleon and without losing the confidence of the other powers.

But however successful a policy, it will not yield results automatically. Metternich had still to translate Allied agreement to his terms into political reality; he had still to create not only the doctrine but the substance of the equilibrium. He could hardly have doubted that this was impossible without war. That Napoleon should relinquish most of his German conquests and throw in Antwerp, without which Britain would not make peace, was beyond all probability. But this fact was not necessarily apparent to the other members of the Austrian Cabinet. If the other powers had difficulty divining Metternich's goals, this was equally true of his colleagues, some of whom considered his policy too risky, while others decried it as dishonourable and shabby in a Europe of universal enthusiasm. The Emperor, remembering four lost wars and always more ready to preserve than to achieve, clung stubbornly to a hope for peace, almost at any price. And all this time the other powers were pleading, cajoling and threatening to end Austrian aloofness.

Once more Metternich began so skilful a balancing act that it was hardly noticeable that the balancer was tipping the scale; so dexterous a performance of juggling that it was not remarked that suddenly, almost imperceptibly, there was only one ball left in the air. He was determined that Austria should emerge as a principal power despite his Emperor's hesitations; but that she should appear at her own time and in a manner best in accord with her domestic structure, whatever the pleas of the Allies. Everything depended on the cause of the war, for that would remove the Emperor's doubts and at the same time irrevocably settle the legitimizing principle of the peace. With this in mind, Metternich set about to transform Austria from an intermediary into a mediator. And while a wave of national enthusiasm swept over Europe and patriotic societies were drawing up plans for a transformed humanity, the cool calculator in Vienna was preparing a *casus belli* which would make all these efforts idle fantasy. Metternich proposed to lead Austria into war and to legitimize the Alliance by what was essentially a logical deduction. He set out to demonstrate the necessity of war by proving the impossibility of peace.

V

The Formation of the Coalition

I

It was of peace then that Metternich spoke as he was preparing the coalition and as the two great armies moved forward into Central Germany. His policy had now reached a turning-point. It had not been welcomed by the "Austrian School" of the aristocracy who would have preferred a war of liberation on the Prussian model. Indeed, in March, Metternich had to suppress a plot, led by Archduke Johann, who planned a national uprising in the Tirol to force the Emperor's hand. But the Emperor had supported Metternich, even if in the interest of different goals. A decade of defeat had developed in the Emperor what was to be a cardinal Habsburg virtue for a century, the quality of endurance, of dogged persistence. But he valued endurance for its own sake, and the goal of his persistence was simply survival. Pedantic and unimaginative, the Emperor confused stability with stagnation and peace with inactivity. Heretofore all of Metternich's measures had conserved, such as the withdrawal of the auxiliary corps. Or they had evaded action, such as the refusal of Napoleon's request for transit through Austrian territory. But could the Emperor be induced to engage in a positive step? Would he recoil when it became clear that Metternich's inactivity had been designed to make possible total commitment?

It was not for nothing that Metternich spoke of peace. In an hour of crisis it is impossible to rail against the domestic structure of the state, and in any case Metternich was never the man to do so. Not in creativity but in the ability to use all available factors, to arrange them in the proper proportion, to achieve seemingly at random the best adaptation to circumstance, lay Metternich's strength. The personality of the Emperor seemed to Metternich more inflexible than the exasperation of the Allies. It was not, therefore, for Austria to conform to the spirit of the hour, but for the hour to wait on the spirit of Austria. "Count Metternich must indulge the very peculiar character of the Emperor," Hardenberg wrote in a dispatch on 2 May. "He would resist everything which would precipitate an outbreak, but, guided one step at a time, he has nevertheless reached the point where a break is unavoidable. . . . But to get here Metternich had to hide all semblance of ambition, indeed even his willingness to risk a war. Even now he has succeeded in getting the Emperor used to the idea of the necessity of war, only in case Napoleon refuses a just peace of equilibrium. . . ."[1] Just like a judo artist, Metternich drew his Emperor along even while seeming to yield and induced him first to create an army in order to protect his neutrality and then to use this army to protect the peace.

He was aided by the inability of Napoleon to come to grips with the new situation. A ruler legitimized by charisma or by force cannot easily accept the fact that henceforth he must seek his safety in self-limitation, that events are no longer subject to his will, that peace depends not on his strength but on his recognition of the power of others. A revolutionary who remembers his opponents when they were still restrained by what they then considered "legitimate", finds it difficult to take seriously their resolution when they have understood the extent of their danger. Because his opponents surrendered easily when they were still conducting wars for limited objectives, the revolutionary is convinced that another successful battle will once more reveal their cravenness. And he cannot believe in the loss of his allies, because he cannot admit the reduction of his power. This was Napoleon's state of mind as he was preparing to leave for his army in April, 1813. Confident that one successful battle would disintegrate the Alliance, he did not doubt that Austria would eventually join his side. He had forgotten, if he ever knew, that his great victories had been due as much to the ease with which his opponents had accepted defeat as to the success of his arms. Not without reason was Metternich more concerned about the resolution of the Allies than about the state of their armies.

The extent of Napoleon's misapprehension was apparent during his interview with Schwarzenberg on 9 April.[2] If Napoleon doubted Austria's intentions, this was not apparent in the propositions he advanced. They amounted to a request for the concentration of an Austrian army of a hundred thousand men in Bohemia and for concerted operations by it and the auxiliary corps in Galicia.

[1] Text, Oncken, II, 221f.
[2] Text, Oncken, II, p. 618f.

Once more, his dearest wish was being offered to Metternich, for an army could now be formed in Bohemia at the request of France, against which it was to be directed. Schwarzenberg did not reply to the proposal regarding the auxiliary corps because he wished to defer explanations to a "more suitable" place and moment. It would have been unsuitable indeed for the commander of the auxiliary corps to explain that the auxiliary corps no longer existed.

For Metternich had decided that with the Allied armies approaching the Elbe, the place of the Austrian army was in Bohemia, the only province still exposed to danger and the best place from which to threaten the flank of the advancing French army. No sooner had Metternich received Lebzeltern's first reports about the Tsar's favourable disposition than he set about to remove the last obstacles to a Russian advance: the threat of a flanking movement from Galicia. Once more this was to be achieved in the name of existing treaties and, if possible, sanctioned by Napoleon himself. On 25 March, Metternich sent a dispatch to Lebzeltern proposing that Russia abrogate the armistice and advance on both flanks of the Austrian auxiliary corps, which would then yield to the force of circumstances.[1] On 11 April, Metternich sent another dispatch indignantly protesting against the Russian failure to advance in Poland: "Our role as French ally is ending; we are preparing to appear on the scene as a principal power . . . it is therefore inexplicable that we receive no news of the abrogation of the armistice."[2] One can imagine Metternich's malicious smile when his desire finally was fulfilled and he drafted an outraged letter of protest to the Tsar, which, to underscore the extent of his discomfiture and surprise, he headed "two o'clock in the morning", and which had no other purpose than to demonstrate his continuing loyalty to his French ally.

Metternich had every reason to assure himself of proofs of his loyalty, for relations with France were being put to a severe test. On 7 April, the French ambassador, Narbonne, had transmitted a demand by Napoleon that Austria increase its army and co-ordinate its movements with Napoleon's. "Napoleon gives one more proof that he is committed to a policy of illusion," Metternich told Hardenberg and set about to exploit his opponent's mistake. For by his request that Austria emerge as a full-fledged partner, Napoleon

[1] Text, Oncken, II, p. 201f.
[2] Oncken, II, p. 205.

admitted that the limited alliance of the previous year was no longer applicable. And if the Emperor could not be induced to forego the status quo even for the sake of regaining Austrian territory, he would certainly resist any effort to embark him on behalf of his son-in-law. But if he would not consent to mobilize his army to enforce a peace of equilibrium, he might agree to do so as a protest against "unreasonable" claims of assistance: "Henceforth, everything depends on us," Metternich told the Emperor. "We must find the means within ourselves which can give this strangest of all moments a happy issue. . . ."[1]

There ensued a contest between Metternich and Narbonne of stylized intricacy and desperate manœuvre, none the less deadly for being carried out with subtle grace. But the psychological advantage was now on the side of Metternich. Napoleon's early successes had resulted from the inability of his opponents to comprehend the enormity of his goals, while he had grasped the limitation of their perspective. Metternich's present superiority was due to his understanding of the limitation of Napoleon's power, while his antagonist was still assuming its omnipotence. In 1805 and 1806, Napoleon had been victorious because his opponents conducted a diplomacy of limited objectives; in 1813, he was defeated because he acted as if he possessed unlimited power. The positions of Metternich and Napoleon had thus been reversed. The superior mobility on which Napoleon had always prided himself, and which had really been only the reflection of his opponents' inflexibility, was now Metternich's. But where Napoleon's mobility had been expressed on the field of battle, Metternich's was exercised in cabinet diplomacy. And just as the rapidity of Napoleon's movements had confounded opponents who adhered to rules which declared them "impossible", so the dexterity of Metternich's moves isolated an opponent who disdained them. Napoleon staked everything on the reality of his power, Metternich on its illusoriness. To rely on the efficacy of diplomacy during a revolutionary period may lead to disaster; but to rely on power with insufficient means is suicide.

It was therefore not mere deviousness which accounted for Metternich's measures—although he dearly loved finesse—but a deliberate choice of weapons. The more intricate the manœuvres, the more surely the contest would be shifted from the plane of patriotic fervour to that of cabinet diplomacy. What appeared as a contest between

[1] Luckwaldt, p. 173.

Metternich and Narbonne was in reality a transformation of the cause of war from a moral to a legal issue, from the liberty of nations to the equilibrium of states. The discussion began, on 7 April, with Narbonne's demand for Austrian military action against the Allies. Metternich suggested in reply that the limitations imposed by the treaty of alliance on Austria's military strength be suspended. And he added ambiguously that the Emperor would not consider himself bound in any case by the stipulated size of the auxiliary corps should his "reasonable" peace proposals be rejected.[1] Here was the first avowal that Metternich was planning "armed mediation" and it should have made it clear that the alliance was finished; but Narbonne persisted and, on 20 April, presented a demand for full Austrian military support. Now Metternich informed him of the withdrawal of the auxiliary corps from Galicia and of the fact that military assistance was out of the question, since the Emperor could hardly act both as mediator and as combatant. Narbonne replied that this was tantamount to a declaration of war. But the threat of Napoleon's power was no longer effective. Not war, but peace was Austria's goal, Metternich insisted, but it was ready to fight for that cause. And the interview ended with an exchange which threw into sharp relief the nature of the conflict between the illusion of power and the power of guile. "But you are not ready," insisted Narbonne, "it is my job to know this." "And mine to hide it," Metternich replied, "let us see who does his job better."[2]

But Narbonne was not to be discouraged. A crumbling world order, even one built on force, finds it as difficult to believe its disintegration as man to visualize his own death. The illusion of permanence is perhaps our most important myth, the one, in any case, which makes life supportable. Narbonne could not believe that Metternich's *sang-froid* in the face of the French threat could be "real", any more than Napoleon's antagonist ten years previously could believe that the eighteenth-century structure had collapsed. But an interview with the Emperor on 23 April gave him pause. For French insistence had manœuvred the Emperor into the only position in which he was capable of assuming heroic proportions, that of dogged perseverance in inactivity. Alarmed by Metternich's report of his conversation with Narbonne, he had given orders

[1] Luckwaldt, p. 75f.

[2] Oncken, II, p. 215. At least this was Metternich's version to Hardenberg and what he wanted to be true even if it was not.

to increase the Bohemian army to eighty-five thousand men.[1] He now told Narbonne that he could hardly attack Russia while engaging in mediation, and in any case the limited alliance with France was not applicable to the new situation. Should Napoleon consider this refusal a breach of the treaty, the rupture would be Napoleon's fault. He was ready, he repeated, to persevere in his policy backed by two hundred thousand men.[2]

Once more Narbonne returned to the charge, but now the period for illusions was drawing to a close. On 29 April, he saw Metternich again and informed him that Napoleon had joined his armies and that this was tantamount to a victorious battle. Would this affect Austria's dispositions? Austrian conduct, Metternich replied coolly, was calculated not on the assumption of Allied victories, but of Allied defeats, and the latter would cause Austria to redouble her efforts. On 1 May, Metternich returned a final reply to the French demands, which announced the emergence of Austria as a contender for the equilibrium: "The Emperor of Austria has adopted the noblest attitude possible . . . that of mediator. As soon as [the Emperor] desires an objective he also desires the means. The means consist of . . . total impartiality and the development of great power. . . . The Emperor desires peace and nothing but peace. It will not be with weak forces that the Emperor will back up his peace messages and *combat the enemies of the interests of France* [my italics], which are inseparable from the interests of his own Empire."[3] With these threateningly pacific phrases, Metternich completed the transformation of Austria from ally to armed mediator. For all its ambiguity, Metternich's reply to Narbonne left no doubt about his real objectives: It was not against France that Austrian mediation was directed, for France was a necessary component of the European equilibrium. The enemy of the real interests of Europe—and therefore of France as well as of Austria—was Napoleon. To give the proof of this postulate was Metternich's next step.

II

War is the impossibility of peace. Metternich's design was as simple as this proposition and as complicated. For Russia and

[1] Luckwaldt, p. 199f. (20 April, 1813).
[2] Oncken, II, p. 217f. (Report of Hardenberg).
[3] Text, Oncken, II, p. 224f, p. 630f.

Prussia, approaching a battle with the man still surrounded by the nimbus of past successes, could not be expected to appreciate the deliberate intricacies of Metternich's policy. It is difficult to understand the importance of stratagem, when confronted with a situation which supersedes all stratagem. Benevolent neutrality is always a tenuous role, for it requires precisely the degree of pretence which will disquiet one's friends, while it may not suffice to reassure the foe. To succeed too completely may involve the loss of allies; to fail prematurely may provoke a sudden attack. A loss of confidence by the Allies would have exposed Metternich to complete isolation; an irrevocable conviction of Austrian treason would have brought down on Austria the full measure of Napoleon's wrath. Already the Tsar, piqued at the Emperor's evasions of his proposals for a personal interview, was muttering darkly that he expected military not diplomatic deeds from Austria; nor was he completely satisfied with Metternich's devious measures with respect to the auxiliary corps.[1] On the other hand, Metternich was afraid that an unexpected reverse might react on Alexander's mercurial temperament and lead to the disintegration of the alliance before it had been fully formed.

To overcome Allied distrust and to convince them of the certainty of eventual Austrian support, Metternich wrote to the Tsar on 29 April. The dispatch represented a plea for understanding and a pledge of aid. This declaration, the most unequivocal yet made by Austria towards Russia, resolved itself into a simple proposition: the war was to be won only by resolution, not in a fit of enthusiasm; the undisturbed marshalling of forces was more important than a dramatic declaration of policy; Austria would be found at the side of the Allies, but in her own time.[2] It began by postulating three basic requirements: (a) the greatest firmness on the part of the Allies in case of disaster, (b) the fullest explanations between Austria and the Allies, (c) the greatest development of Austrian military resources. Austria was prepared to declare without reservation that an Allied defeat would only cause her to redouble her efforts in order to arrest the movements of Napoleon. But, continued the dispatch in a confidential portion designed for the Tsar, the Austrian Cabinet noticed with sorrow the apparent distrust of the Russian court. And yet its measures were only appropriate to Austria's special situation: "Little given to abstract ideas, we accept things as they are and we

[1] Luckwaldt, p. 215.
[2] Text, Oncken, II, p. 630f.

attempt to the maximum of our ability to protect ourselves against delusions about realities."

With this reminder of Austrian determination not to be swept along by outbursts of exaltation, popular or monarchical, Metternich turned to an examination of "reality" as it presented itself to him. In 1809, the Austrian army had been in a complete state of dissolution. In 1811, it would have been impossible to mobilize even sixty thousand men. But now Austria had built the nucleus of a respectable and growing force under the pretext of creating an auxiliary corps and a corps of observation. To be sure, Austria had offered its mediation to France and refused to join the Russo-Prussian alliance. These steps, Metternich argued, were inherent in the nature of the Austrian state. Austria, the state whose existence depended on the sanctity of treaty relations, could not change sides motivated only by the misfortune of its ally; and the financial measures requisite for success could be carried out only under conditions of peace. Moreover, since Austria had foreseen that the decisive battles would be fought between the Elbe and the Oder, it had concentrated its army in Bohemia and delayed its final declaration to Napoleon in order to disrupt his plans as much as possible: "In accordance with the system of complete delusion which has characterized Napoleon since the last campaign, he counted . . . on active support by our *former* auxiliary corps; what is even more incomprehensible, he flattered himself that we would put *all* our forces at his disposal. The opposite is occurring; the auxiliary corps is dissolved . . . upward of sixty thousand men are situated on the flank of the French army. Should Napoleon win the battle, he will have gained nothing, because the Austrian armies will not permit him to exploit his successes; should he lose it, his fate will have been decided sooner, but not more surely. . . . In either case Austria will bear the brunt of the effort. We are not afraid of this prospect; we have given sufficient proof of this during the past twenty years. But it would be inexcusable were we to begin by deluding ourselves about the forces we require and if we did not organize them *before* we place them on the stage. . . ."[1]

This was the declaration of policy of an ancient power, grown wise by many enthusiasms shattered, grown cautious by many dreams proved fragile, grown weary from many battles fought in vain; of a power which had to make up for its narrow margin of safety by

[1] Oncken, II, p. 634.

exactness of calculation. The central position, so often the cause of foreign invasions, was to be utilized for a maximum freedom of action. It was a novel doctrine that the most exposed power should make a virtue of necessity and use the need for her in an hour of crisis to achieve temporary isolation. Dexterity of diplomacy was to create what geographic separation supplied to more favoured states. While Austria was gathering her forces, Metternich was weaving the strands of his diplomacy with an ambiguity which seemed to leave all options open while it slowly inched Austria into the Allied camp. It was paradoxical that it was the Central Empire which appeared on the scene last, after all other powers were committed, and that it was the only state which mobilized its army under conditions of peace.

The success of this policy depended on two factors: the correct assessment of the relative strength of the contenders and the efficacy of its diplomacy. Metternich considered Austria the pivotal state because he was convinced that neither side could achieve a decisive victory without Austrian assistance. And he could translate this estimate into reality because Austria was the only one of the contending parties capable of conducting diplomacy. The relations of France with the Allies were "revolutionary"; they were contending about the nature of the legitimizing principle and diplomacy had necessarily to prove futile. But Austria could appeal to both sides on grounds they considered "legitimate"; to the Allies on the need for a European equilibrium and to Napoleon on the basis of a family compact. To be sure, all of Metternich's finesse would have been of no avail but for Napoleon's delusions. And the most disastrous of these delusions was Napoleon's belief that a father could not make war on the husband of his daughter.

III

Now, as the two armies were approaching each other in Central Europe, Metternich began the armed mediation which was not to end until Austria had joined the Coalition against Napoleon. He sent two plenipotentiaries to the opposing headquarters as if to illustrate that the gulf between the contending parties was too great to be bridged by direct contact, as if the impending battle were designed to illustrate Austria's indispensability. Stadion, who was sent to the Allied headquarters, brought an Austrian proposal for conditions of peace so moderate that they only added fuel to the suspicions of

Austria's motives.[1] But discussions about conditions of peace were still premature. For on 2 May, the Allied army was defeated at Luetzen and, on 16 May, it was defeated again at Bautzen. It was more important to avert disaster than to dispute about the spoils of victory.

The Allied defeat threw the Emperor into panic. Confronted by a seemingly invincible Napoleon, oppressed by the memory of 1805 and 1809, he feared that the French Army might at any moment wheel south and invade his territories. "Had Napoleon demanded a categorical explanation [of Austrian intentions] at this moment," reported Hardenberg, Metternich's channel to Great Britain, "he would without doubt have promised unconditional neutrality. . . . I know that Metternich has had serious clashes with him already about the degree of energy with which Austrian goals are to be pursued."[2] Metternich, therefore, spoke of peace again and dispatched Bubna to Napoleon's headquarters. Originally it had been intended to send Bubna merely for the sake of "diplomatic symmetry" with only the vaguest instructions. But now, at the Emperor's insistence, he was asked to transmit to Napoleon the same conditions of peace that Stadion had brought to the Allies.[3] And in a supplementary instruction Bubna was urged to speak primarily as an Austrian emissary, not as a mediator.[4]

Napoleon, however, had entered the campaign with three illusions. He had counted on a crushing blow which would disintegrate the Alliance. He had believed that he would be able to negotiate a separate peace with Russia any time he chose. He had relied, if not on Austrian assistance, at least on Austrian neutrality. But by the end of May he had won two battles, yet victory had eluded him, partly because his lack of cavalry had made close pursuit impossible, but more importantly because the "rules" of this war precluded surrender or separate peace. On 18 May, he had sent an emissary to the Russian outposts asking for a meeting with the Tsar. But the Tsar had refused, insisting that all negotiations be conducted through Austria.[5] Now Metternich set about to utilize Napoleon's one remaining illusion, his reliance on Austrian good will, to deprive him of the fruits of his victorious battles. While the Allied armies were with-

[1] Instruction to Stadion, 7 May, 1813. Oncken, II, 640f.
[2] Oncken, II, p. 311. See also Luckwaldt, p. 224.
[3] Instructions to Bubna, 11 May, 1813, Oncken, II, p. 314f; 645f. (French).
[4] Luckwaldt, p. 233f.
[5] Luckwaldt, p. 283.

drawing into Silesia, Stadion was instructed to request an armistice to give Austria an opportunity to mediate.

All parties required an armistice: Napoleon to restore his cavalry; Russia and Prussia to reorganize their armies; Metternich to rally the Allies and to complete Austrian mobilization. Napoleon's victories had made necessary a change in Austrian dispositions and the army which had been expected to attack into Northern Bavaria was now deployed to protect the defiles into Bohemia. Furthermore, on 16 May, Stadion had concerted a strategic plan with the Allies which according to the Austrian general staff required a period of between thirty-seven and fifty-seven days to implement.[1] But much more serious than Austrian unpreparedness was the state of mind of the Emperor. The very people who had been loudest in demanding a patriotic war when Napoleon seemed weak, now insisted on peace in the face of his apparent invincibility; and the Emperor frantically sought a formula for returning to complete inactivity. "The Emperor, Duka and all our military are now vociferous in demanding peace . . .," Metternich wrote to Stadion. "An armistice will be the greatest of blessings. . . . It will give us an opportunity to get to know each other, to concert military measures with the Allies and to bring reinforcements to the most threatened points."[2]

On 4 June, an armistice was concluded at Plaeswitz to run until 20 July. Like a commander moving into the field for the decisive operations, Metternich now advanced his headquarters to Gitschin, a castle in Bohemia, about midway between the opposing headquarters. Everything depended on Austria. The Allied route of retreat had been chosen to maintain contact with the Austrian army, and disaster was certain if Austria remained neutral. The exasperation of the Allies was growing. Stewart, the British plenipotentiary at Prussian headquarters, undoubtedly reflected their mood when he wrote to Castlereagh on 31 May: "Our operations have been conducted with implicit faith in Austria: we have . . .

[1] For the deliberations regarding the military plan, see Oncken, II, 320f. and 341f.

[2] Oncken, II, p. 336. Another indication of the Emperor's state of mind is found in a dispatch sent by Stadion to the Emperor at the end of July and contrasting his present brilliant situation with the despair of only six weeks previous: "[After the battle of Bautzen] the Emperor despaired of the Allied cause. He convinced himself that the goal of the war was lost, that nothing remained but to anticipate greater misfortune by concluding a peace even on conditions that corresponded in no respect to the great goals which His Majesty conceived upon sending me on my mission." Oncken, II, p. 443.

committed ourselves to a narrow strip of country where existence for . . . an army becomes very doubtful. We have abandoned Breslau, the direct communication with Kalish and have thus given Poland over to Bonaparte's influence; and still Austria does not declare. . . . I am by no means pleased with the manner things are going, both in the councils and on the battlefields."[1] Metternich had based his policy on the premise that the Allies would permit him to reach an agreed objective in his own manner, the only manner that could be made acceptable to the Emperor. Now he was in danger of failing because no state, however benevolent, will risk disaster because of another power's intricate domestic structure.

All Allied doubts were concentrated on the peace programme which Stadion had brought to headquarters. Austria had suggested the return of Illyria to Austria, the territorial aggrandisement of Prussia in the Duchy of Warsaw, the surrender by France of its possessions on the right bank of the Rhine, and the dissolution of the Confederation of the Rhine, the group of German vassal states of France. The Allied counter-proposal of 16 May added a number of conditions, such as the independence of Spain and a commitment that Prussia obtain the same territorial extent (but not the same territories) as before 1806.[2] But the dispute was much more fundamental than the conditions of peace. The Allies were reluctant to make an agreement with Napoleon, but they wanted their programme to reflect at least the requirements of their security. Metternich, who was convinced that *any* agreement with Napoleon was impossible, was concerned with the psychological impact of the Allied proposals. The Allies were stating conditions of peace; Metternich was elaborating a cause of war. The Allies were worried that Napoleon might accept Austria's moderate terms; Metternich was concerned lest Allied intransigeance give Napoleon a chance to rally the French people and to appeal to the Austrian Emperor.

The real issue then revolved around the purpose of the forthcoming conference. If the conference was designed to achieve agreement, the programmes of the participants had to reflect their maximum demands. But if it was to demonstrate its impossibility, a programme of minimum demands was called for. In a stable international order, demands once formulated are negotiable. In revolutionary periods, demands once made become programmatic. In a stable order the

[1] C.C. IX, p. 21, 31 May, 1815.
[2] Text, Oncken, II, p. 318f.

diplomatic conference attempts to adjust differences among the contenders. In a revolutionary situation the purpose of a conference is psychological; it attempts to establish a motive for action and is directed primarily to those not yet committed. To formulate minimum demands in a stable order is to surrender the advantage of flexibility in negotiation. To formulate exorbitant demands to an antagonist who will in any case reject them is to compound the chief difficulty of a revolutionary period: to convince the uncommitted that the revolutionary is, in fact, a revolutionary, that his objectives are unlimited. It yields to the adversary the advantage of the advocacy of moderation without the risk of its accomplishment. In May, 1813, the uncommitted element was *within* Austria, and Metternich desired a conference to expose Napoleon's goals to his own Emperor.

Everything depended therefore on whether Metternich had judged the situation correctly. Had Napoleon's policy been perfectly flexible, he could have paralysed Metternich by accepting his minimum demands. But perfect flexibility in diplomacy is the illusion of amateurs. To plan policy on the assumption of the equal possibility of all contingencies is to confuse statesmanship with mathematics. Since it is impossible to be prepared for all eventualities, the assumption of the opponent's perfect flexibility leads to paralysis of action. The individual who understands intangibles realizes, however, that no state can give up its vision of "legitimacy" and no individual his *raison d'être*, not because it is physically but because it is psychologically impossible. For Napoleon to make a Continental peace before he knew he could have a maritime peace, and to surrender all his conquests across the Rhine and Illyria would have meant that Napoleon had ceased being Napoleon. Metternich was demanding something more fundamental than the cession of territories: the end of a revolutionary policy. In this sense, his policy can perhaps be said to have been designed to save Napoleon from himself.

When, therefore, the Allied plenipotentiaries discussed the Austrian peace terms with Stadion on 10 June, they insisted on their maximum programme, while Stadion urged them to defer it to the *final* peace conference.[1] This alone should have made clear that Metternich was not interested in a programme to negotiate, but in a cause for which to contend. But lest any doubt remain, Metternich

[1] Oncken, II, p. 340, Report of Stadion.

sent a dispatch to Stadion on 14 June reaffirming his position.[1] The Austrian proposals were essential, Metternich argued, because "the Emperor could never be brought to act until a peace congress had been assembled and the demonstration made that Napoleon will not accept *even* these demands". To formulate excessive demands would be to play Napoleon's game, to give him an opportunity to rally the French people and to fight the war in the name of national honour. The problem, in short, was to demonstrate not the impossibility of a *safe* peace, but the impossibility of *any* peace. And lest Napoleon upset all calculations by accepting Austria's minimum conditions, Metternich added the proviso that their acceptance did not preclude additional demands by the Allies at the peace conference.

These were presumably the arguments which Metternich used towards the Tsar when they met, on 19 June, at Opotschna, where the Tsar had gone on the pretext of visiting his sister. Whatever Metternich's arguments, the negotiations between the Allies and Austria came to a rapid issue after the Tsar's return to headquarters and resulted, on 27 June, in the treaty of Reichenbach, a document of such ambiguity that historians to this day use it to illustrate Napoleon's intransigeance. It stated in effect that Austria, having invited the courts of Russia and Prussia to accept its mediation for a *preliminary* peace, undertook to join the war against Napoleon if the latter refused to accept, by 20 July, the following four conditions: the dissolution of the Duchy of Warsaw; the enlargement of Prussia; the return of Illyria to Austria; the restoration of Hamburg and Luebeck as Free Cities.[2] It did not matter that these conditions were "moderate", that they seemed "soft" towards the conqueror. Their pliability hid a fact of transcendent importance. After seven months of the most ambiguous diplomacy, Austria stood committed to go to war at a definite time and under specified conditions.

The treaty of Reichenbach represents a fitting climax to Metternich's tortuous course of half a year. So gradual had been his movements that a step which a few short months ago would have appeared as the utmost in daring came to be seen as the inevitable reflection of an objective situation. And so adept had been his diplomacy that the very moderation of the Reichenbach proposals hid the fact that

[1] Text, Oncken, II, p. 667f. See also B.D., p. 71. Stewart's report.

[2] Text, Martins, *Recueil de Traités*, p. 106f. The paragraph in question read: "The Emperor of Austria, having invited Russia and Prussia to negotiate with France regarding a preliminary peace to lead to a general peace, undertakes to declare war on France if it does not accept by July 20th the following conditions:"

they were meaningless. For the treaty spoke only of Austrian commitments and not of those of the Allies. It spoke of an offer of mediation by the Emperor of Austria to the Courts of Prussia and Russia, but it did not say under what conditions the Allies were accepting it. It undertook to go to war if France rejected the four conditions, but it was silent about the reaction of the Allies should France agree.[1] Metternich, if not his Emperor, could have no illusions about the possibility of peace, for both the Prussian and Russian ministers had made clear in dispatches sent on 19 June that they accepted the Austrian conditions only as the basis of mediation, not as an expression of their peace terms.[2]

This logical quibble was merely another ambiguity added to the already ominous phrase that Napoleon's acceptance of the Reichenbach conditions would secure him only a *preliminary* peace. Napoleon was being asked in effect to accept the Rhine boundary in return, not for peace, but for the possibility of negotiating it. It was out of the question that the man who had so often identified the fate of his dynasty with the unimpaired existence of his Empire would agree to such a confession of weakness. That Metternich could count so completely on this reaction was the real argument for war. Napoleon, who had staked everything on the supremacy of power, could not be brought to terms until he had learned its limitation—and in the event he did not learn it until too late. The Emperor of Austria, who had staked everything on mere survival, could not be induced to go to war until the incompatibility of Napoleon's claims and a system of equilibrium had been demonstrated. The Treaty of Reichenbach made these two propositions converge with the inevitability of a mathematical equation. Metternich's diplomacy had eventually depended on the correct evaluation of two personalities, the Emperor and Napoleon. Its success proved the reality of intangibles.

IV

Only one short step separated Austria from the Coalition. "It seems now that Metternich is valiant and that the Emperor Francis is the timid person," wrote Stewart to Castlereagh on 16 June. "To wind him up to the proper key . . . and to commit him decisively is

[1] Text, Oncken, II, p. 365.
[2] Oncken, II, p. 359f. See also B.D., p. 78f.

the present aim. . . . His Imperial Majesty Francis does not see things as advantageously as is desirable; and when it is pointed out to him that a movement in Bonaparte's rear . . . would annihilate his son-in-law, he rather looks to reigning in those limits which peaceable arrangements may bring about."[1] The final step in Metternich's diplomacy was to show that peaceable arrangements were incapable of setting limits to Napoleon.

Napoleon himself helped bring matters to a head by one of his precipitate moves, which illustrated his continuing delusion about Austria's attitude. Learning about Metternich's meeting with the Tsar in Opotschna, he invited him to come to his headquarters in Dresden for an exchange of views. "You see," Metternich wrote to Stadion, "that my evil star is calling me to Dresden. . . . The conversation will lead to nothing. . . . I consider the journey the most certain means to get clear about the essence of the question."[2]

Metternich in later life was to write a dramatic account of his meeting with Napoleon in Dresden on 26 June, 1813; of an antechamber full of ministers seeing in him the last chance for peace; of a resplendent Napoleon and an imperturbable Metternich; of a hat flung in a corner and a refusal to pick it up; of a prophecy spoken in parting: "Sire you are lost."[3] Even if it does not report what actually happened, it is true in the sense of the history of the ancients —it is psychologically true. At Dresden the man of will and the man of proportion were confronting each other for the last time, and the man of will was destroyed because he was incapable of the final insight: the recognition of limits. The essence of the conversation is contained in a brief report which Metternich sent to the Emperor shortly after he saw Napeoleon.[4] Its core was a demand by Napoleon to learn the conditions of Austrian mediation and Metternich's insistence that Napoleon first accept the principle of armed mediation; Napoleon's refusal to cede any territory save a part of Poland to Russia because none of the other powers "deserved" any gain, and Metternich's evasion that territorial questions should be raised at the peace conference. Napoleon was arguing as if peace depended on his will, but there was something pathetic about his bluster because he no longer had the power to make his will effective.

[1] Alison, Sir Archibald, *The Lives of Lord Castlereagh and Sir Charles Stewart*, 3 Vols. (London, 1861). Vol. I, p. 667.

[2] Text, Oncken, II, p. 362.

[3] N.P. I, p. 151f.

[4] N.P. II, p. 462f.

Metternich was attempting to assemble a congress to transfer the contest to the plane which he had come to dominate, partly because of his adversary's folly, that of cabinet diplomacy. When Napoleon, in order to commit his elusive opponent and to obtain another paltry extension of the armistice, agreed to Austrian armed mediation and to a congress, he was walking into a trap. For it was no longer peace which was at issue, but the cause of war.

The agreement signed by Metternich and Napoleon on 30 June provided for French acceptance of Austrian mediation, for an extension of the armistice to 10 August and a congress to assemble at Prague by 5 July.[1] Austria's new-found independence was expressed in another act, more symbolic perhaps than even Napoleon's acceptance of Austrian armed mediation: the release of Austria from the French alliance. On 27 June, Metternich had asked that the alliance be suspended during the mediation as incompatible with its purpose. On 29 June, the French Foreign Minister released Austria from all obligations because "France did not wish to be a burden to her friends".[2] Thus, Austria, at the end of June, 1813, had achieved her objectives. She was the controlling element in the Coalition being formed against Napoleon and had assembled one hundred and fifty thousand men undisturbed. Whatever happened, peace or war, Austria's domestic structure would not be threatened, because it would be legitimized by the only guarantees of the Central Empire's continued existence: the European equilibrium and the sanctity of treaty relations. Well might Metternich write to the Emperor from Dresden, not without innuendo: "Where would Austria be today had we confined ourselves to half-measures?"[3]

But Metternich had still to convince the Allies of the necessity of extending the armistice. It was hardly an auspicious beginning for Austrian mediation that its first act involved a violation of the Treaty of Reichenbach, so reluctantly agreed to by the Allies in the first place. Although the Allied ministers did not go so far as Stewart, who wrote to Castlereagh that a secret understanding existed between Austria and France,[4] they nevertheless pointed out the repeated delays in the Austrian commitment from 1 June to 20 July and now to 10 August. How was one to know that Austria could ever be

[1] Text, Fain II, p. 454.
[2] Text, Oncken, II, p. 392.
[3] Oncken, II, p. 395.
[4] Alison, *Lives*, I, p. 674.

brought to action? But Metternich was adamant: he could not prevent the Allies from reopening hostilities on 20 July, but in that case the Emperor would probably declare Austria's unconditional neutrality. He added a reminder that Austria had in fact become the key to the Coalition not only diplomatically but also strategically. Neutrality, he insisted, would preclude the Allied transit through Bohemia, without which Napoleon's position on the Elbe could not be turned. The war, in short, would have to wait while Metternich legitimized his policy domestically.

The Congress at Prague is therefore not significant for the negotiations among the plenipotentiaries but for its impact on the observers, of whom the most crucial was the Emperor of Austria. An exchange between Metternich and the Emperor makes clear the real issues involved. On 12 July, Metternich transmitted a request for instructions to the Emperor which amounted to a plea for steadfastness now that success seemed so near.[1] It began with an assertion, always so distasteful to the Emperor, that decision could no longer be evaded. The power of states, Metternich argued, depends on two factors, their material strength and the personality of their rulers. Austria had achieved the highest point attainable by its present policy, but even the highest point led, inevitably, to a need for decision. The monarchy could be saved only if Metternich could count on the Emperor's greatest firmness and persistence. For anyone familiar with the Emperor's psychology this represented an assertion none the less daring for its submissive tone. It stated, in effect, that failure would be due not to material weakness, but to loss of will; that the moment for commitment had arrived: "We cannot persevere in our present course, which was made necessary by the momentary weakness of the monarchy. Then the admission of weakness represented our sole chance to gather our strength. . . . To be sure, . . . we are still not as strong as formerly, but as weight in the balance. . . . [Austria] is predominant. This consideration, the only correct one, we do not seem to take to heart sufficiently."

With this reminder that calculations of absolute power lead to a paralysis of action and that strength depends on the *relative* position of states, Metternich turned to an examination of the eventualities confronting Austria at the Congress of Prague. It was a truism of Austrian policy, he declared, that mediation could take place only *in favour* of the Allies, that Austria would declare war only if *France*

[1] N.P. II, p. 463f.

rejected the Reichenbach basis. Should the Allies reject the four Austrian conditions, it was inconceivable that Austria should join Napoleon. For this eventuality, Metternich reserved the right to submit his recommendations at the proper time. But Metternich's real fear had nothing to do with the Allies and he summed it up in the following query: "Can I count on the firmness of Your Majesty if Napoleon rejects the Austrian conditions; is Your Majesty . . . determined in that case . . . to entrust the just cause to the arbitrament of arms. . . .?" Metternich knew only too well that the exasperation of the Allies and the increasing displeasure of Napoleon might furnish a sufficient bond to crush the perfidious Austria should it be found hesitating again. Ambiguity could force a commitment of others, but this commitment represented a claim, however deferred. "[If we delay again]," Metternich concluded, "we would bring about neither peace nor a favourable war . . . but the probable collapse of the monarchy . . . and I would have become, with the best of intentions, the tool of the destruction of all political consideration, of the moral substance and the dissolution of the machinery of state." All of Metternich's obliqueness could not obscure the fact that the fate of Europe depended on the resolution of one man.

The turn of mind of that man is best illustrated by his answer to his minister. In its pedantic craving for safety, in its timid consciousness of all dangers, it furnished the best reply to those who had wanted to embark Austria on a crusade on the Prussian model: ". . . Peace, lasting peace," it read, "is the most desirable goal of any decent man, all the more so for me on whom falls so heavily . . . the suffering of such decent subjects and such beautiful provinces. This must be our goal . . . we must not be deceived by temporary advantages. . . ."[1] This man, who saw in the Austrian Empire a personal possession, to be thriftily administered by careful husbandry, was not to be inspired by considerations of the European equilibrium, much less by the liberty of nations. To demonstrate his readiness for peace he even offered to forego the "Austrian" condition in the Reichenbach convention, the claim to Illyria. But should Napoleon refuse these "reasonable" demands, he affirmed, then war was the only solution. Emperor Franz entered what came to be known as the "War of Liberation" with all the resolution of a shopkeeper defending himself against a competitor who cannot be brought to see that splitting up the market is the best insurance for mutual harmony.

[1] N.P. II, p. 467f.

Metternich, however, was almost at his goal. At Kalish, he had obtained Russian acceptance of Austrian mediation; at Dresden, Napoleon had consented; now, and this was not his meanest accomplishment, the Emperor had submitted to the implications of his own policy. What did it matter that each had his own reason for accepting Metternich's policy; the Tsar to secure Austria as an ally, Napoleon to paralyse her and the Emperor to avoid commitment? What difference did it make that the Tsar saw in Austrian mediation a weapon for victory, Napoleon for conquest, and the Emperor for peace? All the strands were now in Metternich's hands and only the last knot remained to be tied.

The Congress of Prague never really met. To show his disdain or to gain time, Napoleon did not dispatch his plenipotentiary until 25 July. The Tsar sent the Alsatian, Anstett, a calculated affront to Napoleon. The British envoys, Stewart and Cathcart, waited in the wings, prepared to animate the faltering by the promise of subsidies or the threat of their withdrawal. There was no occasion to falter, however. Secure in his belief in Austrian pusillanimity, Napoleon had left his headquarters on a tour of inspection. Since Caulaincourt, his plenipotentiary, was obliged to refer all proposals to him for final decision, no agreement even on procedure could be reached. "Our affairs here," Metternich wrote to Stadion on 30 July, "leave no doubt that 10 August will be the final day of our relations with France. . . . Caulaincourt has confirmed what I realized at Dresden, that Napoleon is deluding himself completely about the real situation. All his calculations having long since been frustrated, he now clings to those ideas which flatter his preconceptions. He seems just as convinced now that Austria will never take up arms against him, as he was in Moscow that Alexander would negotiate."[1]

So it came about that Napoleon's one peaceful effort to give permanence to his dynasty, the marriage to Marie-Louise, had turned into a means to hasten his downfall. Even Caulaincourt asked for Austrian firmness, at least so Metternich reported to the Emperor.[2] "Conduct us back to France either by war or by armistice and thirty million Frenchmen will thank you," Metternich quoted him as saying. On 8 August, Metternich transmitted to him the

[1] Oncken, II, p. 440. See also B.D., p. 79 (Report by Stewart).

[2] During his stay at Prague, Metternich transmitted extensive reports in which Caulaincourt and Fouché use arguments deceptively similar to his own. See, for example, Oncken, II, p. 433f.

Austrian conditions in the form of an ultimatum. So complete was his mastery of the situation, that he succeeded in pledging Caulaincourt to secrecy about their content and thus made impossible their utilization by Napoleon to rally the French people. In vain did Caulaincourt appeal to Napoleon to "dissolve the hostile Coalition by peace". Napoleon thought he could count on his father-in-law's cowardice, if not on his loyalty. 10 August passed without word from Napoleon. When, on 11 August, a messenger brought Napoleon's counter-proposals, in any case inadequate, Metternich merely replied: "Yesterday we were mediators, but not today. French propositions must henceforth be addressed to the three *Allied* Courts."

V

The bonfires on the hills of Bohemia, which told the Austrian army on 11 August that it was now at war, signalized the end of an extraordinary diplomatic campaign. Cool and deliberate, it had enabled Austria to emerge as the unchallenged spokesman of the Coalition. It had not produced any great conceptions; nor had it used the noble dreams of an impatient generation. Its skill did not lie in creativity but in proportion, in its ability to combine elements it treated as given. Starting from the assumption of the special requirements of the Austrian central position and peculiar domestic structure, Metternich had succeeded in building a coalition around the sanctity of treaties and the legitimacy of sovereigns. He had transformed Austria from an ally of France into its enemy, with Napoleon's approval at every stage. He had transformed the war from a war of national liberation into a cabinet war for the equilibrium, as an offer from the Tsar. He had built an army right under the noses of the French. And he had led Austria into war for a cause which would insure a peace compatible with Austria's structure—with the approval of his Emperor.

Philosophers may quarrel with the moral stature of this policy, but statesmen can study it with profit. An ancient Empire, barely recovering from two disastrous wars, cannot be reformed while it is about to struggle for survival. The statesman cannot choose his policies as if all courses were equally open. As a multi-national state, Austria could not fight a national war; as a financially exhausted state, it could not fight a long war. The "spirit of the age" was against the continuation of a polyglot Empire, but it is too much to ask its statesman to elevate national suicide into a principle of policy. To be sure, Metternich would hardly have conducted a different policy even had the Austrian domestic structure been more flexible. The reason for his success lay in the correspondence between his convictions and the requirements of the Austrian situation. But this is no more than saying that Metternich was not a cynic where his deepest values were concerned.

His policy, both in content and in form, symbolized the nature of the Austrian Empire. Austria could not join a crusade, for crusades make universal claims and Austria's survival depended on a recognition of limits, on the sanctity of treaties, on legitimacy. The deliberate measures, the cool calculations, the careful manœuvres all testified to the quest for a world in which universal claims would disappear and hegemony would become impossible. Since Austrian policy could not draw its strength from the inspiration of its people, it had to achieve its aims by the tenacity and subtlety of its diplomacy. Few diplomatic campaigns demonstrate more clearly that policy is proportion, that its wisdom depends on the relation of its measures to each other, not on the "cleverness" of individual moves. Every individual measure was ambiguous, each step subject to differing explanations. But the result was a Coalition whose moral framework was well tested, whatever one may think of its content, and whose accomplishment was the restoration of peace after a quarter-century of war.

All the elements of Metternich's later policy are already apparent in this period: the careful preparation, the emphasis on obtaining the widest possible moral consensus, the utilization of the adversary's psychology to destroy him more surely. Its crowning accomplishment was its success in identifying the domestic legitimizing principle of Austria with that of the international order. With justice could the Emperor tell a Prussian visitor in his crude Austrian dialect: "Look here, was I not smarter than you? Did I not do in an orderly fashion what you wished to do in disorder?"[1]

That it was accomplished in an orderly fashion was not his merit, but that of his Foreign Minister. Disaster had been averted; the Coalition was formed; Austria had survived once more. Friedrich

[1] Springer, Anton, *Geschichte Oesterreich's seit dem Wienen Frieden von* 1809, 2 Vols. (Leipzig, 1863). Vol. I, p. 222. "Schaun's war ich nicht gescheiter wie Sie? Hab' ich nicht in Ordnung getan, was Sie in Unordnung tun wollten?"

von Gentz thus summed up Metternich's accomplishments: "In the sunlight of a state's health and power and with unlimited means, it is not too difficult to play a role in the world. . . . But to guide a ship, battered by storms for twenty years, through cliffs and maelstroms, through a thousand obstacles and contending pressures and back to the open sea is an art not given to many."[1]

Metternich was to prove later that to divine the direction on a calm sea may prove more difficult than to chart a course through tempestuous waters, where the violence of the elements imparts inspiration through the need for survival.

[1] Srbik, I, p. 128.

VI

The Testing of the Alliance

I

WHILE Metternich was engaged on his tortuous course, the statesman of the power which had fought Napoleon the longest and most unrelentingly could only wait with impotent impatience. To Castlereagh, Napoleon's bad faith seemed so self-evident that any attempt to demonstrate it could hide only cowardice or profound design. To hold a conference solely for the psychological impact of its failure appeared to him a meaningless evasion. A defensive conception of foreign policy imparts a great singleness of purpose against a power felt as a threat. But it cannot persuade those still uncommitted. If the danger were understood it would be unnecessary to invoke it. Until it is experienced, the pleas for common action will appear like exhortations to fight in a foreign cause, all the more irritating because of their self-righteousness. For this reason Britain had stood alone while one Continental power after another succumbed to the illusion of separate arrangement or the impotence of isolation. For this reason, too, Britain had to stand aside while the nature of Napoleon's inability to accept limits was being demonstrated through his refusal of even the most moderate conditions.

For Metternich had excluded the British representatives at Allied Headquarters from all negotiations about conditions of peace. His formal reason was the British refusal of Austrian mediation. But his real reason was his fear that Britain would insist on terms which would have nullified his efforts to convince the Emperor of the necessity of war. No wonder that the British representatives to the Allied courts, Sir Charles Stewart at the Prussian and Lord Cathcart at the Russian headquarters, regarded Metternich with undisguised dismay.[1] A power which has never suffered disaster finds it difficult to comprehend a policy conducted with a premonition of catastrophe. The attempt of a less favoured ally to hedge its risks cannot but

[1] See, for example, C.C. IX, p. 13, 18 May, 1813.

appear to it as the outgrowth of a decadent cleverness. The role of Baron Wessenberg, Metternich's envoy to London, could not have been more miserable. Shunned by society, never officially received by the Prince Regent, under virulent attacks by the press, he was barely tolerated and, at one time, thought seriously of withdrawing to the countryside to escape the wrath of the populace.[1] And Stewart, true to his self-appointed mission of penetrating base intrigue, wrote from Allied Headquarters: "I cannot help thinking . . . that Metternich will attempt some family alliance. . . . If things turn to a Congress pray send a very able man. Depend upon it he will be required. . . . You will want a devilishly clever fellow there."[2]

As Castlereagh contemplated the European scene in the spring and early summer of 1813, he had little reason for satisfaction. To be sure, Allied armies stood in the centre of Europe but they seemed paralysed by the vastness of their opportunity. Britain, although no longer isolated, was nevertheless not yet part of the concert of powers, partly because of difficulties of communication, but primarily because a power which is absolutely committed has no negotiating position. Her most effective bargaining weapon, the threat to withhold subsidies for the Allied armies, could not prevent negotiations of peace, as was indicated by the Treaty of Reichenbach, concluded only three days after the signature of subsidy treaties.[3] Metternich's measures, although largely misunderstood, were nevertheless an indication that Britain was still not completely part of Europe, that a Continental peace to the exclusion of Britain was at least conceivable. Britain was fighting, not the least, for an international order which would make purely Continental arrangements impossible.

The reverse side of the fear of a Continental peace was the determination never to stand alone again. Almost any arrangement would be preferable to the continued exclusion of the balancer from the balance of power, to the implied threat that the opposite mainland was capable of a policy *against* the island power. If necessary, Britain would be willing to agree to a peace far below her expectations if it

[1] For Wessenberg's role in London, see Luckwaldt, p. 122f.

[2] C.C. IX, p. 23, 6 June, 1813.

[3] Metternich's negotiations were, of course, completely misunderstood. We have seen that Britain was to be excluded only from the preliminary peace, that she was to participate in the general peace, and that Russia and Prussia had specifically reserved this right. Webster is quite misleading on this point. See, however, B.D., p. 78. (Hardenberg's letter to Stewart.)

could be concluded *together* with its allies. "You must guard against a Continental peace being made to our exclusion," Castlereagh wrote to Cathcart. "Impracticability on our part may hazard this, notwithstanding our treaties. . . . For this purpose our readiness to treat with our allies must be avowed, so that they have no reproaches to make against us."[1] Only the independence of Spain, Portugal and Sicily, the fulfilment of British obligations to Sweden and, of course, maritime rights were not negotiable.[2] The island power had to retain some points of influence on the Continent, if not at its centre, at least on the periphery guarding sea lanes.

Castlereagh went even further. On 13 July, yielding to the pleas of the Prussian and Russian ambassadors, he accepted Austrian mediation, albeit with some churlishness.[3] He immediately qualified it by pointing out that the peace might prove so imperfect as not to tempt Great Britain to surrender any of her colonial conquests.[4] This was tantamount to reserving the right to veto a settlement, since only the return of France's lost colonies could induce Napoleon to accept the Austrian conditions. In another letter, Castlereagh multiplied the obstacles to even a preliminary peace and concluded with an exhortation which was at the same time an expression of his extreme distrust of Metternich's incomprehensible policy: "Bonaparte has had a severe lesson, but whilst he has such a force under arms, he will not *submit* to any arrangement which even *Count Metternich would have the face to sign his name to* [my italics], as providing on solid principles for the repose of Europe."[5] He was not aware how completely he and Metternich agreed in their analysis of the situation. Britain, in any case, had not fought alone for a decade to be negotiated now out of the fruits of her victory.[6]

By the time the British acceptance of mediation arrived, the die had been cast, and it was in fact not transmitted to the Austrian court until after the Austrian declaration of war and then only as a token of good faith.[7] Castlereagh, henceforth, saw his task in translating the fact of the alliance into a consciousness of its necessity. He confessed to Cathcart that the Congress of Prague, however unlikely its success,

[1] C.C. IX, p. 30, 6 July, 1813.
[2] B.D., p. 6f.
[3] B.D., p. 12.
[4] C.C. IX, p. 36, 14 July, 1813.
[5] C.C. IX, p. 40, 7 August, 1813.
[6] See B.D., p. 79f.
[7] C.C. IX, p. 45, 1 September, 1813.

had filled him with great anxiety.[1] His dispatches during September and October abound with statements of the need for common action; with assertions stressing the common danger, and presented with an eloquence seldom found in his pedantic writing: "The sovereigns of Europe . . .," he wrote to Cathcart, "have successively found that no extent of submission could procure for them either safety or repose, and that they no sooner ceased to be objects of hostility themselves than they were compelled to become instruments in the hands of France for . . . the conquest of other unoffending states. . . . *It is this common danger* [my italics] which ought always to be kept in view as the true basis of the alliance. . . . As opposed to France, a peace concluded in concert, though less advantageous in its terms, would be preferable to the largest concessions received from the enemy as the price of discussion. . . . This alone can bring down the military force of the enemy to its natural level and save Europe from being progressively conquered by its own spoils."[2]

Only Austria still seemed irresolute. Not without justice did Castlereagh continue to suspect Metternich of lack of determination. For Metternich continued to be less interested in triumph than in balance, less in a French collapse than in limiting French power. Metternich, who attempted to avoid *any* preponderance, sought to prevent a vacuum which would whet Russian ambitions. Castlereagh, who feared only *French* preponderance, attempted to animate the Coalition to maximum efforts. So concerned was he about Austrian determination that he poured forth a flood of advice to transform the war into a war of nations, not of states, to appeal to the popular enthusiasm, in short, to do all the things Metternich had worked so craftily to avoid. "It really appears to me quite impossible," he wrote to Cathcart, "to mistake the true issue and the sooner the Austrian minister makes up his mind to it . . . the less risks he runs. . . . It is become a contest of nations and not a game of statesmen and he will play into Bonaparte's hands if he deals with it on any other principle."[3] The fear of Austrian defection even made Castlereagh go so far as to assert a social foundation for the international order: "It appears," he wrote to Aberdeen, "that [Metternich's] ears could hardly yet bear the sound of war and that he is disposed to whisper rather than din it into the ears of the nation. . . . The whole military

[1] See f.e., B.D., p. 103, 15 October, 1813.
[2] B.D., p. 20, 18 September, 1813.
[3] B.D., p. 34, 14 October, 1813.

history of the Revolution has taught us to dread that the monster once engendered on French ground may break loose to seek its sustenance elsewhere. . . . The people are now the only barrier. They are against France and this is the shield above all others that a State should determine to interpose for its protection which is so wholly destitute as Austria of a defensible frontier."[1] Thus one of Castlereagh's rare excursions into social philosophy added up to just one more argument for steadfastness against France.

Castlereagh's exhortations to Austria were in fact based on a misconception. It was not a lack of awareness of the French threat which caused what seemed to be Austrian hesitations, but Metternich's concern with another danger as yet undiscerned by Castlereagh. For while Castlereagh was still looking to concerted action by the "unselfish" powers, Great Britain and Russia, to define the conditions of the European equilibrium, the Tsar was perfecting plans which threatened to place Central Europe at his mercy. While Castlereagh was exhorting Metternich about the dangers of universal dominion, he did not know how well his words were being heeded. Except that Metternich was watching Napoleon with one eye and the Tsar and Poland with the other.

II

It was paradoxical that a state which had ceased existing in 1795 and a monarch who prided himself on the nobility of his principles should have provided the elements of discord in the Great Coalition. Poland, partitioned for the third time in 1795, had lived only as the inspiration of its patriots until, in 1807, Napoleon resurrected the Duchy of Warsaw out of Prussia's Polish possession and added to it portions of Austrian Poland after the war of 1809. In 1812, Napoleon had utilized Polish patriotism as a tool in the Russian campaign. His declaration that he considered the war a Polish war had augmented his forces by eighty thousand men, the remnants of which were still with the French armies in 1813. The retreat from Moscow had shattered the vision of a Poland extending to the Dnieper. As Russian armies swept westward no other fate seemed in store for Poland than the return to the partitioning powers of their old possessions.

But Poland has often been better served by the fervour of her

[1] B.D., p. 105, 15 October, 1813.

patriots than by their ability to choose the winning side. As Russian armies were approaching Poland, Adam Czartoryski, whose father had presided over the proclamation of the Confederation of all Poles under Napoleon's auspices and who himself had on that occasion resigned from the Russian army, remembered the friend of his youth, the Tsar Alexander. On 6 December he sent a letter to the Tsar which included the following passage: "If you should enter our country as victor, will you take up again your old plans regarding Poland? Will you, in subjugating it, also conquer its hearts?"

The ambiguity of this letter was matched by the instability of the man to whom it was addressed. Napoleon said of the Tsar that he had great abilities but that "something" was always missing in whatever he did. And since one could never foresee which particular piece would be missing in any given instance, he was totally unpredictable. Metternich described him as "a strange combination of masculine virtues and feminine weaknesses. Too weak for true ambition, but too strong for pure vanity".[1] At the same time mystic and cunning, idealistic and calculating, he presented an ambivalent mixture of universal principles justifying specifically Russian gains, of high motives supporting aspirations considered selfish in lesser men. He was capable of great self-abnegation, as he proved repeatedly during the period of the Holy Alliance. But he could also be cruel and treacherous. "He was not for nothing the son of [the mad] Tsar Paul," Talleyrand said of him. That he was convinced of the identity of his goals with the claims of universal justice cannot be doubted. That these claims generally coincided, at least during his early period, with the national interest of Russia is even less open to question. He had been greatly influenced in his youth by his Swiss tutor, La Harpe, who had sought to raise him as the ideal ruler of the Enlightenment, as the philosopher-king who would govern on the basis of universal maxims and bestow on his people the blessings of his liberality. While still a Grand Duke, Alexander had promised Adam Czartorisky to work for the liberation of Poland. It was this promise to which the letter referred.

The reply Alexander returned to Czartorisky's letter revealed the duality of his nature. "Vindictiveness is a feeling unknown to me," it read. "It is my sweetest delight to repay evil with kindness." After asserting that his aims with respect to Poland had not changed, he discussed the opposition he would encounter both within Russia and

[1] N.P. I, p. 316f.

from Austria and Prussia. A precipitate declaration would keep Austria and Prussia from joining the Coalition and might throw them into the arms of France. He promised, however, that his plans would become increasingly apparent as the military situation developed.[1] Nobility of soul might supply the motive for Polish independence, but cunning was to be the mode of its accomplishment.

Alexander proved a man of his word. The Treaty of Kalish had significantly avoided any promise to return its Polish territories to Prussia, and, during the course of the negotiations, Saxony was mentioned as a possible compensation. But although the Tsar carefully refrained from revealing the full extent of his ambitions, Metternich, as we have seen, was well aware of them. And Austria could not be indifferent either to the extension of Russia deep into Central Europe or to the transformation of Prussia from an Eastern into a predominantly German power. Russian expansion almost to the Oder would transform Prussia, with an indefensible Eastern frontier, into a Russian satellite; while a Prussia deflected into Germany might compete with Austria for predominance. Metternich was therefore in no hurry to crush France completely, and thereby create a vacuum which would merely serve to strengthen Russia's bargaining position, particularly while Britain's attitude was still not clear. For it was still unknown whether Great Britain would identify the European equilibrium with anything other than the defeat of Napoleon; or whether it could be brought to realize that Antwerp was best defended in Poland.

Castlereagh was, as yet, unaware of these problems; and had he known of them, he would in all likelihood have blamed them on Metternich's chicanery. For him, the war was still a contest for the restoration of the equilibrium by powers so chastened by the experience of foreign rule as to limit their ambitions. That any power other than France should again disturb the peace seemed so inconceivable that no reference to it can be found, direct or implied, in any of Castlereagh's numerous dispatches of this period. Instead, he tended to pursue the course charted by the Pitt plan: to create the European equilibrium in co-operation with the other "satisfied" power, Russia; to restrain the historical rivalries of the Central Powers, to animate the Alliance and to guarantee the European settlement. For this reason, as provided in the Pitt plan, all proposals for a post-war settlement were invariably first submitted to the Tsar.

[1] Text, Oncken, I, p. 226.

It was not until he came to the Continent that Castlereagh realized that Britain's natural ally was Austria, the Continental power, which, whatever its differences in domestic structure, also represented the claims of the equilibrium and of repose.

This misunderstanding led to a dialogue with Alexander which was all the more exasperating because the real cause of its inconclusiveness did not immediately become apparent. In his first dealings with the Tsar, Castlereagh was advancing purely British conditions, whose achievement was either assured by the fact of British possession, such as the independence of Spain, Portugal or Sicily, or which remained still academic, such as the independence of Holland or the exclusion of maritime rights from any peace conference. Whatever his concern for the Coalition, Castlereagh pursued these goals with an almost fanatic singlemindedness. This was particularly true with respect to Holland and the maritime rights. As early as 10 April, he had written to Cathcart to "direct the Tsar's anxious attention to Holland. Nothing short of driving the French across the Rhine, and providing a safe existence for that country, can give us a good barrier against France and a safe communication with our Allies on the Continent".[1] The independence of Holland was to be pressed at every opportunity. But as Allied armies were still far away, the Tsar's noncommittal replies could be taken as but a reflection of the military situation.

The same impasse occurred with the maritime question. Despite the fact that Castlereagh attempted to avoid any discussion of this point, the Tsar brought the matter to a head by offering to arbitrate between Great Britain and the United States. Since that war had been fought very largely on the issue of the British "right" to search neutral vessels, Great Britain was touched on a raw nerve, and Castlereagh returned a very sharp warning. "I cannot omit [stressing]," he wrote to Cathcart, "the importance of awakening the Emperor's mind to the necessity of pre-emptorily excluding from the general negotiation every maritime question. If he does not, he will risk a . . . misunderstanding between those Powers on whose union the safety of Europe now rests. . . ". When the Russian ambassador in London again raised the controversial question, Castlereagh replied with an even longer dispatch. He reiterated that no British minister could dare compromise the maritime rights and he added ominously that, if the Powers of Europe were interested in establish-

[1] C.C. VIII, p. 359, 10 April, 1813.

ing a counterpoise against France, they should not risk dissension among themselves by introducing this subject.[1] Here was indeed a paramount British interest, one that superseded even the great Coalition.

Another difficulty arose when Castlereagh attempted to implement the basic idea of the Pitt plan, the negotiation of the General Alliance which would define the conditions of the European equilibrium. He appealed to the Tsar within a few days of learning of the break-up of the Congress of Prague: "Were either of the [powers] to attempt a separate peace, it must leave France master of the fate of the others. It is by the war in Spain that Russia has been preserved and that Germany may be delivered; it is by the war in Germany that Spain may look to escape subjugation. . . . To determine to stand and fall together is their only safety and to achieve this the confederates must be brought to agree to certain fixed principles of common interest."[2] The war was thus legitimized entirely by the need to subdue France and the proposed conditions reflected this goal: They called for the independence of Holland, Sicily, Spain and Portugal, the removal of French influence from Italy and from the Confederation of the Rhine, and the restoration of the Austrian and Prussian monarchies to the territorial extent and influence they enjoyed before their defeat by Napoleon.

Castlereagh evidently had no doubt that these proposals would be accepted without hesitation. He urged Cathcart to assure the Tsar of the imperishable impression his conduct had made on the British government; he proposed that Britain and Russia jointly invite the other Powers to accede to the Alliance. If any difficulty was expected, it would be from Austria, although Castlereagh reassured himself that the best way to make a cautious power bold was to convince it that it possessed temperate but determined allies.[3] But the Tsar proved strangely difficult. Castlereagh's dispatch arrived while the Allied armies were pursuing a routed foe after the battle of Leipzig, and the Tsar evaded several meetings by pleading military concerns. When Cathcart finally saw him on 26 October, the Tsar expressed agreement in principle with the proposed alliance and suggested a discussion of its provisions with his minister, Nesselrode.[4] At sub-

[1] B.D., p. 32.
[2] B.D., p. 19f., 18 September, 1813.
[3] B.D., p. 30.
[4] B.D., p. 35, 30 October, 1813.

sequent meetings he became increasingly reticent, however. He invoked his good faith, which would make a formal engagement unnecessary; he raised once more the question of maritime rights; he insisted that Britain specify the colonies conquered during the war it intended to return and he demanded a firm commitment of future subsidies. He remarked enigmatically that the conditions of the peace would have to reflect the "real situation", but he failed to make clear just what he understood by that term. It was odd, reported Cathcart, that Austria, the power which had been expected to cause most difficulties, should seem so pliable and that the Tsar should prove so obdurate.[1] This, too, was a misapprehension, for Metternich was so pliable precisely because the Tsar had been so difficult.

The Coalition had in fact arrived at the critical point where an avowal of goals might demonstrate the tenuity of the protestations of harmony. It is the essence of a coalition, by definition almost, that the differences between its members and the common enemy are greater than their internal differences among each other. Since the appearance of harmony is one of its most effective weapons, a coalition can never admit that one of its members may represent a threat almost as great as the common enemy and perhaps an increasingly greater one as victories alter the relative position of the powers. Coalitions between status quo and acquisitive powers are always a difficult matter, therefore, and tend to be based either on a misunderstanding or an evasion. A misunderstanding, because such a coalition will tend to solve peripheral questions—those of concern to only some of its members and which do not affect the basic power relationship—relatively easily, by a mutual recognition of special claims. And an evasion because the longer the settlement of fundamental questions is delayed during a successful war, the stronger the position of the acquisitive power becomes both militarily and psychologically. The total defeat of the enemy removes, if nothing else a weight in the balance and confronts the status quo power with the alternative of surrender or a war with an erstwhile ally whose relative position has improved with the enemy's defeat.

A status quo power must therefore attempt to force a definition of war aims at as early a stage of the conflict as possible, in effect by adding the weight of the enemy, or the fear of the enemy, to its own side. As long as the gulf between the acquisitive ally and the common enemy is sufficiently wide, the desire for victory or the fear of revenge

[1] B.D., p. 37, 11 November, 1813.

may suffice to force the issue. This had been Metternich's design in the diplomatic campaign ending with Austria's entry into the Coalition. It was to remain his policy throughout the war.

By contrast, the acquisitive power will attempt to defer a final settlement as long as possible. In this effort all advantages are on its side. If it insists that the final arrangement must depend on the military situation, it will tend to bring about a total war which creates a power vacuum through the complete destruction of the enemy. The greater the vacuum, the greater the disturbance of the equilibrium and the more "natural" unlimited claims will appear. Only a separate peace can forestall this, but the status quo power will always have great difficulty, psychologically if not physically, in ending the war by violating existing treaties; for its real war aim, stability, depends on the recognition of the sanctity of treaty relations. And if the acquisitive power maintains that its objectives are really "limited" and offers its good faith as a surety, it shifts the onus for the rupture of the Alliance on the very powers which have most to gain from an assumption of their ally's good faith. They cannot be sure that their ally's protestations are insincere until he has demonstrated it, and he will attempt to avoid having to demonstrate it until it is too late. As the Allied armies were sweeping westward, the Tsar spoke grandly of a peace based on the military situation and sanctified by his good faith.

But Castlereagh's proposals confronted Alexander with a dilemma. They were intended to restrain France but, by inference, they also limited Russia. For if the Tsar agreed to the alliance, the other powers would have been guaranteed their major objectives while he had not even avowed his aims. But if he made explicit his Polish plans, he might force a separate peace between France and Austria. If all the powers had obtained their interests, it was dangerous to defer the Polish question to the final settlement because they might then unite against Russian pretensions. But if he attempted to include the Polish question among the goals of the alliance, there might be no final settlement left to negotiate. And Metternich was equally reluctant to commit himself. While the Tsar was concerned lest his agreement to the objectives of his allies would remove their incentive to agree to Russian compensations, Metternich was afraid that Britain would withdraw from the Continent once her special conditions were satisfied. It was not yet clear whether Britain identified her security with the mouth of the Scheldt or with the European equilibrium. Until

Britain had made its attitude plainer, Metternich proposed to use its obsession with Holland to frustrate the Tsar in Poland.

The Tsar and Metternich both evaded the alliance, then, if for diametrically opposite reasons. Metternich saw in the proposed treaty one more tool for obtaining a British commitment to European defence; the Tsar considered it a means to establish a claim. But Metternich, aware of the Tsar's intentions, used him as a stalking horse. He repeatedly avowed his willingness to sign the Alliance but urged that it would be meaningless without Russia.[1] At other times he offered to guarantee eventual Russian acquiescence. "And now my dear Aberdeen," Metternich said on one occasion to the gullible Aberdeen, Britain's new ambassador to Austria, "make my compliments to Lord Castlereagh and ask him what is the next proof of our loyalty and zeal that he requires."[2] Finally, when it became quite clear that Russian acquiescence could not be obtained, Metternich proposed to Aberdeen that he sign an agreement in effect expressing his willingness to sign an agreement.[3] But Aberdeen refused, as Metternich undoubtedly expected.

Castlereagh was thus looking for support from a power which he was destined to oppose, even at the risk of war, while he distrusted the state which was to become his chief support. Until this misapprehension was eliminated, British policy had to be beside the point. Castlereagh summed up his growing doubts in a dispatch to Cathcart. In its tone of studied reasonableness and outraged probity, it testified to the legacy of Pitt which made it impossible to think of Russia as an acquisitive power.[4] It began by dealing with the Tsar's protestations of good faith and his reference to the developing military situation: The charge that the offer of an alliance indicated distrust of the Tsar was unreasonable, for Great Britain had singled out Russia for its earliest confidence and had rested on its "enlarged views" the chief reliance for the success of the measure. Nor was the Tsar's reference to the developing military situation any more comprehensible. Allied successes had made the common objectives easier to attain and should therefore have removed, rather than multiplied, the difficulties in concluding the Alliance. Castlereagh indignantly rejected the Tsar's proposal that Britain enumerate the colonial con-

[1] B.D., p. 119, 9 December, 1813.
[2] Webster, I, p. 175.
[3] C.C. IX, p. 105, 19 December, 1813.
[4] B.D., p. 56f., 18 December, 1813.

quests it intended to return. The return of the colonies had been a spontaneous offer, but they could not be specified until the Continental powers had agreed on the outline of the peace settlement. In short, the colonies were to be used to make certain that any settlement would safeguard Britain's fundamental interests. And Castlereagh concluded with one more appeal which, in its repetitious insistence, expressed both his surprise and his disbelief in the Tsar's hesitations, as if the obstacles to an agreement were due to a failure of communication which a patient teacher might remove by frequent reiteration. Great Britain had approached Russia first, he repeated, not because it distrusted her, but because Britain and Russia were the two powers least in need of such an alliance: ". . . Amidst the fluctuating policy of states . . . it appeared to me not less an act of wisdom, than of duty to the world, that Great Britain and Russia should take this opportunity of solemnly binding themselves . . . to oppose hereafter a barrier to the oppression of France. [This] determination . . . would afford to Europe the best, perhaps the only protection of a durable peace. . . . The British government [are] from principle disposed to pursue *their own interests through the general interests of the Continent.* [my italics] . . . but, if not, England [will not be] the first state to suffer from an insulated policy."

As things turned out, this proud dispatch was never delivered. An event had occurred which caused Castlereagh to decide to go to the Continent and to participate personally in the deliberations of the Allies. It had to be a grave turn which induced a British Foreign Secretary to go to the Continent for the first time in history. The Alliance was indeed being tested. For Metternich, not willing to see a complete overturn of his cherished equilibrium, had offered peace to Napoleon in the name of the Alliance.

III

When Austria declared war on Napoleon on 11 August, 1813, its leadership of the Coalition was an established fact. An Austrian field-marshal was commander-in-chief of the Allied armies, and it was doubly ironical that he proved to be the former commander of Napoleon's auxiliary corps, Prince Schwarzenberg. Metternich was in effect the Prime Minister of the Coalition. It was he who spoke for the Allies during peace negotiations; it was he who negotiated with those of Napoleon's vassals who, in increasing numbers, attempted to join the winning side. On 7 September, he had adhered to the Alliance of Prussia and Russia through the Treaty of Teplitz, which provided for the liberation of Germany up to the Rhine and its organization on the basis of sovereign states. The Treaty of Teplitz represented merely one more recognition by the Allies that the war was not fought in the name of nationalism.

There was another reason for Metternich's emergence as spokesman of the Coalition. Unwilling to the last to believe in Austria's entry into the war, Napoleon now flattered himself that her resolution was as weak as her entry had been delayed. Already on 18 August the Duke of Bassano had offered a renewal of negotiations. On 26 September, Napoleon's adjutant had appeared at the Austrian outposts with a letter to the Emperor appealing for peace to prevent further misfortune. On 17 October, the first day of the battle of Leipzig, Napoleon sent another emissary, the captured Austrian general, Merveldt, with an offer of peace. Nothing illustrates better the difficulty of a settlement when two legitimacies confront each other than the fate of these overtures. However eager Napoleon might have been to end the war and however sincere, the Allies remembered his skill in dissolving coalitions through peace overtures and refused to deal with him. Only after Napoleon had lost his army at Leipzig, when, in short, his impotence might guarantee his good faith, did Metternich consider his proposals and then only because French weakness increased his fear of Russia.

As the remnants of the French Army were seeking shelter behind the Rhine, Metternich was confronted with what must have seemed to him the last possible moment to prevent the war from becoming total. All stipulated goals had been achieved. Another defeat of Napoleon would transfer the war to a plane where no agreements limited claims and the European equilibrium would be seriously threatened. But to arrest the advance during the negotiations might break up the Coalition and give Napoleon a chance to rally his forces. Napoleon, the man of power, could not be brought to terms until he had accepted his impotence. But if his impotence became too evident, one of the most important counterpoises to Russia would be lost. How to achieve a peace of proportion against an opponent bent on self-destruction? How to prevent a vacuum when confronted with an adversary who considered the recognition of limits dynastic suicide? By offering a peace of moderation, Metternich replied, and by continuing the advance. "Let us always carry the sword in one hand and the olive branch in another," he had written during the disastrous war of 1809, "always ready to negotiate but negotiating only while advancing." The time had come to put these maxims into practice. A moderate peace offer would represent a limitation on Russian claims and at the same time undermine Napoleon's domestic position by appealing to the desire of the French nation for peace. It would, wrote Metternich, "forge for the Allies weapons with the [French] people".[1]

But how to induce the Allies, particularly Russia and Britain, to negotiate in a moment of triumph? Fortunately for Metternich the chief actors, with the exception of Castlereagh, were all assembled at Allied Headquarters: three monarchs and their ministers, accompanied by their general staffs and, not least, by three British plenipotentiaries, represented just the proper field of activity for a diplomat of Metternich's skill. On what proved the first of many such occasions, Metternich succeeded in dominating all of the protagonists. He established extremely cordial relations with the Tsar, always susceptible to flattery. "The Emperor Alexander is his own minister," Cathcart wrote. "His regular ministers are at St Petersburg and the few confidential servants he employs here cannot assume the authority of ministers. . . . H.I.M. is fully aware of the ability of the Austrian minister. . . . Prince Metternich has ready access to him, and H.I.M. certainly listens to his suggestions with confidence. . . . Prince Metternich, of course, cultivates this advantage by every observance, and his frank . . . manner is in the highest degree prepossessing."[2] An appeal to national interest had failed to obtain the Tsar's concurrence with an alliance; an appeal to his idealism resulted in his approval of an offer of peace.

Lord Aberdeen, the British ambassador to Austria, proved even easier to deal with. Only twenty-nine years old, barely able to speak French, he was not a match for a diplomat of Metternich's subtlety. His stiffness and self-confidence only played into Metternich's hands. "Metternich is extremely attentive to Lord Aberdeen," reported Cathcart. The results were not long delayed. Metternich had once described the diplomat's task as the art of seeming a dupe, without being one, and he practised it to the fullest on the high-minded Aber-

[1] Fournier, August, *Der Congress von Chatillon* (Vienna, 1900), p. 242 (Appendix), 9 November.

[2] B.D., p. 43f., 28 November. 1813.

deen. "Do not think Metternich such a formidable personage . . .," Aberdeen wrote to Castlereagh. "Living with him at all times . . ., is it possible I should not know him? If indeed he were the most subtle of mankind, he might certainly impose on one little used to deceive, but this is not his character. He is, I repeat it to you, not a very clever man. He is vain . . . but he is to be trusted. . . ."[1] For his mixture of condescension and gullibility, Aberdeen earned himself Metternich's sarcastic epithet as the "dear simpleton of diplomacy".[2]

At a conference, on 29 October, between the Tsar, Metternich and Aberdeen, it was decided to reply to Napoleon's overtures of 17 October. The method chosen was one of those subtle, symbolic acts so dear to the heart of the Austrian minister. Napoleon had offered peace through a captured Austrian officer; it was therefore only appropriate that the Allies should reply through a captured French official. The French *chargé d'affaires* in Weimar, St Aignan, the brother-in-law of Caulaincourt, Napoleon's plenipotentiary at Prague, was selected for the mission. At a meeting between Nesselrode, Metternich and Aberdeen it was decided to offer France her "natural" boundaries, the Rhine, the Alps, and the Pyrenees; Holland was to be independent, although its boundary towards France was left subject to negotiation; the ancient dynasty was to be restored in Spain.[3] Metternich insisted that the military operations continue during the negotiations. So complete was Metternich's domination over Aberdeen that the latter strongly defended these conditions both to Nesselrode, who wanted to advance much more severe terms, and to Castlereagh.[4]

But before he permitted events to take their course, Metternich added a final touch, which testified to his eagerness to end the war. On 9 November, he arranged a meeting between Nesselrode, himself, and St Aignan, which Aberdeen joined as if by accident, to explain Britain's desire for peace and her willingness to grant to France those maritime rights "to which she could justly pretend". Whatever this enigmatic phrase meant, and despite Aberdeen's disavowal that it represented a surrender of any part of the maritime code, it was clear that Aberdeen had missed the vital point: maritime rights had for Britain a symbolic as well as a substantive importance.

[1] Webster, I, p. 174.
[2] Fournier, *Congress*, p. 91.
[3] B.D., p. 110.
[4] B.D., p. 107.

By discussing them in this context, Aberdeen agreed to their *negotiability*, something British statesmen had consistently denied. In his eagerness to gain the glory of pacifying Europe, Aberdeen forgot that no power can agree to negotiate about what it considers the condition of its existence.

The terms were more moderate than the military situation warranted, because Metternich was above all concerned that France remain a powerful weight in the European balance. France was to be left territories for which generations of Frenchmen had fought in vain, Belgium and the left bank of the Rhine. And to reinforce this generous offer, Metternich sent a private letter to Caulaincourt on 10 November. France, he warned, should not miss this opportunity for making peace. New Allied successes would lead to more severe demands, while French victories could not reduce them. If, as he feared, Napoleon would not yield, the consequence would be upheavals without point and without limit.[1] The offer of the Rhine boundary was thus no longer a plea for self-limitation but a definition of Napoleon's real, perhaps even of his maximum strength. It was an appeal to Napoleon to give up his delusions, not indeed because Metternich wanted to save Napoleon, but because he wanted to save Saxony and Poland. For this end, Metternich proposed to find out whether it was possible for the Emperor of the French to become, in Talleyrand's phrase, King of France.

But these subtleties were not apparent in London, where it was not even realized that there was to be a contest about Poland. Aberdeen's dispatches had not been reassuring. The Pitt plan had wanted to confine France to the "ancient", pre-revolutionary boundaries, which excluded Belgium and the left bank of the Rhine, but the St Aignan note had offered to settle on the basis of the "natural boundaries". No provision had been made for a barrier for Holland in the Low Countries, and in its absence Holland would be little more than a French appendage. Fortunately for Aberdeen, the British Cabinet did not yet realize the full implications of his cavalier attitude regarding maritime rights. But Castlereagh's lack of enthusiasm was reflected in his first reaction to Aberdeen's exuberant reports. In its cautious approval of the Allied measures as an accomplished fact, it revealed that the only contingency Britain dreaded more than peace on these terms was the dissolution of the Alliance. "You will not be surprised to learn," Castlereagh wrote, ". . . that this nation is

[1] Fournier, *Congress*, p. 32.

likely to view with disfavour any peace which does not strictly confine France within her ancient limits. Indeed, peace with Napoleon on *any* [my italics] terms will be far from popular. . . . We are still ready to encounter, with our Allies, the hazards of peace. . . . But I am satisfied we must not encourage our Allies to patch up imperfect arrangements."[1]

Nor was Castlereagh reassured by the silence of the Frankfurt proposals with respect to Antwerp. "I must particularly entreat you to keep your attention upon Antwerp," he wrote insistently. "The destruction of that arsenal is essential for our safety. To leave it in the hands of France is little short of imposing upon Great Britain the charge of a permanent war establishment. After all we have done for the Continent in this war they owe it to us and to themselves to extinguish this fruitful source of danger to both."[2] In another dispatch, Castlereagh warned that under existing circumstances Britain would give up her colonial conquests only to gain a better frontier for Holland and Italy.[3] And his disquiet vented itself finally in a protest against the term "natural boundaries". Not a claim of right, but considerations of expediency had inspired the Allied offer which, once refused, need not be maintained.[4] Castlereagh left no doubt that Britain would find it difficult to reconcile itself to peace on these terms, even after twenty years of war.

But, once more, Napoleon removed all embarrassments. Just as his acceptance of the Reichenbach basis could have frustrated all of Metternich's calculations, so his acceptance of the Frankfurt proposals might have dissolved the Coalition. But the conqueror could still not believe in the determination of his foes. On 23 November, a note was received from the Duke of Bassano simply proposing Mannheim as the conference site and evading any reference to the Allied conditions, except to what was declared British willingness to make sacrifices for the general peace. The idea that Britain might end its war with Napoleon by concessions on maritime rights filled the British Cabinet with outrage. Castlereagh sent two sharp notes to Aberdeen, instructing him to protest in writing to the Allies about this construction of his remarks.[5] Before Aberdeen could discharge this task, however, Metternich, on 25 November, had replied on

[1] C.C. IX, p. 74, 13 November, 1813.
[2] C.C. IX, p. 75.
[3] B.D., p. 115, 30 November, 1813.
[4] B.D., p. 117, 7 December, 1813.
[5] B.D., p. 116f.

behalf of the Allies that negotiations could not begin until the Frankfurt basis had been accepted.

Napoleon had missed the psychological moment. He had delayed accepting the Frankfurt proposals in order to gain time to increase his armaments. But by putting the issue on the plane of a contest for power, he merely gave the Allies an opportunity to become fully aware of their relative strength. While the Allied army wheeled south for a flanking movement through Switzerland, Metternich drafted a manifesto to the French people so conciliatory that Caulaincourt was to say later that it did more damage than a lost battle. The war was not directed against France, the proclamation read, but against French predominance. For this reason the first use the Allies had made of their victory was to offer peace. But Napoleon had replied with a new conscription. The Allies wished to see France great and powerful, greater in fact than it had ever been under the kings, but they also desired a peaceful existence for themselves and would not rest until they had achieved a just equilibrium of power.[1] As long as he was writing the proclamations, Metternich meant to see to it that the war would not become a crusade. If the Tsar's designs could not be thwarted by preserving the equipoise of France, Metternich proposed to restrain him by committing him to moderate pronouncements.

If the proclamation was designed, as Metternich asserted, to increase the desire for peace of the French people and thus to exert pressure on Napoleon even within France, it was hardly necessary. Bowing to popular discontent, Napoleon replaced the Duke of Bassano as Foreign Minister with Caulaincourt, well-known as an advocate of peace. But when Caulaincourt accepted the Frankfurt proposals on 2 December, it was too late. While the Allied armies were preparing to invade France, Metternich merely forwarded Caulaincourt's note to London and suggested that Britain appoint a plenipotentiary.

IV

This, then, was the situation in December, 1813: British hopes for a General Alliance had been disappointed. The Allies might agree on the need to defeat Napoleon, but, surprisingly for Britain, this did not imply a consensus on the new structure of Europe. The danger of French predominance might be obvious, but, unexpectedly, this

[1] Fournier, *Congress*, p. 23f.

did not provide an adequate impetus for organizing the equilibrium anew. At the very moment that Caulaincourt accepted the Frankfurt basis, the efforts to agree on a treaty of alliance had reached a stalemate at Allied Headquarters and had been transferred to London. But, since the Allied ambassadors had not been given full powers, the negotiations proved inconclusive once more. The dealings with St Aignan had demonstrated that even the aims of the immediate war effort were being variously understood and that some of the Allies were only slightly less afraid of victory than of defeat. Great Britain's influence had not been proportionate to the extent of her sacrifices. The difficulty of communication caused Castlereagh's dispatches always to lag at least ten days behind events, while the divided authority among the British representatives on the Continent reduced their effectiveness. The British Sanhedrin, as Hardenberg called the triumvirate of Stewart, Aberdeen, and Cathcart, was beset by internal rivalry. Aberdeen had kept the St Aignan negotiations a secret from his colleagues, a slight which almost caused Stewart's resignation. None of the British representatives was really up to his task. Aberdeen was too young, Stewart too vain, Cathcart too phlegmatic. In any case, Stewart and Cathcart were soldiers chafing at the bit, while Aberdeen could never fully suppress a certain pity for Napoleon's misfortune. To give authority to British counsels, to gain a measure of control over the pending negotiations, the British Cabinet on 20 December took the unprecedented step of sending its Foreign Secretary on a mission to the Continent.

Castlereagh's instructions, largely drafted by himself, reflected Britain's view of the struggle: the importance of the Coalition as the symbol of opposition to Continental hegemony, of Holland as the expression of the security of an island power, of good faith as the sufficient link of common action.[1] Appropriately enough, they began with a reference to the maritime rights: "Having previously received from the ministers of the [Allied] powers satisfactory assurances on the maritime question, H.R.H. [the Prince Regent] has been pleased . . . to direct His Majesty's Secretary of State for Foreign Affairs to proceed forthwith to the headquarters of the Allies. . . ." With the most fundamental British interest thus assured, Castlereagh was to establish an understanding with the Allies, so that, in negotiations with the enemy, one common interest could be represented. Since the Cabinet still believed that the inability to achieve

[1] Text, B.D., p. 123f., 26 December, 1813.

agreement had been due largely to a misunderstanding of British motives, Castlereagh was "to evince a desire to conform as far as possible to the general interests of the Continent; to give to the Allies the most unequivocal assurance of a firm determination to support them in contracting for an advantageous peace and to avoid everything that might countenance a suspicion that Great Britain was inclined to push them forward in our own purposes."

But it was evident that the mind of the Cabinet was primarily on British objectives. The instructions were therefore as significant for what they omitted as for what they said. They revealed that Britain had still not overcome the habits of a decade of isolation; that it had still not made the transition from an insular to a European policy. To be sure, Britain spoke of common interests, but it meant the military defeat of France; it advocated a European equilibrium, but it was really thinking about Antwerp. Only the most cursory attention was paid to the organization of Italy and Germany; but considerable space was devoted to getting a large Allied force into Holland. The problem of Poland was not mentioned; but a special memorandum on the maritime peace enumerated some of the colonies Britain would return in the event of satisfactory arrangements in the Low Countries. The Alliance was to continue after the war, but the *casus feoderis* was to be an attack by France on the European possessions of the contracting parties. So absorbed was Britain in the struggle against Napoleon, that the question whether there might exist other threats to the equilibrium was not even considered.

As Castlereagh left on his mission to the Continent, the danger of French hegemony was past, but the outline of its alternative not yet apparent. The Coalition was formed but it was barely held together by the consciousness of a common danger. As the enemy was reduced in power, the centrifugal elements in the Alliance were becoming increasingly evident. It was likely that Napoleon would be defeated, but uncertain whether universal dominion could be replaced by anything but the chaos of contending factions. Britain's policy was still based on the twin illusions of a "satisfied" Russia and a European equilibrium maintained by good faith and the self-evidence of its necessity. It was not yet certain whether Britain could transcend its narrow insular outlook, whether it could be brought to see that the independence of Holland and therefore the security of Great Britain was but an aspect of the European equilibrium.

Much depended on the man who was hastening to Allied headquarters. It was he who would have to decide whether security resided in isolation or in commitment; whether the need for peace could be made as effective a bond as the fear of France; whether the Coalition could generate its own goals after the defeat of the enemy; whether it could achieve self-limitation free from outside pressure. Aloof from the parochial quarrels of Continental states, he could emerge as the arbitrator of Europe. It was for him to translate the Coalition from a fact into reality.

VII

The Crisis of the Coalition

I

NOTHING in Lord Castlereagh's background indicated that perhaps the most European of British statesmen was about to sail for the Continent. Up to now all of his measures had been imposed by events. The necessity of a Coalition against Napoleon was so basic a doctrine of British policy that the Foreign Secretary's problem resolved itself into the essentially technical task of how best to implement it. The control of the mouth of the Scheldt or the freedom of the peninsulas in the Mediterranean represented truisms of British strategy, well charted in the Pitt plan. But as Castlereagh was preparing to sail for the Continent, Britain had reached the point, perhaps more difficult than heroic persistence in adversity, where a nation must generate its own objectives. The outside world was no longer so overpowering that it supplied all the challenges; Britain would have to fashion a new interpretation of reality. It was only appropriate that an island power should begin this task with a discussion about the nature of security and that Napoleon should be, once more, the focal point.

An insular power at the periphery of events finds it difficult to admit that wars may be produced by intrinsic causes. Since its involvement is usually defensive, to prevent universal dominion, it will consider the need for peace a sufficient legitimization for the equilibrium. In a world in which the advantages of peace seem so patent—the conception of a power with no unsatisfied claims—wars can be caused only by the malice of wicked men. Because it will not be understood that the balance of power may be *inherently* unstable, wars tend to become crusades to eliminate the "cause" of the upheaval. In no country, even those he had occupied, was Napoleon more detested than in Great Britain; no country proved more reluctant to conclude a peace which would preserve his dynasty.

Even before Castlereagh left England, news of victories from every quarter made it appear that the fate of Napoleon might depend on the will of the Allies. Allied armies had invaded France through Switzerland; British forces under Wellington crossed the Pyrenees and were greeted enthusiastically by the local population. Now was the time, Wellington suggested, for a Prince of the House of Bourbon to show himself in France.[1] While the ship which was to take Castlereagh to the Continent was still fog-bound at Harwich, the Cabinet transmitted Wellington's letter to him and made no secret of its favourable sentiment. It seems to have occurred to no one that the alternative to Napoleon could be somebody other than the "legitimate" head of the house of Bourbon, Louis XVIII, the brother of the last King of France. Castlereagh was being asked, in effect, to assist in the overthrow of the very government with which he had been sent to negotiate.

There is no doubt that the Cabinet reflected the sentiments of the country.[2] But Castlereagh was not prepared to identify British security with the fate of an individual. None of the popular manifestations in France, he argued, warranted British separation from the Allies, who would consider any effort on behalf of the Bourbons as a subterfuge to get rid of the negotiations altogether: "We ought always to recollect that we are suspected of having an *arrière pensée* on the question of peace and we should act with the more caution. . . . If Bonaparte will give you your own terms you ought not to risk . . . the confederacy in the labyrinth of counter-revolution."[3] It was the first enunciation of a cardinal principle of Castlereagh's policy: the unity of the Alliance superseded all but the most basic British interests; or better, the Coalition of Europe *was* a basic British interest.

This did not mean that purely British interests were to be neglected, but that they would be sought within the framework of Allied unity. After reaching the Continent, Castlereagh stopped at The Hague, where he arranged for the marriage of the Princess of Wales with the hereditary Prince of Orange and promised to work for the incorporation of Belgium into Holland. He obtained the cession of the Cape of Good Hope to Great Britain in return for a sum of money to be used for the construction of barrier fortresses against France.[4] Having thus

[1] Wellington, Duke of, Dispatches, 13 Vols. Edited by Curwood. (London, 1837.) Vol. XI, p. 306, 21 November, 1813.

[2] See C.C. IX, p. 137, 5 January, 1813, and Webster, I, p. 514 (Appendix), 12 January, 1813.

[3] C.C. IX, p. 124, 10 December, 1813.

[4] C.C. IX, p. 153, 8 January, 1814.

safeguarded the most essential British interests, Castlereagh set out for Allied Headquarters. It was on this journey that he told his companion, the Earl of Ripon, of his intention to serve as a mediator, to bring the parties into unrestricted communication, to remove irritations and to modify pretensions.[1] If the war had been caused by bad faith, goodwill was to provide the remedy.

It was to be sorely needed. The dispatches of his ambassadors were making it increasingly evident that only the prospect of Castlereagh's arrival was postponing an explosion at Headquarters. "With relation to the enemy, our situation is as good as possible," wrote Aberdeen on 6 January. "Among ourselves it is quite the reverse. Everything which has been so long smothered is now bursting forth. Your presence is absolutely providential. If you come without partiality . . . you will be able to perform everything; and no words are sufficient to express the service you will render."[2]

Castlereagh was reaching Headquarters at the precise moment when the increasing weakness of the enemy had radically transformed relations among the Allies. As long as the enemy is more powerful than any single member of a coalition, the need for unity outweighs all considerations of individual gain. Then the powers of repose can insist on the definition of war aims which, as all conditions, represent limitations. But when the enemy has been so weakened that each ally has the power to achieve its aims alone, a coalition is at the mercy of its most determined member. Confronted with the complete collapse of one of the elements of the equilibrium, all other powers will tend to raise their claims in order to keep pace. It was no accident, therefore, that as the Allies were advancing almost unopposed into France and complete victory seemed to depend only on their will, or even on the will of each individual ally, the Great Coalition of 1814 should be rent by a contest between the Tsar and Metternich.

For the completeness of the victory revealed that Metternich had miscalculated. He had been confident that Napoleon could be brought to terms only through a combination of psychological and military pressure; through a war fought in the name of peace and peace offered with the threat of war. He had therefore insisted on a winter campaign, as much for its psychological as for its military impact. He had, almost single-handedly, engineered the flanking

[1] C.C. I, p. 128 (Full quotation, see Chapter III).
[2] C.C. IX, p. 142, 6 January, 1814.

movement through Switzerland over the violent opposition of the Tsar, who did not wish to violate the native country of his revered teacher, La Harpe, and against the hesitations of the King of Prussia, who wanted to clinch his gains. He had done so because he believed that Napoleon was still strong enough to defeat each ally in single combat, so that the limits of the campaign could always be defined by the threat of Austria's withdrawal.

These limits Metternich had sought in one of those finely balanced solutions which to the eighteenth century expressed the fitness of a universe conceived as a "great clockwork". He had fought Napoleon's foreign policy for its revolutionary attack on the international order. But he had admired Napoleon's domestic policy for its ability to master a decade of social upheaval. He therefore attempted to eliminate Napoleon as a threat to the international equilibrium while preserving him as the protector of the social balance. But no policy can combine all advantages. The very qualities which had made Napoleon an autocrat domestically caused him to be a revolutionary in foreign affairs. The very intransigeance which had led him to crush domestic opposition made it impossible for Napoleon to come to terms in time with his foreign foes. As the Allies traversed the plateau of Langres, the road to Paris seemed open; France appeared eliminated as a weight in the balance; the war fought in the name of the equilibrium had lost its necessary limitation.

Henceforth, every advance would further weaken an already impotent foe and thus strengthen the relative position of Russia. Austria could not be secure until Napoleon had been reduced within certain limits; but it would be equally insecure with Central Europe at the mercy of Russia and with a revolutionary government in power in France. Each step forward merely increased Metternich's dread that Russia might remain, in Castlereagh's words, mistress of the Polish question after the war. In the contest now beginning, all the advantages, moreover, were on the side of the Tsar. Metternich's great period had occurred when Austria was the pivotal state, both militarily and diplomatically. In June, 1813, a decisive Allied victory had been impossible without Austrian assistance, and Austria had been the only power capable of conducting diplomacy, because it possessed a "legitimizing principle" recognized by both sides: the family compact by Napoleon and the restoration of the equilibrium by Russia and Prussia. But now the Tsar could speak of pressing on alone and, more important still, he, not Metternich, "owned" the "legitimizing principle" of the common effort.[1]

For war has its own legitimacy and it is victory, not peace. To talk of conditions of peace during total wars appears almost as blasphemy, as petty calculation. When power reigns supreme, *any* conditions seem restrictive and a threat to the exhilaration of common action. Austria's strongest bargaining weapon was a separate peace; the Tsar's final appeal was the enemy's defeat. When the Tsar told Cathcart that a peace settlement should be deferred until after complete victory,[2] he was talking, in the mythology of Coalitions, "good sense". When Metternich argued for another peace effort with Napoleon, he was exhibiting, in terms of the same mythology, "timidity". Moderation in an hour of triumph is appreciated only by posterity, rarely by contemporaries to whom it tends to appear as a needless surrender. "The sole remaining evil," wrote Metternich to Hudelist, the chief of his chancellery, "is an excess of riches. We are protected against this . . . only by my moderation. . . . I need not tell you that I am as much embarrassed by the plenitude of success as heretofore by the plenitude of disaster."[3]

The dispute between the Tsar and Metternich, although in form usually concerned with peripheral questions, was therefore in substance a contest over the nature of a stable international system. Alexander sought to identify the new international order with his will; to create a structure safeguarded solely by the purity of his maxims. Metternich strove for a balance of forces which would not place too great a premium on self-restraint. The Tsar proposed to *sanctify* the post-war period by transforming the war into a moral symbol; Metternich attempted to *secure* the peace by obtaining a definition of war aims expressing a physical equilibrium. As usual with Alexander, it was difficult to disentangle personal rancour and reason of state, moral claims and national ambition. But since these motives, as always, tended to reinforce each other, their disentanglement is perhaps not too important. The disagreement began over the invasion of Switzerland, which the Tsar threatened to treat as a declaration of war against Russia. But Metternich, who considered a direct communication with Italy more important than Imperial displeasure, arranged one of his intricate manœuvres by which the Swiss

[1] C.C. IX, p. 148, 8 January, 1814.
[2] C.C. IX, p. 112, 24 December, 1813.
[3] Fournier, *Congress*, p. 48, 9 January, 1813, and p. 251, 20 January, 1813.

invited Austrian troops to protect their neutrality. Metternich confronted the Tsar with an accomplished fact, yielding to him, as he told Aberdeen, the principle of the measure after having obtained its substance.[1] Despite many protestations of friendship, the breach thus opened did not fully heal for some months.

But more fundamental differences soon appeared. Metternich tried to prevent the war from becoming a crusade; but his bargaining position was weakened by the increasingly evident impotence of France. He therefore attempted to substitute hesitation in military operations for French resistance and, on 8 January, ordered Schwarzenberg to advance but "cautiously" and "to utilize the desire of the French common man for peace by avoiding warlike acts".[2] Alexander, by the same token, sought to keep the situation fluid. He never tired of invoking his good faith, the impossibility of peace with Napoleon, and the wisdom of avoiding a detailed discussion of postwar boundaries until after victory was won.[3] As an alternative to the physical elimination of French power, the Tsar proposed to reinsure himself in two ways: through a treaty by which the Allies would exclude Napoleon from the settlement of any issue beyond France's borders[4] and through installing the Prince Royal of Sweden, Napoleon's former Marshal Bernadotte, as King of France in case of Napoleon's overthrow. The Tsar thus proved that he was crafty, as well as mystical. The exclusion of France from a voice in European affairs would have eliminated France from the balance of power by diplomatic means; while the installation of Bernadotte as King of France would, in effect, have reinstated the Franco-Russian alliance with Russia as the dominant party.

But Metternich, who in 1813 had risked disaster in order to found the war on the principle of the legitimacy of thrones, was not prepared to end it with the installation of a ruler who was himself of revolutionary origin. Any alternative to Napoleon would be weak; any weak government must seek to be popular; any popular government would call forth the Jacobins. If Napoleon's overthrow proved unavoidable, Metternich would not accept a marshal who would lack Napoleon's charisma while leaning on the elements of his power, but only a ruler who possessed a legitimacy independent of the popular

[1] C.C. IX, 111, 24 December, 1813.
[2] Fournier, *Congress*, p. 51.
[3] See, for example, C.C. IX, p. 112, 24 December, 1813; p. 149, 8 January, 1814.
[4] C.C. IX, p. 170, 15 January, 1814.

will. Not even the prospect of a Habsburg regency under Marie-Louise could tempt Metternich, who remembered the fate of Marie-Antoinette only too well. The only alternatives he admitted were the existing or the "legitimate" dynasty; the man who had transcended the social revolution, or the dynasty which could exist only in opposition to it.

And Metternich did not propose to stand idly by while the spectre of a Franco-Russian alliance reappeared as the result of a victorious war. He returned once more to his favourite idea of a strong Central Europe and sought to detach Prussia from Russia by offering to acquiesce in the annexation of Saxony if Prussia opposed the Tsar on the Polish question.[1] Nor would Metternich permit an Austrian commander-in-chief to superintend the complete destruction of the equilibrium. On 16 January, Schwarzenberg was ordered to stop the advance of the Allied army until further instructions. Austria, whose existence depended on a recognition of limits, both domestic and foreign, and which had fought Napoleon for this reason and no other, did not propose to inaugurate a new era in Europe by conducting a crusade. "All our engagements are fulfilled," Metternich wrote to Hudelist, "all former goals of the Coalition have been not only achieved but even exceeded. Now we must get clear once more about our purpose, for it is with alliances, as with all fraternizations, if they do not have a strictly determinate aim they disintegrate."[2]

As Castlereagh was approaching Allied headquarters, the Coalition was in greater danger of dissolution from Napoleon's seeming impotence than it had been from his military strength. The degree of Allied rivalry was revealed by the fact that two quarters awaited Castlereagh in Basel, one in the Russian section close to the Tsar, the other in the Austrian wing of headquarters near Metternich.[3] Fortunately, the Tsar's eagerness to animate the advance on Paris, which seemed unaccountably to have stalled, overcame his desire for the earliest possible conversation with Castlereagh. Two days before Castlereagh's arrival, Alexander left for Schwarzenberg's headquarters. It was clear that Castlereagh's attitude would decide the fate of the Coalition and the result of the war. If Britain limited its objectives to the security of the Narrows, Poland was lost and

[1] Fournier, *Congress*, p. 361 (Hardenberg diary); C.C. IX, p. 171, 15 January, 1814.

[2] Fournier, *Congress* (Appendix), p. 250, 17 January, 1814.

[3] C.C. IX, p. 164, 14 January, 1814.

Russian would be substituted for French predominance. If, on the other hand, Castlereagh understood that the security of Great Britain depended on the stability of the Continent, it might yet prove possible to construct a peace of equilibrium.

Castlereagh arrived with few preconceptions. He was determined that the unity of the Allies supersede all considerations of local gain, but he did not yet realize that the question at issue was so difficult precisely because it was not local in nature. He reached Basle on 18 January and immediately was confronted with the issue which nearly dissolved the Coalition: whether to make peace with Napoleon or to continue the advance on Paris. For, on 9 January, Caulaincourt had presented himself at the Allied outposts and had asked for safe conduct to Headquarters to negotiate a peace. But the dispatch of a Foreign Minister to the enemy's headquarters without the assurance of his being received, was interpreted as merely one more symptom of Napoleon's impotence and spurred the Tsar's eagerness to push forward. At his urging, Caulaincourt was told to await Castlereagh's arrival and that he would be informed when the Allies were ready to begin negotiations.[1] While the Allies were debating Napoleon's fate, as if it depended merely on their will, Caulaincourt was waiting in Luneville.

Between 18 and 22 January, Castlereagh and Metternich had several conferences about the future of the Coalition. Castlereagh learned to his amazement of the Tsar's plans with respect to Bernadotte. Characteristically, his primary concern was not their effect on the European equilibrium, but on the prosecution of the war: "If there be no other evil in the scheme, its effect in paralysing the Allied army must be conclusive. I have reason to believe that until this intention is disavowed the Austrian army will not advance much further. . . ."[2] Here then was the issue of Napoleon's fate raised again and from a totally unexpected quarter. Castlereagh had resisted the Cabinet's desire to overthrow Napoleon for the sake of Allied unity. But now Allied unity appeared broken on this very issue, seemingly leaving Britain free to pursue her own objectives.

Castlereagh made his decision from the European, not from the insular, point of view, however. "I cannot praise Castlereagh enough," reported Metternich. "His attitude is excellent and his work as direct as it is correct. I cannot find a single point of difference

[1] Fournier, p. 61.
[2] B.D., p. 133f., 22 January, 1814.

with him and assure you that his mood is peaceful, peaceful in *our* sense."[1] The two great statesmen of stability had met and understood each other. "The Austrian minister is charged with more faults than belong to him," reported Castlereagh. "But he has great ability in carrying forward the machine."[2] Castlereagh preferred a Bourbon France as a guarantee against political upheaval, but he was willing to negotiate with Napoleon for the sake of Allied unity. Metternich preferred a Napoleonic France to prevent a social revolution and to forestall a Franco-Russian alliance, but he was willing to make peace with the Bourbons for the sake of British friendship. They agreed that Napoleon and the Bourbons were the only alternatives and that both Bernadotte and a Regency under Marie-Louise were to be excluded.[3] The choice would be left to the French nation, but at the same time the possibility of peace with Napoleon would be explored. "We must not encumber ourselves with anything that can bear the appearance of initiative on such a question [Napoleon's overthrow]," Castlereagh wrote to Liverpool. "We cannot press *our* demands to the utmost, if we are at the same time mixed in a question which, as far as relates to the existing government of France, supersedes all terms."[4] "Paris will decide with whom to make peace," reported Metternich. "Are we wise in making the experiment with whom to deal? Were I alone and could I act independently, I would not do so. But in the present situation the requirement of unity outweighs all other considerations."[5]

In this manner, with hesitations and misgivings, began a co-operation which was to last until Castlereagh's death. It was only appropriate that Castlereagh, who saw in the Coalition an end in itself, should emerge as the mediator of its differences; while Metternich, who conceived it as the outgrowth of a legitimizing principle, should act as its spokesman. As Castlereagh and Metternich travelled together to Langres to meet the Tsar both had cause for satisfaction: Castlereagh because he had learned that Austria, although it did not welcome, would not oppose the overthrow of Napoleon if peace could be won in no other manner and because Metternich had proved favourable to a barrier for Holland in the Low Countries; Metternich because he had been reassured regarding Bernadotte and

[1] Fournier, p. 61.
[2] B.D., p. 160, 26 February, 1814.
[3] B.D., p. 137, 22 January, 1814.
[4] C.C. IX, p. 185, 22 January, 1814.
[5] Fournier, *Congress* (Appendix), p. 256.

because, even if it should prove impossible to save Napoleon from himself, Austria would not stand alone in Europe.

II

But before the conferences at Langres started, Metternich attempted once more to force a definition of war aims which would be compatible with the European equilibrium. He was given the opportunity by a memorandum to the Emperor in which the commander-in-chief, Schwarzenberg, gave expression to Austrian disquiet as the war seemed to become transformed into a total effort, so inconsistent with the spirit of the Austrian state. In the pedantically "objective" manner the mediocre assume to shift the responsibility for their own preference, he assembled the arguments for and against a continued campaign which, under the guise of asking for the Emperor's decision, left no doubt about his fears.[1] He admitted the advantages of a continued advance, but he also emphasized the risks inherent in the exposed flanks, the increasing rate of disease in the army, and the difficulty of supply. Schwarzenberg's major concern was not defeat, however, but victory. The impending negotiations impelled him to point out, so his memorandum read, that Langres represented the last stop before Paris, the last point from which peace with Napoleon was still possible. With the practised skill of a soldier feigning innocence of matters profoundly political, he emphasized that henceforth the struggle would take on the character of a civil war and that it was for the Emperor's superior knowledge to make the choice: "The steps we will have to take are too important that I should not feel . . . honour-bound to request Your Majesty's unequivocal order on the following proposition: Whether I should remain in my present position, to give my troops a much-needed rest, to await supplies and to give my flanks a chance to catch up. Or whether I should descend into the plain there to begin a struggle of incalculable consequences. . . ." In thus posing the alternative between stability and chaos, both military and political, Schwarzenberg made clear the Austrian dilemma: beyond Langres lay victory, but victory would prove hollow. For it would involve so violent a shock to the equilibrium as to threaten the state whose existence depended on the denial of total transformations.

[1] Text, Klinkowstroem, Alfons, *Oesterreich's Theilname an den Befreiungskriegen*, (Vienna, 1887), p. 810f.

Schwarzenberg's views were by no means without support. The Prussian King and his immediate environment, although not his generals, Blücher and Gneisenau, were in substantial accord. Even Stewart sent Castlereagh a memorandum based on essentially similar arguments.[1] Metternich now used the opportunity to appeal to his monarch for direction and to his allies for a definition of war aims, to restate Austria's conception of security as balance and of peace as proportion. He began his memorandum with a reminder of the days preceding Austria's entry into the war.[2] The greatest Allied achievement, he argued, had been psychological, to have deprived Napoleon of the pretence of moderation. Should the Allies now reverse themselves and engage in a war of conquest? Was there any other purpose to the war except to confine France within limits compatible with the European equilibrium and to restore Austria and Prussia to the scale of 1805? Metternich was significantly silent about Russian gains. The equilibrium could evidently only be disturbed by them. As to whether to negotiate with Napoleon, a few conferences with Caulaincourt would reveal Napoleon's sincerity, and in any case Napoleon's ultimate fate could be decided only by the French nation, not by the Allies. But what if Napoleon rejected the Allied terms? In that case, Metternich replied, there would exist no choice but to continue the advance and to appeal to the French nation by publishing the Allied conditions.

Thus, whatever contingency Metternich considered he resolved into a plea for a definition of limits, for it was plain that he desired an Allied proclamation as much as a means to commit the Tsar as for its impact on the French people. And he concluded by summarizing the issues in a number of queries which amounted to still another effort to lure Alexander into avowing his aims while there was yet a French army in the field. He inquired whether the Allies were still prepared to make peace with France; whether they would impose a ruler on France or leave the dynastic issue to the French nation; whether, finally, and this was the crucial question, the Allies were prepared to inform each other of their demands beyond the re-establishment of the conditions of 1805.

But during the ascendancy of Coalitions it is difficult to force the hand of an acquisitive power, because, in the absence of agreement, each day improves its relative position. Alexander's crafty reply

[1] C.C. IX, p. 525f., 27 January, 1814.
[2] Fournier, *Congress*, p. 62f.

avoided any discussion of war aims, explaining that such a discussion would only disturb the existing harmony, all the more so as the conditions of peace depended on the military situation.[1] They had been defined differently in Basel than in Frankfurt, in Langres than in Basel, and they would have to be redefined with changing circumstances. Provided the advance continued, he was ready to negotiate with Napoleon. The Tsar was thus posing a dilemma which could end only with Napoleon's collapse. He agreed to discuss the European equilibrium, but only *after* the settlement with France. He was ready to negotiate with Napoleon, but he would make the terms depend on the progress of military operations. Since these were changing daily in favour of the Allies, the Tsar reserved the right constantly to raise his terms. In short, Austria could learn Alexander's conditions of peace only by assisting in the elimination of French power. If Napoleon had sought to conquer England in Moscow, it was not unreasonable for Alexander to attempt to win Warsaw in Paris.

Castlereagh, who was misinformed about the Tsar's Polish plans[2] and who, in any case, had not yet reached the point where he could admit the existence of any other threat to peace than Napoleon, also pressed for the continuation of military operations. The result was one of those specious compromises by which Coalitions maintain the façade of unity and obscure the fact that a shift in the balance within the Alliance has occurred. It was decided to negotiate with Napoleon, but also to continue the advance. Castlereagh rejected the Tsar's proposal that France be excluded from even inquiring into the conditions of the European settlement, but his substitute formula was only a token improvement: the conditions of the settlement were to be submitted to France, but simply for its agreement, not for negotiation.[3] France was temporarily eliminated as a factor in the balance. As the Allied ministers prepared to discuss the conditions to be submitted to Napoleon, it was becoming increasingly clear that the war would end only at Paris; that the war for the equilibrium was creating a vacuum; that Europe would have to rescue its sense of proportion, if at all, from the threat of chaos.

But the conferences at Langres also revealed that, however the new

[1] Fournier, *Congress*, p. 67f.

[2] Cathcart had erroneously reported on 16 January that the Tsar confined his demands to the Vistula boundary. Castlereagh seems to have believed this for he showed the dispatch to the Tsar at Vienna as a token of his understanding of the question. C.C. IX, p. 169.

[3] Castlereagh report, B.D., p. 141f., 28 January, 1814.

settlement was arrived at, Britain would play an integral role. For Langres marked an important step in the transformation of Castlereagh into a European statesman. He emerged as the mediator of the Coalition, and this fact enabled him to obtain Allied agreement to one further step in the direction of obtaining a "barrier" in the Low Countries, by placing Belgium under the temporary administration of Holland. By 1 February, he could instruct Clancarty, his Ambassador at the Dutch Court, that the Prince of Orange would be quite safe in attempting to rouse sentiment for annexation in the Low Countries up to the Meuse.[1] Finally, the Allies, abandoning the Frankfurt basis, agreed to restrict France to its ancient limits. Castlereagh had obtained these concessions from Austria because it was becoming increasingly evident that he intended to seek British security in Continental stability, even if he still tended to identify stability with the restraint of France. His treatment of the colonial question was symptomatic. When he specified the conditions which would induce Great Britain to surrender part of her conquests, he added to the previous demands of the ancient limits and a barrier for Holland in the Low Countries, the requirement of an amicable agreement between the Continental powers "so that . . . having reduced France by their union, they were not likely to re-establish her authority by differences among themselves."[2] Metternich meant to see to it that no settlement that left the Tsar in possession of Poland would be amicable.

Although Metternich failed at Langres in forcing the Tsar into avowing his ambitions, he accomplished something perhaps more important. As the Allied armies prepared themselves, in Schwarzenberg's symbolic phrase, to descend into the plain, Metternich knew that in traversing it he was likely to have Castlereagh at his side.

III

The Congress of Chatillon, which opened on 3 February, represented the final effort to determine whether Napoleon could be brought to accept a peace of equilibrium. But it only served to put into sharp focus the difficulty of bridging the chasm between opposing systems of legitimacy. The negotiators could never even approach agreement, because the concept of security of the Allies and Napoleon's concept

[1] C.C. IX, p. 224.
[2] B.D., p. 146, 6 February, 1814.

of the requirement of his dynasty were incompatible. Napoleon believed that he could not make peace at the expense of any of his conquests, while the Allies were not prepared to make peace until Napoleon had been restricted to the very limits he thought would cost him his throne. Thus the issue became one of pure power and the Congress of Chatillon an illustration of the difficulty of achieving self-limitation under such conditions. During its course Napoleon was willing to make peace only at its very beginning and at its very end, when he seemed decisively defeated and his fate subject entirely to the will of the Allies. He refused to consider peace when victories had restored a measure of the balance and peace depended in part on his will. That he was confronted by another mercurial temperament in the Tsar merely complicated matters.

So it happened that the final act saw a hesitant army march on Paris, while all the time an inconclusive peace congress was debating conditions which never proved acceptable to the party which seemed to have the momentary ascendancy. The war was becoming total because the two sides could never agree on the precise power relationship and, above all, because Napoleon could not bring himself to accept the legitimacy of a Europe independent of his will. The period of the Congress of Chatillon is therefore more significant for the relationship among the Allies than for their negotiations with Napoleon.

When the negotiators were assembling at Chatillon on 3 February, Napoleon had just been defeated at La Rothière and it seemed certain that the Allies would reach Paris within two weeks. Each Ally was represented at Chatillon, although they had agreed to act as a body and to let the Austrian plenipotentiary, Stadion, serve as their spokesman. The entire British contingent of Cathcart, Stewart, and Aberdeen had been assembled, supervised by Castlereagh, who was however not himself a plenipotentiary. But the requirements of unanimity doomed the Congress to futility and placed it at the mercy of the power which had most to gain from delay. During the first stage at Chatillon, this was Russia, whose plenipotentiary had been ordered to sign nothing without Alexander's approval.

This led to a strange series of sessions. The Allies were reluctant to make a peace which might represent Napoleon's only hope for retaining power, even on terms beyond anybody's wildest dreams six months previously; while Caulaincourt did not dare to accept the "ancient limits" without the express approval of Napoleon. In the meantime, Castlereagh had made the return of the colonies dependent on the general European settlement, which in turn the Tsar refused to discuss until the peace with France had been concluded. This set up another circular dispute: French acceptance of the "ancient limits" was impossible without the return of her colonies, but the return of the colonies presupposed the peace with France which would induce the Tsar to discuss the European settlement. "We are playing a comedy," wrote Stadion to Metternich, "interesting only because of its platitude. . . . It is unworthy to play such a game with diplomatic customs."[1] Little doubt remained that the key to peace lay not in Chatillon but at Allied Headquarters at Troyes and that it had come to depend on Alexander as much as on Napoleon. It was symbolic that on the very day, 9 February, that Caulaincourt accepted the "ancient limits" in a letter to Metternich, the Russian plenipotentiary left Chatillon to return to Headquarters "for instructions". The first phase of the Congress of Chatillon was over.

Alexander no longer made any secret of his determination to advance on Paris, to overthrow Napoleon and to call an Assembly of Notables to elect a new ruler. And his insistence on total victory caused Metternich to force a showdown which nearly broke up the Alliance. It was one thing to advance on Paris while demonstrating at each step the impossibility of peace, because the very continuation of negotiations symbolized a quest for proportion and for a world of determinate goals. But a blind rush towards Paris was a march into infinity. The Central Empire could fight wars only according to "rules" which permitted the translation of victory into precise political terms. A state situated amidst contending powers could afford neither a vacuum nor an unbridgeable schism; nor could a power so sensitive to domestic transformations in other countries end the war with a revolution. Austria was more afraid of the open road to Paris than of Napoleon's army.

At Headquarters in Troyes, Metternich therefore once more prepared a questionnaire to force an avowal of goals and, in the process, to group the contending points of view. And just as the alliance against Napoleon had been prepared under the guise of mediation, so the isolation of Russia—the only means left to determine how far the Tsar was prepared to go—occurred under the pretext of defining the objectives of the Alliance. Metternich's questions posed the problems

[1] Fournier, *Congress*, p. 93.

of what to reply to Caulaincourt's offer; how to determine the will of the French nation; how to deal with the Bourbons; how to govern Paris if it fell.[1] These questions could not, as at Langres, be evaded by pleading the pressure of military operations, for they pretended to agree with the Tsar's desire to advance on Paris in order to force him into a definition of his aims.

Castlereagh's reply showed how far he had come since the time when he had opposed the overthrow of Napoleon merely to maintain the unity of the Alliance.[2] Not Allied unity, but the requirements of the equilibrium were now his primary concern. He defined the problem as the choice between "accepting the peace on *our* terms or making the peace more secure by the dethronement of [Napoleon]", and therefore left little doubt that, in his opinion, the objective of the war had been achieved. To attempt to overthrow Napoleon, he argued, would be both unwise and in violation of existing engagements; it had never been the object of the invasion to transform the French government, but to "conquer a peace which could not be found on the Rhine". The Allies were incompetent to raise the question of the Bourbons now that the *legitimate* [my italics] objects of their war were within reach. Almost imperceptibly, Castlereagh had come to accept the Austrian interpretation of the goal of the war. He was soon to learn how much it differed from that of the British people.

A conference of the ministers on 12 February made the schism in the Alliance explicit. After Hardenberg had answered Metternich's questions in the same sense as Castlereagh, Nesselrode transmitted Alexander's reply, which proved peremptory. The goal of the campaign was Paris, insisted the Tsar, where an Assembly of Notables should decide the future ruler. The Bourbons were to be neither supported nor discouraged. A Russian military governor should rule Paris and supervise the elections as a tribute to the power which had fought Napoleon the longest.[3] The Tsar was proposing nothing less than to be appointed arbiter of the fate of Europe.

But Metternich had not nursed Austria so tenaciously to this point to establish an international order based on the will of one man. He submitted a memorandum replying to his own queries which rejected the Tsar's argument that the moral vindication of the

[1] Fournier, *Congress*, p. 111.
[2] B.D., p. 155f., 13 February, 1814.
[3] Fournier, *Congress*, p. 121.

Alliance was to be sought in Napoleon's overthrow.[1] On the contrary, the war had been fought for the restoration of the equilibrium, not for the domestic transformation of France, and the conditions accepted by Caulaincourt at Chatillon represented the maximum weakening of France compatible with the balance of power. To demand more would be to overturn the moral principle of the Alliance. But should Napoleon be forced to abdicate, Metternich continued, Louis XVIII, the legitimate head of the House of Bourbon, was the only alternative, because foreign powers could not appeal to the people in a dynastic question without undermining the existence of *all* thrones. The House of Habsburg, Metternich was saying in effect, whose survival depended not on its acceptance but on its sanctity, and therefore the sanctity of all legitimate rule, would not risk a battle to give the popular will a chance to be consulted.

Everything depended now on the Tsar's determination and on his power. If the Tsar was strong enough to advance alone, as he threatened, Metternich would be able to achieve his goal only through a change of sides to which Castlereagh would never agree and which was contrary to all the principles of sound Austrian policy. But if Napoleon had still some strength left, his weight would in effect be added to the Austrian side and the requirement of unity might bring Alexander to terms. Thus, when on 12 February Napoleon defeated Blücher, he made Metternich master of the situation. For the failure of the Prussian army, which had advanced precisely to demonstrate the dispensability of Austria, proved instead that, however weakened, Napoleon was not to be defeated in single combat. Austria was needed again, and Metternich meant to exploit his pivotal position to the utmost. To insist on a definition of war aims in front of the enemy may not be heroic and is never popular. But to create a vacuum without necessity may lead to permanent revolution.

At the next meeting of the ministers on 13 February, Metternich forced the issue by declaring that Austria was not fighting to reestablish a tyranny and that it would conclude a separate peace.[2] Confronted with the disintegration of his cherished Coalition when success seemed so near, Castlereagh gave up his role of mediator. He proposed that the negotiations at Chatillon be resumed, that Metter-

[1] Fournier, *Congress*, p. 123f.

[2] Münster to the Prince Regent, 14 February, 1814, Fournier, *Congress* (Appendix), p. 298f.

nich write to Caulaincourt expressing the readiness of the Allies to conclude an armistice if France accepted the "ancient limits", and he undertook to obtain the Tsar's acquiescence to this programme. Six weeks after he had set out for the Continent with the vision of a Europe united by the self-evident threat of French supremacy and stabilized by British-Russian co-operation, Castlereagh emerged as a contestant for the equilibrium against the Tsar.

There ensued the first of the many stormy interviews Castlereagh was to have with Alexander. Alexander reiterated his determination to reach Paris, there to call an Assembly of Notables, his distrust of the Bourbons, his displeasure with Austrian timidity. Castlereagh represented the undesirability of engaging in a civil war within France, the difficulty of eliciting the sense of the nation, the dangers of a contest without goal. But the Tsar proved adamant. He had learned that British public opinion violently opposed peace with Napoleon and produced a letter from his ambassador in London stating that Lord Liverpool shared this feeling. Castlereagh remained firm, however. He told the Tsar that "acting in discharge of a responsible trust, I must be guided by the dictates of my own judgment and not suffer myself to be biased by any supposed wishes formed in England in ignorance of the real circumstances upon which we are now called upon [*sic*] to decide".[1] Castlereagh's strength and his failure are contained in this sentence: the proud assertion of responsibility, not for the mechanical execution of the popular will, but for the evaluation of interests not apparent to the multitude; and the refusal or the inability to influence the public sentiment. Castlereagh's was the statesmanship which had the courage to refuse the easy solution and the tragic isolation of the hero, who, because he cannot communicate, must walk in solitude.

Castlereagh's mission to the Tsar failed in its immediate objective, but it completed Russia's isolation. The answers to Metternich's questionnaire had resulted in what was in effect a Coalition against Russia within the Great Alliance. Metternich did not hesitate to press his advantage. When he threatened, once more, to withdraw Austrian troops, Prussia, afraid to be left at the mercy of its two volatile neighbours, agreed to guarantee Austria's objectives in the form of a convention, which Castlereagh approved although for reasons of domestic policy he did not formally join it. The Convention of 14 February represented another compromise, but one which

[1] Castlereagh's report of the conversation, B.D., p. 147f., 16 February, 1814.

demonstrated Austria's pivotal position: it provided that no conditions exceeding the Chatillon basis would be imposed, no matter how crushing the defeat of Napoleon; that peace would be concluded with Napoleon unless he was overthrown by a *spontaneous* popular movement; that in this case, the Allies would deal only with the Bourbons and with Louis XVIII, unless he should voluntarily step aside; that Paris, if occupied, would receive a Russian military governor, but that the actual administration should be in the hands of a council representing each of the Allied powers.[1] If the Tsar agreed, the advance could continue; otherwise, Austria would leave the Coalition.

In his quest for a total victory, the Tsar had attempted to exploit Austria's desire for stability by refusing to state his terms until Paris had fallen. Metternich now turned the tables and used the Tsar's desire to capture Paris to commit him both to the territorial extent and the domestic structure of France. And because Alexander's obsession with Paris outweighed all other considerations, he agreed, on 15 February, to Metternich's treaty draft. Whatever happened henceforth, France would remain a factor in the balance and whoever ruled, Napoleon or the Bourbons, was not likely to be too friendly towards the Tsar. The campaign could resume.

But it is the characteristic of a policy which bases itself on purely military considerations to be immoderate in triumph and panicky in adversity. When, on 14 February, Blücher was defeated again, the Tsar was one of the first to press for an armistice, which Schwarzenberg offered to the French commander on 17 February, on the pretext that a preliminary peace was to be signed at Chatillon at any moment. Castlereagh was outraged. He had used his powerful negotiating position to obtain Allied agreement to the principle of using Belgium to augment Holland, to the stipulation that no ships were to be turned over to France as a result of the peace, and that the maritime rights were not even to be discussed at a conference.[2] Now the Coalition, so long awaited and so painfully created, seemed to disintegrate at the very moment when Napoleon had appeared finally ready to come to terms and all "British" objectives had been realized. Little wonder that Castlereagh wrote an indignant letter to Metternich, which proved that he, at least, had not lost his sense of proportion: "You will . . . make a fatal sacrifice both of moral and political consideration, if under the pressure of those slight reverses

[1] Fournier, *Congress*, p. 133f.
[2] Fournier, *Congress*, p. 137.

which are incident to war and some embarrassments in your Council which I should hope are at an end, the great edifice of peace were suffered to be disfigured in its proportions. . . . If we act with *military* and *political* prudence how can France resist a just peace demanded by six hundred thousand warriors? Let her if she dares and the day we declare the fact to the French nation rest assured Bonaparte is indeed subdued."[1]

These brave words could not hide the fact that Castlereagh was deeply discouraged. He was bitter about the Allies: "At one time too proud to listen to anything; at another so impatient to be delivered from the presence of our enemy as to make the prolongation of Chatillon seem almost ludicrous."[2] And he added an exasperated letter to Liverpool which would have seemed like heresy to him only two months previously. "The criminations and recriminations between the Austrians and Russians are at their height and my patience is about worn out combating both. . . . We must not go to sea looking for adventures with such a bark as we sail in." The Coalition must indeed have lost its lustre when Castlereagh could even threaten to continue the war alone: "Nothing keeps either power firm than the consciousness that without Great Britain peace cannot be made. . . . I have explicitly told them that if they neither will nor can make a peace based upon a principle of authority, we must for their sake as well as our own rest in position against France."[3]

But the crisis in Troyes had served a useful purpose. Gone were the halcyon days of hope when protestations of eternal friendship were taken as the guarantee of permanent stability. They were replaced by a recognition that the problems of peace, although less exhilarating than those of war, have their own logic and that they alone justify the suffering of nations. The Tsar began to learn that he might conquer territories but not the right to them, that his good faith was a less useful guarantee than the location of his boundaries. The Tsar was confronted by a united front of the other powers and, in contrast to Napoleon, he accepted it. However vast his claims, there was a prospect that he would place legitimacy above conquest. As the Allied negotiators returned once more to Chatillon, the outline, not of the substance, but of the form of a European settlement, began to appear at last. The Coalition had established the nature of its internal

[1] B.D., p. 158f., 18 February, 1814.
[2] C.C. IX, p. 290, 25 February, 1814.
[3] B.D., p. 160, 26 February, 1814.

relations; and although many crises were still to await it, the Allies had lost their illusions, the most painful crisis in the life of men as well as of nations, and survived. In the tougher awareness of their new-found maturity, they could now confront the remaining problem: the possibility of Napoleon's acceptance of a Europe whose structure was independent of his will.

VIII

The Treaty of Chaumont and the Nature of Peace

I

NOW, if ever, was the moment for Napoleon to make peace. At Langres, Metternich had extorted the agreement to negotiate with a seemingly impotent foe from the reluctant Allies. But because peace had then appeared as an act of grace, it could not be concluded. In the meantime, Napoleon had demonstrated a measure of strength, however, and in the crisis of Troyes the Allies had decided that even a Bonapartist France, if restrained within the "ancient limits", would be compatible with the equilibrium of Europe. In order to hasten the peace, Castlereagh had enumerated the colonial conquests Britain proposed to return to France. When Metternich finally replied to Caulaincourt's letter of 9 February with an exasperated plea for a speedy settlement and a remark about the difficulty of acting as minister of a coalition which contained fifty thousand Cossacks,[1] it was clear that everything depended on Napoleon.

But Napoleon again misunderstood the situation. If any doubt remained about the impossibility of the peaceful co-existence of a revolutionary system and a "legitimate" equilibrium, the second stage of the Congress of Chatillon removed it. An individual who has legitimized himself by charisma or by force will tend to ascribe failure to the malice of fortune, for he could not survive the admission of personal inadequacy. And he will confuse each success with total triumph, for a limited victory would be almost as bad as a defeat; it would represent a confession of finite power. When Napoleon spoke of driving the Allies across the Rhine, he was not being unreasonable, but obeying the logic of charismatic rule, which has its laws as do all human activities. So it happened, that the long retreat from the Elbe to just before Paris had taught

[1] Fournier, *Congress*, p. 148, 16 February, 1814.

Napoleon nothing. At the very gates of his capital he still could not accept the fact that his resources were limited, that even a succession of victories would avail him nothing, that the Allied offer reflected the reality of the power relationship. He was reinforced in his obstinacy by two contradictory beliefs: on the one hand he imagined that, no matter how severely he was defeated, he would always be able to make peace on the basis of the "ancient limits", as if domestic transformations within France were impossible. On the other hand, he did not think his rule could survive the loss of all his conquests. The exclusive reality of power and the illusoriness of its legitimacy, these were in fact the definition of the gulf between Europe and Napoleon.

There ensued in Chatillon the second act of the "comedy" as Stadion called it, but, in order to show the contingency of all human plans the gods had reversed the roles. Now the Allies were pressing for a peace and Caulaincourt, who had received orders to hold out for the "natural boundaries", procrastinated. The Allies submitted a treaty draft for a preliminary peace, but Caulaincourt replied with an abstract discussion about the nature of the equilibrium and the inconsistency of restraining France within her pre-Revolutionary boundaries while all other powers were gaining in strength. The Allies offered to forego certain military clauses in the treaty draft referring to the surrender of French fortresses, but Caulaincourt could only plead for delay. In the meantime, on 21 February, Napoleon wrote a peremptory letter to the Emperor of Austria attacking the Tsar's vindictiveness and demanding a peace on the basis of the "natural boundaries".

But as the days passed, the Allies came again to a realization of their strength. A military victory always has two components, its physical reality and its psychological impact, and it is the task of diplomacy to translate the latter into political terms. The Allies as well as Napoleon, remembering Austerlitz and Jena, had confused tactical reverses with a strategic stalemate. But while the Allies could afford this error, it was catastrophic for Napoleon. His victories had been due to the dexterity of his manœuvres, but they had left the basic situation unchanged, because in a contest of attrition even victories undermine the relative position of the weaker power. It soon became apparent that Napoleon was no longer the victor of 1805 and 1809, not because he had lost his skill but because he had lost the power to make it effective. Napoleon's real victory had been psychological, to have forced a superior foe into a willingness to make peace. He now destroyed himself because he could not accept any peace he did not dictate. When, on 25 February, the Allies insisted on a definite reply by a certain date, Caulaincourt must have known that the answer he promised for 10 March would not be forthcoming.

In the interval there occurred a struggle between Metternich and Napoleon, similar to many that had gone before, and more than ever, the object was Napoleon's soul. Every encounter between Napoleon and Metternich had this quality of Faustian doom. It was through an exploitation of Napoleon's pride—the attitude of a man who defines himself by what he seems, not by what he is—that Metternich had lured him step by step towards the abyss which ended in Prague. It was this same pride which now frustrated Metternich's efforts to save Napoleon. The end of the war thus taught a dual lesson: while Napoleon was experiencing the boundaries of power, Metternich was learning the limits of manipulation, that spirits once called forth cannot be banished by an act of will. Metternich had never intended more than the limitation of Napoleon's power, if only because the overthrow of *any* dynasty was a dangerous symbol for Austria. Because he needed a strong France, Metternich now attempted to reverse the fate of which he had himself been the agent, to demand of Napoleon what he must have known was impossible, the recognition of limits. And just as in Greek tragedy the warning of the oracle does not suffice to avert the doom because salvation resides not in knowledge but in acceptance, so now Napoleon disregarded Metternich's entreaties, not because he failed to understand their arguments but because he disdained them.

It was in vain that the Emperor rejected Napoleon's accusation of Russian vengefulness and reiterated the willingness of the Allies to make an immediate peace on the basis of the "ancient limits". It was in vain that Caulaincourt and Metternich added pleas for peace. "Are there no means to enlighten [Napoleon] about his situation?" Metternich wrote to Caulaincourt in exasperation. "Has he irrevocably placed his fate and that of his son on the carriage of his last gun? Does he think his daring and his courage will protect him against being crushed by superior force? . . . If the Emperor of Austria could cede Tirol in 1809, why can Napoleon not cede Belgium in 1814?"[1] But even this appeal, so subtly adjusted to Napoleon's

[1] Fournier, *Congress*, p. 194, 3 March, 1814.

never-ending quest for "legitimacy", proved futile. Metternich might declare the House of Habsburg and the House of Bonaparte as equivalent, but the key to the situation was that Napoleon was oppressed by their disparity. For Napoleon never tired of pointing out that legitimate rulers could return to their capitals no matter how many battles they lost, but that he, the son of the Revolution, could not afford this luxury. Because he had been unable—or thought he had been unable—to translate force into obligation, Napoleon had to stake everything on exhibiting his power. Because power is the expression of an arbitrary and therefore insecure world order, he succeeded only in uniting Europe in a war for his destruction.

Napoleon's intransigeance on the brink of disaster completed the demonstration which even his triumphs had not been able to achieve: that his continued rule was incompatible with the peace of Europe, that any agreement with him would amount to no more than an armistice. Whatever the differences among the Allies, the threat of Napoleon was now paramount. Even Metternich was coming to realize that the danger to the equilibrium inherent in the complete collapse of France was less important than the threat posed by the continued rule of Napoleon. The attempt to balance the Tsar with Napoleon and to defeat the social revolution by its political expression had been a little too subtle. A revolution cannot be ended by an act of will or because the world would be more "reasonable" without it. Napoleon simply refused to play according to the rules of the balance of power. The war was becoming total, despite Metternich's victory over the Tsar, because a revolutionary finds it easier to destroy himself than to surrender.

The result was that the treaty of General Alliance so laboriously and patiently sought by Castlereagh finally came into being. Napoleon's armies in Central Europe had not sufficed to bring about a unity of purpose, but Napoleon pushed back to the gates of his own capital had finally removed all illusions. As 10 March was approaching and peace seemed increasingly unlikely, the Allies finally agreed on the common measures and on the goals of their effort.

The Treaty of Chaumont, which was signed on 4 March, was primarily concerned with the prosecution of the war against France.[1] Each of the four Allies agreed to put a hundred and fifty thousand men in the field and Britain, in addition, undertook to pay subsidies

[1] Text, Martens, G. F., *Nouveau Receuil de Traités*, 16 Vols. (Göttingen, 1817–1818). Vol. III, p. 155f.

to the amount of five million pounds. Each signatory bound itself not to conclude a separate peace. But these were the conventional clauses of any military alliance, significant only for the scale of the British effort. The real importance of the Treaty of Chaumont lay in its assumption that France would continue to be a threat even after Napoleon's defeat. The alliance was to continue for twenty years and each power undertook to furnish sixty thousand men against French aggression, although Britain reserved the right to supply the equivalent in subsidies. Since the Treaty of Chaumont was concluded on the assumption that peace would eventually be concluded with Napoleon, this provision made clear the prevailing distrust.

But the Treaty of Chaumont also represents the measure of the skill of Metternich and Castlereagh in obtaining their special objectives. An additional clause provided for the independence of Spain, Switzerland, Italy, Germany, and Holland. Holland was to have both a territorial extension and a "suitable" boundary; Germany was to be organized in a confederacy of independent, sovereign states. Nothing was said about Poland. The extension of Holland included at least Antwerp and the "suitable" boundary referred to Belgium. While a Germany of sovereign states amounted to a recognition that the dreams of a unified Germany and the aspirations of Prussian hegemony in the North were equally doomed to frustration. In this manner, Austria and Britain had been satisfied before Russia after all. To be sure, the Tsar attempted to make his agreement to the Dutch point conditional on Britain's assumption of the Russian debt in Holland.[1] But by pressing this subsidiary claim, he admitted, by inference, the principle of the annexation of Belgium to Holland. The Tsar had succeeded in deferring the settlement of the Polish question, but in the process, by his insistence on peripheral objects, by his phobia about Paris and his pettiness about Holland, he had lost his bargaining position.

Castlereagh was triumphant. The special British objectives had been achieved *through* the Coalition; the Alliance had been constructed, legitimized by the threat of France. "I send you *my* [my italics] treaty," he reported proudly and in a strange tone of whimsy, "which I hope you will approve. We four ministers when signing happened to be sitting at a whist table. It was agreed that never were stakes so high at any former party. My modesty would have prevented me from offering it, but, as they chose to make us a

[1] C.C. IX, p. 326, 8 March, 1814.

military power, I was determined not to play second fiddle. The fact is . . . our engagements are equivalent to theirs united. . . . What an extraordinary display of power! This, I trust, will put an end to any doubts as to the claim we have to an opinion on Continental matters."[1] Here was the essence of Castlereagh's achievement: After twenty years of isolation, Britain was once more a part of Europe.

On 9 March, Blücher defeated Napoleon at Laon. The war was now decided because Napoleon, who could not make use of his victories, could no longer afford a defeat. And only twenty-four hours separated the Allies from the deadline of the Congress of Chatillon. In his unofficial capacity as Prime Minister of the Coalition, Metternich instructed the plenipotentiaries to refer to him any answer Caulaincourt might make on 10 March, partly to keep the thread of negotiations in his own hands, partly to delay the seemingly inevitable rupture. This provoked an outburst from Stewart, who inquired what the Allies should do if Caulaincourt accepted their own demands.[2] But he was to be relieved of all embarrassment. Caulaincourt's reply proved ambiguous because Napoleon's instructions had been scanty. It amounted to no more than a slightly modified insistence on the "natural limits". Only procedural questions delayed the break-up of the Congress. On 15 March, Caulaincourt's final offer was transmitted to Headquarters and, on 17 March, a proclamation drafted by Metternich announced the end of the last Allied effort to make peace with Napoleon.

Even at this late moment Metternich could not reconcile himself to ending the war for the political equilibrium by threatening to overturn its social base, or to seeing the French Revolution, transcended in the Napoleonic Empire, break loose again with its collapse. On 17 March, after the Congress of Chatillon had already broken up, he therefore appealed again to Caulaincourt in a tone of desperate urgency which revealed that the last victory had eluded Metternich: to bring Napoleon to a sense of reality, to defeat the French Revolution by its own product: "On the day on which you are ready to bring the inevitable sacrifices for peace, come here to our headquarters, but do not come as the advocate of impracticable projects. The issues are too serious to permit the continued writing of novels without endangering Napoleon's fate. What do the Allies risk? At most to have to leave the territory of old [pre-revolutionary] France. And

[1] C.C. IX, p. 336, 10 March, 1814.
[2] C.C. IX, p. 322f., 8 March, 1814.

what would Napoleon gain? The Belgian people would rise in arms; so would the left bank of the Rhine. . . . Austria's wishes are still for the preservation of a dynasty with which it is closely connected. The peace still depends on your master. In a little while this will no longer be true. I will do my best to keep Lord Castlereagh here for a few days. Once he is gone, peace will be impossible."[1]

Like an exasperated professor Metternich thus exhibited, for the final time, the elements of his cherished equilibrium, as if it were inconceivable that reality could elude its beholder. But if revolutionaries had a sense of reality, or at least if their sense of reality were not incommensurable with the "legitimate" one, they would not be revolutionaries. By the time Caulaincourt replied, on 25 March, that he was now ready to come to Headquarters to conclude the peace, the die had been cast. Napoleon's last desperate attempt to cut the line of communications of the Allies had failed. The road to Paris was once more open. And the curt reply which Metternich returned to Caulaincourt, that the Emperor was away from Headquarters, indicated that the peace, now so imminent, would not be concluded with Napoleon.

Metternich's letter may, in any case, have overestimated Castlereagh's pliability, for, unlike Metternich, Castlereagh was not concerned about a social revolution in France. He had acquiesced in negotiations with Napoleon because he considered the "ancient limits" and an enlarged Holland a sufficient political guarantee for British security. But his agreement to deal with Napoleon had been intended as a proof of British good faith, not as an indication of a British preference. He had maintained this position despite increasingly ominous letters about public reaction in Great Britain. The permanent Foreign Office officials, Cooke and Hamilton, not less than Liverpool and Clancarty, agreed that peace with Napoleon would prove difficult to defend. "The voice, no peace with Napoleon, is as general as ever," reported Hamilton on 19 March. "The disposition of the country for *any* peace with Napoleon becomes more unfavourable every day," wrote Liverpool on 17 February. "I hear it from all quarters and from all classes of the people."[2] On 19 March, the Cabinet ordered Castlereagh to refer any treaty back to London before signature.[3] This dispatch arrived too late to affect events, but

[1] Text, Fournier, *Congress*, p. 226.
[2] Webster, I., p. 514 (Appendix).
[3] B.D., p. 166, 19 March, 1814.

it left no doubt that peace with Napoleon would be a sacrifice brought to Allied unity and would be signed by Britain only as a last resort.

When the Congress of Chatillon broke up, Castlereagh could therefore justly feel that he had carried out any obligation imposed upon him by good faith and that he was now free to pursue his own goals. "I wish it had been possible," he reported to the Cabinet, "with less sacrifice in point of time, to have ascertained . . . the impracticability of concluding peace with the existing ruler of France, but it has at length been accomplished in a manner which . . . can leave no doubt in the view even of the French nation that Napoleon is the true and only obstacle to an early, honourable and solid peace."[1] Since Napoleon's power was disintegrating rapidly, no reason for concluding peace with him existed any longer. While Napoleon, with a last desperate show of daring, bared the road to Paris in order to interpose his army in the Allies' rear, his fate was being decided. He had had absolute power for so long that it had not occurred to him that, by the time he returned to Paris, the city might have declared against him.

Between 20 and 22 March, the Allies took the first steps towards recognizing the Bourbons. All during the campaign the royal dukes had been in France, but they had been ignored by the Allies. Now their emissary, Vitrolles, was received at Headquarters and encouraged to organize a movement on their behalf. The Allies promised to turn over to the Bourbons the revenue of any occupied province that declared itself and to protect the advocates of the Bourbon cause in case peace should be concluded with Napoleon.[2] In addition Castlereagh advanced British funds. On 24 March, Bordeaux went over to the Bourbons. Metternich now knew that the die had been cast, that Napoleon had been eliminated as a factor in the balance, that stability both domestic and foreign would have to be sought with a Bourbon France. "You may rest tranquil about our course," he wrote to Hudelist. "Be assured . . . that I remain true to my eternal principle that events which cannot be avoided must be directed and that only weak individuals hold back."[3]

The events to which Metternich was referring were taking shape in Paris, where Talleyrand, Napoleon's erstwhile Foreign Minister, was

[1] B.D., p. 168, 22 March, 1814.
[2] B.D., p. 170, 22 March, 1814.
[3] Fournier, p. 231, 23 March, 1814.

arranging a plot which would end with the restoration of the Bourbons. Of all his contemporaries, the one most similar to Metternich was Talleyrand. He possessed the same nonchalance, the same subtlety and an even more trenchant wit. This was no accident. Both Talleyrand and Metternich were products of the eighteenth century, grand seigneurs caught up in a contest they could not but consider gross and even loutish. Both were sufficiently aristocrats to be concerned not only with the substance but with the form of their achievements. Both identified tranquillity with balance and proportion.

Still these similarities hid basic differences. For fate had not been kind to Talleyrand; it had not given him the opportunity to live his values. To be an aristocrat is not a dogma but a fact; but in Talleyrand there was always an incongruity between his professions and his performance. Forced into the priesthood as a young man, he became Bishop of Auteuil, only to renounce the Church during the Revolution. After breaking with the Revolution, he had become Foreign Minister of Napoleon; and now with the Allied armies approaching Paris, Talleyrand was working for the Restoration of the Bourbons. It is possible, of course, to find a certain consistency in this behaviour, an effort to balance by his changes of side the excesses of his contemporaries. Still one cannot blame his contemporaries for distrusting Talleyrand, because they had to judge him by his actions, not by his explanations of them. To be sure, in more tranquil times, Talleyrand would have found more conventional outlets for his talents. But there are two ways of defeating turbulence, by standing above it or by swimming with the tide; by principle or by manipulation. Talleyrand failed of ultimate stature because his actions were always too precisely attuned to the dominant mood, because nothing ever engaged him so completely that he would bring it the sacrifice of personal advancement. This may have been due to a sincere attempt to remain in a position to moderate events; outsiders may be forgiven if they considered it opportunism. Thus Talleyrand's greatest strength always lay in the dexterity of his manœuvres, in the manipulations of the principles of others, in devising formulae for achieving an agreed goal.

But whatever Talleyrand's shortcomings, the situation in Paris in the spring of 1814 was tailor-made for his special abilities. The Tsar, at the gates of Paris, might flatter himself that all options were still open and that a grateful populace might decide even on a

Republic if it wished. The cool calculators in Dijon, the seat of Allied Headquarters, and in Paris meant to see to it that no dangerous experiments were attempted. On 31 March, the Tsar entered Paris in triumph, while Metternich and Castlereagh remained behind in Dijon. They left the glory of entering Paris to the Tsar because they knew that foreign occupations, however eagerly awaited, appear in retrospect as national humiliations. The very people who have cheered loudest upon the conqueror's entry will, in the atmosphere of regained self-confidence, blame their degradation not on their cravenness but on the force of circumstance, and will tend to purge themselves by the rigidity of their hostility against the foreigner. Nor was the Tsar's exposed role in the restoration of the Bourbons an unmixed blessing. A weak government, suspected of being the tool of foreign powers, cannot legitimize itself more easily than by an attack on the very power to which it owes—or is thought to owe—its existence. In the exultation of victory this was not apparent, however. On 6 April the Senate, under Talleyrand's direction and with the Tsar's acquiescence, passed a new Constitution which recalled Louis XVIII to the throne of France. The contest against Napoleon had ended with the triumph of legitimacy both on the battlefield and in Paris.

To be sure, the legitimacy of the Bourbons was a tenuous one. They had been recalled by the popular will and had been forced to accept a constitution they had never seen. But this is no more than saying that "legitimacy" can never be restored by an act of will. Its strength is its spontaneity; it is strongest when it is never talked about, indeed when it cannot be talked about. But once the question regarding the existing pattern of obligations has been raised, expressed in the existence of a significant revolutionary party, the social structure will never be the same again, even should the "legitimate order" triumph. It is not given to social structures to recapture their spontaneity, any more than to man to regain a lost innocence.[1] But if the Bourbons could never go back to the *ancien régime*, they might establish a claim through the recognition of their legitimacy by the foreign powers. If they had to depend in part on the popular will, they might best begin by bringing the peace Napoleon had been unable to conclude. And since their legitimacy depended to such an extent on foreign recognition, the conditions of the peace about to be concluded would reflect their international standing. As the

[1] See Chapter XI for development of this point.

Allies began their deliberations, not only the European equilibrium but also the domestic equilibrium of France was at stake.

II

Although every war is fought in the name of peace, there is a tendency to define peace as the absence of war and to confuse it with military victory. To discuss conditions of peace during wartime seems almost indecent, as if the admission that the war might end could cause a relaxation of the effort. This is no accident. The logic of war is power, and power has no inherent limit. The logic of peace is proportion, and proportion implies limitation. The success of war is victory; the success of peace is stability. The conditions of victory are commitment, the condition of stability is self-restraint. The motivation of war is extrinsic: the fear of an enemy. The motivation of peace is intrinsic: the balance of forces and the acceptance of its legitimacy. A war without an enemy is inconceivable; a peace built on the myth of an enemy is an armistice. It is the temptation of war to punish; it is the task of policy to construct. Power can sit in judgment, but statesmanship must look to the future.

These incommensurabilities are the particular problems of peace-settlements at the end of total wars. The enormity of suffering leads to a conception of war in personal terms, of the enemy as the "cause" of the misfortune, of his defeat as the moment for retribution. The greater the suffering, the more the war will be conceived an end in itself and the rules of war applied to the peace settlement. The more total the commitment, the more "natural" unlimited claims will appear. Suffering leads to self-righteousness more often than to humility, as if it were a badge of good faith, as if only the "innocent" could suffer. Each peace settlement is thus confronted with the fate of the enemy and with the more fundamental problem whether the experience of war has made it impossible to conceive of a world *without* an enemy.

Whether the powers conclude a retrospective peace or one that considers the future depends on their social strength and on the degree to which they can generate their own motivation. A retrospective peace will crush the enemy so that he is *unable* to fight again; its opposite will deal with the enemy so that he does not *wish* to attack again. A retrospective peace is the expression of a rigid social order, clinging to the only certainty: the past. It will make a "legitimate" settlement impossible, because the defeated nation, unless completely dismembered, will not accept its humiliation. There exist two legitimacies in such cases: the internal arrangements among the victorious powers and the claims of the defeated. Between the two, only force or the threat of force regulates relations. In its quest to achieve stability through safety, in its myth of the absence of intrinsic causes for war, a retrospective peace produces a revolutionary situation. This, in fact, was the situation in Europe between the two World Wars.

It is to the credit of the statesmen who negotiated the settlement of the post-Napoleonic period that they resisted the temptation of a punitive peace. This may have been due to the very quality which is usually considered their greatest failing: their indifference to popular pressures. But whatever the cause, they were seeking equilibrium and not retribution, legitimacy and not punishment. Instead of considering the domestic transformation of France an added bonus or speaking of a meaningless façade, the statesmen of the Coalition of 1814 were willing to accept the consequences of their own myth. The full implications of Metternich's tenacious diplomacy, which had seemed so timidly obtuse while defeat of the enemy was the primary consideration, now became apparent. He had talked so much about the war for an equilibrium that no other basis appeared conceivable. He had issued so many proclamations declaring the war an effort to bring Napoleon to "reasonable" terms that no serious proposals for dismemberment were advanced. Only the Prussians spoke of an inherently wicked France, and they were soon brought to terms. So deliberate had been the conduct of the war, so careful the preparation of each step that although the war had become total, it did not seem so. Infinity achieved by finite stages loses its terrors and its temptations. This is the final meaning of Metternich's policy in 1813–14.

Even more remarkable was Castlereagh's attitude. The statesman of the nation in which feelings ran perhaps the highest, he nevertheless became one of the chief advocates of moderation. He had resisted the temptation of joining the Tsar in a march on Paris. He was now to resist the blandishments of "absolute" security. In this manner the final settlement of the Napoleonic wars was accomplished in three stages: the abdication of Napoleon and the treaty settling his fate; the peace with France; the settlement of the European equilibrium.

The fate of Napoleon was of no immediate consequence in the European balance, but it served as a touchstone of the state of mind of the Allies. The early nineteenth century was not yet a period which measured the extent of its triumph by the degree of personal retribution exacted. Even Stewart wrote to Castlereagh that Napoleon's predicament deserved the pity which is extended by Christians to the most unfortunate of their fellow-men.[1] Whatever Alexander's faults, they did not include the absence of magnanimity, and it was he who negotiated the Treaty of Fontainebleau with Caulaincourt. Under its provisions Napoleon was to keep the Imperial title and to be given an annual revenue of two million francs out of French funds. The island of Elba was established as an independent principality to be possessed by Napoleon in full sovereignty. The Empress was granted the Duchy of Parma. Provisions were made for Napoleon's family, his divorced wife, and even his adopted son, Eugene Beauharnais, the Viceroy of Italy. Napoleon was permitted to take a ship and a bodyguard of French soldiers to Elba. Perhaps from a psychological point of view this treaty was not as generous as it sounded. For it must have been crushing for the conqueror of Europe to be reduced to the status of a third-rate Italian prince.

When Castlereagh and Metternich arrived in Paris, the negotiations were already completed. In vain did Metternich protest against Napoleon's sovereignty over Elba in view of its proximity to France and Italy. He even predicted a new war within two years. Nor was Castlereagh completely satisfied. Like Liverpool he would have preferred a "more suitable" station for Napoleon than Elba. And Britain was not prepared to grant the defeated Napoleon a recognition it had refused him at the height of his power. Castlereagh succeeded in limiting the Imperial title to Napoleon's lifetime and acceded only to those parts of the treaty which referred to the territorial settlement. On 16 April, Napoleon commenced his movement southward. The Allies could now turn to making peace with France.

As in all negotiations which were concerned with adjustments within a given framework, Castlereagh emerged as the leading figure. He was now at the height of his influence. He had kept the Coalition together despite the hesitation of the Allies. He had negotiated with Napoleon despite the clamour of public opinion and in doing so had laid the moral basis for the Restoration. As is usual in such cases,

[1] C.C. IX, p. 449, 6 April, 1814.

the public now interpreted the violence of their attacks as a token of their good faith and the Cabinet ascribed to profound, if somewhat incomprehensible, design what had been due at least in part to Napoleon's inability to come to grips with reality. "Be assured," wrote Cooke, "that the fullest justice is done to the great abilities you have displayed throughout the whole of the transaction which you have so successfully and wonderfully managed. Your superiority and authority are now fixed."[1] Castlereagh was well aware of his position. When Liverpool urged him to return immediately for the session of Parliament, since Parliament might prove unmanageable without him, he replied: "It may appear presumptuous in me to say so but my remaining . . . is beyond all comparison more important than my original mission. You must therefore manage it. . . ."[2]

One of Castlereagh's major concerns was to solidify the authority of the Bourbons and to rely for the security of Europe not on a prostrate but on a pacific France. He urged the Bourbons to accept the Constitution drafted by Talleyrand, however defective, rather than "engage in a dispute about political metaphysics". He sought to arrange for the earliest possible withdrawal of Allied troops.[3] Since the Bourbons had agreed before the Restoration to accept the "ancient limits", nothing seemed to stand in the way of a speedy settlement. But as one power after another achieved its aims, Prussia, seeing the available compensations for the probable loss of its Polish possessions to Russia dwindle away, attempted to force a settlement of *all* outstanding questions, to redraw the map of Europe before concluding peace with France. This was not an unreasonable demand. Although an acquisitive power has most to gain from deferring a settlement until after the conclusion of hostilities, it also has most to lose from a series of partial arrangements. The more powers are satisfied, the less motive there is for concessions. On 29 April, the Prussian Chancellor, Hardenberg, therefore submitted the draft of a peace settlement which would have given the major part of Poland to Russia, while annexing Saxony to Prussia.

But the Tsar, always torn between the desire for universal approbation and the necessities of reason of state, was not ready to avow his claims. He may also have believed that the longer he delayed, the more Britain would disinterest itself in the final settlement, and he

[1] C.C. IX, p. 454, 9 April, 1814.
[2] C.C. IX, p. 458, 13 April, 1814.
[3] C.C. IX, p. 459, 13 April, 1814.

promised himself great things from his impending visit to London. No other choice remained, therefore, but to conclude a treaty with France and to defer the settlement of the Polish and Saxon question. Under the provisions of the Treaty of Paris, France renounced all claims over Holland, Belgium, Germany, Italy, Switzerland, and Malta. Britain obtained the colonies of Tobago, Santa Lucia and Ile de France, and Spain received the French portion of Santo Domingo. A secret article provided for the independence of Germany and its organization as a confederation. By another secret article, France recognized the incorporation of Belgium into Holland. A third secret article fixed the Austrian border in Italy at the Po and Lake Maggiore and reinstated the Habsburg lines in Tuscany.

Well might Castlereagh feel that this treaty carried out his intention of stripping the arrangement of any appearance of excessive distrust.[1] France retained not only her ancient limits but was given an extension in Savoy and the Palatinate, augmenting her pre-Revolutionary population by six hundred thousand. No restrictions were placed on the size of her army. Britain returned most of the colonial conquests, and those retained were thought to have strategic rather than commercial importance. Holland sold the Cape Colonies to Great Britain, in part to obtain funds to construct barrier forts, but was restored the Dutch East Indies whose value was not then fully understood. France was permitted to retain the art treasures which had been accumulated in Paris during twenty-five years of conquest. No reparations were exacted, causing Cooke to write in protest: "It will be hard, if France is to pay nothing for the destruction of Europe, and we are to pay all for saving it."[2]

The treaty of Paris was thus a peace of equilibrium, based on a recognition that stability depends on the absence of basic cleavages, that the task of statesmanship is not to punish, but to integrate. Ignored was the myth of "absolute security" which measures safety entirely by the position of the boundary-posts and which, by seeking to restrict only one power, creates an imbalance among all the others. When the plenipotentiary of Geneva insisted on certain frontier rectifications on the grounds of strategic necessity, Castlereagh replied: "These arguments about . . . strategic boundaries are pushed too far. Real defence and security comes from the guarantee which is given by the fact that they cannot touch you without declaring war on

[1] C.C. IX, p. 472, 19 April, 1814.
[2] C.C. IX, p. 454, 9 April, 1814.

all those interested in maintaining things as they are."[1] In this manner the war against Napoleon ended, not in a paean of hatred but in a spirit of reconciliation, with a recognition that the stability of an international order depends on the degree to which its components feel committed to its defence. It was not a peace which took account of the great ideals of an impatient generation. Its motivation was safety, not the realization of abstract ideals. But safety, after a quarter-century of turmoil, was not a mean achievement.

To be sure, the European equilibrium was not yet completed. The complementary questions of Poland and Saxony awaited the attention of a European congress. But the shape of the settlement was becoming apparent. In Troyes the elements of the new European order had begun to group themselves. Through the Treaty of Paris, France emerged as a possible factor in the balance. True, it was invited to the Congress only to ratify its decisions. But the Restoration had made France an "acceptable" ally; no "ideological" gulf separated it any longer from the rest of Europe. Would any nation accept an unfavourable verdict without attempting to reinforce its side of the scale by France? The answer to this poser in the limits of self-restraint was to be given by the Congress of Vienna.

[1] Webster, I, p. 268.

IX

The Congress of Vienna

I

ARTICLE XXXII of the Peace of Paris had provided for a congress to be held in Vienna which was to settle the problem of the European equilibrium and to which all the powers engaged on either side during the war were invited. When this article was drafted, the Congress was expected to have a primarily symbolic significance, as the beginning of an era based on the reciprocal respect of sovereign states. The elements of the new equilibrium were to have been settled in London, where the Tsar, the King of Prussia, and Metternich repaired after the conclusion of the Treaty of Paris. It was almost an accident, therefore, that the Congress became the scene of a contest none the less bitter for the festivities surrounding it and all the more acrimonious because of the realization that the ultimate issues could no longer be evaded. For here at Vienna the final decision had to be taken whether out of the wars with Napoleon there could emerge a "legitimate" order, an order, that is, accepted by all the major powers, or whether relations would have to remain revolutionary, based on the unsupported claims of power.

Any international settlement represents a stage in a process by which a nation reconciles its vision of itself with the vision of it by other powers. To itself, a nation appears as an expression of justice, and the more spontaneous its pattern of social obligations, the more this is true; for government functions effectively only when most citizens obey voluntarily and they will obey only to the extent that they consider the demands of their rulers just. To others, it appears as a force or an expression of will. This is inevitable because external sovereignty can be controlled only by superior force and because foreign policy must be planned on the basis of the other side's capabilities and not merely of its intentions. Could a power achieve all its wishes, it would strive for absolute security, a world-order free from the consciousness of foreign danger and where all problems have the manageability of domestic issues. But since absolute security for one power means absolute insecurity for all others, it is never obtainable as a part of a "legitimate" settlement, and can be achieved only through conquest.

For this reason an international settlement which is accepted and not imposed will always appear *somewhat* unjust to any one of its components. Paradoxically, the generality of this dissatisfaction is a condition of stability, because were any one power *totally* satisfied, all others would have to be *totally* dissatisfied and a revolutionary situation would ensue. The foundation of a stable order is the *relative* security—and therefore the *relative* insecurity—of its members. Its stability reflects, not the absence of unsatisfied claims, but the absence of a grievance of such magnitude that redress will be sought in overturning the settlement rather than through an adjustment within its framework. An order whose structure is accepted by all major powers is "legitimate". An order containing a power which considers its structure oppressive is "revolutionary". The security of a domestic order resides in the preponderant power of authority, that of an international order in the balance of forces and in its expression, the equilibrium.

But if an international order expresses the need for security and an equilibrium, it is constructed in the name of a legitimizing principle. Because a settlement transforms force into acceptance, it must attempt to translate the requirements of security into claims and individual demands into general advantage. It is the legitimizing principle which establishes the relative "justice" of competing claims and the mode of their adjustment. This is not to say that there need be an exact correspondence between the maxims of legitimacy and the conditions of the settlement. No major power will give up its minimum claim to security—the possibility of conducting an independent foreign policy—merely for the sake of legitimacy. But the legitimizing principle defines the marginal case. In 1919, the Austro-Hungarian Empire disintegrated not so much from the impact of the war as from the nature of the peace, because its continued existence was incompatible with national self-determination, the legitimizing principle of the new international order. It would have occurred to no one in the eighteenth century that the legitimacy of a state depended on linguistic unity. It was inconceivable to the makers of the Versailles settlement that there might be any other basis for legitimate rule. Legitimizing principles triumph by being taken for granted.

Although there never occurs an exact correspondence between the maxims of the legitimizing principle and the conditions of the settlement, stability depends on a certain commensurability. If there exists a substantial discrepancy *and* a major power which feels disadvantaged, the international order will be volatile. For the appeal by a "revolutionary" power to the legitimizing principle of the settlement creates a psychological distortion. The "natural" expression of the policy of a status quo power is law—the definition of a continuing relationship. But against a permanently dissatisfied power appealing to the legitimizing principle of the international order, force is the only recourse. Those who have most to gain from stability thus become the exponents of a revolutionary policy. Hitler's appeal to national self-determination in the Sudeten crisis in 1938 was an invocation of "justice", and thereby contributed to the indecisiveness of the resistance: it induced the Western powers to attempt to construct a "truly" legitimate order by satisfying Germany's "just" claims. Only after Hitler annexed Bohemia and Moravia was it clear that he was aiming for dominion, not legitimacy; only then did the contest become one of pure power.

The major problem of an international settlement, then, is so to relate the claims of legitimacy to the requirements of security that no power will express its dissatisfaction in a revolutionary policy, and so to arrange the balance of forces as to deter aggression produced by causes other than the conditions of the settlement. This is not a mechanical problem. If the international order could be constructed with the clarity of a mathematical axiom, powers would consider themselves as factors in a balance and arrange their adjustments to achieve a perfect equilibrium between the forces of aggression and the forces of resistance. But an exact balance is impossible, and not only because of the difficulty of predicting the aggressor. It is chimerical, above all, because while powers may appear to outsiders as factors in a security arrangement, they appear domestically as expressions of a historical existence. No power will submit to a settlement, however well-balanced and however "secure", which seems totally to deny its vision of itself. No consideration of balance could induce Britain to surrender the maritime rights or Austria its German position, because their notion of "justice" was inseparable from those claims. There exist two kinds of equilibrium then: a general equilibrium which makes it risky for one power or group of powers to attempt to impose their will on the remainder; and a particular equilibrium which defines the historical relation of certain powers among each other. The former is the deterrent against a general war; the latter the condition of smooth co-operation. An international order is therefore rarely born out of the consciousness of harmony. For even when there is an agreement about legitimacy, the conceptions of the requirements of security will differ with the geographical position and the history of the contending powers. Out of just such a conflict over the nature of the equilibrium the Congress of Vienna fashioned a settlement which lasted for almost exactly a century.

For the problem at Vienna was not just the simple one of the status quo powers, Britain and Austria, confronting the acquisitive Russia and Prussia, while Talleyrand was gleefully watching at the periphery of events. Neither the claims of the acquisitive powers nor the resistance of the conserving states were of the same order. Russia's demand of Poland threatened the equilibrium of Europe; Prussia's insistence on Saxony merely imperilled the balance within Germany. When Castlereagh spoke of the equilibrium, he meant a Europe in which hegemony was impossible; but when Metternich invoked the equilibrium, he included a Germany in which Prussian predominance was impossible. Castlereagh was interested in creating a Central Europe which would be strong enough to resist attack from both the West and the East; Metternich desired the same thing, but he was also concerned about Austria's relative position within Central Europe. To Castlereagh the Continental nations were aspects of a defensive effort; but to the Continental nations the general equilibrium meant nothing if it destroyed the historical position which to them was the reason for their existence. To Castlereagh the equilibrium was a mechanical expression of the balance of forces; to the Continental nations, a reconciliation of historical aspirations.

This led to a diplomatic stalemate, all the more inflexible because Britain and Austria had secured most of their special interests, so that few bargaining weapons were left for Russia or Prussia; a stalemate which could be broken only by adding an additional weight to one side of the scales. Since the sole uncommitted major power was France, the former enemy emerged as the key to the European settlement. Thus grew up a myth about Talleyrand's role at the Congress of Vienna, of the diabolical wit who appeared on the scene and broke up a coalition of hostile powers, who then regrouped them into a pattern to his liking by invoking the magic word "legitimacy" and who emerged, finally, as the arbiter of Europe.[1] It is a legend spread by those who confuse results and causes and by professional diplomats wont to ascribe to mere negotiating skill what can be achieved only through the exploitation of more deep-seated factors. It has gained currency because Talleyrand, whose monarch had not come to Vienna, was obliged to write voluminous reports, and, in order to cement his shaky domestic position, the former Foreign Minister of Napoleon tended to emphasize his indispensability.

To be sure, since the Treaty of Paris had settled France's boundaries, Talleyrand could afford perhaps the most disinterested approach. His wit and caustic comments became famous, so that Gentz could say of him that he had both the laughers and the thinkers on his side. But arguments not dissimilar to Talleyrand's, at least with reference to Russia's acquisitiveness, had been used six months previously by Napoleon without effect, because nobody trusted him. The real transformation in the situation had been wrought, not by Talleyrand's memoranda, but by the Bourbon restoration and the Treaty of Paris. Talleyrand could be effective because these acts had ended a revolutionary situation and inaugurated a "legitimate" era. He could be successful, not because he invented the concept of "legitimacy", but because it was there for him to exploit.

It was only natural that France, excluded from the European settlement by being forced to renounce, in the Treaty of Paris, any influence outside her boundaries, should attempt to construct a group of powers as a wedge to break up the Coalition; and it was equally natural that it should resist the attempt to shift Prussia's centre of gravity into Germany. But these efforts would have availed little, had not the threat of France been eclipsed by the danger from the East, had not the differences among the Allies become greater than their common fear of France. So long as the Coalition still believed that the memory of the common war-time effort would provide the motive force of a settlement, Talleyrand was powerless. Once this illusion was shattered, the issue became one of the limits of self-restraint, whether a power would fail to add a factor to its side merely for the sake of the appearance of harmony. The logic of the situation provided the answer. France came to participate in European affairs, because they could not be settled without her.

[1] See, for example, Nicolson, *Congress of Vienna*; Cooper, *Talleyrand*; Brinton, *Talleyrand*; Ferrero, *The Reconstruction of Europe*.

As the plenipotentiaries were assembling in Vienna, however, the course of events was by no means this clear. It was still thought that the settlement would be rapid, that France would appear as but a spectator, that the rest of Europe would only have to ratify an instrument drafted in relative harmony. Prussia appeared to contend for Saxony, Russia for Poland, Austria for the German equilibrium, Castlereagh for that of Europe, and Talleyrand for French participation in European affairs. Nobody seems to have believed that these positions might prove incompatible.

In the process of bringing about a reconciliation of the contending aspirations, the Congress of Vienna went through five phases: (*a*) an initial period dealing with the essentially procedural problem of organizing the Congress around the anti-French Coalition; (*b*) an effort by Castlereagh to settle the outstanding problems, particularly the Polish-Saxon question, first by a personal appeal to the Tsar and then by attempting to rally the powers of Europe against him; (*c*) a complementary effort by Metternich to separate the Polish and Saxon problems and to create a combination of powers united by a consensus of historical claims; (*d*) the disintegration of the anti-French Coalition and Talleyrand's introduction into the Allied deliberations; (*e*) the negotiation of the final settlement.

II

As Castlereagh was preparing to leave for the Continent once more, there was no longer any question that British interests would be sought in European stability. Whatever reservations the Cabinet might have about the involvement of its Foreign Secretary in Continental affairs, the success of his policy during the course of the year had put him beyond immediate attack, all the more so since the Tsar's sojourn in London had led to disenchantment. The hero of the war against Napoleon had emerged as a self-willed autocrat who conspired with the Opposition against the Government and succeeded only in alienating both sides of the House of Commons. By confusing public acclaim with public support, Alexander helped to give credence to Castlereagh's repeated warnings that the peace of Europe might be soon disturbed by the Tsar's intransigeance. At the same time, dispatches from British representatives in the most different parts of Europe were painting a picture of Russian intrigue too consistent to be ignored. From Berlin, Jackson reported the remark of a Russian general that, with six hundred thousand men under arms, there was little need to negotiate.[1] And from Palermo, A'Court complained about Russian interference in the domestic affairs of Sicily.[2] Whatever the Tsar's real intentions, the actions of his representatives gave rise to a fear that one conqueror might have been overthrown merely to ease the task of another. In these circumstances there could no longer be any doubt that the issue of Poland would be contested and that Britain would emerge as one of the chief protagonists.

But Castlereagh left Britain with three misconceptions: He still hoped that Alexander might be restrained by exhibiting the unreasonableness of his claims. If persuasion failed, he preferred to assemble the requisite force against Alexander *within* the anti-French Coalition and he thought this a relatively simple matter, at least as simple as demonstrating the threat to the equilibrium represented by Russia's possession of Poland. Finally, in case a contest was unavoidable, he believed that he could use France as a reserve to bring forward when a stalemate was reached, as if France would be content with so passive a role. The lengths to which Castlereagh was willing to go were revealed in a dispatch on 7 August to Wellington, who served as British ambassador to Paris. Wellington was instructed to inquire "whether France was prepared to support her views on the [Polish] question by arms" and to ask for French support in urging Prussia to resist Russian claims in Poland.[3] On 14 August, Castlereagh suggested that on his way to Vienna he stop at Paris for an exchange of views with Talleyrand. "The situation of the world," Wellington replied to this proposal, "will naturally constitute England and France as arbitrators of Europe, if these powers *understand* each other; and such an understanding may preserve the peace."[4]

Castlereagh arrived in Vienna on 13 September and immediately began discussions preliminary to the formal Congress which was to open on 1 October. He still hoped that the basic decisions might be taken before that date and that he could use the fact of his sojourn in Paris to bring the Russian minister to terms.[5] As things turned out, however, most of the preliminary discussions were taken up by pro-

[1] C.C. x, p. 96, 19 August, 1814.
[2] C.C. x, p. 75, 6 August, 1814.
[3] C.C. x, p. 76, 7 August, 1814.
[4] C.C. x, p. 93, 18 August, 1814.
[5] B.D., p. 192, 3 September, 1814.

cedural questions. It soon became apparent that Castlereagh's overture to Talleyrand had been premature and that the other powers were willing to admit France into their concert only as a last resort and after all other combinations had failed. For the memory of wartime still provided the impetus for international relationships. Unity was still considered an end in itself; harmony the cause, not the expression, of amity. And since the wartime unanimity had been produced by the threat of France, the Allies dealt only hesitatingly and ambiguously with the most fundamental problem of a "legitimate" order: whether it can construct spontaneous relationships or requires the myth of an enemy as a motive force. They agreed that decisions would be taken by the "Big Four", but that they would be submitted to France and Spain for their approval and to the Congress for ratification. If the Allies were in accord, opposition would be of no avail. What would happen in case of disagreement was not even considered, because it would have represented an admission that the requirement of unity did not supersede all other considerations. The only dispute arose over the manner in which this procedure was to be made effective, whether it should be embodied in a formal resolution by the Congress, as Prussia proposed, or simply carried out as an informal arrangement as Castlereagh preferred.[1] At this point, on 23 September, Talleyrand arrived in Vienna, prepared to use the legitimizing principle of the anti-French Coalition in order to dissolve it.

For if "legitimate" rulers represented the guarantee for the repose of Europe, no reason existed for excluding a Bourbon France from the discussion. And if "legitimate" rule was sacrosanct, Prussia had no "right" to dispossess the traditional King of Saxony by annexing his territory. To be sure, the Allies had developed an ingenious subterfuge for this violation of their legitimizing principle by accusing the hapless King of treason for his failure to join the Allied side in time. But Talleyrand had no difficulty exposing the tenuity of this argument: "Treason," he said acidly, "is evidently a question of dates."

Talleyrand's heaviest fire was concentrated on the Allied procedural scheme, however. He protested against the exclusion of France and the minor powers from the deliberations of the Congress. He denied the legal existence of the "Big Four", and he threatened to

[1] For full discussion of procedural questions, see Webster, Sir Charles, *The Congress of Vienna*, (London, 1934), pp. 149–65.

transform France into the advocate of all the secondary powers chafing under their direction. But despite his brilliance and sarcasm, Talleyrand achieved only a few minor concessions. It was decided to adjourn the formal opening of the Congress until 1 November and in the meantime to have the pending questions examined by the eight signatories of the Treaty of Paris, the "Big Four" plus France, Spain, Portugal, and Sweden. The "Big Four" left no doubt, however, that they intended to continue their private discussions and to treat the "Eight" merely as a ratifying instrument or to settle peripheral issues.

Talleyrand's first sally failed, because a logical inconsistency is not sufficient to dissolve coalitions. A mere appeal to a legitimizing principle is of no avail against the united opposition of all other major powers acting as if the appealing government still represented a threat to their existence. There existed in fact two relationships, that within the Coalition and that of the Coalition towards France, which was an ambiguous mixture of distrust and pretence of normality, which could not decide whether to rely on force or on legitimacy. Only after the claim of special righteousness, which is characteristic of coalitions, had disappeared in a conflict of the Allies among each other, could Talleyrand emerge as an equal partner. But first one more test of the efficacy of the "internal legitimacy" of the Coalition had to be made. It still remained to be determined whether the Tsar could be induced to limit his claims without the threat of force. So well had Castlereagh established himself as the prime contender for the European equilibrium that it was he who entered the arena to try the Tsar's resolution.

III

All efforts to induce the Tsar to state the nature of his goals in Poland had heretofore proved futile. Neither at Langres, nor at Troyes, nor yet at Paris had Alexander defined his precise claims. It was known that he wanted to re-establish a kingdom of Poland with a liberal constitution, connected with Russia only through the person of the monarch; but nothing could be learned either about its territorial extent or the nature of its internal arrangements. This secrecy was not only a crafty bargaining device to delay a final decision until France had been eliminated as a factor in the balance and Britain had disinterested itself in the Continent. Nothing in the Tsar's complex make-up ever worked so simply. When the Tsar demanded a free hand in Poland to fulfil the pledges of his youth, he was undoubtedly sincere; but this made a legitimate order all the more difficult to establish. When Alexander insisted on the major part of Poland, not on grounds of expediency but as a moral "right", he was not raising the issue to a more elevated plane, but posing a dilemma which might unleash a new round of violence. For a "right" is established by acquiescence, not by a claim, and a claim not generally accepted is merely the expression of an arbitrary will. Moreover it is the essence of a moral claim that it cannot be compromised, precisely because it justifies itself by considerations beyond expediency. Thus, if the Tsar was "really" sincere in his protestations of moral duty, he was making a revolutionary contest—a contest based on the mere assertion of force—inevitable. This is the paradox which the fanatic, however well-intentioned and however sincere, introduces into international relations. His very claim to moral superiority leads to an erosion of all moral restraint.

There ensued a strange and unreal series of interviews between Castlereagh and Alexander; strange, because their bitterness was accompanied by protestations of unending friendship, and unreal, because Alexander and Castlereagh could never agree on basic premises. In order to obtain a framework for negotiation, the protagonists constantly shifted positions, pretending to agree with the other's principles, but interpreting them in a manner which reduced them to absurdity. Thus Castlereagh at one stage became an avid defender of a completely independent Poland, while Alexander on another occasion defended his Polish plan as a contribution to European security. That Alexander proposed to rest his claims on the sanctity of his maxims became apparent on the occasion of his first interview with Castlereagh on the day after his arrival.[1] For the first time, he was explicit about his Polish plans. He proposed to keep all of the Duchy of Warsaw with the exception of a small portion to be ceded to Prussia in pursuance of the Treaty of Kalish. These claims, Alexander argued, were not the result of ambition, but the outgrowth of a moral duty and motivated by the sole desire of achieving the happiness of the Polish people. In short, since they were not advanced in the name of security, they could not threaten anyone. Castlereagh, in reply, urged the threat represented by a constitutional Poland to the tranquillity of Austria's and Prussia's remaining Polish

[1] Castlereagh's report. See B.D., p. 197f., 2 October, 1814.

provinces, and he added the dubious proposition that an independent Poland would be generally welcomed, even by Austria and Prussia, but that a Russian appendage extending deep into Central Europe would constitute a constant source of disquiet. But the Tsar left no doubt that he was not prepared to withdraw from his Polish possession and to create a truly independent Poland. The first interview between Castlereagh and Alexander had merely served to demonstrate the duality of the Tsar's nature and the incommensurability of the two positions.

The contest was renewed, on 13 October, with Alexander attempting to refute Castlereagh's assertion that the possession of Poland represented a threat to the equilibrium.[1] Although he did not admit that the requirements of security limited his moral claims, Alexander was quite prepared to invoke them when they seemed to support his designs. He therefore advanced the curious argument that his Polish scheme, far from extending Russian power, would actually ameliorate it by leading to a withdrawal of Russian troops beyond the Niemen. But when Castlereagh pointed out that security depends on the total strength of states, not on the position of their armies, Alexander retreated again to his moral duty. It was in vain that Castlereagh emphasized Alexander's inconsistencies; his moral claims on one side of the partition line but not on the other; his duty limited by the claims of Russian national interest. When Castlereagh declared that it "depends exclusively upon the temper [of] your Imperial Majesty . . . whether the present Congress shall prove a blessing to mankind or only exhibit . . . a lawless scramble for power," he merely revealed the exasperation induced by their inability to agree on what constituted a reasonable claim. When the Tsar replied that the Polish question could end only in one way since he was in possession, it was clear that a stalemate had been reached.[2] The dispute between the Tsar and Castlereagh had thus made it evident that persuasion would prove unavailing and that relations would have to be based on force or the threat of force.

[1] Castlereagh's report, B.D., p. 206f., 14 October, 1814.

[2] The exchange continued through October with an exchange of memoranda, Castlereagh to the Tsar, 12 October, 1814, W.S.D. IX, p. 332; the Tsar's reply: October 30, W.S.D. IX, p. 386; Castlereagh's reply, 8 November, W.S.D. IX, p. 410.

IV

While Castlereagh was negotiating with the Tsar, he made every effort to assemble such a force. As an abstract problem in diplomacy his task seemed simple. If the Tsar's pretensions threatened the European equilibrium, the obvious counter-measure was to marshal the resources of Europe against him. But although the equilibrium may be indivisible, it does not appear so to its components. The Tsar could not be resisted without a united front of the rest of Europe, but the powers of Europe were not at all in accord regarding the real danger. They did not wish to see the general equilibrium overturned, but they were not prepared to resist at the sacrifice of that part of it on which their historical position depended. A strong Russia might dominate Europe, but a too powerful Prussia would outstrip Austria and a united Germany might menace France.

So it came about that Castlereagh, the representative of the insular power which had no Continental position to defend, was the only statesman contending for the general equilibrium. Hardenberg, the Prussian Minister, was more interested in Saxony than in Poland; Talleyrand was almost as afraid that the problem of Poland would be settled *without* him as that it would be settled *against* him; and Metternich's attitude was as complex as the dilemmas confronting Austria: Austria could not be indifferent to the extension of Russia into Central Europe, because this threatened Austria's European position; or to the extension of Prussia into Central Germany, because this threatened its German position. But Austria's geographic location made open resistance foolhardy, for it would cause the brunt of the effort to fall on the most exposed power and surrender the policy of close co-operation with Prussia, which Metternich considered the key to Austrian security. The easiest solution was to return Prussia's Polish provinces to her in exchange for the independence of Saxony. But Prussia's Polish provinces were beyond reach until the Tsar was defeated. This, in turn, was impossible without Prussian support, which Prussia made conditional on Austrian acquiescence in the annexation of Saxony. On the other hand, Metternich could not thwart Prussia in Saxony without British or French assistance. But Castlereagh would contend only for European, not for German, concerns and French support at an early stage in the proceedings would have alarmed the secondary German Powers.

In this situation, Metternich adopted a policy of procrastination in order to exploit Austria's only bargaining weapon, that the other powers required Austrian acquiescence to make their annexations "legitimate". For several weeks he was unavailable because of "illness". After he "recovered", festivities succeeded each other in endless profusion and his love affairs and abstractedness became notorious. Metternich was determined to separate the Polish and the Saxon question, so that he could defeat his opponents in detail; to use their impatience for a settlement to lure his adversaries into a precipitate step which would provide him with a moral basis for action. He therefore assumed what he was wont to call the strongest position: the defensive, the expression of the ethos of a status quo power. "I barricade myself behind time," he told the Saxon envoy, "and make patience my weapon."[1]

Thus Castlereagh's efforts to create a united front against Russia led to an ambiguous series of constellations, of half-hearted coalitions and tentative betrayals, of promises of unyielding support coupled with hedges against bad faith. All during October Castlereagh laboured indefatigably, but, as in the previous year, he encountered incomprehensible hesitation and quibbling delay. Again he conceived his task to animate the wavering while refusing them the only solace that could spur their effort, British support for their special claims. When Castlereagh exhorted Hardenberg and Metternich to joint action, he found himself forced to admit that "there was a certain mutual distrust . . . which does not justify me to speak confidently of the result".[2] He complained about Metternich's incomprehensible "timidity" and asserted that the Austrian Minister seemed without any fixed plan. And he admonished Talleyrand, gleefully exploiting Allied embarrassments from the sidelines, that "it was not for the Bourbons, who had been restored by the Allies, to assume the tone of reprobating . . . the arrangements which had kept the Alliance together."[3]

Matters were finally brought to a head by Prussia, the power which could least afford delay. To be sure, the treaties of Kalish, Teplitz, and Chaumont had guaranteed Prussia its territorial extent of 1805; but they had never specified where Prussia might find the requisite territories, particularly if it lost its Polish possessions to Russia. The

[1] Schwarz, Wilhelm, *Die Heilige Allianz*, (Stuttgart, 1935), p. 13.
[2] B.D., p. 202, 9 October, 1814.
[3] B.D., p. 203f., 9 October, 1814.

available compensations, composed of former provinces or former satellites of France, primarily in the Rhineland, were inadequate. And they were undesirable because of their geographic separation from the main part of the Prussian monarchy and the Catholic religion of their inhabitants. Thus Prussia came to look towards Saxony, coveted since the time of Frederick the Great, contiguous with its own territories and with a predominantly Protestant population. But Prussia's negotiating position was the weakest of the major powers. Unlike Russia, it was not in possession of its prize. Unlike Austria, it had not made its participation in the war dependent on obtaining its special conditions. If now the Polish question was settled before that of Saxony, Prussia would have paid the penalty for its total commitment; for having fought the war with so much fervour that its participation had never been negotiable; for neglecting the peace because the war, in effect, had become an end in itself. And Prussia required Austrian acquiescence in the annexation of Saxony, because the organization of Germany, the indispensable condition of Prussia's security, would become illusory if Austria emerged on the Saxon issue as the protector of the secondary powers.

It is not surprising, therefore, that on 9 October, Hardenberg submitted a memorandum agreeing to the wisdom of an "intermediary system based on Austria, Prussia and Britain".[1] But he made Prussia's co-operation on the Polish question dependent on Austrian agreement to the annexation of Saxony and to the provisional occupation of Saxony by Prussia as a token of good faith. In its tentative quest for allies, in its pedantic effort to achieve the advantage of every course of action, the Hardenberg memorandum merely served to illustrate Prussia's dilemma: Russian support might gain it Saxony but not legitimacy; while Austrian support might yield it Poland, but not Saxony. The Hardenberg memorandum was a plea not to leave Prussia dependent on the goodwill of the Tsar; to create a European order based on Austro-Prussian friendship, but also on Prussian possession of Saxony.

But this effort to combine incompatible policies provided Metternich with the means to separate the Polish and Saxon question by one of his intricate manœuvres. On 22 October he transmitted two notes to Hardenberg and Castlereagh, whose tone of grudging agreement to Hardenberg's proposal obscured the fact that the moral frame-

[1] Text, d'Angeberg, Comte de, *Le Congrès de Vienne et les Traités de* 1815, 2 Vols. (Paris, 1863–4). Vol. II, p. 1934.

work which was being created to resist in Poland would prove equally effective to resist in Saxony, and that Hardenberg, in his effort to hedge his risks, had made his defeat inevitable. The note to Castlereagh began with a summary of the reasons against the destruction of Saxony:[1] the baneful symbol of the overthrow of a "legitimate" ruler, the danger to the German equilibrium, the difficulty of constructing a German confederation if the intermediary states lost confidence in the major powers. Nevertheless Austria would bring this sacrifice to the European equilibrium provided Prussia resisted in the Duchy of Warsaw and agreed to an equal division of influence within Germany. Castlereagh seems not to have noticed, or if he noticed, considered it unimportant, that the definition of Austria's sacrifice for the European equilibrium also marked the extent of her claim for support in the defence of the German equilibrium, should the sacrifice prove in vain. And he ignored an enigmatic reservation: that Prussia's annexation of Saxony should not lead to a "disproportionate aggrandizement", a condition clearly impossible of fulfilment if Prussia first regained her Polish provinces.

The note to Prussia coupled an appeal for close Austro-Prussian co-operation with an account of Austria's support of Prussia during the critical period leading up to the Treaty of Kalish and thus implied that Prussia owed its present position to Austria even more than to Russia.[2] Austrian policy would continue to be based on the most intimate relations with Prussia reinforced by a German Federation, but its effectiveness depended on thwarting Russia's designs on Poland. For this reason and despite Austria's reluctance to witness the destruction of a friendly state, Metternich agreed to the Prussian annexation of Saxony on three conditions: conformity of views in the Polish question, the fortress of Mainz as part of the South German defence system, and the Moselle as the Southern limit of Prussian power in the Rhineland. This alone should have made clear that Metternich was more concerned with the German than with the European equilibrium. But his eagerness to obtain Saxony blinded Hardenberg and caused him to overlook still another subtle reservation, that Metternich's offer was conditional not on the *fact* of resistance in Poland but on its *success*.

Thus, while Metternich was preparing the moral framework for an effort to separate Prussia and Russia, Castlereagh was looking only to

[1] Text, d'Angeberg, II, p. 1939f.
[2] Text, d'Angeberg, I, p. 316f.

Poland, as if the European equilibrium could be created with the certainty of a mathematical equation. On 23 October, he finally succeeded in getting Austria and Prussia to agree on a common plan of action against Russia on the basis of Metternich's memorandum.[1] The three powers undertook to force the issue by confronting the Tsar with the threat of bringing the Polish question before the full Congress if a reasonable settlement could not be obtained by direct negotiations. They proposed three acceptable solutions: an independent Poland as it existed prior to the first partition, a rump Poland on the scale of 1791, or the return of the three partitioning powers to their former possessions.[2] It was clear that Polish independence was advanced primarily as a bargaining weapon and for British domestic consumption, because the Tsar was not likely to agree to surrender territory considered Russian for two generations as the result of a victorious war.

The threat of an appeal to Europe in Congress was the last effort to settle the European equilibrium by a combination within the anti-French Coalition. When Metternich called on the Tsar to present the ultimatum on the Polish question, he was dismissed haughtily and even challenged to a duel, another indication of the Tsar's conception of foreign affairs in personal terms. And when, on 30 October, the three sovereigns left to visit Hungary, Alexander appealed to his brother monarchs against their ministers. He failed with the Austrian Emperor, but it was different with the stodgy and unimaginative Prussian King who had always admired the mercurial Tsar for his intrepidity in disaster and for the brilliance of his intellect. It did not prove too difficult to convince him now that the secret negotiations of the three ministers were an act of bad faith. When the monarchs returned to Vienna, Hardenberg was ordered, in the presence of the Tsar, to refrain from any further separate negotiations with his Austrian and British colleagues.

In this manner, on 5 November, the contest over Poland ended for the time being. Castlereagh's personal appeals had failed because Alexander had insisted on resting his claims on a "right" transcending the requirements of European security; the attempt to marshal a superior force had proved futile because there did not exist sufficient resolution within the anti-French alliance to bring the Tsar to terms and because complex problems are not soluble by declaring them

[1] Castlereagh's report, B.D., p. 212, 29 October, 1814.
[2] Memorandum re procedure, B.D., p. 213f.

simple. The effort to achieve an international order based on agreement and not on force seemed to have returned to its starting point.

V

But this was a mistaken impression. For if Castlereagh's failure had proved that the equilibrium could not be achieved through a demonstration of its necessity, Metternich's almost imperceptible complementary effort had created the moral framework for reopening the issue by an appeal to legitimacy. And if defeat in Poland could be translated into victory in Saxony, perhaps victory in Saxony might provide a means to extort concessions in Poland. The procrastination which had proved so maddening to Castlereagh had in fact been Metternich's most effective means to overcome his dilemmas, for delay strengthened Austria's chief bargaining weapon, that legitimacy can be conferred but not exacted, that it implies agreement and not imposition. His measures during October had therefore been designed primarily to break up the Russo-Prussian front and to provide a moral framework for action in the direction which proved most vulnerable. "Metternich's greatest art," reported Talleyrand, "is to make us waste our time, for he believes he gains by it." So the weeks had passed while Europe complained about the frivolity of the Austrian minister and the old school of Austrian diplomats raged that their "Rhenish" minister, whom they nicknamed Prince Scamperlin, was betraying the Empire to Prussia. But in the admiration for the famous phrase of the Prince de Ligne: "Le Congrès danse, mais il ne marche pas," it was overlooked that the Congress was dancing itself into a trap.

When Hardenberg offered Metternich his co-operation, he may have believed that he was clinching his gains and that he was obtaining a guarantee of Saxony, however the Polish negotiations ended. But because Metternich's reply had made Austrian agreement to the annexation of Saxony conditional on the *success* of their common measures, the effort to connect the two issues became a means to separate them. For if the Polish negotiations succeeded, Prussia would lose her moral claim to Saxony in the eyes of Europe. If Prussia regained her Polish possessions, the annexation of Saxony would represent the "disproportionate aggrandizement" against which Metternich had warned Castlereagh. Nor would it be necessary in that eventuality that Metternich bear the brunt of the opposition.

Talleyrand was certain to resist, indeed he could be restrained only with difficulty during October, and the secondary German states would rally around him. The Tsar, frustrated in Poland, was only too likely to enjoy Prussia's discomfiture; while Castlereagh, under attack in Parliament because of Saxony in any case, could not possibly have supported Prussia's demand for annexation. Castlereagh, at any rate, seems to have foreseen the possibility of such a development. "In the event of success attending the common effort with respect to Poland," he wrote to Liverpool, "[France] would have improved means of urging amicably upon Prussia some modification of her demands upon Saxony."[1]

But if the Polish negotiations failed, Prussia would lose her claim to Saxony in the eyes of Austria. Prussia's isolation was assured none the less surely, because the fact of resistance was almost as certain to alienate the Tsar as its success. Having demonstrated Austria's European concern by yielding in Saxony, intransigeance could now be defended by the requirements of the European and not the German equilibrium. And Castlereagh, having obtained Austrian support in the Polish negotiations, could no longer treat the Saxon issue as an internal German affair. There could be no doubt of the attitude of France or of the smaller German states. Prussia, in its effort to obtain reinsurance, had only succeeded in achieving its isolation.

When, on 7 November, Hardenberg informed Metternich of the King's orders and of the difficulty of carrying out the agreed plan with respect to Poland, Metternich finally had the moral basis for action.[2] He waited until 18 November before he insisted on the fulfilment of the three conditions of the memorandum of 22 October. He suggested that, since the King's command had made it impossible to utilize Castlereagh as an intermediary, Hardenberg conduct the negotiations with the Tsar himself.[3] But this only served to supply Metternich with yet another proof of Austrian good faith and another reason for resisting in Saxony, because, in view of the Tsar's dominance over the Prussian King, there could be no doubt

[1] B.D., p. 213, 24 October, 1814.

[2] D'Angeberg, I, p. 406. (Hardenberg's note to Metternich.) There is yet another indication, although no proof, that Metternich never intended the Polish negotiations as anything but a means to isolate Prussia on the Saxon question: his dismal defeat during his interview with Alexander. At no other time in his career did Metternich choose a frontal attack, negotiate so ineffectively or surrender so easily.

[3] D'Angeberg, I, p. 418, 18 November, 1814; also B.D., p. 238.

about the fate of a solitary Prussian overture. Hardenberg was obliged to report that the Tsar had again invoked the purity of his intentions, but that the only concession he was willing to make was to declare Thorn and Cracow free cities.[1] Although Alexander had slyly made this concession dependent on Austrian acquiescence in the annexation of Saxony, the Saxon negotiation thus became a means to restore fluidity to the Polish issue. For the Tsar's offer, however contingent, was his first admission that the territorial extent of Poland was not irrevocably settled after all.

Metternich submitted the final Austrian reply on 10 December.[2] Austria was interested in the closest relationship with Prussia, but not at the price of the destruction of Saxony. The German Federation, on which their common welfare depended, would remain stillborn, because none of the secondary German states would join an organization based on the destruction of one of their number. Having been forced to tolerate Russian aggrandizement in Poland, Austria could not acquiesce in Prussian aggrandizement within Germany without upsetting the equilibrium completely. Metternich suggested an alternative plan which maintained a nucleus of Saxony, while giving a large part of it to Prussia together with other compensations in the Rhineland. But all protestations of friendship could not hide the fact that Prussia was outmanœuvred, that Metternich had lost out in Poland only to win in Saxony and then partially to restore the situation in Poland by means of Saxony.

It did not matter that, on 8 November, the Russian military governor of Saxony turned over the provisional administration to Prussia, nor that the Prussian military were threatening war. Russia, at the periphery of Europe, might rest its claim to Poland on the fact of possession, but a power situated in the centre of the Continent could survive only as the component of a "legitimate" order both within Germany and in Europe. Thus, although by the middle of December the Congress of Vienna seemed to have reached a complete stalemate, behind the scenes a fundamental transformation was preparing itself. A stalemate is not total until all the factors are engaged and France was still uncommitted. The contests during October and November had exploded the myth of Allied unity and the threat of France no longer loomed larger than that of the erstwhile ally. It was becoming plain that the memory of a common

[1] D'Angeberg, II, p. 1941, 2 December, 1814; also B.D., p. 248.
[2] Text, d'Angeberg, I, p. 505.

effort would not suffice to restrain any power from attempting to add France to its side of the scale.

While Castlereagh was despairing about the Polish failure[1] and accusing Metternich of never having really intended to resist, a combination was forming on the Saxon question which was to give a new direction to the contest. For the coalition which could resist in Saxony was, by definition, also the coalition which could resist in Poland. And if the claims of power were defeated in one quarter, this would, almost necessarily, limit the assertions of arbitrariness in the other. So it was proved, after all, that the equilibrium was indivisible, although the solution did not come about through a consciousness of this. It was not in the name of Europe that Europe was saved, but in the name of Saxony.

VI

But before this new combination could be formed, domestic pressures on Castlereagh nearly wrecked Metternich's finely-spun plan. An insular power may fight its wars in the name of the European equilibrium, but it will tend to identify the threats to the equilibrium with threats to its immediate security. Because its policy is defensive and not precautionary, it will make the cause of war depend on an overt act which "demonstrates" the danger. But the danger to the equilibrium is never demonstrated until it is already overturned, because an aggressor can always justify every step except the crucial last one as the manifestation of limited claims, and exact acquiescence as the price of continued moderation. To be sure, Britain had entered the fray against Napoleon at an early stage and continued the contest with great persistence. But the threat to the equilibrium had become manifest through an attack on the Low Countries and the balance of power had come to be identified with the possession of Antwerp.

Now the issue was Poland, however, a "distant" country both geographically and psychologically. It was not clear until it was "proven" that the Rhine was best defended along the Vistula or that there existed any threat to peace except France. In this frame of mind the Cabinet considered the Polish dispute an irritating outgrowth of Continental rivalry, threatening a peace dearly won, and dealt with it primarily under the aspect of its impact on British domestic politics. This led to a discussion between the Cabinet and Castle-

[1] B.D., p. 248f.

reagh in which both sides were trying hard to convince themselves that the disagreement was really a misunderstanding produced by insufficient information. Whereas the gulf separating them was hardly less than that separating the Tsar from Castlereagh. For while the Tsar attempted to guarantee Continental security by his good faith, the British Cabinet wished to identify safety with an insular position. The arbitrariness of power and the irresponsibility of isolation, these were the Scylla and Charybdis between which Castlereagh was forced to navigate.

On 14 October, Liverpool wrote Castlereagh that the "less Britain had to do with [Poland] . . . the better" and pointed out that, from the Parliamentary point of view, the Tsar's plan was preferable to a new partition because it preserved the principle of Polish independence.[1] Liverpool repeated these arguments on October 28 and transmitted a memorandum by the Chancellor of the Exchequer, Vansittart, who simply denied the reality of the Russian danger. With the petulance of mediocrity convincing itself that the easy way out is also the course of wisdom, Vansittart argued that the absorption of Poland would add an element of weakness to the Russian state while proving conducive to British commerce.[2] These dispatches forced Castlereagh into one more statement of the connection between British and Continental security. He insisted that he was not opposing Russia for the sake of Poland but for the sake of Europe. If the Polish question were settled against the Central Powers, the remaining issues would resolve themselves into a contest between Austria and Prussia within Germany, transforming Russia into the arbiter of Central Europe and leaving Holland defenceless. The security of even the most immediate British interests thus depended on a European policy: "It appeared to me, that it was better for Great Britain to contend for a European question of the first magnitude in the true spirit of the policy that has marked her conduct throughout the war, than . . . to reserve herself for one object, viz. the Low Countries . . . which might be exposed to a very unpleasant question under a discussion between the great German Powers."[3]

But Liverpool's reply left no doubt that the Cabinet feared France more than Russia and war more than any threat to the balance of power. A war now, argued Liverpool, might turn into a revolutionary

[1] B.D., p. 210f.
[2] B.D., p. 220f.
[3] B.D., p. 229f.

struggle, while even two years of peace might bring about a stability under which the limited wars of the eighteenth century would again become the rule.[1] On 22 November, the Cabinet sent its first instructions to Castlereagh since his arrival in Vienna: "It is unnecessary," wrote Bathurst, "for me to point out to you the impossibility of . . . consenting to involve this country into hostilities . . . for any of the objects which have hitherto been under discussion at Vienna."[2]

Thus, at the crucial point in the negotiations, Castlereagh was deprived of his only means of exerting pressure and at a moment when the issue was becoming one of pure power. For Prussia was being drawn by Metternich's temporizing into precipitate action. As it observed its moral and material basis slipping away, its tone became increasingly bellicose. Its military were openly speaking of war and even the more moderate Hardenberg hinted at extreme measures. But if possession without legitimacy was illusory, legitimacy through force proved chimerical. Castlereagh was merely defining Prussia's dilemma when he told Hardenberg that "he [Hardenberg] could not regard an unacknowledged claim as constituting a good title and that he never could in *conscience* or *honour* . . . make the mere refusal of a recognition a cause of war. . . ."[3] In this situation Castlereagh did not propose to follow his Cabinet's instructions. To announce British disinterest would remove the major deterrent to war and, in its effort to guarantee peace, the Cabinet would have brought about what it feared most. Or else, British withdrawal from the contest would lead to an Austrian surrender and to a complete overturn of the equilibrium.

So it happened that Castlereagh and Metternich again found themselves on the same side in a battle whose moral framework had been defined by the wily Austrian Minister. The more intransigeant Prussia's attitude, the stronger became Metternich's position. Without the necessity for abstract discussion Austria emerged as the protector of the secondary powers. When Metternich proposed an alliance to Bavaria and Hanover and the construction of a German League without Prussia, he was simply giving expression to a general consensus. As the contest was becoming transformed into a test of power, Metternich had again achieved the position where he was resisting claims which could be represented as exorbitant and unjust.

[1] W.S.D. IX, p. 285, 25 November, 1814.
[2] B.D., p. 247f.
[3] B.D., p. 255, 7 December, 1814.

But as the test of strength approached, it also became necessary to marshal a maximum force. It was at this point, when the last vestiges of the Alliance were disappearing, that Talleyrand reappeared on the scene. He emerged because Metternich put him on the stage and his eloquence was but a reflection of Metternich's desire for anonymity, for Metternich was not interested in appearing as the agent of Prussia's humiliation. It was Metternich's desire that events should come about "naturally", because this minimized the danger of personal schisms; it was Talleyrand's wish that they should appear "caused", for that would cement his shaky domestic position.

Talleyrand was given his opportunity by Metternich, who communicated to him the Austrian reply to Hardenberg of 10 December and thus made clear that the Big Four had not been able to settle the issue.[1] Talleyrand replied in a trenchant memorandum, which asserted the superiority of the claims of legitimacy over the requirements of the equilibrium and denied the possibility of deposing kings, because sovereigns could not be tried, least of all by those who coveted their territories. It was not for Prussia to state what she would take, Talleyrand argued boldly, but for the "legitimate" king of Saxony to define how much he would yield.[2] It was a masterly summary of all the inconsistencies of two months of acrimony, but this was not its significance. Talleyrand had served France better by remaining "available" than by writing memoranda. The real importance of the exchange lay in the fact that France was once again part of the concert of Europe.

In the meantime Prussia was becoming panicky. To expose Metternich's trickery, Hardenberg transmitted some of Metternich's letters on the Polish question to the Tsar, an unheard-of breach of diplomatic etiquette. But here again Metternich's dilatoriness during October paid dividends. For almost every action of Metternich had been in response to a Prussian initiative and when Hardenberg had withdrawn from their agreement, he had justified it as deferring the contest with the Tsar to a more convenient time. When, therefore, Metternich sent *all* of his letters to the Tsar, Hardenberg was again out-manœuvred for he did not dare produce his own.[3] But this exchange of pinpricks had a salutary consequence, because it demonstrated to the Tsar how he had disquieted the other powers by his

[1] N.P. II, p. 503f.
[2] N.P. II, p. 509f, 19 December, 1814.
[3] W.S.D. IX, p. 483, 17 December, 1814.

Polish plans. After his intransigeant attitude during October and November, Alexander had in any case undergone one of the sudden shifts of mood which characterized him. Gone was his earlier militancy, to be replaced by the first symptoms of the religious exaltation which was to dominate him for the next decade. When Emperor Francis called on him to clear up the misunderstanding, Alexander accordingly offered to cede the district of Tarnopol, with a population of 400,000, back to Austria as a token of his good faith. The Tsar might emerge with the greater part of Poland, but only through a process of adjustment, which symbolized his need for the recognition of other powers.

In desperation Prussia now proposed to transplant the King of Saxony to the Rhineland, into territories earmarked for Prussia. But neither Metternich nor Castlereagh was ready to acquiesce: Metternich because it would have transformed the King of Saxony from an ally of Austria into a Prussian vassal; Castlereagh because, true to the Pitt plan, he wanted to see a power of the first order protect the Rhineland and back up Holland.[1] And all the time the balance was shifting against Prussia, because Castlereagh and Metternich were slowly insinuating France into the Allied councils. Since part of the dispute between Austria and Prussia dealt with the technical question of where to find the territories to reconstitute Prussia to the scale of 1805, Castlereagh proposed the creation of a Statistical Commission to determine the population of disputed territories. When under Austrian and British pressure a French delegate was admitted to this commission, it was becoming evident that the Coalition against France was in the process of being dissolved.

Only a short step separated Talleyrand from full participation in the deliberations. Castlereagh, who had hoped to avoid so drastic a step, finally agreed on 27 December. On 31 December, Castlereagh and Metternich proposed that henceforth Talleyrand participate in the meetings of the Big Four. Prussia was now completely isolated, for the emergence of Talleyrand was a symbol that the special claims of the Alliance had ceased before Prussia had gained the fruits of its war. Even the Tsar, in Castlereagh's words, "would not advise Prussia to resist now that he has secured his own arrangement in Poland". Thus driven back on its last resources, Prussia threatened war.

But the reaction merely served to indicate Prussia's impotence.

[1] B.D., p. 270, 24 December, 1814.

Castlereagh replied sharply that "such an insinuation might operate upon a power trembling for its existence but must have the contrary effect upon all alive to their own dignity; and I added that if such a temper really prevailed, we were not deliberating in a state of independence and it was better to break up the Congress".[1] That same day, Castlereagh proposed a defensive alliance between France, Austria, and Britain. To be sure, Talleyrand was required to guarantee the Low Countries and to reaffirm the provisions of the Treaty of Paris. But Talleyrand's greatest achievement at Vienna was precisely this exhibition of self-restraint, this refusal to attempt to sell French participation in the alliance for a territorial advantage, an effort which would have united all the other powers against him. As a result he gained something more important, the end of the isolation of France and the recognition of its equality.

Thus, almost exactly one year after he first sailed for the Continent, Castlereagh, in direct violation of his instructions, dissolved the Alliance he had striven so hard to create for the sake of the very equilibrium it was supposed to perpetuate. It was a bold and a courageous step. A defensive conception of international relations involves the danger of inflexibility, the tendency to base foreign policy on the last and not on the current danger. By the proposal of a pact with the erstwhile enemy, Castlereagh demonstrated his awareness that no policy, however successful, can be an end in itself. By his decisiveness at a crucial moment, he made clear his conception of the responsibility of the statesman: that opportunities once lost are irretrievable; that the timing of a measure could not, at least under conditions of the early nineteenth century, depend on the availability of instructions. That he went even further and considered himself free to *violate* his instructions shows both his dominance domestically and his conviction that his justification resided in the confidence of the Cabinet in his basic policy and not in their approval of every step.

And the alliance of 3 January marked the culmination of another of those diplomatic campaigns by which Metternich isolated his opponents in the name of universal reason and not reasons of state. An alliance with France against Prussia in October would have provoked the horrified protest of Europe. That same alliance in January was hailed as the defence of the equilibrium. Resistance to Prussia in October would have been construed as the expression of a short-sighted egotism; that same resistance in January was greeted as the

[1] B.D., p. 277f., 1 January, 1815.

protection of legitimacy against the claims of power. Just as in the spring of 1813, Metternich had prepared his moral position by outwaiting his opponent, by using his impatience for a decision to commit him irretrievably. Because Prussia required Austria's acquiescence in the annexation of Saxony, Hardenberg had offered joint measures against the Tsar. The Saxon problem was thus transformed from a German into a European issue on Prussia's initiative, and it was separated so dexterously from the Polish question that Hardenberg did not realize what had happened until it was too late. And because the Tsar had become eager to demonstrate his beneficence, he had offered as a free concession in Poland what Castlereagh had not been able to elicit by threats. It was Castlereagh, not Metternich, who bore the brunt of the final negotiation on the Saxon question, and it was he, not Metternich, who proposed the alliance of 3 January. Metternich's was the statesmanship which understood the value of nuance; that the *mode* was as important as the *fact* of accomplishment and sometimes more so. The issue at Prague had been for Metternich not the fact of war but its cause; the issue at Vienna was not to rescue the equilibrium but the manner of saving it. Saxony saved by an assertion of Austrian power was the start of unending conflict; saved in the name of Europe it created a wound which could heal.

VII

If the defensive alliance provided the crisis of the Congress of Vienna, it also paved the way for its resolution. In any negotiation it is understood that force is the ultimate recourse. But it is the art of diplomacy to keep this threat potential, to keep its extent indeterminate and to commit it only as a last resort. For once power has been made actual, negotiations in the proper sense cease. A threat to use force which proves unavailing does not return the negotiation to the point before the threat was made. It destroys the bargaining position altogether, for it is a confession not of finite power but of impotence. By bringing matters to a head, Prussia found itself confronted by three powers whose determination could not be doubted, although the treaty itself remained secret. And the Tsar proved a lukewarm ally. A series of partial settlements had isolated Prussia, because "satisfied" powers will not fight for the claims of another, if an honourable alternative presents itself.

It was up to Metternich to see that this alternative was presented. Already in his memorandum of 10 December, he had advanced a plan by which Prussia could be reconstituted to the scale of 1805 by acquiring territories in the Rhineland together with a portion of Saxony. This plan was now taken up by Castlereagh, when it became apparent that Prussia would not carry out her threat of war. By 3 January, after Metternich and Castlereagh had declared that they would not negotiate without Talleyrand, Hardenberg, to save face, himself recommended Talleyrand's participation.[1] On 5 January, Castlereagh could report that "the alarm of war is over".[2] The Saxon question was henceforth officially discussed by the now Big Five and was resolved largely through unofficial negotiations, in which Castlereagh played the role of the intermediary between Metternich and Talleyrand on the one side and the Tsar and Hardenberg on the other.

The negotiations leading to the final settlement again revealed Castlereagh's special qualities in their most favourable light. The framework was once more determinate; it was clear that none of the powers, and Russia perhaps least of all, were ready for war. There remained the essentially technical task of adjusting conflicting points of view through patience, perseverance and good will. Gentz reported that Castlereagh worked indefatigably day and night to bring the issue to a conclusion. There was a special reason for this. With a Parliamentary session approaching, Liverpool pleaded with him, as during the previous year, to return lest the House of Commons prove unmanageable. But, as then, Castlereagh refused, insisting that he would return as soon as possible, but that "you might as well expect me to run away from Leipzig (if I had been there) last year . . . as to withdraw from hence till the . . . contest is brought to a point; and I think you do both too much injustice to your own supporters and too much honour to me in supposing my presence so necessary."[3]

In his endeavour to achieve a final settlement, Castlereagh had to resist a new attempt by Prussia to move the King of Saxony to the left bank of the Rhine and an effort by Austria to save the Elbe fortress of Torgau for Saxony. But with the aid of the Tsar, he convinced Prussia that in the interest of the European equilibrium she would have to assume the defence of the Rhineland, and he made

[1] B.D., p. 280.
[2] B.D., p. 282, 5 January, 1815.
[3] C.C. x, p. 247, 30 January, 1815.

clear to Austria that the defensive alliance extended only to an actual attempt to overthrow the European equilibrium, not to internal German arrangements.[1] The danger of war had also made the Tsar more pliable. When Castlereagh suggested some concessions in Poland in order to make the Saxon arrangement more palatable to Prussia, Alexander agreed to return the city of Thorn to Prussia. Metternich immediately used this opportunity to attempt to lure Alexander into another series of adjustments and to shift on him the onus for Prussia's unsatisfactory boundaries. He offered to cede the district of Tarnopol back to Russia in exchange for further concessions to Prussia.[2] Although the Tsar refused, the Saxon question had become a means to limit Russia's Polish aspirations. What could not be exacted for the sake of the general equilibrium of Europe was obtained through a number of concessions which made local arrangements possible.

On 11 February, a final agreement was reached. In Poland, Austria retained Galicia and the district of Tarnopol, while Cracow was constituted a free city. Prussia retained the district of Posen and the city of Thorn which controlled the upper Vistula. The remainder of the Duchy of Warsaw with a population of 3.2 million became the Kingdom of Poland under the Tsar of Russia. In Germany, Prussia obtained two-fifths of Saxony, Swedish Pomerania, much of the left bank of the Rhine, and the Duchy of Westphalia. Austria had already been assured compensation in Northern Italy and predominance in all of Italy through the establishment of dependent dynasties in Parma and Tuscany. Thus, the equilibrium of Europe was established after all and with a modicum of harmony. It was not achieved with the necessity of a mathematical axiom, as Castlereagh had imagined, because while states may appear to the outsider as factors in a security arrangement, they consider themselves as expressions of historical forces. It is not the equilibrium as an end that concerns them—this is the conception of an insular power—but as a means towards realizing their historical aspirations in relative safety. It was no accident therefore that the contest over Poland fought in the name of abstract considerations of balance of power proved inconclusive, but that the dispute over Saxony involving the historical problem of Germany provided the key to the settlement.

On 9 June, 1815, the Final Acts of Vienna were ratified by Europe

[1] B.D., p. 295, 29 January, 1815.
[2] D'Angeberg, I, p. 676.

assembled in congress. It was the only meeting of the Congress of Vienna.

VIII

There are two ways of constructing an international order: by will or by renunciation; by conquest or by legitimacy. For twenty-five years Europe had been convulsed by an effort to achieve order through power, and to contemporaries the lesson was not its failure but its near success. It is not surprising, then, that in their effort to create an alternative, the statesmen in Vienna looked back to a period which had known stability and that they identified this stability with its domestic arrangements. The statesmen at Vienna were not interested in transforming humanity, because in their eyes this effort had led to the tragedy of a quarter-century of struggle. To transform humanity by an act of will, to transcend French nationalism in the name of that of Germany, would have seemed to them to make peace by revolution, to seek stability in the unknown, to admit that a myth once shattered cannot be regained.

The issue at Vienna, then, was not reform against reaction—this is the interpretation of posterity. Instead, the problem was to create an order in which change could be brought about through a sense of obligation, instead of through an assertion of power. For the difference between a revolutionary order and a *healthy* legitimate one is not the possibility of change, but the mode of its accomplishment. A "legitimate" order, as long as it is not stagnant, achieves its transformations through acceptance, and this presupposes a consensus on the nature of a just arrangement. But a revolutionary order having destroyed the existing structure of obligations, must impose its measures by force and the Reign of Terror of *any* revolution is inevitably an almost exact reflection of its success in sweeping away the prevailing legitimacy. A "legitimate" order limits the possible by the just; a revolutionary order identifies the just with the physically possible. A legitimate order confronts the problem of creating a structure which does not make change impossible; a revolutionary order faces the dilemma that change may become an end in itself and thus make the establishment of any structure impossible. In neither case is reform carried out through a sudden act of insight; this is the illusion of Utopians. Nor is it possible to construct an order which will have no defenders of the status quo *or* no reformers, and the attempt to do so leads either to the frenzy of the totalitarian state or to stagnation. The health of a social structure is its ability to translate transformation into acceptance, to relate the forces of change to those of conservation. The statesmen at Vienna had experienced an effort to establish this relation by force; it was not strange that they attempted to construct an alternative based on "legitimacy".

Whatever one may think of the moral content of their solution, it excluded no major power from the European concert and therefore testified to the absence of unbridgeable schisms. The settlement did not rest on mere good faith, which would have put too great a strain on self-limitation; nor on the efficacy of a pure evaluation of power, which would have made calculation too indeterminate. Rather, there was created a structure in which the forces were sufficiently balanced, so that self-restraint could appear as something more than self-abnegation, but which took account of the historical claims of its components, so that its existence could be translated into acceptance. There existed within the new international order no power so dissatisfied that it did not prefer to seek its remedy within the framework of the Vienna settlement rather than in overturning it. Since the political order did not contain a "revolutionary" power, its relations became increasingly spontaneous, based on the growing certainty that a catastrophic upheaval was unlikely.

That the Vienna settlement came to be so generally accepted was not a fortunate accident. Throughout the war Castlereagh and Metternich had insisted that theirs was an effort for stability, not revenge, justified, not by crushing the enemy, but by his recognition of limits. If we compare the outline of the Vienna settlement with the Pitt plan and its legitimization with that of the instructions to Schwarzenberg, we find that luck, in politics as in other activities, is but the residue of design. This is not to say that the settlement revealed a prescience that made all events conform to a certain vision. Castlereagh, in giving up his conviction of the mechanical equilibrium for that of an historical balance, maintained through confidential intercourse among its members, increasingly separated himself from the spirit of his own country. Metternich, by attempting to maintain predominance in both Italy and Germany, was forced into a policy beyond his resources. His increasingly inflexible struggle for legitimacy revealed a growing consciousness of the insufficiency of Austria's material base for the European task he had set for her. If a policy of pure power is suicidal for an Empire located in the centre of a continent, reliance on unsupported legitimacy is demoralizing and leads to stagnation. Finesse can substitute for strength when the goals are determinate, but it is no substitute for conception when the challenges have become internal. And Prussia, with misgivings and hesitations, with a feeling of national humiliation and grudging surrender, was forced into a German mission in spite of itself. Extending now from the Vistula to the Rhine, it symbolized the quest for German unity. Scattered in enclaves across Central Europe, its need for security, if not its conception of a national mission, forced it into becoming, albeit reluctantly, the agent of a German policy. Situated athwart the major waterways and land routes, Prussia came to dominate Germany economically before it unified it physically. The defeat in Saxony, so bitterly resented, became the instrument of Prussia's final victory over Austria.

But this was still fifty years in the future, and a truly successful policy may have been impossible for Austria in a century of nationalism. Tragedy can be the fate of nations, no less than of individuals, and its meaning may well reside in living in a world with which one is no longer familiar. In this sense, Austria was the Don Quixote of the nineteenth century. Perhaps Metternich's policy should be measured, not by its ultimate failure, but by the length of time it staved off inevitable disaster. As the Congress of Vienna ended, disaster seemed to have been transcended, however. For the first time in twenty-five years statesmen could turn to the problems of peace rather than the preparation for war. They were yet to learn that these problems, although less overpowering, may prove even more intricate. But they had at least created a structure which might survive this process of adjustment. And before they had even begun this task, they were driven to a consciousness that, whatever their differences, they were part of a greater unity. Nothing illustrates better the legitimacy of the order just agreed on than the reaction of the powers to the incredible news that now reached Vienna.

For on 7 March it was learned that Napoleon had escaped from Elba.

X

The Holy Alliance and the Nature of Security

I

"ON the night of 6–7 March," Metternich wrote in his autobiographical fragment, "there had been a meeting . . . of the plenipotentiaries of the Five Powers. Since the meeting had lasted until three in the morning, I had forbidden my valet to disturb my rest. . . . In spite of this prohibition, the man brought me, at about six in the morning, an express dispatch marked Urgent. Upon the envelope I saw only the words 'From the Imperial and Royal Consulate in Genoa.' . . . I laid the dispatch, without opening it, upon the table beside my bed. . . . But having once been disturbed I was unable to rest again. At about 7.30 I decided to open the envelope. It contained only the following six lines: 'The English commissioner Campbell has just entered the harbour inquiring whether anyone had seen Napoleon at Genoa, in view of the fact that he had disappeared from the island of Elba. The answer being in the negative, the English frigate without further delay put to sea.' "[1]

In this manner, which testified to its conviction that a fundamental crisis capable of disrupting the ordered flow of life was no longer possible, Europe learned of the tenuity of its new-found legitimacy. It was expressive of the nature of revolution as an assertion of will, that a solitary individual whose whereabouts were still unknown, could fill all of Europe with terror. And the fear indicated that a settlement can draw boundaries and sometimes even establish rulers, but that only duration can bring about self-confidence. So it happened that the statesmen at Vienna discussed Napoleon's movements as if all options were open to him, as if the symbol of the revolution could transform it into actuality in any quarter of Europe. "He will land on some part of the Italian coast and fling himself into Switzerland," said Talleyrand, proving that even a cynic cannot easily believe in the collapse of his world-order. "No," replied Metternich, who better than anyone understood the structure of

[1] N.P. I, p. 209.

revolutions, if not their causes, "he will make straight for Paris." For Paris was the key to the European settlement; it was there, and there alone, where Napoleon had a claim to his own kind of legitimacy—that of charismatic rule. While these discussions were taking place, Napoleon was advancing up the Rhone valley. And on the night of 20 March he entered Paris.

But the extent of its fear also demonstrated the degree of Europe's unity. It had been possible to conceive of peace with Napoleon while the memory of his triumphs still created the illusion of the invulnerability of his power. But now an international order based on incompatible domestic structures could no longer be accepted. On 13 March, only six days after learning of Napoleon's escape, the "Big Eight"—Austria, Britain, Prussia, Russia, Sweden, Spain, Portugal, and France, in the person of Talleyrand—published a declaration which promised the King of France the requisite assistance to re-establish public tranquillity. At the same time it proclaimed that Napoleon, as the disturber of world repose, had placed himself outside the pale of civil and social relations. The armies, on the verge of demobilization, were again set in motion. Before the Vienna settlement had even been ratified, Europe once more found itself at war; and, giving its final symbolic expression to the culmination of an era, war was declared not against a nation, but against an individual.

It was in vain that Napoleon accepted the Peace of Paris. It was in vain that he sent the Tsar a copy of the secret treaty of 3 January, which had been left behind in the Tuileries. Nor did Metternich reply to his entreaties. For Napoleon was no longer the ruler who had transcended the Revolution, but a revolutionary chieftain. He might invoke his desire for peace, but, even if he was sincere, he had lost the capacity to make it effective. The Napoleon of 1814, for all of his setbacks, still had the charismatic qualities of the victor of Jena and Austerlitz. The Napoleon of 1815 was the vanquished of 1814, and the memory of his defeat limited his claim to power. His return was not in the nature of a triumph but of a protest, brought about by the usual revolutionary coalition of all the disaffected. Napoleon, the man of will, had become a symbol, a principle by which to fight the hated principle of "legitimacy;" he had to prove, in his last appearance on the stage, that although men can conquer ideas, ideas outlast men. The Revolution reclaimed its own and Napoleon could legitimize himself only by basing his government on the Jacobins and by liberalizing the Bourbon constitution. But if Metternich had hoped to bring a conquering Napoleon to a recognition of the limits of power, a Napoleon basing himself on revolution domestically was no longer an acceptable factor in the balance. On 3 May the Allied powers agreed that "they were in a state of hostility with the existing ruler of France because experience has shown that no reliance can be placed on his professions. . . . They are at war for the purpose of securing their own independence, and for the reconquest of a permanent tranquillity because France under its present chief can afford no security whatever".[1]

But if the Allies were agreed about the incompatibility of Napoleon's continued rule with the equilibrium of Europe, they were far from unanimous about the remedy. The new outbreak of war reopened all the issues so acrimoniously settled at Langres, Troyes, and Vienna. For the advocates of all the causes that had been defeated during the past year drew from Napoleon's re-emergence the conclusion that it had been due to the disregard of their counsel. The Tsar recalled his opposition to the Bourbons, the Prussians their demand for a harsh peace, and the Liverpool Cabinet their displeasure with the Treaty of Fontainebleau. All the advocates of vengeance, barely restrained during the previous year, broke forth again. It seemed that if the revolution could not conquer Europe, it might at least draw it into a maelstrom which would erode all restraint.

It was on Castlereagh that the major burden fell. The Austrian army was in Italy, the Russian army still deep in Poland. Only British and Prussian forces, hastily assembled in the Low Countries, were available. None of the Allies were in a financial condition for war. But while during the previous year Castlereagh had been forced to animate the wavering, he now had, if anything, to restrain the eager from rushing into a war, the cost of which, it was generally agreed, would not again fall on the victors. On 25 March Wellington, Castlereagh's replacement in Vienna, renewed the subsidy arrangements of the Treaty of Chaumont, only that this time all of the secondary German powers joined. "If we are to undertake the job," Castlereagh wrote to Wellington, "we must leave nothing to chance. . . . It must be done on the largest scale . . . you must inundate France with force in all directions."[2]

[1] B.D., p. 331, 6 May, 1815; *British and Foreign State Papers*, (London, 1841). Vol. II, p. 301. Henceforward referred to as B.F.S.P.

[2] C.C. x, p. 285, 26 March, 1815.

But it was one thing to inundate France with force, it was anotl to determine in the name of what that force was to fight. Brit: might be the most eager of the powers to restore the Bourbon: second time, but its domestic legitimization did not permit fighti a war for that cause. Non-interference in the domestic affairs of otl states was too cardinal a principle of British policy to permit violation even for the Bourbons. "[Louis XVIII]," Castlereagh wrc to Clancarty, "cannot wish us to feel more decisively the importan of his restoration than we do, and most assuredly every effort w be made to conduct the war so as to lead to this result, but we ca: not make it a *sine qua non*. Foreign powers may justly covenant f the destruction of Bonaparte's authority as inconsistent with the safety, but it is another question avowedly to stipulate for his succe: sor. This is a Parliamentary delicacy."[1] And he added in a letter to S Charles Stewart, his ambassador with the exiled Bourbon kin "... John Bull fights best when he is not tied and ... although w can with good management connect the cause of the Bourbons wit the *avowed* [my italics] object of the war, we never could sustai [it] as a principle. ..."[2]

Throughout April and May, while the Tsar spoke darkly of pre ferring even a Republic to another Restoration,[3] Castlereagh hac to contend with Parliamentary pressures which forced him to pretenc complete impartiality in the domestic arrangements of France. Whil the Bourbons were appealing for succour and the Continent fo financial aid, Castlereagh had to prepare a cause of war compatibl with the ethos of an insular power. But however great his difficulties, he refused to legitimize his policy by an appeal to popular passions which called for the "punishment" of France. He told the House that the Bourbons had given France a social character and put her within the family of nations, and that Napoleon had returned only because the army had found peace contrary to its view.[4] The war was a struggle of a united Europe against the threat of Napoleon and its aim was the reintegration of France, not its chastisement. On 26 May, the address of war finally carried the House and Castlereagh could report to Nesselrode: "It required some management to embark the country heartily in a new war. ... You may rely upon it that it has

[1] C.C. x, p. 301, 8 April, 1815.
[2] Webster, I (Appendix), p. 545, 19 April, 1815.
[3] B.D., p. 324f., 15 April, 1815.
[4] Hansard (Commons), 29 April, 1815.

been well done and that we shall not be wanting to our allies and to the good cause. . . ."[1]

It came none too soon. On 18 June the battle of Waterloo was fought. On 22 June Napoleon abdicated once more in favour of his son. Castlereagh was thus spared the embarrassment of another Coalition war. For while the Tsar was pushing on to Paris accompanied only by a small escort of Cossacks in the hope of repeating his triumph of the previous year, Wellington arranged a second Restoration in which Louis XVIII, the "legitimate" ruler of France, was recalled by a Jacobin National Assembly. And just as in April, 1814, Talleyrand confronted Alexander with an accomplished fact in the name of the Tsar's magnanimity, so now Wellington and Castlereagh presented him with another in the name of moderation. Alexander's was a life whose fulfilments were found only in anticipation.

France was "social" again. But as the four powers assembled to draw up another peace, the hopes of the previous year had been shattered. It seemed clear that revolutions were not to be ended merely by exhibiting their alternative and that France could not be integrated into the community of nations simply by altering its domestic structure. In 1814 the war had been fought avowedly to reduce France to the "ancient limits" and Napoleon's overthrow had been an incidental by-product. Nevertheless the Restoration of the Bourbons was taken as an essential transformation of the situation. In 1815 the war had been fought to overthrow Napoleon, but, paradoxically, the achievement of this aim only produced new misgivings. Forgotten were the brave words of the previous year, of the community of nations restrained by the legitimacy of their aspirations. Europe was beginning to organize itself by the fear of an enemy, and in the process its spontaneity was being lost. In the self-righteousness of victory the four powers met again to impose a peace on France, but it seemed unlikely that a sense of proportion would animate them a second time.

There was one man at Paris, however, who for a brief three months represented the conscience of Europe. It is difficult to explain why it should have been Castlereagh who resisted the Prussian clamour for the dismemberment of France in which even Metternich joined to the extent of demanding the permanent dismantling of the outer belt of French fortifications.[2] Or why he should have refused

[1] C.C. x, p. 365, 28 May, 1815.
[2] D'Angeberg, II, p. 1482.

to go along with the Cabinet and Parliament, both urging a punitive peace. Yet France was spared and the equilibrium of Europe saved by the representative of the insular power which stood in least danger from immediate attack. At no other time in his career did Castlereagh show to greater advantage than in his battle for the equilibrium at Paris. Misunderstood at home, without the support of the moral framework which Metternich had provided in previous frays, he conducted himself with his customary methodical reserve, cumbersomely persuasive, motivated by an instinct always surer than his capacity for expression. This was the man on whom Europe for two generations heaped opprobrium as the destroyer of its liberties, because so much had the political equilibrium come to be taken for granted that the social contest overshadowed all else; to the extent that it was forgotten that without the political structure so resolutely preserved by Castlereagh, there would have been no social substance left to contend for.

II

As Castlereagh prepared to discuss the treaty of peace, all pressures operated against moderation. An impotent enemy is a fact; a reconciled enemy a conjecture. A territorial accretion represents the surety of possession; to integrate an opponent into the community of nations through self-restraint is an expression of faith. It is no accident that the advocates of "absolute security" always have popular support on their side. Theirs is the sanction of the present, but statesmanship must deal with the future.

For however "reasonable" the arguments for absolute security, they will lead to a revolutionary situation within the international community. By their insistence on only a single cause for war, they create a physical and psychological imbalance. The more punitive the peace, the more insistent will be the demand for a system of collective security, legitimized by the threat of the erstwhile enemy. But such a system is a confession of rigidity, of a peace maintainable only by overwhelming force. In an order containing a permanently dissatisfied power, harmony becomes an end in itself, and this places the settlement at the mercy of its most ruthless member, the one most ready to come to terms with the revolutionary power. The apparent weakness of the prostrate power is therefore deceptive, and the very effort to guarantee its permanent weakness may improve its relative position. For by violating the legitimizing principle of their settlement, or by their inability to exact its voluntary acceptance from the erstwhile enemy, the victorious powers create a psychological distortion. No longer can the status quo powers appeal to "legitimacy" in defence of their position. Against the victim of a punitive peace, they must rest their claims on force. Those most in need of stability thus become the exponents of an essentially revolutionary policy. It is no accident that a punitive peace tends to be more demoralizing for the victor than for the defeated. The quest for absolute security leads to permanent revolution.

But in Paris, in July, 1815, this was apparent to but very few. Confronted by the exorbitant demands of Prussia and to a lesser degree of Austria, under pressure from his own government, Castlereagh was forced, for one of the few such occasions in his career, into a theoretical defence of his position. He was outraged by the depredations of the Allied troops and by the eagerness of the German powers to move as many of their troops as possible into France in order to be relieved of the expense of their maintenance.[1] He was becoming testy about the increasing intransigeance of the Cabinet. In order to shift some of the onus for his policy, Castlereagh now prevailed on the Tsar, deep in a mood of religious exaltation, to make a proposal for a peace settlement, which amounted to a reaffirmation of the first Treaty of Paris coupled with a demand for a moderate indemnity. He sent this to the Cabinet with a letter which implied that Russia should not obtain the sole credit for a lenient peace.[2]

But the Cabinet was no more willing to defer to the Tsar than to Castlereagh. Already on 15 July, Liverpool had argued that the forbearance of the French government with regard to the "traitors" demonstrated its unreliability; that safety therefore resided in diminishing the means of French aggression; that the Allies had the right to strip France of all the conquests of Louis XIV; but that as a minimum they should dismantle the major fortresses along the Northern and Eastern border and inflict an indemnity.[3] The result of a magnanimous policy had proved disappointing and Britain "owed it to herself to provide in the best manner for its own security". And, as

[1] C.C. x, p. 484f., 17 August, 1815. Also Wellington's view, Gurwood, xii, p. 558; B.D., 342f.
[2] B.D., p. 353, 29 July, 1815.
[3] C.C. x, p. 431f., 15 July, 1815.

always in such periods, final recourse was had to military considerations, as if the military component of security had a morality of its own, as if the reliance on purely military considerations were not itself a symptom of the abdication of policy. The popularity of Louis XVIII, declared Liverpool, should not affect the disposition of French fortresses which depended entirely on the military judgment of Wellington: "However desirous we may be of seeing the government of Louis XVIII popular in France, we do not feel that we should be justified in endeavouring the object by the sacrifice of everything which is judged important for the general security of Europe."[1]

Thus Castlereagh was forced into his most exhaustive statement of the nature of security. In two memoranda, of 12 August and 17 August, he dealt with the question of integration or punishment, of a peace of reconciliation or a settlement of dismemberment. The memorandum of 12 August dealt with the issue of territorial cession. If dismemberment represented a guarantee of security, Castlereagh argued, it might be risked despite the disunion which the disposition of the spoils would evoke. But instead dismemberment would only provoke the military temper of France, without any assurance that the other powers, particularly Russia, would prove resolute in opposing renewed aggression: "How much better is it for Europe to rest its security on what all the Powers will stand to, than to risk the Alliance by aiming at measures of *extreme* precaution." In short, the mirage of absolute security destroys what it seeks to accomplish. By exalting the physical component of stability, it overlooks its moral aspect and, while assembling the force to restrain the defeated enemy, it undermines the resolution to make it effective: "The continued excesses of France may, no doubt, yet drive Europe . . . to a measure of dismemberment . . . [but] let the Allies take this further chance of securing that repose which all the Powers so much require, with the assurance that if disappointed . . . they will again take up arms not only with the commanding positions in their hands, but with that moral force which can alone keep such a confederacy together. . . ."[2]

If the memorandum of 12 August amounted to a definition of the nature of security, that of 17 August was a denial that policy could

[1] C.C. x, p. 431, 15 July, 1815; C.C. x, p. 454f., 3 August, 1815; C.C. x, p. 479, 11 August, 1815.
[2] B.D., p. 361, 12 August, 1815.

be conducted by deference to the short-run swings of public opinion.[1] "I have no doubt," he wrote to Liverpool, "that the middle line would be most popular and that, in extorting the permanent cession of one or two fortresses of great name, our labours would carry with them an *éclat*, which is not likely to attend them. . . . But it is not our business to collect trophies, but to try, if we can, to bring the world back to peaceful habits. I do not believe this to be compatible with any attempt . . . to affect the territorial character of France . . . neither do I think it a clear case . . . that France, even within her existing dimensions, may not be found a useful, rather than a dangerous member of the European system." It was a measure of Castlereagh's growth as a statesman that the most implacable foe of Napoleon, the minister who but fifteen months previously could conceive only a Europe organized by the fear of France, should emerge now as the advocate of a peace of harmony. And it is symptomatic of his conception of the duty of statesmanship that Castlereagh, even at this moment when he stood practically alone, disdained concessions to popular opinion.

In this manner, with exasperated insistence on the side of Castlereagh and with grudging agreement on the part of the Cabinet, was defined the role of Britain in the new settlement. That this role rested on the convictions of a single individual did not affect the actual negotiation of the peace treaty. But that its motivation could not command the enthusiasm, or even the comprehension, of the nation came to prevent its implementation. A peace constructed in the name of Europe could be maintained only by the consciousness of a European role. And this consciousness diminished as the memory of the great danger subsided and as Britain, looking across the Channel, saw Antwerp in friendly hands for so long that it forgot that things could ever have been different.

Castlereagh had succeeded in overcoming the hesitations of his Cabinet; he was next confronted with the avarice of the Continental powers. For Prussia, which had inundated France with 280,000 men exacting an often barbaric retribution for Prussia's past suffering, did not propose to be deprived of the revenge for its national humiliation a second time. It was supported by the secondary powers, which had everything to gain and nothing to lose, since their territorial gains would perforce have to be guaranteed by the major powers. Castlereagh was furious and inveighed against "the spirit of plunder which

[1] C.C. x, p. 484f., 17 August, 1815.

had been the misery of Germany for the past century".[1] The extent of his exasperation is shown by the fact that he even threatened to withdraw the British guarantee of the Low Countries if the latter persisted in their excessive demands.[2]

But a peace as generous as the first Treaty of Paris was now out of the question. It was agreed that France should assume the costs of the war as well as part of the expense of constructing barrier fortresses in the Netherlands, and the indemnity was fixed at 700,000,000 francs. An army of occupation in Northern France was to enforce the execution of the treaty and to protect the King. Finally, Prussia and the minor German powers succeeded in obtaining a frontier rectification. France was reduced to her pre-Revolutionary boundaries by stripping her of the additional territories conferred by the first Treaty of Paris: Saarlouis, Landau, and Savoy. And the art treasures acquired during the Revolutionary wars were returned to their original owners.

If this treaty lacked the magnanimity of the first Peace of Paris, it was nevertheless not so severe as to turn France into a permanently dissatisfied power. The territories lost were of strategic rather than of commercial or symbolic significance and contained, in any case, a population of less than a million. The indemnity was paid within three years and the army of occupation withdrawn at the end of that period. Thus a peace of moderation was made a second time and, within the space of less than fifteen months, the temptations of total victory were successfully withstood twice by the same statesmen who, for over a century, were to be criticized for their blindness to the great emotions sweeping across Europe. But the representatives of these emotions, like Stein, whatever their social insight, were all defenders of a peace of vengeance which would have exposed Europe to unending political strife.

III

But the era of the legitimate equilibrium could not begin without two acts which in their self-consciousness made explicit that the memory of revolutions may be more dangerous than their reality, that only "established" orders *are*, while creations must be explained. It was only natural that these acts should represent the two aspects of the quest for order: the Quadruple Alliance of 20 November, 1815, stood for the equilibrium of power and the reality of good faith; the Holy

[1] B.D., p. 375, 4 September, 1815.
[2] B.D., p. 376, 4 September, 1815.

Alliance of 26 September, 1815, announced the reconciliation of aspirations and the pervasiveness of moral principles. It was appropriate that Castlereagh should develop the political framework, but the creator of its moral expression was a paradoxical figure: the Tsar of Russia, who in the year previous had brought Europe to the brink of war, but who now, satiated with glory, in a mood of mystic exaltation, sought renown in the realization of the beneficent maxims of Christianity.

Already on 17 July Castlereagh had written to Liverpool that he had committed a great error when last in Paris "in not opposing the barrier of a stipulation [of a European interdiction] against Napoleon's return, for there is no doubt he . . . made both the nation and the army believe he might be restored and peace be nevertheless preserved."[1] Thus was born the Quadruple Alliance, which represented an ambiguous mixture of the concept of international relations of an island power and of the knowledge of the elements of stability of a statesman with a European vision.

As in all of its relations with the revolution, Britain was confronted by a conflict of its desires with its domestic legitimization, of the wish to preserve the Bourbons with the principle of non-interference in the domestic concerns of other states. The result was a compromise which guaranteed Europe against French aggression, while evading a definite commitment of common action against domestic upheavals. Its avowed aim was the protection of the territorial arrangements of the Second Treaty of Paris and this was undoubtedly the aspect which appealed most strongly to the British Cabinet. Since the territorial balance had been repeatedly disturbed by Napoleon, an exception to the principle of non-interference was made in his case in the second article of the Alliance which provided for the exclusion of the Bonaparte family from the throne of France. But what if France should undergo a revolution other than Bonapartist? To make the fact of a revolution a cause of war was to give up the principle of non-interference. But to remain aloof might lead to another series of revolutionary contests. This dilemma was solved by an evasion by which the insular power admitted that European stability had a social component, while hedging its commitment in deference to public opinion: the Allies agreed to remain "watchful" in case "revolutions should again convulse France . . . and to take the measures necessary for the safety of their respective states". Revolu-

[1] B.D., p. 349, 17 July, 1815.

tion in France was thus declared a potential threat, even if it did not engage in any act of physical aggression, but it was not automatically a cause of war.

Fifteen months previously these provisions, together with additional clauses stipulating the forces each power undertook to contribute for collective measures, would have been considered by Castlereagh as the culmination of his effort. And it is certain that nobody in the Cabinet identified British security with anything other than the restraint of France. But in the interval Castlereagh had become the victim of a temptation encountered by many statesmen of great Coalitions. In the mythology of Coalitions the diplomacy preceding the war appears overly subtle, petty and a contributing cause to a climate of distrust. In the exuberance of concerted action or while its memory is still fresh, the desire for peace seems a sufficient motive for its accomplishment. Castlereagh accordingly had come to see the unity of purpose imposed by a common enemy as the normal pattern of international relations. In the satisfaction of a triumphant "reasonableness", he forgot the process of painful adjustments of the previous year. Increasingly, he considered confidential relationships not the expression, but the cause, of harmony and the requirements of a peaceful order as unambiguous as the measures to achieve military victory. He therefore urged that the powers of Europe should remain in intimate contact not only to control France, as the Tsar proposed, but to consider general problems of European repose. The conception that stability might reside in commitment and not in a mechanical balance, in precaution and not in defence, was so much beyond the imagination of the British Cabinet that no one protested against Article VI of the Treaty of Alliance drafted by Castlereagh which provided for periodic meetings "by the High contracting Parties . . . for the consideration of the measures which shall be considered the most salutary for the repose and prosperity of nations. . . and the peace of Europe."[1]

The Conference system by which Europe was governed for seven years thus came about almost as an afterthought. But in any political situation there are factors which are not amenable to will and which cannot be changed in one lifetime. This is the guise Necessity assumes for the statesman, and in the struggle with it resides his tragic quality. Whatever the merit of Castlereagh's vision, the experience

[1] For an extended analysis of the treaty, see Webster, II, pp. 54–6. Text of Quadruple Alliance, Martens, *Recueil*, IV, p. 27ff.

of Great Britain prevented it from comprehending its Foreign Secretary. In the public mind the English Channel was to remain a more certain guarantee of British security than Continental stability. Only a misunderstanding kept the conflict from becoming apparent in 1815: while Castlereagh was thinking of Europe, the Cabinet and the country had their attention fixed on France.

There was another man at Paris also aiming at an unattainable perfection. Ever since the contest at Vienna, Alexander's mind had been taking an increasingly mystical turn. The glory and the approbation, so long and eagerly sought, had somehow eluded him and even his victories had proved increasingly hollow. The first march on Paris had not resulted in a moral vindication of the burning of Moscow, but in a complicated intrigue which restored the Bourbons. And the Congress of Vienna had not led to a surrender to the self-evidence of ethical maxims, but to a tenacious contest for seemingly peripheral issues. It is proper, of course, that policy is not conducted in the mood of a moment of exaltation, because statesmen must be as interested in preserving as in conquering the world. But this is no consolation for the fanatic—or for the prophet. The statesman lives in time; his test is the permanence of his structure under stress. The prophet lives in eternity which, by definition, has no temporal dimension; his test is inherent in his vision. The encounter between the two is always tragic, because the statesman must strive to reduce the prophet's vision to precise measures, while the prophet will judge the temporal structure by transcendental standards. To the statesman, the prophet represents a threat, because an assertion of absolute justice is a denial of nuance. To the prophet the statesman represents a revolt against reality, because the attempt to reduce justice to the attainable is a triumph of the contingent over the universal. To the statesman, negotiation is the essence of stability, because it symbolizes the adjustment of conflicting claims and the recognition of legitimacy; to the prophet, it is the symbol of imperfection, of impure motives frustrating universal bliss. It was no accident that Alexander always felt misunderstood or that his colleagues always distrusted him. Their safety was a recognition of limits; his security a moment of transcendence. Castlereagh and Metternich, whatever their differences, sought a world of intermediary nuance; Alexander one of immediate perfection.

As he followed the armies towards France once more, the Tsar began to ascribe the squabbles at Vienna to the lack of religious inspiration of the protagonists and he recurred to a proposal submitted on his behalf to the Congress which had called for a fraternal association of the sovereigns, guided by the precepts of Christianity.[1] When, in this frame of mind, Alexander was surprised by the visit of a Baroness Kruedener, a religious fanatic who considered him the Saviour of Europe, it was not difficult to interpret her appearance as a hint from God or to see in the new contest a Divine trial. No sooner had the Tsar reached Paris than he invited the Baroness to join him with the following letter: "You will find me living in a little house at the edge of town. I chose this domicile because in its garden I found my banner, the cross."[2] On 10 September, the Tsar staged a tremendous review of his troops for the benefit of his brother sovereigns. But instead of a military parade there took place a Mass at which Baroness Kruedener officiated.

In this mood the Tsar had supported Castlereagh in his quest for a lenient peace. He now set about to sanctify this work by relating it to the religious principles before which all activity was judged. After consultation with Baroness Kruedener, he proposed the draft of a declaration, worthy only of Sovereigns and for their signature alone, of which the Austrian Emperor said that he did not know whether to discuss it in a council of ministers or at the confessional. It began with an invocation of the Holy Trinity and of Divine Providence: because of the plenitude of His beneficence, the Sovereigns had decided that "the course, *formerly* adopted by the powers in their mutual relations had to be *fundamentally* changed and *that it was urgent* to replace it with an order of things based on the exalted truths of the eternal religion of our Saviour." This was followed by three articles, symbolizing the Trinity, which called on the monarchs and the people to consider each other as brothers and the nations as provinces of a Christian commonwealth; it exhorted them to govern with benevolent care and to extend mutual succour to each other.[3]

But however Metternich might ridicule this effort and even if he ascribed it to the fact that the Tsar's mind was affected, it represented to the careful calculator of Vienna not a religious but a political document of the first magnitude. "[Metternich] was un-

[1] D'Angeberg, I, p. 571, 31 December, 1814.
[2] Quoted Schwarz, *Die Heilige Allianz*, p. 50.
[3] Schwarz, p. 52f. Italicized phrases were later eliminated by Metternich. See below.

willing," reported Castlereagh, "to thwart [the Tsar] in a conception which, however wild, might save him and the rest of the world much trouble as long as it should last. In short, seeing no retreat, after making some verbal alterations the Emperor of Austria agreed to sign it."[1] But these alterations were of fundamental importance. For Metternich transformed the Tsar's generalities into statements of a policy compatible with the sober spirit of the Central Empire and he did this so skilfully that Alexander affirmed that they implemented the spirit of his effort.[2] In its altered form the Holy Alliance substituted a patriarchal association of monarchs for the community of peoples, and its preamble, quoted above, read: "The Allied Sovereigns have become convinced that the course which the relations of powers had assumed, must be replaced by an order of things founded on the exalted truths of the eternal religion. . . ."[3]

Gone was the urgency and the reference to the need for fundamental reform; gone too was the reference to the *former* relations of states which was an indictment of the political concert of Europe. Its new version could rather be read, and more logically, as an attack on the transformations wrought by the Revolution, as a promise to return to order, as an assertion of the primacy of law over will. The Tsar had conceived the Holy Alliance as programmatic, as the proclamation of a new era transcending the pettiness of history; Metternich used it to announce the end of a revolutionary period and the re-entry into history. So it happened that Alexander's second crusade on Paris again yielded unexpected results. In the Tsar's life of anti-climaxes, the treaty he had envisioned as the tool to reform the world was to become the means for the protection of the European equilibrium.

There was still some difficulty about obtaining British agreement. Castlereagh, who called the Holy Alliance "a piece of sublime mysticism and nonsense", realized that no formal accession to such an instrument would ever be accepted by Parliament. He therefore proposed that the Prince Regent accede in his own name to a treaty "where the objection lies rather in the excessive excellence than the quality and nature of the engagement".[4] But even this proved too

[1] B.D., p. 383, 28 September, 1815.

[2] Schwarz, p. 57.

[3] For a discussion of all of Metternich's changes, see Werner Naef, *Geschichte der Heiligen Allianz* (Berner, Untersuchungen zur Allgemeinen Geschichte), p. 8f.; Text of treaty, Martens, *Recueil*, II, p. 656f.

[4] B.D., p. 382f., 28 September, 1815.

strong for the Cabinet who escaped their dilemma by stressing the inconsistency of Castlereagh's proposal with the principles of the British Constitution. The Prince Regent finally sent a letter to his brother monarchs expressing his personal sympathy with their efforts.[1] Thus with misgivings and hesitations, with an exalted vision and a sober calculation, was born the Holy Alliance, the symbol of an era.

As the monarchs prepared to leave Paris at the end of September, 1815, peace seemed finally assured, the revolutionary period over at last. So unobtrusively had the settlement been constructed, that its greatest achievement, the possibility of its universal acceptance, went largely unnoticed. And at Paris had been created the two instruments which guided Europe for the next decade and, at the same time, marked the tragic fate of their advocates: the Quadruple and the Holy Alliance, the hope for a Europe united by good faith and the quest for a moral consensus, the political and the ethical expressions of the equilibrium. It was thus that a vision of a united Europe destroyed the two most different personalities of the period: the sober, pedantic Castlereagh and the fantastic, exalted Tsar; Castlereagh, through an intuition beyond the experience of his people; Alexander, through an effort beyond the experience of the international order.

There was one man at Paris who knew the limits of his possibilities, however; knew them too well as things turned out. Not for Metternich were policies of idealistic construction or of reforming the ethos of his people. The statesman of the Empire perhaps most in need of adaptation saw only an unyielding framework, and he conceived his task in attempting to force the international order to conform to its structure. Almost alone of the statesmen at Paris, he considered the peace not an end, but a beginning. The political struggle was over, the social struggle about to commence. Metternich proposed to enter this contest with his usual tactics: to defeat his opponents not by constructiveness but by patience, not by transcending but by outlasting them. As Metternich began to gird for his new battle, the nature of his social convictions became of paramount importance.

For Europe was waiting to see what the self-styled "doctor of Revolutions" would prescribe for it.

[1] B.D., p. 385f., 3 October, 1815.

XI

Metternich and the Conservative Dilemma

I

So it was that peace came to Europe at last, only to confront the Central Empire with its most serious dilemma. For while the pressure of the Conqueror still seemed pervasive, Austria's special problems were submerged in the common danger. But henceforth each country would have to find its own challenges and confront its particular difficulties. Yet Austria was the sole power on the Continent which could enter the peacetime era without commitments. Its soberness while Europe was swept by the dreams of a reformed humanity, its insistence that each step be translatable into concrete political terms, were but the reverse side of the conviction of its minister that the social goals were all negative: to rescue a sense of obligation out of chaos, to defeat the revolution, not through a counter-revolution, but through an insistence on legitimacy. The deviousness of Metternich's diplomacy had been the reflection of a fundamental certainty: that liberty was inseparable from authority, that freedom was an attribute of order. Austria, under Metternich, was not interested in reform until it had saved its moral substance, nor in change until it had conserved its values. "The world is subject to two influences," wrote Metternich, "the social and the political. . . . The political element can be manipulated; not so the social element whose foundations must never be surrendered."[1] In the period of peace now beginning, everything depended therefore on the conception of the nature of the social foundation held by the Austrian minister.

The conservative in a revolutionary period is always somewhat of an anomaly. Were the pattern of obligations still spontaneous, it would occur to no one to be a conservative, for a serious alternative to the existing structure would be inconceivable. But once there exists a significant revolutionary party, even more once a revolution has actually triumphed, two complementary questions have been

[1] N.P. VIII, p. 340.

admitted as valid, more symbolic in their very appearance than any answer that may be given: What is the meaning of authority? What is the nature of freedom? Henceforth stability and reform, liberty and authority, come to appear as antithetical; the contest becomes doctrinal and the problem of change takes the form of an attack on the existing order, instead of a dispute over specific issues. This has nothing to do with the label of political parties. There have been societies, such as the United States or Britain in the nineteenth century, which have been basically conservative, so that existing parties could be considered at once conservative and progressive. There have been others, such as France for over a century, where all issues have been basically revolutionary, however the parties consider themselves, because of the existence of a fundamental social schism.

But what is a conservative to do in a revolutionary situation? A stable social order lives with an intuition of permanence, and opposition to it is either ignored or attempted to be assimilated. Voltaire was "fashionable" in the eighteenth century, not because it was a revolutionary period, but because revolution was inconceivable. A revolutionary period, on the other hand, is characterized by its self-consciousness, because political life loses its spontaneity once the existing pattern of obligations has been challenged. The motivation of a stable order is a concept of *duty*—the assertion of the self-evidence of the social maxims—where alternative courses of action are not rejected but inconceivable. The motivation of a revolutionary period is a concept of *loyalty*, where the act of submitting the will acquires a symbolic and even ritualistic significance, because alternatives seem ever present. An ethic of duty involves a notion of *responsibility* which judges actions by the orientation of the will. It is for this reason an ethic of *motivation*, striving to achieve identification of the individual code with a standard of morality which, no matter how rigid, must become individually accepted in order to be meaningful. An ethic of loyalty involves a notion of *orthodoxy*, because it is a means to achieve a group identity. It does not exclude the identity of the individual with the social code, but it does not require it. "Right or wrong my country"—this is the language of loyalty. "So act that your actions could become by your will universal laws of nature"—this is the language of duty. Duty expresses the aspect of universality, loyalty that of contingency.

In this manner the conservative, when he organizes himself

politically, becomes, in spite of himself, the symbol of a revolutionary period. His fundamental position involves a denial of the validity of the questions regarding the nature of authority; but the questions, by exacting a reply, have demonstrated a kind of validity. To the revolutionary, the conservative's position therefore becomes an *answer*, a victory even should the immediate battle end adversely. For what does it profit a conservative to emerge victorious in a battle of wills? His battle is not personal but social, his justification not individual but historical. It is no accident that in revolutionary contests the conservative position comes to be dominated by its reactionary—that is, counter-revolutionary—wing, the group which fights in terms of will and with an ethic of loyalty. For the true conservative is not at home in social struggle. He will attempt to avoid unbridgeable schism, because he knows that a stable social structure thrives not on triumphs but on reconciliations.

How then can the conservative rescue his position from the contingency of conflicting claims? How can that which *is*, persuade when its self-evidence has disintegrated? By fighting as anonymously as possible, has been the classic conservative reply, so that if the answer must be given it will transcend the will, so that the contest occurs at least on a plane beyond the individual, so that obligation can become *duty* and not *loyalty*. To fight for conservatism in the name of historical forces, to reject the validity of the revolutionary question because of its denial of the temporal aspect of society and the social contract—this was the answer of Burke. To fight the revolution in the name of reason, to deny the validity of the question on epistemological grounds, as contrary to the structure of the universe —this was the answer of Metternich.

The difference between these two conservative positions is fundamental. To Burke the ultimate standard of social obligation was history; to Metternich it was reason. To Burke history was the expression of the ethos of a people; to Metternich it was a "force" to be dealt with, more important than most social forces, but of no greater moral validity. Burke denied the revolutionaries' premise that reason supplied the sufficient basis for social obligation and his challenge was therefore destined to have no immediate effect. Metternich accepted this premise, but drew from it conclusions diametrically opposed to that of his opponents and his was therefore a mortal challenge. To Burke a revolution was an offence against social morality, the violation of the sacred contract of a nation's historical constitution. To Metternich it was a violation of the universal law governing the life of societies, to be combated, not because it was immoral, but because it was disastrous. Historical conservatism abhors revolution as undermining the *individual* expression of a nation's tradition; rationalist conservatism fights it as preventing the implementation of *universal* social maxims.

It was this rationalist conception of conservatism which imparted the rigidity to Metternich's policy and to his interpretation of the complementary issues of the nature of freedom and the meaning of authority. The West has produced two basic replies: freedom as the absence of restraint or freedom as the voluntary acceptance of authority. The former position considers freedom to reside outside of the sphere of authority; the latter conceives freedom as a *quality* of authority. The negative version of freedom is the expression of a society transcending its political structure, a society which, as in Locke, exists prior to the state and whose political organization becomes like a company of limited liability organized for the achievement of determinate goals. In such a society the issue of conservatism against reform tends to appear as a question of emphasis, of greater or lesser change on problems of specific form and content. Since the significant field of activity occurs outside the governmental sphere, politics has a utilitarian, but not an ethical function; it is useful, not moral. A society based on Locke's concept of freedom is always conservative, whatever form its political contests take. Were it not, it could not operate a system whose strength resides in its social cohesiveness, in the things "which are taken for granted". Burke's defence of conservatism had for this reason no applicability to the British domestic scene, but was directed against its misapprehension by foreigners.

But the Continent has never been able to accept the Anglo-Saxon version of freedom. Before the French Revolution, this was because Locke's became the philosophy of an *accomplished* revolution, a doctrine of reconciliation which lacked the logical rigour of a call to action. Afterwards, it was because the French Revolution, unlike the British, had produced a fundamental social schism. Cohesive societies can regulate themselves through custom which reveals that disputes are peripheral. Societies which contain fundamental schisms must rely on law, the definition of a *compulsory* relationship. Thus Kant and Rousseau, not Locke, were the representatives of the Continental version of liberty which sought freedom in the identification of the will with the general interest and considered government freest, not when it governed least, but when it governed justly. To the British conservative, the social problem was one of adjustment: to protect the social sphere by timely political concession. But to his Continental counterpart, the problem was one of conservation in the literal sense, because to him political concession was equivalent to social surrender. For one can make concessions only *to* something. When state and society are two different entities, this is no problem. But when they are identical, a concession is a confession of failure, a recognition of an unbridgeable social schism. Thus even at the end of his life, after his era had long ended, Metternich could still object to a speech by a British Peelite, Sir James Graham, that the statesman's wisdom consisted of recognizing the proper moment for making concessions: "My conception of statesmanship differs completely. The true merit of a statesman . . . consists of governing so as to avoid a situation in which concessions become necessary."[1]

This did not mean that the conservative statesman had to oppose *all* change. To be a conservative, wrote Metternich, required neither return to a previous period, nor reaction, but carefully considered reform.[2] True conservatism implied an active policy.[3] Yet reform had to be the product of order and not of will; it had to assert the universality of law against the contingency of power. "The word freedom," wrote Metternich in his political testament, "has for me never had the character of a point of departure but of a goal. The point of departure is order, which alone can produce freedom. Without order the appeal to freedom is no more than the quest of some specific party for its special objectives and will in practice always lead to tyranny. Because I have been a man of order, my efforts were directed towards the attainment of a real, not a deceptive, freedom. . . . I have always considered despotism of any kind a symptom of weakness. Where it appears, it condemns itself; most intolerably where it appears behind the mask of advancing the cause of liberty."[4]

But what was the meaning of these assertions if they represented only a personal conviction? They would have constituted a "system", one more construction of the kind whose contest had convulsed

[1] N.P. VIII, p. 562.
[2] N.P. III, p. 415.
[3] N.P. VIII, p. 288.
[4] N.P. VII, p. 633f.

Europe for a generation. This dilemma led to Metternich's insistent battle against giving his name to his period. The correctness of the epithet "Metternich system" would have marked the defeat of the conservative statesman almost as surely as the victory of the revolution. Not as an individual but in the name of reason, not because of personal opposition but for the sake of universality, did Metternich fight his battles. Hence his insistence that he represented eternal principles not a system; his assertion of superior knowledge of the *real* foundation of states;[1] his pose of the doctor treating "ill" social organisms, of revolution as a malady, of conservatism as truth. At the end of thirty-nine years of power Metternich could still observe a collapsing world with a bitter-sweet resignation, mixed with pity for his opponents whose ignorance of the *real* social forces would unleash a terrible holocaust: "For thirty-nine years I played the role of rock, from which the waves recoil . . . until finally they succeed in engulfing it. They did not become calm afterwards, however, for what caused their turmoil was not the rock but their inherent unrest. The removal of the obstacle did not alter the situation, nor could it have . . . I would like to call out to the representatives of social upheaval: 'Citizen of a world, that exists but in your dreams, nothing is altered. On 14 March,[2] nothing happened save the elimination of a single man.' "[3]

It was thus that the Enlightenment retained deep into the nineteenth century its last champion, who judged actions by their "truth", not by their success, an advocate of reason in an age of philosophical materialism, who never surrendered his belief that morality could be known and that virtue was teachable. "These maxims have been proved true," he wrote in 1822, "[policy is based] not on novels, but on history; not on faith, but on knowledge."[4] When another Napoleon appeared on the scene, thirty-five years after the defeat of his great predecessor, Metternich did not consider this a personal failure, but the illustration of a philosophical insight: "The millions of votes for Louis Napoleon are only the expression of an instinctive feeling, that without order there can exist no social life, and without authority no order. Today this truth calls itself Louis Napoleon; so old has the world become that truth must assume a

[1] N.P. VIII, p. 236.
[2] 14 March, 1848, the date of Metternich's resignation as Staatskanzler.
[3] N.P. VIII, p. 232.
[4] N.P. III, p. 542.

personal name, because all other roads have been closed to it."[1] Truth must assume a personal name—this is the tragedy of the rationalist conservative, just as history with a personal name is that of the historical conservative. And the anonymity of truth was also the paradox of the Enlightenment: when truth is strong, its foundation is faith, if only in a theory of knowledge. When truth is challenged, it becomes a dogma.

But only a cynical age is capable of such an insight. It was unattainable for the intellectual contemporary of Kant and Voltaire, who prided himself on his soberness, which is merely the reverse side of a belief in the self-evidence of philosophical axioms, and who when asked to inscribe a picture of himself dedicated it with: "Above all no pathos". Into his old age Metternich retained a profound interest in the natural sciences, engaging in extended correspondence with scientists, particularly in the experimental sciences. And when the Tsar attempted to implement his religious exaltation in the social sphere, Metternich, in 1817, wrote him the following note: "The world suffers from a very special disease, which, as all epidemics, will pass away, that of mysticism. . . . It would be easier today to renew the sermons of Peter the Hermit, than to make clear to the afflicted that God demands another service than the shedding of blood, and that no man can judge the conscience of his fellows."[2] This was not only the conservative protesting against mass movements of *any* kind, it was also the accusation of the Enlightenment against Romanticism.

II

What then were the insights which Metternich's maxims revealed to him? They showed a universe governed by law, not in the modern sense of an *interpretation* of events but as their *attribute*. To disregard this law and its dictates of harmony and equilibrium was not so much morally wrong as physically disastrous. And just as in the political world the equilibrium reflected a balance between the forces of aggression and the forces of resistance, so the social order revealed an uneasy tension between the conserving and the destructive tendencies inherent in any body social. It was the task of statesmanship to distinguish the form and the substance of this contest and

[1] N.P. VIII, p. 197.
[2] N.P. III, p. 52f.

to create the moral foundation of an order on which only time could confer spontaneity. This led to another distinction, so often considered by the rationalist as the solution and not the definition of a problem: Man can only create Chartes, which have the value of programmatic announcements; it is time which makes constitutions.[1]

Metternich therefore opposed the efforts of his contemporaries to construct ideal constitutions for two reasons. They overlooked the factor of "time", not in Burke's sense of an almost hallowed entity, but as one of the most potent social forces. And they were unrealistic because the whole discussion about constitutions was beside the point. Anything that existed was subject to laws and the expression of law in the political world is a constitution: "A state without a constitution is an abstraction, just as an individual without a corresponding psyche".[2] It was for this reason contradictory to attempt to achieve freedom by means of constitutional guarantees. "Rights", according to Metternich, could not be created, they existed. Whether they were affirmed or not was an incidental, essentially technical, question and had nothing to do with freedom. Nobody could transgress laws, not even kings, an idea reminiscent of Grotius' famous phrase that not even God could make 2 + 2 equal 5. To guarantee rights was therefore a paradox; it was to clothe in the language of power what could only be a statement of fact, to endow with an arbitrary existence what has eternal validity: "Things which ought to be taken for granted lose their force when they emerge in the form of arbitrary pronouncements. . . . The mania of law-making is a symptom of the disease which has ravaged the world for 62 years. . . . Natural, moral or material forces are not fit subjects of *human* regulation. What would one say of a Charte which side by side with the Rights of Man exhibited the laws of gravitation? . . . Objects mistakenly made subject to legislation result only in the limitation, if not the complete annulment, of that which is attempted to be safeguarded."[3]

Here, then, was the rationalist belief in rights as an attribute of the universe, the aristocrat's vision of the inseparability of power and responsibility, the Enlightenment's faith in the connection between order and freedom. While it asserted the existence of "rights" transcending any human construction, indeed from which human

[1] N.P. VII, p. 636; VIII, p. 525.
[2] N.P. VII, p. 635.
[3] N.P. VIII, p. 557f.

construction could only detract, it emphasized a fundamental contradiction of democratic theory: the view of human nature which insisted on man's capacity for self-government was combined in the same theory with another view of human nature which limited the scope of this government. Why if man is conscious of arbitrary oppression should he wish to oppress others? Why should universal rights be guaranteed? This has, of course, never been a problem in Anglo-Saxon countries where the relation between state and society has had a juridic, not an ethical foundation. In such cases constitutional guarantees have the value of the difference between explicit and implicit limitations on a government in any case understood as limited. But in an "ethical state" an explicit limitation on government is meaningless. If the state justifies itself, not by its utility, but by its morality, there exists no tribunal before which to appeal its measures. If the sanction is not juridic but ethical, limitation can come about only by self-restraint, not by constitutional guarantees.

This was the challenge of the conservative statesman to his liberal opponents: If the conservative became an unwilling symbol of a revolutionary period by being forced into a definition of the nature of authority, the liberal contradicted himself by answering his own question about the nature of freedom. To be sure, Metternich did not have an answer of his own to the query regarding freedom, because he thought it inseparable from the notion of authority. But, equally, his opponents had not really dealt with the problem of authority which they thought exhausted in the definition of freedom. And yet they were closer than they realized: For had one asked Metternich as to the limits of authority and his opponent as to the limits of freedom, they would have both answered with one word, which indicated that to them the question was essentially meaningless: reason, self-evident and sovereign, which proved its applicability in its very conception, would trace the boundary of freedom as well as of necessity. That the categorical imperative was capable of differing interpretations was inconceivable to Kant. That a Sovereign should substitute force for law was not inconceivable to Metternich, but he considered it suicidal and therefore unlikely. It is this which gave the dispute between Metternich and the liberals the bitterness of a civil war, at least on the "democratic" side. For Metternich was an opponent who fought liberalism in the name of the very universality it claimed for itself, whose *mode* of argument represented as much of a challenge to his opponents as their existence to him. It is difficult, indeed, for a rationalistic philosophy to survive the demonstration that the same premise can lead to two diametrically opposed conclusions.

III

If Metternich considered the quest for formal constitutions chimerical, he saw in revolutions a physical disaster. In a universe characterized by a balance between the forces of conservation and those of destruction, revolution was due to a disturbance of the equilibrium in favour of the latter. But since the equilibrium was the "natural" condition, a revolution could achieve no more than a dislocation straining towards a new integration. The disorders attendant on revolutions were therefore symptoms of a transitional period and their violence a reflection of the ignorance of their advocates: "Revolutions are temporary disturbances in the life of states. . . . Order always ends up by reclaiming its own; states do not die like individuals, they transform themselves. It is the task of statesmanship . . . to guide this transformation and to supervise its direction."[1] The difference between a conservative and a revolutionary order was not the fact of change, but its mode: "A consideration the liberal spirit usually ignores . . . is the difference in the life of states, as of individuals, between progress by measured steps or by leaps. In the first case, conditions develop with the consequence of natural law; while the latter disrupts this connection. . . . Nature *is* development, the ordered succession of appearances; only such a course can eliminate the evil and foster the good. But leaping transitions wind up by requiring entirely new creations—and it is not given to man to create out of nothingness."[2] Civilization, then, was the degree to which change could come about "naturally", to which the tension between the forces of destruction and of conservation was submerged in a spontaneous pattern of obligation. Thus true civilization has come only with the advent of Christianity, which made authority inviolable, obedience sacrosanct and self-abnegation divine[3]—the rationalist's functional interpretation of religion.

It is expressive of the conservative dilemma that Metternich's pronouncements on the nature of authority are truistic—because a

[1] N.P. VIII, p. 468.
[2] N.P. VII, p. 638.
[3] N.P. VIII, p. 242.

conservative takes it for granted; and those on the meaning of freedom are skimpy—because he considered the question meaningless. But his analysis of the nature of revolutions is lucid and powerful. In 1820, while arranging the series of congresses designed to defeat the revolutionary outbreaks, Metternich wrote a "profession of faith" which coupled an analysis of the nature of revolution with a philosophy of history.[1] Up to the sixteenth century, Metternich maintained, the forces of conservation and of destruction had been in an increasingly spontaneous balance. But then there occurred three events which in time caused civilization to be supplanted by violence and order by chaos; the invention of printing and of gunpowder and the discovery of America. Printing facilitated the exchange of ideas which thereby became vulgarized; the invention of gunpowder changed the balance between offensive and defensive weapons; and the discovery of America transformed the situation both materially and psychologically. The influx of precious metals produced a sudden change in the value of landed property which is the foundation of a conservative order, and the prospect of rapid fortunes brought about a spirit of adventure and a dissatisfaction with existing conditions. And then the Reformation completed the process by overturning the moral world and exalting man above the forces of history.

All this gave rise to a type of individual who symbolized the revolutionary era: the presumptuous man, the natural product of a too-rapid march of the human spirit towards seeming perfection: "Religion, morality, legislation, economics, politics, administration, all seem to have become a common good and accessible to everyone. Science appears intuitive, experience has no value for the presumptuous; faith means nothing to him, and he substitutes for it the pretence of a personal conviction, to arrive at which, however, he dispenses with analysis or study, for these seem too subordinate activities to a mind which believes itself capable of embracing at one blow the whole ensemble of issues. Laws have no value for him, because he did not contribute to their preparation, and it is below the dignity of a man of his quality to recognize limits traced by ignorant and brute generations. Power resides in himself; why submit to what can have use only to men deprived . . . of insight? That which was appropriate for an age of weakness is no longer adequate for that of reason. . . . [All this] tends to an order of things which

[1] N.P. III, p. 400f.

individualizes all the elements which compose society. . . ." It would be difficult to find a more tragic statement. What was intended as sarcasm—the exhibition of an incommensurability between pretence and reality—amounted to no more than a description of the objectives of his opponents. That which Metternich believed he merely needed to exhibit to reduce to absurdity, his opponents thought required only an affirmation in order to be validated. It was the inevitable revolutionary misunderstanding, the reluctance to admit that "truth" may not be self-evident. While Metternich desperately attempted to protect "reality" against its enemies, the issue increasingly became a debate about its nature and the nature of "truth". Had "reality" still proved unambiguous, he would not have needed to affirm it. By the increasing insistence of his affirmation, he testified to its disintegration.

Metternich next distinguished the presumptuous by type and by origin. They were composed of levellers and theoreticians: the former, men of powerful wills and strong determination; the latter, abstract theoreticians living in a world of their own. But whatever guise presumption assumed, its place of origin was the middle class. The revolutionary aristocrat was a lost soul, destined to become the victim of the Revolution or to be degraded by being forced to play the role of courtier to his inferiors. And the mass of the population always distrusted change and craved only the equal protection of laws in order to pursue their hard calling. But the middle class, the lawyers, the writers, the bureaucrats, the half-educated, owning the means of communication, ambitious but without goal, dissatisfied but unable to offer an alternative, this was the real organ of revolution. It was no accident, concluded Metternich, that the revolution occurred, not in the poorest, but in the richest country of Europe; not in the most backward, but in the most advanced state, so demoralized that "the revolution had already triumphed in the palace of the kings and in the boudoirs of the towns before it even began to prepare itself in the mass of the people".

The Revolution could not have triumphed then but for the weakness of the government and for the belief in a myth whose literal application proved ruinous: that British institutions could be transplanted to the Continent: "Among the causes of the tremendous confusion characterizing present-day Europe," wrote Metternich in later life, paralleling his profession of faith, "is the transplantation of British institutions to the Continent where they are in complete contradiction to existing conditions, so that their application becomes either illusory or distorted. The so-called 'British school' has been the cause of the French Revolution, and the consequences of this revolution, so anti-British in tendency, devastate Europe today. The concepts of freedom and order are so inseparable in the British mind that the last stable-boy would laugh in the face of the reformers if they appeared by preaching his freedom."[1] The wars of the French Revolution had spread these principles across Europe. The hatred for Bonaparte delayed their baneful impact for but a little while, and this through a misunderstanding. For the war, fought by the kings against Napoleon, was fought by the people in part against their own masters in the hope of obtaining from them the realization of the promises of the French Revolution. The wise peace concluded in 1814 might have inaugurated a period of tranquillity, but Napoleon's return from Elba undid in one hundred days the anti-revolutionary achievement of fourteen years of Bonapartist rule. By unleashing again the revolution in France, Napoleon exposed Europe to unending social strife.[2]

IV

This was a powerful analysis of the cause of the unrest sweeping across Europe. But its power was at the same time its bane. For if the revolutionary spirit was so widespread, how could it be combated? If the causes of the revolution were so fundamental, dating so far back in history, what possible remedy could exist? If the middle class was so potent, how could it be dealt with? By gradual integration, a representative of historical conservatism, such as Burke, might have answered, by learning moderation and the need for adaptation. Even Castlereagh could still advise Louis XVIII that revolutionaries "are nowhere so little to be dreaded as in office, mixed up with other material. Tyrants may poison an obnoxious character but the only means a constitutional monarch has to restrain him is to employ him".[3] But to Metternich, the rationalist conservative, this solution was a dangerous evasion. To the product of the Enlightenment political problems had to assume the precision of logical antinomies, and he therefore sharpened the differences instead of smoothing

[1] N.P. VIII, p. 218.
[2] N.P. III, p. 409.
[3] Webster, I, p. 547 (Appendix).

them over. If the forces of destruction were rampant, it was the task of the conservative to strengthen those of order. If the cry for reform was universal, it was all the more imperative to resist in the name of authority.

In this manner the equation, freedom = voluntary submission to order, became in practice a definition of sterility and unexceptional maxims turned into justifications for inaction. So it happened that Metternich never tired of comparing concessions to popular clamour to squandering capital; therefore his basic maxim "that in the middle of agitated passions one cannot think of reforming; wisdom in such situations confines itself to maintaining".[1] Therefore, his increasingly rigid opposition to *any* change, for change symbolized the possibility of yielding to pressure: "Where everything is tottering, it is above all necessary that something, no matter what, remain steadfast, so that the lost can find a connection and the strayed a refuge."[2] This accounted for his preference of Napoleon over the Bourbons despite the "legitimacy" of the latter; to Metternich legitimacy was not an end but a tool and when it conflicted with the requirements of stability, it had to yield. Therefore, paradoxically, Metternich became a defender of existing institutions however much he might deplore them, because their overthrow would be an even more dangerous symbol. When in the panic of 1820 the Grand Duke of Baden offered to abolish his constitution, Metternich replied: "Every order lawfully established bears within itself the principle of a better system. . . A Charter, in any case, is not a constitution. It is up to the government to separate good and evil, to strengthen public authority and to protect the repose and the happiness of nations against hostile attack."[3]

It was a futile contest, a *tour de force* leading to self-destruction, this effort to bring about change through order and to identify order with tranquillity in the middle of a revolutionary period. It was really, despite its protestations to the contrary, an effort to recapture a lost innocence, a quest for a period when obligation was spontaneous, an aristocratic notion of government as the reciprocal execution of duties. The "Metternich system" answered the question of the cause of revolution, but it gave no indication of how to cope with it once it had occurred. It spoke abstractly of its readiness to re-

[1] N.P. III, p. 415.
[2] Srbik, I, p. 354.
[3] N.P. III, p. 375.

form but it never discussed what specific measures it would consider appropriate. As late as 1851 Metternich could give no better advice to his successor, Schwarzenberg, than to strengthen the landed aristocracy, as if the middle class could still be crushed. The assertion that revolutions were always the fault of governments, that only action could conserve, was unexceptionable. But in practice it led to a vicious circle, because Metternich, although not opposed to reform in principle, wanted it as an emanation of order, while his opponents desired the same thing in the name of change. The result was a stalemate, a triumph of form over substance.

Metternich's thus became a never-ending quest for a moment of tranquillity, for a suspension, if only for an instant, of the flux of life, so that what happened, perhaps inevitably, could be represented as a universal principle instead of an assertion of will and of indeterminacy. It was as if a physicist, unable to measure both position and velocity of the electron accurately, bent all his energies to making the electron hold still, if only a fraction of a second, because this would enable him to chart its course for eternity. Or as if the driver of a car heading out of control in an unknown direction down a precipitate mountain road sought desperately to capture the wheel; for if he could but do this, his inevitable descent would represent order and not chaos. So it happened that Metternich's insights, however powerful, became increasingly dogmatic. While he might have been right in asserting that those who have never had a past cannot own the future, those who *have* had a past may doom themselves by seeking it in the future.

And still in all this obtuseness there was an element of grandeur. For Metternich had no illusions about the probable developments; he saw his task in ameliorating their inevitable consequences: "The existing society is on the decline. Nothing ever stands still . . . and society has reached its zenith. Under such conditions to advance means to descend. . . . Such periods appear interminable to contemporaries, but what are two to three hundred years in the annals of history? . . . My life has fallen into a terrible period. I was born either too soon or too late. . . . Formerly I would have enjoyed life, later I could have helped in the reconstruction. Now I spend my time shoring up decaying buildings."[1] He did not fight the revolution because it was impossible, but because it was "unnatural". And he combated democracy because "authority is an expression of the

[1] N.P. III, p. 347f.

power of permanence; while in [parliamentary government] power appears under the aspect of transitoriness . . . I understand that little minds like to think of themselves as the expression of power, but it is equally without doubt that the opponents of *all* authority like to see it reduced to personal terms, because it will facilitate their effort to eliminate it. . . ."[1] Because he considered order the expression of the equilibrium and equilibrium the reflection of the structure of the universe, he was certain that the "basic interests" of states would reassert themselves in the end. But he predicted that the revolutionaries would be horrified by the world they were bringing about.[2] The greater the dislocation, the more violent the interregnum of chaos. Despotism, to Metternich, was not the absence of guaranteed rights, but government without universal maxims. Tyranny was not the cause of revolutions, but their likely result. And the more the forces of destruction succeeded in undermining the social order, the more authority—the inevitable expression of society—would have to assume personal shape, the conservative's vision of arbitrariness.

It was thus that Metternich posed the conservative challenge as the need to transcend the assertion of the exclusive validity of the will and as the requirement to limit the claims of power. It was a redefinition of the classic theological version of humility, "Thy will be done", only that reason took the place of God. It represented an effort to deal with the most fundamental problem of politics, which is not the control of wickedness but the limitation of righteousness. To "punish" the wicked is a relatively easy matter, because it is a simple expression of public morality. To restrain the exercise of righteous power is more difficult, because it asserts that right exists in time as well as in space; that volition, however noble, is limited by forces transcending the will; that the achievement of self-restraint is the ultimate challenge of the social order. Metternich dealt with this problem by asserting that excess in any direction was disruptive of society. The individual will was contingent because man was an aspect of forces transcending him: of society and its historical expression, the state, which were products of nature as surely as man himself, for they reflected his basic needs for justice and order. Because they were "natural", states had a life cycle just as human beings, only they were incapable of the ultimate human solace: they

[1] N.P. VIII, p. 467. He did not apply this to Great Britain where he saw the permanence of authority expressed in the phrase, "His Majesty's Government".
[2] N.P. VIII, p. 235.

could not die, they had to pay the price of *all* their transgressions.[1]

It was only appropriate, therefore, that the last act of the conservative statesman was of a symbolic nature, a plea for the anonymity which alone could justify his maxims. When in 1848 a deputation of the victorious revolution called his resignation "generous", the aged Metternich replied: "I protest solemnly against this term. Only a Sovereign can be generous; my action is the result of my sense of right and my concept of duty." Thus, the final gesture of the "doctor of Revolutions" was a last desperate assertion of order, of the precedence of right over will even in defeat after half a century of struggle. And when one of the deputies insisted on using the term "generous", Metternich replied: "In resigning I anticipate another claim, that I have carried the monarchy away with me. But this is not the case. No individual has shoulders strong enough to carry an Empire; if states disappear, it is because they lose faith in themselves."[2] This was also the final symbolization of the conservative dilemma: that it is the task of the conservative not to defeat but to forestall revolution; that a society which cannot *prevent* a revolution, the disintegration of whose values has been demonstrated by the *fact* of revolution, will not be able to defeat it by conservative means; that order once shattered can be restored only by the experience of chaos.

V

There was, however, another reason for the rigidity of Metternich's maxims; indeed, their rigidity in many respects merely reflected the structure of the Empire he represented. In each period there exist anachronisms, states which appear backward and even decadent to those who fail to realize that they are dealing with the most tenacious remnant of a disintegrated world order. But the very quality of obtuse toughness which enabled these relics to survive also limits their adaptability. Confronted by a world which no longer understands them, rigidity becomes their instinctive reaction to the forces of dissolution.

This was the situation of the Austrian Empire in the nineteenth century. Built through the tenacity of a single dynasty, grown powerful as the bulwark of Europe against the East, its territories combined

[1] N.P. I, p. 334.
[2] N.P. VII, p. 626; VIII, p. 212.

the most polyglot nationalities and levels of civilization, united only by the common Emperor. Alone of the great feudal structures of the medieval period, the Austrian Empire had survived into the modern period, still connected by principles of reciprocal fealty, by a series of complex understandings, by the self-evidence of its necessity. "Austria," wrote Metternich, "is a juridically uniform, but administratively diverse state. It is diverse, not through an act of will, but through fundamental reasons, the most important of which is the difference in nationalities. . . . The foundation of the Empire is therefore the maintenance of the different legal codes of the various components of the Empire; this is our only protection against the levelling of all concepts which is characteristic of our period."[1]

But what was a dynastic state to do in an era of centralization and nationalism, of rationalized administration and codified legislation? The impact of modernity was dissolving for so complex, indeed so subtle, a structure. For how could organic institutions be rationalized, when relationships were so intricate that the very attempt to define them would merely serve to accentuate differences? What was the applicability of the French lesson of the efficacy of a highly centralized government in a state where the effort to centralize was only too likely to consume all energies in internal strife? Austria had had the experience of the effort of the great Emperor Joseph to apply the lessons of the Enlightenment, and it had nearly torn the Empire apart. And if the Austrian Empire was slow to learn, it never forgot a lesson, and its memory proved as much its undoing as its inflexibility.

Metternich therefore fought Liberalism not only on theoretical, but also on eminently practical grounds. He considered the quest of the Austrian liberals for a modern, centralized state as chimerical, because it was based on a conception of government which did not apply to Austria. "Vienna is not Paris," wrote Metternich after the liberal revolution of 1848 attempted to transform Austria into a unitary state, "it is not the city which consumes the life of the whole Empire and which can therefore prescribe its laws at discretion. It is nothing but the shell in which the heart of the Empire happens to be situated. . . . It is the capital of the whole complex of states only because the Emperor happens to reside there and the reason for this is technical, its central situation. . . . All components of the Empire look towards the Emperor—its true and visible head. Does any one

[1] N.P. VIII, p. 474.

look towards a ministry which represents only itself? Will Hungary obey its commands? Indeed how can it, for does the ministry wear the Crown of St. Stephan? . . . The Emperor is everything, Vienna is nothing."[1] Again it was a magnificent analysis of a dilemma and again it offered no remedy, because Austria's tragedy was precisely that the legitimacy of personal loyalty was no longer sufficient, that the nineteenth century increasingly reduced government to an abstract expression which justified its acts by the rationality of each measure, not by the historical "truth" of its ruler.

His analysis of the structure of the Austrian Empire caused Metternich to reject the notion of ministerial responsibility, not because he believed that the power of the Emperor was absolute, but because his notion of responsibility applied to a different realm of discourse than that of his opponents. Responsibility implied a juridical concept, Metternich argued, and for this reason, in Parliamentary states, Parliament was the high court of justice. But Austria could not afford a Central Representation, precisely because its bond was dynastic and not national. A responsible ministry implied popular sovereignty, but popular sovereignty involved the dissolution of Austria.[2] This situation would not be changed by creating legislatures in the various parts of the Empire, for, while monarchical sovereignty could be extended to several nations, popular sovereignty was indivisible. Nor would a hierarchical arrangement of the Parliaments of different nations prove a solution, as the experience of Great Britain and Ireland had demonstrated. The call for responsible government was therefore a demand for total irresponsibility. Since there existed no Austrian nation, the ministry would be responsible only to itself. Austria, the product of history and of a dynastic vision, could find responsibility only in the maxims of its monarch, in the embodiment of its only vision of itself the Emperor.

Again a splendid antinomy. But how was the monarch to rule in a century of nationalism? By strengthening the government so that it really governed and by decentralizing the administration, Metternich replied. The polyglot Empire could survive only by demonstrating the beneficial effect of a central authority and its compatibility with cultural diversity. This was Metternich's remedy for the fundamental malady of the Austrian Empire, the confusion of statesmanship with administration. As the nineteenth century progressed, the anachron-

[1] N.P. VIII, p. 424f.
[2] N.P. VIII, pp. 427, 465, 471, among many examples.

istic Empire increasingly looked for determinacy of calculation, and this can be found more easily in the application of bureaucratic norms than in the adjustment to changing conditions. Administration creates the illusion of "running by itself"; the routine which is its mode of assimilating mediocrity appears to the outsider as the condition of its success. The motivation of a bureaucracy is its quest for safety; it measures success by errors avoided rather than by goals achieved; it prides itself on objectivity which is a denial of the necessity of great conception—all qualities which to a disintegrating structure may symbolize a means to rescue certainty from impending chaos. It is understandable, even if it proved disastrous, that Austria increasingly applied purely administrative considerations to the solution of its complex domestic problems. But while it was true that Austria could not make the transition from a dynastic to a centralized state without disintegrating, it did not follow that it had to import the mode of government of the eighteenth and earlier centuries into the modern period. It was the measure of the sterility of Austrian statesmanship that it confused the nature of its domestic legitimization with the structure of its bureaucracy and that an outmoded administration therefore confronted the rapidly multiplying problems of industrialization, nationalism, and liberalism. In this manner the Austrian monarchy lost the opportunity to justify itself through performance and the opposition was enabled to add the charge of inefficiency to the doctrinal differences.

The system of administration was nothing less than a continuation of the patriarchal pattern of obligations of the feudal period. The Emperor was not only the sole source of authority juridically but the actual centre of both policy and administration. The government was conducted not by means of ministries, but through departments of the Imperial Court. Their heads were not ministers but "Hofräte", permanent chiefs of departments. For almost a decade, Metternich was the only official with the title of minister, and he paid for his eminence by being jealously deprived of all domestic influence. Beside the Emperor, no less than three organs were charged with co-ordinating the different departments; but they were in the nature of inter-departmental committees, composed of officials of the departments concerned, and their structure and function were so confusing that an eminent Austrian historian in 1884 was unable to account for them precisely.[1] At any rate, they met but at the pleasure

[1] Springer, I, p. 120.

of the Emperor and considered only the matters he chose to bring before them. The Austrian administration has been described as a contraption whose wheels revolved with an infernal noise without advancing one inch. Well might Metternich say in later life that he had sometimes governed Europe, but never Austria.

It was in vain that one of Metternich's first acts on assuming the foreign ministry was to propose its reorganization, or that soon after he submitted a plan to introduce a Reichsrat, an Imperial Council, to co-ordinate and develop basic policy.[1] All these efforts, as so many others, ran afoul of the obstinacy of the Emperor. Emperor Franz was one of those mediocrities who believe that the lesson of experience resides in mechanical remembrance. His notion of success was the opposite of failure, his notion of causality was succession in time. Because the centralizing tendencies of his predecessor, Joseph II, had led to civil strife, all reform was to be avoided. Because the attempt to rally the people had not succeeded in achieving victory in 1809, no reliance whatever was to be placed on popular support. Dour and suspicious, unimaginative and pedantic, he had seen so many convulsions that he regarded mere persistence an ethical value. His most characteristic quality was a pretentious stoicism which reflected an absence of sensibility. "He hates reflection," his uncle, the great Joseph II, said of him. "He does not communicate his thoughts because he is afraid of learning the truth. . . . Because he has seen that obstinacy . . . makes his environment pliable, he uses it so that he can persist in his comfort. . . . One threat affects him, the most unpleasant of all, because it reveals an insensitive character, namely fear of vexation. This makes him small, pliable, free with promises without however changing his opinions in which he persists because of a falsely understood pride in his birth."[2]

This was the man who ruled Austria for over a generation and in perhaps the most crucial period of its history. A trivial mind, he thought himself capable of resolving all problems personally, because to the uninspired all problems are equally difficult—and equally easy. A succession of disasters had taught him only that change was the cause, not the expression, of transformations. He therefore attempted to avoid it at all costs and by any means. His system of police supervision was notorious, and he delighted in reading even

[1] N.P. II, pp. 315, 444f.
[2] Springer, I, p. 110.

its most unimportant reports. Jealous of his prerogatives, he was careful to divide the power among his subordinates to avoid any preponderant influence. Even Metternich, despite all his successes in foreign affairs, felt impelled to introduce any discussion of domestic problems with a subservient disclaimer which indicated their relation to foreign policy.[1] It was not surprising that such a man sought refuge in the determinacy of bureaucratic norms, that he interfered in every detail of administration, that not even the most trivial decision could be taken without his concurrence. His industry was stupendous, but industry is the sop to the conscience of mediocrity. "He deals with affairs like a drill," Metternich said of him once in a rare moment of exasperation, "which penetrates ever deeper, until suddenly and to his surprise he emerges somewhere without having done more than make a hole in a memorandum."[2]

In these circumstances, Metternich's careful manipulations become understandable. For unless the Emperor was brought to a decision so imperceptibly that change could be accomplished with the illusion of stability, he was certain to resist. Metternich was not too far from the truth when he said whimsically: "We have had a saint who went to heaven because he stood for years on a pillar on one foot. . . . His merit was the uncomfortable position; my position is no better."[3] But the impact of the personality of the Emperor was even more baneful domestically, and again it is Metternich who has left us the best capsule description: "I wanted the government to *govern*, my colleagues sought to *administer* according to existing norms. . . . In this situation measures only came to my attention after they had run the gamut of all subordinate departments, where their final formulation was prepared and whence they reached me only if an urgent decision was required, which in turn made it impossible to do anything except to concur with the administrative proposal. . . . The greatest mistake in the Austrian Empire . . . was the concern of the government with matters which should have been dealt with administratively. This paralysed the machinery of government, overwhelmed the highest level with trivia and absolved the lowest of responsibility. Should I have forced the administration into a different direction? For this I did not have sufficient power. Should I have smashed the machinery? This would only have led to paralysis.

[1] See, for example, N.P. II, p. 432.
[2] Srbik, I, p. 447.
[3] N.P. III, p. 333.

My task was not to govern nor to administer, but to represent the Empire towards foreign countries."[1]

This then was the task of the conservative statesman as he contemplated the international order in 1815: To represent his country abroad, to cover its weaknesses, to delay the inevitable as long as possible. In this task he was aided by a marvellous diplomatic skill, which for a time transformed weakness into a diplomatic asset and which enabled him to emerge as the conservative conscience of Europe. Its attempt to identify the domestic legitimization of Austria with that of the international order was not so much a symptom of rigidity as perhaps the only possible policy in a domestic structure which Metternich had no choice but to take as given. It was thus diplomacy *par excellence*, pure manipulation, and that it lacked ultimate stature was due as much to the force of circumstances as to the lack of creativity of Metternich. "In what times have I lived?" Metternich wrote in his political testament. "Let anyone look at the situations which Austria and all of Europe confronted between 1809 and 1848 and let him ask himself whether one man's insight could have transformed these crises into health. I claim to have recognized the situation, but also the impossibility to erect a new structure in our Empire . . . and for this reason all my care was directed to conserving that which existed."[2]

This is the epitaph of the conservative statesman: History is greater than the individual, but although it teaches its lessons surely, it does not do so in a single lifetime. And the statement also marks the limits of Metternich's abilities. For statesmen must be judged not only by their actions but also by their conception of alternatives. Those statesmen who have achieved final greatness did not do so through resignation, however well founded. It was given to them not only to maintain the perfection of order, but to have the strength to contemplate chaos, there to find material for fresh creation.

[1] N.P. VII, p. 619.
[2] N.P. VII, p. 640.

XII

The Congress of Aix-la-Chapelle and the Organization of the Peace

I

WHEN peace finally came to a Europe grown accustomed to incessant strife, it was greeted not only with relief but with a feeling of disillusion as well. The suffering of a period of revolutionary war can be sustained only by millennial hopes, by the vision of a world free of problems. Because the conflict seems so overpowering, peace is conceived as merely the absence of war, order is assumed the natural consequence of the equilibrium and harmony the self-evident maxim of self-preservation. Yet the greater these expectations, the more severe the inevitable disenchantment. There must come a point when it is realized that the exaltation of war is not transferable to the problems of peace, that harmony is an attribute of coalitions but not of "legitimate" orders, that stability is not equivalent to the *consciousness* of universal reconciliation. For the objective of a war is determinate, the defeat of the enemy. But the goal of peace is contingent, the adjustment of the differences among the components of the equilibrium. The motivation of a war is imposed from the outside by the threat of a common enemy. The motivation of peace is the attempt to realize a state's historical objectives within the framework of a system of order. Long periods of peace have for this reason not necessarily been accompanied by a consciousness of harmony; this is the illusion of posterity—or of island powers. On the contrary, only periods convinced that irretrievable disasters are impossible are capable of conducting cabinet diplomacy with its shifting alliances, which testify to the absence of unbridgeable schisms; with its seeming cynicism, which indicates that risks are limited; with its limited wars, which reveal that differences are peripheral.

"Everything that occurred after 1815," Metternich wrote in 1819, "belongs to the course of ordinary history. Since 1815, our period is left to its own devices; it advances because it cannot stop, but it is no longer guided. . . . We have relapsed again into an epoch where a thousand small calculations and petty opinions form the history of the day. The sea is still tumultuous at times, but only from passing storms. To be sure, it is possible to capsize on such a sea; one is even more likely to drown in it, because the wind is more difficult to calculate than the storm; but the spectacle is no longer grandiose."[1] The petty calculations to which Metternich was referring were a symptom that stability was coming to be taken for granted. When total transformations have become impossible or inconceivable, statesmanship must concentrate on the almost imperceptible changes whose cumulative effect may result in upsetting the equilibrium. When absolute claims have abdicated, the contingent reigns supreme. And while the spectacle it presents is not grandiose, it is the mode by which legitimate orders implement their intuition of permanence. War involves the suppression of nuance; peace witnesses its re-emergence.

It was a symptom of the stability of the Vienna settlement that disputes after 1815 increasingly took the form of a conflict over the interpretation of the three sets of treaties which had established the new international order: (a) the treaties of peace and the Final Acts of the Congress of Vienna; (b) the treaties of alliance (the Treaty of Chaumont and the Quadruple Alliance); (c) the Holy Alliance. The treaties of peace and the Final Acts of the Congress of Vienna had settled the territorial arrangement of Europe. But it was still a moot point whether they represented at the same time a guarantee of this arrangement. Which was correct, the British interpretation that the treaty structure of 1814–15 was designed to deal only with the problem of renewed French aggression, or that of Alexander who insisted that it implied a guarantee of the existing order, both domestic and territorial? This was to be the problem of the Congress of Aix-la-Chapelle. The treaties of alliance directed against France made evident that Europe was being organized, at least in part, by the fear of a common enemy. But with the proviso of periodic conferences, Castlereagh had introduced something entirely new in the diplomatic relations of the major powers: a vision of European government. And the issues which would be considered proper topics for international discussion were still undefined. Was the threat to the

[1] N.P. III, p. 297.

equilibrium political or social? Could diplomacy by conference be legitimized domestically in Great Britain? These were the problems of the Conferences of Troppau and Laibach. The Holy Alliance, which all sovereigns save the Pope and the Sultan soon joined,[1] was an assertion of the pervasiveness of moral principles and of the fraternal association of monarchs. But ethical maxims make universal claims which can be used to justify general interference as well as self-restraint. Would the Tsar's increasing mysticism become a revolutionary weapon or a means to limit Russian expansion? This was the issue which led to the Congress of Verona.

It was only appropriate that a series of Congresses should mark the stages of an attempt to organize Europe under the tutelage of the Great Powers. It was at these congresses that it became apparent that unity was not an end but a series of conditions, that its interpretation depended on the geographical and historical position of the protagonists and, finally, that it was limited by the possibility of legitimizing the international consensus domestically. But in 1815 the habits of wartime were still powerful; harmony was still invoked as a magic solvent of discord and good faith as a sufficient remedy for problems conceived as misunderstandings. It was not yet apparent that the three chief protagonists meant something entirely different by the "unity" so frequently invoked: that Castlereagh considered it the cause, not the expression, of international co-operation; Metternich, a means to achieve a moral sanction for Austrian policy; and the Tsar, a step towards the bliss of a reconciled humanity.

II

The period immediately following the Peace of Paris was marked by the closest co-operation between Castlereagh and Metternich. It was a co-operation tested during the various crises of the Coalition and, as then, their unity of purpose was in part a result of an identity of interests, in part imposed by the pressure of the Tsar. As long as Britain sought its security in Continental stability Austria was its natural ally. Both Britain and Austria were status quo powers, Britain because stability was its only Continental interest, Austria because stability was the condition of its survival. Both agreed in their interpretation of the elements of the equilibrium, that a strong

[1] The Prince Regent of England having expressed his sympathy for its objectives in a personal letter.

Central Europe was a requirement of European tranquillity and that a powerful Austria was the key to Central Europe. And they were both confronted by a restless Russia, which in one generation had advanced its frontiers from the Dnieper to beyond the Vistula.

For despite his increasing mysticism Alexander remained a source of disquiet. It soon became apparent that the general formulae of the Holy Alliance were capable of various interpretations. The brotherhood of peoples might have been eliminated from the text, but the spirit which produced it continued to hold sway. Reports from all parts of Europe spoke of the activity of Russian agents. In Sicily, they intrigued with the Jacobin faction; in Spain, the Russian ambassador negotiated for the sale of Russian ships to replace the Spanish fleet—a direct, if meaningless, challenge to Great Britain. And, after the Princess of Wales refused to marry the Hereditary Prince of Orange, the Russian court profited from the British embarrassment by arranging for the marriage of a Grand-Duchess to the jilted Prince. In part, these activities were due to the new adviser of the Tsar, Capo d'Istria, a Greek noble, who managed to combine the liberal maxims of the Enlightenment with service to an autocrat and whose dogmatism and suspected Pan-Hellenism soon earned him the almost obsessional dislike of Metternich. In part, the Russian activities were caused by the insecurity of a young and backward nation, still unaccustomed to being at the centre of events. "All Russians are peculiarly alive to unfavourable comparisons," reported Cathcart. "They are hurt at any apparent superiority. . . . They hate us for what they cannot do and, without any particular object of immediate advantage, will always feel inclined rather to abate than increase our power."[1]

Nor did the Tsar's religious exaltation involve a withdrawal from political activity. On the contrary, it seemed to furnish him with another pretext to interfere in the domestic affairs of other states. Even Austria was not spared, although Metternich saw to it that the situation did not get out of hand. When Nesselrode inquired whether Austria had suppressed Pietist sects, Metternich dryly denied it, but added immediately that they had not been suppressed only because they had never been permitted. He concluded with the attack on mysticism quoted in the preceding chapter[2] and forwarded the whole exchange to the Emperor with the following sarcastic note:

[1] C.C. XI, p. 265. 1 July, 1816.
[2] See ante, p. 197.

"If I have discussed some strange matters, it is because I wanted to put an end to the discussion about *biblical subjects* and *religious police* before it fairly got started. . . . All ideas of the Emperor Alexander always amount to the same thing, to solicit proselytes. For this reason he solicits the Jacobins in Italy and the Pietists in the rest of Europe. Today the 'Rights of Man' have been replaced by a concern for Readers of the Bible".[1] The problem of relations with Russia was therefore still the same as at Langres, Troyes, and Vienna; the attempt of one man to identify the European order with his will. "Alexander desires the peace of the world," reported an Austrian diplomat, "but not for the sake of peace and its blessings, rather for his own sake; not unconditionally, but with mental reservations: he must remain the arbiter of this peace; from him must emanate the repose and happiness of the world and all of Europe must recognize that this repose is his work, that it is dependent on his goodwill and that it can be disturbed by his whim. . . ."[2] It was his consciousness of a mercurial, unstable, meddling Russia which shaped Metternich's policy during Alexander's lifetime.

But while Metternich and Castlereagh agreed about the elements of the equilibrium and the likely danger, they were not necessarily at one about the policy to combat it. To Castlereagh, the fact of a conference was a symbol of good faith, and good faith was the sufficient motive for European harmony. To Metternich, the conference was merely a framework which would have to be given content through diplomatic skill. To Castlereagh, unity was the cause of harmony; to Metternich, the expression of moral identity. Castlereagh proposed to moderate the Tsar by demonstrating to him that he had nothing to fear; Metternich sought to restrain Alexander by obtaining his assent to a doctrine of self-limitation. Castlereagh's policy conceived the danger to Europe as political. Metternich considered the real threat as social, and his energies were devoted to preventing what he called the revolutionary party from obtaining the political support of a major power.

This divergence reflected the difference in domestic structures as well as in geographic location. The insular power, secure in the belief of the unassailability of its domestic institutions, could rest its policy on the doctrine of non-interference in the domestic affairs of other

[1] N.P. III, p. 51–4.

[2] Text, Nicolas Mikhailovitch, *Les Rapports Diplomatiques du Lebzeltern* (St Petersburg, 1915), p. 37f.

states; the polyglot empire, conscious of the anachronism of its institutions, had to attempt to *prevent*, not to limit, transformations. Britain, at the periphery of Europe, could afford to take a chance on a mistake in the evaluation of the intentions of another power. Metternich had no such margin of safety. Thus, while both Castlereagh and Metternich represented status quo powers and conducted essentially defensive foreign policies, Metternich's "boiling point" was lower. Living with the conviction of invulnerability, Castlereagh could gamble on the reality of good faith. Living with a premonition of catastrophe, Metternich had to look for a more tangible expression of security.

"Our insular position *places us sufficiently out of the reach of immediate danger* [my italics] to permit our pursuing a more generous and confiding policy," Castlereagh wrote in a circular dispatch on 31 December, designed to allay the fears of British representatives regarding Russian motives. "In the present state of Europe, it is the province of Great Britain to turn the confidence she has inspired to the accounts of peace, by exercising a conciliatory influence. . . . The immediate object to be kept in view is to inspire the states of Europe . . . with a sense of the danger they have surmounted by their union, of the hazards they will incur by a relaxation of vigilance. . . ."[1] With the self-confidence of insular safety, Castlereagh lectured Metternich about his "timidity" and his excessive caution. When the Tsar, in the spring of 1816, came up with a plan for a general disarmament, Castlereagh took this as a vindication of his policy. Although he evaded the proposal by suggesting that Russia follow the example of Austria and Prussia and disarm unilaterally, Castlereagh sent his reply to Metternich pointing out that "a frank and conciliatory system of diplomacy, holding fast to the principle of the Alliance . . . is likely to bring the motives of internal economy to bear with the most effect upon the military expenditure of Russia."[2] And when Metternich suggested that Britain and Austria co-ordinate their steps *vis-à-vis* Russia, Castlereagh replied: "Should the alarms to which the Austrian dispatch points unfortunately be realized, it might be reasonable to suppose that Prussia and France might be disposed, in concert with Austria and Great Britain, to take an active part in opposing [Russia], but there is reason to believe that neither power regard the danger at the present moment to be imminent. In

[1] Webster, II, p. 67; C.C. XI, p. 104, 28 December, 1815.
[2] Webster, II, p. 99.

this state of things I . . . submit to Prince Metternich whether it may not be prudent to moderate the language of alarm."[1] When, finally, Metternich attempted to transform the Ambassadorial Conference, established in Paris to supervise the execution of the Treaty of Peace, into a centre to collect police reports from all over Europe, Castlereagh protested sharply: "It may be too much to assert that no case could occur in Europe to render an authoritative remonstrance of the Great Powers conjointly to any particular Court expedient, but such a mode should not be a habitual occurrence and especially ought not to proceed from the ministers in conference at Paris."[2]

But in the period immediately following the Peace of Paris these exchanges were merely hints of divergences, the full implications of which were not to become fully apparent for some years, and they were submerged in a larger identity of interests. As long as the social danger did not become more evident, Metternich was content to deal with it as an Austrian, not a European, problem. As long as Alexander continued so erratic, it was risky to attempt to transform the Alliance into the government of Europe. Above all, Metternich's energies were concentrated on consolidating Austria's position in both Germany and Italy, and Castlereagh's doctrine of non-interference provided a splendid shield behind which to accomplish it free from Russian meddling. As long as the problem was the political and essentially negative task of restraining Russian influence, Castlereagh and Metternich could march side by side. If there occurred occasional disagreements, they were not fundamental and extended to methods rather than goals. It was, therefore, with considerable anticipation that Castlereagh looked forward to the first meeting of a European congress in peacetime. The Congress at Aix-la-Chapelle, which assembled at the end of September, 1818, was to prove the efficacy of diplomacy by conference, to dispel misunderstandings and exhibit again the self-evident advantages of good faith. And while Metternich's motivations were more complex, he, too, hoped to turn the Congress to good use, if only to begin to create a moral framework for the social contest he knew must inevitably come.

[1] Webster, II, p. 107.
[2] Webster, II, p. 72.

III

The period after 1815 was the first attempt in peacetime to organize the international order through a system of conferences, and the first explicit effort by the great powers to assert a right of control. Throughout the immediate post-war period, Ambassadorial Conferences in Frankfurt, London and, most importantly, Paris, dealing with the territorial arrangements of Germany, the suppression of the Slave Trade, and the execution of the Treaty of Paris, respectively, had symbolized the new trend. But since they were confined to specific problems, the main outlines of which had been well charted, they did not represent a true test. As the plenipotentiaries were preparing for the Congress of Aix-la-Chapelle, however, the whole range of European problems lay before them. And as they discussed the agenda, the membership, and even the authority under which the Congress was to be assembled, it became increasingly evident that the achievement of unity was not as simple as the desire for it.

For the Congress of Aix-la-Chapelle not only brought to a focus the differences among the Allies regarding the interpretation of the international order, but also the incompatibility of Castlereagh's intentions with what he could legitimize domestically. Castlereagh was in a difficult and tragic position. He had originated the conference system, but it proved beyond the comprehension of the Cabinet or the British people, to whom problems of *general* European repose meant a dangerous meddling in the affairs of other states. To Castlereagh, the Alliance was the expression of European unity; but to the British people and the Cabinet, an alliance had to be directed *against* someone and they could conceive of no enemy save France. This forced Castlereagh into a succession of ambiguities: what in his dealings with foreign powers he represented as the dictates of good faith, he made appear to the Cabinet as a reluctant surrender to foreign pressure. What he desired as the symbol of European harmony, could be legitimized in Britain only as a mechanism to control France. This became apparent as soon as the discussion turned to the authority under which to convene the Congress. The choice lay between the Fifth Article of the Treaty of Paris, which provided for a review of the Allied relations with France at the end of three years, or Article VI of the Quadruple Alliance, which had instituted the conference system for *general* problems of European repose. Castlereagh preferred to base the Congress on the

Quadruple Alliance, because this would have symbolized the new method of diplomatic relations. But the only European congress the Cabinet would even consider attending was one which would deal with French problems and was assembled under the obligations of the peace treaty.

To complicate matters further, there occurred a similar difference of opinion between Castlereagh and Metternich. For while Castlereagh's vision went far beyond that of the Cabinet, it did not go far enough for Metternich. Castlereagh was still sufficiently British to base the Alliance on no more than an identity of *political* interests. But the very pragmatism of this approach made it insufficient for Metternich, who sought a principle on which to organize Europe for the social struggle. He was not opposed in principle to the Russian scheme of a guarantee of the existing order, but he realized that a system of collective security justifies universal interference, as well as common defence; that it makes local conflicts impossible and reduces action to the level of the least enterprising member of a coalition. Metternich had no intention of giving Russia, the most restless power, a voice in every European concern or of making Austrian policy dependent on Alexander's consent. Castlereagh attempted to utilize the Congress to demonstrate "a new discovery in the European government, at once extinguishing the cobwebs with which diplomacy obscures the horizon, bringing the whole bearing of the system into its true light and giving to the counsels of the Great Powers the efficiency and almost the simplicity of a single state".[1] Metternich saw in the Congress an opportunity to teach a moral lesson to Europe, of the sanctity of treaties and also of the difference between the Tsar's pretensions and his ability to realize them. For this reason, he sided with the British Cabinet in their effort to base the Congress on the Treaty of Paris because he was above all concerned to prevent the Tsar from opening up the whole range of European problems. However different their motivation, Metternich and the British Cabinet carried the day, and the Congress of Aix-la-Chapelle met finally under the authority of Article V of the Treaty of Paris.

The instructions of Castlereagh and Metternich reflected this difference. The British instructions, largely drafted by Castlereagh but attuned to the sensibility of the Cabinet, dealt exclusively with the problem of France, as if Europe could be organized only *against* someone. They listed the issues under four headings: the withdrawal

[1] C.C. XII, p. 54, 20 October, 1818.

of the army of occupation; the pecuniary demands of the Allies; the problem of military precaution against France after the withdrawal of the army of occupation; and the diplomatic relations of the Allies towards France.[1] The first three headings presented few problems, since Wellington had already advocated the withdrawal of the army of occupation and since the French Chamber had voted the money to meet Allied pecuniary demands. A new system of military precaution after the evacuation of France was unnecessary, the instructions argued, because the Quadruple Alliance had been devised for precisely this contingency. Everything therefore depended on the Cabinet's interpretation of the Quadruple Alliance.

But the Cabinet's analysis revealed its reluctance to undertake Continental commitments. It did not object to treating either French aggression or a Bonapartist revolution as a cause of war. But it was far from happy about the clause providing for Allied consultation in case of a domestic upheaval other than Bonapartist. Castlereagh was instructed to undertake no new engagement on this point without the explicit authority of the Cabinet, lest Parliament interpret them as "menacing France with a systematic interference in her internal affairs which threatened her independence and compromised her dignity". And French membership in the Alliance was declared out of the question with the lame excuse that it "would place the King in an altogether false position towards his own people". To be sure, the Cabinet agreed to invite France to join the general deliberations under Article VI, but in a manner which only served to demonstrate that Britain could conceive of no other purpose for these meetings except the restraint of France: French participation in the conference system was justified exclusively as a means to consult the King in case of Allied measures against revolution in France and because, in any case, "*the Alliance is essentially founded on a French basis*". [My italics.]

If Castlereagh's instructions expressed the inability of an island power to consider foreign policy on any other terms than defensive, Metternich's programme, contained in a letter to the Emperor, reflected the quest of the Continental statesman for a moral symbol.[2] Where the Cabinet spoke only of France, Metternich, whose major concern was Russia, barely mentioned it. While Castlereagh defended the Congress as opening a new era of international relations, Metter-

[1] Webster, II, p. 134f.
[2] N.P. III, p. 139f.

nich defended it because it was provided for in the Peace of Paris and because it would therefore represent a symbol of the sanctity of treaty relations. Appropriately enough, Metternich's letter began with an analysis of Russian intentions: Alexander, torn between conflicting motives, was not likely to disturb the repose of Europe, if only because of his increasing religious mania. But while Alexander's religiosity made an aggressive policy unlikely, it nevertheless introduced an element of unrest because it involved an unending quest for moral and religious proselytes. "Therefore the many intrigues which confuse almost all the governments; therefore the flood of emissaries and apostles."

Metternich accordingly rejected the Russian arguments for a Congress on the model of that of Vienna. The gist of these arguments was that a meeting confined to the major powers would arouse the jealousy of the secondary states, and that the lack of concrete results might compromise the conference system altogether. No cause for jealousy existed, Metternich maintained, because the Congress would only deal with France and met in pursuance of existing treaty obligations. As for the danger of inactivity, "the most advantageous result of the Congress will be its failure to change the existing order of things; this result will be the greatest triumph for Your Majesty and all other Cabinets which since 1815 . . . have refused to cater to the mania for innovations. For that court, however, which has paid homage to the 'spirit of the times' at every opportunity, which raised the hopes of all reformers and sectarians by its *words*; this court will indeed be profoundly compromised, and precisely in the eyes of the reformers, *as long as everything remains unchanged*." Here was another illustration of Metternich's diplomacy, of his use of inaction as a weapon, and of a conference for its psychological impact: "Our calculations," Metternich concluded, "have so far carried the day and I do not doubt that this will also be true at Aix-la-Chapelle. . . . Much depended on the first step. We took it in time and have therefore avoided being compromised. . . . We have gained so much ground with the British and Prussian Cabinets that I do not anticipate any possible deviation from a deliberate conduct of our negotiations."

IV

Metternich was not to be disappointed. The Tsar's progress across

Europe was marked by his usual ambiguities: An address in Warsaw expressing the hope that Poland's liberal institutions might soon become the model of other European states was followed by protestations of his peaceful intentions as he made the rounds of the German courts. When he arrived at Aix-la-Chapelle, Alexander seemed motivated by the most conciliatory sentiments. He assured Castlereagh that he considered the Quadruple Alliance the key to European stability and insisted that its dissolution would represent a criminal act. There could be no question of French membership, even less of separate engagements with France as Metternich had feared. In this mood it was not difficult to settle the relationship of France to the Quadruple Alliance in a manner consistent with Castlereagh's instructions. On 2 October, it was agreed to withdraw the Allied troops from France. Ten days later it was decided to renew the Quadruple Alliance and not to allow France to become a member of it. In order to spare French sensibilities, this decision was to remain secret while a public protocol was to invite France to participate in the reunions under Article VI. So far the course of events seemed to have justified Castlereagh's faith in the efficacy of the conference system. "The review that has been taken of our existing engagements," he reported proudly, ". . . could not have been taken by the ordinary course of diplomatic intercourse . . . [but] placed as the Cabinets now are side by side to each other, misconceptions have been immediately obviated and a divergence of opinion is likely to be avoided."[1]

But it was soon to become apparent that the very rapidity of progress of the congress gave rise to illusions which mortgaged the future of the conference system. As the fear of France subsided and France was admitted to the concert of Powers, the period of a purely defensive policy came to an end. Common action henceforth would have to be based on the creation of a moral consensus and, as was to be expected, it was the Tsar who gave this realization its most extreme formulation. A Russian memorandum, dated 8 October, finally revealed the reason for the Tsar's exalted frame of mind, which Castlereagh had noticed at their first interview. For what emerged in a lengthy, philosophical disquisition was an appeal for a Treaty of Guarantee of both territories and domestic institutions.[2] The Quadruple Alliance, asserted the memorandum, was the political ex-

[1] Webster, II, p. 146.
[2] W.S.D. XII, p. 723f.

pression of a general alliance embodied in the treaties of peace and the Final Acts of Vienna. It was designed to deal with the twin problems of the post-war period, the fear of foreign aggression, and the threat of internal revolutions. To defeat these dangers, Alexander proposed nothing less than an affirmation that the existing treaties amounted to an *Alliance Solidaire* and that the Quadruple Alliance was charged with protecting Europe both against aggression and domestic upheaval. With tranquillity thus assured, the memorandum concluded ominously, social progress would be facilitated and greater liberties could be granted to the peoples.

This was a doctrine of general interference in the domestic concerns of all states superimposed on a system of collective security. Obviously Castlereagh could never agree to such an arrangement. Nor was Metternich, much as a guarantee of the existing order appealed to him, prepared to justify his policy by its suitability for social reform, or to let Alexander march his armies across Europe to combat the Tsar's conception of revolutionary danger. But although Castlereagh and Metternich were agreed in opposing the Tsar's scheme, they differed in their method of dealing with it, and this difference again indicated the schism behind the appearance of amity. Castlereagh rejected the *principle* on which the Russian memorandum was based as impractical and as a violation of the doctrine of non-interference; while Metternich, eager to keep his Russian option open, accepted the Tsar's principle but invoked Alexander's own creation, the Holy Alliance, to demonstrate that an *Alliance Solidaire* was unnecessary. For what was to be the first of many similar occurrences, Metternich induced the Tsar to forego a cherished project by convincing him that he did not really desire it.

Metternich's memorandum, dated 7 October, had been drafted in anticipation of the Russian proposal. It thus dealt ostensibly with the new political relations of Europe after the end of the occupation of France and not with the memorandum of the Tsar. Nevertheless its import was unmistakable. It began with a legalistic analysis of existing treaty relations: The Treaty of Chaumont still existed in full force because the lapsing of clauses contingent on the war with France could not affect the permanent provisions; while the Quadruple Alliance had been concluded for a period of twenty years, without any provision for its abrogation. French membership was therefore impossible, because the addition of a new member would transform the Alliance as fundamentally as the withdrawal of an original signatory. But these legalistic arguments were merely preliminary to an eloquent discussion of the moral problem, so dear to the heart of the Tsar. Since the Quadruple Alliance, argued Metternich, had reflected a fundamental principle of political morality and since the Allies could not accept a guarantee of their domestic structure from the country against which all their measures of security had heretofore been directed, a new alliance would have to confine itself to an enunciation of *general* principles. But this was not only unnecessary but even impious, given the existence of the Holy Alliance: "A transaction in general terms could only encroach upon the Holy Alliance, *which exists* [Metternich's italics] as well as on the Treaty of Chaumont, the instrumentalities most useful as well as worthy of the intentions of their august founders."[1]

The appeal to the Holy Alliance proved unanswerable. By exalting the moral contribution of Alexander, Metternich made it impossible for him to insist on the reformulation of the treaty structure. By keeping the prevailing order unchanged, he obtained a symbol of stability in a Europe clamouring for reform. As was his custom, Metternich let the brunt of the effort of frustrating the Tsar fall on others, and Castlereagh, under pressure domestically, was only too eager to enter the fray. In a strong memorandum, dated 20 October, he took issue with the Russian interpretation of existing treaties.[2]

While Metternich had accepted the principle of the Tsar's proposal but denied the need for it, Castlereagh rejected Alexander's conception of the international order out of hand. Far from representing an application of universal moral principles, the Quadruple Alliance was directed against specific dangers explicitly enumerated. The Conference system was not designed for superintending the government of Europe, but merely to interpret the provisions of existing treaties in the light of changing conditions. The *fact* of upheaval, domestic or otherwise, could never be made the cause of war. Rather, the Allies would have to consider from case to case whether a given change represented a sufficient threat to warrant intervention. "The problem of an universal Alliance for the peace and happiness of the world,"

[1] Hans Schmalz, *Versuch einer Gesamteuropäischen Organisation* 1815–20 (Berner Untersuchungen zur Allgemeinen Geschichte), p. 38f. See also N.P. III, p. 160f. for Metternich's distinction between the Quadruple Alliance and a General Alliance.

[2] Although the memorandum was designed to demonstrate Castlereagh's vigilance to the Cabinet and was not shown to the Tsar, similar, if less sharp, arguments were undoubtedly used during the negotiations.

concluded Castlereagh, "has always been one of speculation and hope, but it has never yet been reduced to practice, and if an opinion may be hazarded . . . it never can. The idea of an *Alliance Solidaire* . . . must be understood as morally implying the previous establishment of such a system of general government as may . . . enforce upon all nations an internal system of peace and justice. . . . Till then, a system of administrating Europe by a general alliance of its States can be reduced to some practical form, all notions of general and unqualified guarantee must be abandoned, and States must be left to rely for their security upon the justice and wisdom of their respective systems, aided by such support as other states may feel prepared to afford them. . . ."[1]

This was the issue between Great Britain and the Continent in its most fundamental form, and no amount of "good will" could obscure it: The British conception of international affairs was defensive: Britain could act co-operatively only in case of an overriding danger. But the policy of the Continental powers was precautionary; their crucial battle was the first, not the last; their effort was to prevent an overriding danger from materializing. Britain wanted to limit the scope of physical aggression, the Continental powers attempted to keep aggression from taking place at all. On the Continent, exactness of calculation, which appears as pettiness to an insular power, had to be substituted for physical isolation. The gap between the exaltation of the Tsar, the insistence on the widest attainable moral consensus of Metternich, and an insular mentality, could not be bridged by good intentions, nor by a European vision, however noble.

How well advised Castlereagh had been in refusing to entertain the Tsar's proposal was revealed in a dispatch by the Cabinet on 20 October. Before the news of the Tsar's proposal had even reached London, the Cabinet had taken alarm at the prospect that the Congress might end with a declaration announcing periodic meetings as a regular institution of European diplomacy. Nothing illustrates better the gulf separating Castlereagh from the Cabinet than their reaction of pained surprise at this interpretation of Article VI of the Quadruple Alliance, which in turn Castlereagh considered his proudest achievement. In its attempt to hedge its commitment as far as possible, in its sour-grape acceptance of the announcement of *another* meeting as long as a reference to periodic congresses was eliminated,

[1] Text, Webster, *Congress of Vienna*, p. 166f.

the dispatch made clear, once more, that the conception of a Europe organized by anything other than a common danger was simply beyond the scope of British mentality. To be sure, the difficulties of meeting a new Parliament of "doubtful affections" were given as a primary reason, but the real difficulty was more fundamental: "We approve [a general declaration] on this occasion, and with difficulty too, by assuring [the secondary powers] that we only intended to treat the simple subject of the evacuation; but in announcing to them a system of periodic meetings we must declare that they are to be confined to one . . . subject, or even . . . to one power, France, and no engagement to interfere in any manner in which the Law of Nations does not justify interference. . . ."[1] In fact, one faction in the Cabinet, led by Canning, objected to the *principle* of periodic meetings as contrary to the traditions of British policy, because it would involve Britain in all Continental quarrels, whereas "our true policy has always been not to interfere except in great emergencies and then with commanding force". Although the dispatch specifically denied that the Cabinet shared this opinion, nothing could obscure the fact that Britain participated in the conference system only because of the personal dominance of its Foreign Secretary and because the Cabinet could think of no honourable way of thwarting him.

By the time this dispatch arrived, the crisis, as so often before, had passed. Confronted by Castlereagh's intransigeance and Metternich's evasion, the Tsar had withdrawn his proposal for an *Alliance Solidaire*. Alexander insisted on salvaging something, however, if only a vague expression of the moral unity of Europe. Although Castlereagh was eager to attract as little attention as possible in order to smooth over his domestic difficulties, he was obliged to accept a declaration by which the Allies announced that France under its legitimate and constitutional ruler had given sufficient proofs of its peaceful intentions to join the conferences of the Quadruple Alliance. At the same time, the Allies reaffirmed the Quadruple Alliance in a secret protocol.[2] Despite some grumbling at the phrases *légitime et constitutionel*, the Cabinet accepted Castlereagh's assurance that they were merely part of the sacramental language of the Tsar and devoid of meaning.[3]

At this moment, just when the Congress seemed ready to conclude

[1] C.C. XII, p. 394.
[2] Documents in B.F.S.P. VI, pp. 11–19.
[3] C.C. XII, pp. 71, 75.

on a high note of harmony, there arose another dispute, which revealed once more that in the absence of more tangible guarantees the appearance of harmony does not suffice to reassure Continental nations. This time it was Prussia which sought safety in a system of collective security. Extending from the Vistula to beyond the Rhine, composed of two major parts separated by enclaves, Prussia was no little disquieted by Castlereagh's insistence that the Alliance required interpretation from case to case. She therefore proposed a Treaty of Guarantee, extending only to the territorial possessions of the major powers and including the Netherlands and the German Confederation. There could be no doubt about the Tsar's reaction to the prospect of realizing at least part of his favourite project. But even Metternich was tempted. Characteristically, he favoured the treaty not only because it would represent an admission of self-limitation by Russia, but, more importantly, as a means to reduce the influence of the military party, always hostile to Austria, within Prussia.[1] He consequently attempted to find a formula by which Britain could express its moral approval without undertaking the obligatory commitments of the treaty. But the difficulty of drafting so comprehensive a document proved insuperable and the Congress ended with the appearance of unity, as Castlereagh had desired, and with nothing changed, as Metternich had planned.

But behind the façade of harmony the incompatibility of the various motivations was becoming manifest. With France integrated into the concert of powers, the political contest was finally over and with it disappeared the only motive which could make British participation in Continental affairs acceptable domestically. As Britain increasingly hedged its commitments, a vicious circle was set in motion: the stronger Britain's isolationist tendencies, the more Metternich, aware of Austria's material weakness, came to rely on his most effective weapon of restraining the Tsar: the appeal to Alexander's moral fervour. But the more Metternich flattered the Tsar's exaltation, the more difficult it became for Castlereagh to engage in any joint action. As the Congress of Aix-la-Chapelle ended, both were eager to obscure this, however: Metternich because his bargaining position towards Russia depended on the illusion of his British option; Castlereagh because of his European vision, which he still hoped he could make prevail against the obtuseness of his Cabinet and the, to him, petty quest for safety of his Allies. Yet he must have

[1] N.P. III, p. 159.

sensed that the time for illusions was coming to an end. For at this moment Metternich engaged in an act which left little doubt that the next battle would be fought on a plane where Castlereagh, could not follow, whatever his personal sympathies. He submitted two memoranda to the King of Prussia advising him on the administrative structure of his state and urging the impossibility of fulfilling the promise, made during the passionate days of 1813, of granting a constitution to his subjects.[1] The precise arguments used by Metternich are less interesting than this first step which indicated Metternich's intention to function as the conservative conscience of Europe.

[1] N.P. III, p. 171f.

XIII

The Carlsbad Decrees and the Domination of Central Europe

I

METTERNICH'S major concern in the immediate post-war period was the construction of the strong Central Europe which he considered the condition of European stability and Austrian security. Because he was convinced that a powerful Austria was the key to Central Europe, domestic reorganization became his primary concern. In 1817, he submitted a plan for the reform of the Austrian governmental apparatus, involving the decentralization of administration and the appointment of four chancellors, one for each nationality.[1] It was an attempt to create an identity for a polyglot Empire through administrative excellence, not dissimilar to the parallel effort conducted successfully by Prussia in the north. But the Emperor had not fought Napoleon to begin the peacetime era with a programme of reform, and he saw no reason to alter fundamentally the system which had seen Austria through a revolutionary period. It was a symptom of Metternich's impotence domestically that he was reduced to an attempt to dominate Central Europe entirely by diplomatic means; by creating a political structure which would by its inner logic have to rely on Austrian support; by calling into being a multiplicity of sovereignties which would have a joint interest with Austria in frustrating the twin movement of nationalism and liberalism. To be sure, neither Germany nor Italy could remain immune to the current sweeping across Europe. But social unrest, as long as it did not get out of hand, actually favoured Metternich's design by discouraging the secondary powers from attempting solitary policies. In the immediate post-war period, Metternich was therefore less interested in suppressing than in localizing opposition, less in conducting an anti-revolutionary crusade than in preventing his

[1] N.P. III, p. 69f.

opponents from obtaining the support of a major power. Metternich's efforts were therefore still primarily political: to paralyse the two powers he considered revolutionary, Russia in Europe and Prussia in Germany.

This proved a relatively easy matter in Italy. Austria dominated Northern and Central Italy by virtue of its geographic position and the dependent dynasties in the secondary states. And it concluded a treaty with the Kingdom of Naples, which placed the Neapolitan army under Austrian control and by which the restored King undertook not to alter his domestic institutions without Austrian consent. When Metternich visited the Italian courts in 1817, he reported the existence of widespread Carbonari activity, fomented to a considerable extent by Russian agents. But he was confident of his ability to frustrate the revolutionary movement, in part by associating more Italians with the administration of Austria's Italian provinces, in part by giving the widest publicity to Russian activities, so that the Tsar would be forced either to disavow or to stop them.[1]

The situation in Germany was more complex. There Austria possessed neither a preponderant geographic position, nor did it have to deal merely with secondary powers. Located at the periphery of Germany, faced by a powerful Prussia, Austria could not hope to dominate Germany physically; and the twin currents of nationalism and liberalism threatened Austria's moral position. Throughout the passionate days of 1812, while Prussian patriots were dreaming of a reformed Germany and the Liberals were drawing up plans for a nationalist panacea, Metternich had therefore worked tortuously, tenaciously, and craftily to frustrate these aspirations. A unified Germany would have led to the exclusion of Austria from the source of its historical strength, for Austria, the polyglot Empire, could never be part of a structure legitimized by nationalism. A Germany of Parliamentary institutions, or even one based on linguistic unity, represented a constant challenge to a state built on the myth of the interdependence of historical structures. For this reason Metternich had procrastinated in 1813 until the Coalition was formed around a principle which could assure Austrian survival. The insistence on the sanctity of historical sovereigns guaranteed a Germany of a multiplicity of sovereignties, where the claims of the common nationality would be submerged in those of the dynasties, which could be

[1] N.P. III, p. 175f. (Metternich's final report regarding Italian conditions.)

governed only by agreement—the formal expression of a moral consensus—and not by dominion.

Metternich's German policy was therefore a gamble on the reality of moral connections. He had disdained reassuming the Imperial Crown for Austria because he wanted to base Austrian supremacy in Germany on the myth of equality. And he had permitted the shifting of Prussia's centre of gravity from Eastern Europe into Germany and that of Austria from Germany into South-eastern Europe, because he believed that Austria's moral position did not depend on a commensurate territorial base within Germany. In the protection of the dynasties against the popular will, in the guarantee of secondary states against claims of power, Metternich saw the moral strength of the Austrian position. A Prussia whose possessions were fragmented across the Confederacy and which could find security only in organizing Germany for defensive purposes could be counted on to provide the outside pressure which would cause the secondary states to look to Austria for support.

While the chief actors at Vienna had contended for the European equilibrium, a German committee composed of Austria, Prussia, Hanover, Bavaria, and Württemberg had attempted to call into being the German Federation so often and so ambiguously promised during the war. For while acts of state, such as the Treaties of Teplitz and Chaumont, had called for a Germany of many sovereignties, the Russo-Prussian Proclamation to the German people, which had announced the beginning of the War of Liberation, had promised a national constitution. But the Austrian constitutional goal could be simply defined: to create a structure which forced the people to act, if at all, through their dynasties and channelled national enthusiasm into the realm of cabinet diplomacy. Since the negotiations were conducted by the representatives of dynastic states, jealous of their sovereignty, the issue could not be in doubt. The result was the Act of Confederation, which established Germany as a confederacy composed of sovereign states. The German states abjured war among each other and promised to submit internal disputes to mediation. They created an assembly composed of representatives of the individual states, appointed by their governments, with the eleven major states each having one vote while the remainder were organized into six curies voting as units. Decisions were to be taken by a simple majority except for certain major questions such as war and peace which required a two-thirds majority. All that was left of the promised constitutional reform was a programmatic clause, Article XIII, which Metternich was soon to deprive of all meaning: "Each state will create a constitution based on assemblies."

No instrument better calculated to frustrate popular action could have been devised. The Assembly of the Confederation was composed of representatives not of the people, but of the governments. The disproportionate weight given to the vote of small states, the prohibition of war with each other which put a premium on factiousness, the requirement of unanimity for constitutional amendments, the presidency of Austria, all emphasized that action was obtainable only by *influence* and not by *power*. And the necessities of their situation made the secondary states look to Austria for protection both against domestic revolution and against Prussian predominance. So it came about that fear of the national mission of Prussia became the unifying element within the German Confederation under Austria's tutelage; that the national structure for which so many patriots had hoped was held together primarily by anti-nationalist motives. But Metternich's problem was more complex than simply isolating Prussia. A dissatisfied Prussia, in rebellion against the fetters of the Confederation, might become the spokesman of the national movement and transform the vague unrest from a nuisance into a conflagration. To dominate Germany through a moral consensus of the secondary powers and *with* Prussian support, might be considered incompatible efforts. But they were the core of Metternich's German policy.

Metternich was aided by the difficult position into which the Vienna settlement had placed Prussia and by the indecisiveness of Prussian policy which never could opt between its basic alternatives: between security on a national basis by unifying Germany or on a Cabinet basis through friendship with Austria. Sprawled across Central Europe, with arbitrary and indefensible frontiers, afraid of French designs on the Rhineland and Russian ambitions on Poland, it was natural that Prussia sought security in a militarily strong Confederation. But an aggressive German policy was certain to frighten the secondary powers, jealous of their sovereignty. On the other hand, Prussia thought Austrian support indispensable in any war with Russia or France, and this in turn was incompatible with an effort to strengthen the Confederation.

Not for fifty years was Prussia to solve her dilemma: that the most exposed European power had at the same time the most indefensible frontiers. In the immediate post-war period, however, it led to a half-hearted groping to correct the mistakes of the Vienna settlement, without a very clear conception in what precise direction; an uncertain striving for a powerful German position without any exact idea of its preconditions. The bane of Prussian diplomacy throughout the War of Liberation, the attempt to combine the advantages of all policies, again asserted itself. While seeking a formal recognition of parity with Austria within the Confederation, Prussia tried to insure Austrian co-operation *vis-à-vis* France and Russia. While conducting an extra-German policy conditional on Austrian friendship, it carried out an intra-German policy achievable only by neutralizing Austria.

Such inconsistencies were fatal with an opponent of Metternich's subtlety; whose subtlety, in fact, consisted precisely in obscuring the fact of his opposition. The more erratic Prussia's measures, the stronger became Austria's moral position. The more insistent Prussia, the more Austria could withdraw to the ground of existing treaty obligations. Prussia was thus cast in the unenviable position of demonstrating to the secondary powers the validity of Austria's moral claims. Nothing sums up Metternich's German policy better than his first instructions to his representative at the Assembly at Frankfurt, Buol, who according to the Acts of the Confederation was to function as presiding officer. After urging Buol not to emphasize this title, Metternich continued: "It is more important to eliminate the claims of others than to press our own. . . . It will be your task to utilize the Presidency conferred by the Act of Confederation as advantageously as possible for [our] interests, without [however] attracting attention which might excite distrust . . . and to confound the ambiguous designs of other confederates through a certain correctness in the conduct of your office. With such a demeanour it is to be expected that most of the [German states] will feel themselves attracted by our reticence and that they will not only accept our advice, but actively seek it. . . . We will obtain much in proportion as we ask little."[1]

In such a situation Prussia was frustrated wherever it turned. When the Prussian representative in Frankfurt proposed that Austria and Prussia share the direction of the Assembly and the military control of Germany, he merely furnished Metternich a means to

[1] Stern, Alfred, *Geschichte Europas seit den Vertraegen von* 1815 *bis zum Frankfurter Frieden von* 1871, 10 Vols. (Munich-Berlin, 1913–24). Vol. I, p. 298.

exhibit Austrian predominance. The proposal was secretly communicated to the other German courts, while Metternich replied that Austro-Prussian friendship was so firm that it required no formal treaty and that, in any case, overt co-operation would only unite the secondary powers against them. In order to cover its retreat, Prussia had no choice but to recall its representative. When Prussia demanded numerical parity with Austria in the army of the Confederation, Metternich, with fine indirection, ordered the Austrian delegate to vote with Prussia, secure in the knowledge that the secondary states would defeat the proposal.[1] And when the King of Prussia asked to have his Polish provinces included in the Confederation, Metternich used this confession of weakness to demonstrate Austria's indispensability. He first induced the Prussian King to withdraw his proposal, by convincing him that it would only antagonize the Tsar without any prospect of approval by the secondary powers, and he then offered a secret Austro-Prussian defensive alliance as a substitute.[2] The exchange symbolized the basis of Metternich's German policy: he proposed to control the secondary German states through their fear of Prussia and Prussia through its fear of France and Russia.

In this manner, the German Confederation, launched with such high hopes, increasingly became a means to give the widest moral base to Austrian policy. The Assembly was transformed into a meeting of diplomats and its impotence emphasized by Metternich's insistence that the Austrian representative delay his vote until the arrival of instructions. Article XIII of the Acts of Confederation, which had promised each state a constitution based on assemblies, was interpreted by Metternich as programmatic, as a symbol of good faith whose execution was left to the wisdom of each government. Austria's predominance was emphasized not only by the presidency of its representative, but by the meeting-place of the Assembly which was the Austrian Embassy and by the seal of the Confederation which, until 1848, was the Austrian seal. Prussia could have broken this stranglehold only by a national policy based on an alliance with the patriotic societies and the liberal movement. But, although this was favoured by a few, the King and his advisers were even more afraid of revolution than of foreign attack. No wonder that the hopes raised to such heights during the war gave place to a corresponding

[1] Stern, I, p. 530.
[2] Stern, I, p. 633 (Appendix).

bitterness; that the younger generation, above all, felt cheated of its national aspirations and that the universities, in many respects the most truly national institutions, should become the focal point of protest. But protest was of no avail in the face of Austria's domination of the machinery of the Confederation. And the hopes placed on the Tsar were no less doomed to disappointment. It became increasingly apparent that his vague generalities were more likely to become a force for repression than a crusade for liberty. Metternich only gave another proof of his power of diagnosis, if not of his creativity, by his statement prior to the Congress of Aix-la-Chapelle that the Tsar's moral position would be shattered if everything remained unchanged.

Thus, by the end of 1818, Metternich had achieved a stable Central Europe and Austria was its key. But the rumblings were not to be stilled, nor was the social struggle to be avoided simply by exhibiting a monolithic unity. It was expressive of the feeling of frustration within Germany, and also of the disenchantment with the Tsar, that the first overt revolutionary act was the assassination of a Russian publicist, who had distinguished himself by his monarchical writings, and that it should be carried out by a demented student from the University of Jena. The assassination of Kotzebue marked the end of Metternich's effort to organize Central Europe entirely by political measures. Henceforth he would use policy primarily as a means to obtain a moral base for social repression, in a never-ending quest for the moment of order which would signal the end of the revolutionary wave and the survival of the Central Empire.

II

Metternich learned of Kotzebue's assassination in Rome, while accompanying the Emperor on a tour of the Italian courts. He was informed through a series of hysterical letters by his associate and publicist Gentz, who was not free from the fear that Kotzebue's fate might be in store for him as well. Gentz urged immediate repressive steps and Austrian leadership of an anti-revolutionary crusade, by-passing the Confederation. But Metternich was too sober to conduct policy in the mood of a moment of hysteria. He saw in Kotzebue's murder not so much a challenge but an opportunity to teach the minor German courts the wisdom of Austrian homilies. True to his unfailing tactic, he therefore set about to hedge his risks by utilizing the panic in Germany to have Austria offered her objectives by the other courts, to demonstrate Austria's indispensability by a policy of aloofness. For the situation seemed precisely designed to vindicate all of Metternich's preaching over the past three years. Alone of the major German powers, Austria appeared immune to the revolutionary danger. No patriotic societies disturbed the tranquillity of Austrian universities, nor was its press an organ of anti-governmental propaganda. If this was more a tribute to the excellence of Austria's police than to its moral homogeneity, it nevertheless furnished a useful basis from which to operate.

There began again one of Metternich's periods of maddening inactivity, designed to force his potential allies into revealing the extent of their commitment. Metternich was quite prepared to head an anti-revolutionary crusade, but he wanted to be sure to involve the maximum number of other powers, and Prussia above all. He was more than willing to by-pass the Confederation, if only to demonstrate that important problems could be solved better on the basis of pure cabinet diplomacy than by a national organ, however attenuated. He wanted to do this, however, not as an act of Austrian self-will, but by demonstrating the impotence of the Confederation so that the other courts would realize "spontaneously" that Austrian assistance was their only protection. For anyone familiar with Metternich's diplomacy it is not surprising, therefore, that he opened his diplomatic campaign—by doing nothing. He returned a very non-committal reply to Gentz, which in its tone of abstracted indifference was designed to make evident his mastery of the situation. He devoted one paragraph to Kotzebue's murder, which he ascribed to a national conspiracy, and several pages to reflections on the architectural marvels of Rome, and to the relationship between scale, beauty, and spirituality.[1] Gentz, who could barely restrain his hysteria, suggested in reply that the real problem was not to repress a national conspiracy but to reform the system of university education which had produced it, and he enclosed a letter by an Austrian consul in Saxony which blamed the whole turmoil on the Reformation. But, once again his ardour was cooled by Metternich, who was convinced that maximum measures were certain to be advanced in other quarters if Gentz's letters were an even approximate reflection of the spirit among the German powers. He showed his unconcern by leaving for Naples, one stage further removed from

[1] N.P. III, p. 227f.

the seat of the turmoil, and replied that educational reform should be confined to the system of academic discipline. "As for the Reformation," he wrote acidly, "I cannot deal with Dr. Martin Luther from the Quirinal and I hope that it will prove possible to do some good without uprooting Protestantism at its very core."[1]

In the meantime, the other German governments were becoming panicky. The King of Prussia instituted a commission to investigate revolutionary tendencies and immediately recalled all Prussian students from Jena, an example followed by many other courts. So powerful was this trend that the Grand-Duke of Weimar, who had distinguished himself by his liberalism, but who had the misfortune that the offending university was located in his territory, proposed that the Assembly of the Confederation develop a uniform system of academic discipline for all of Germany. It did not matter that the unfortunate Duke protested his devotion to academic freedom and to his constitution, one more opponent of Metternich had been lured into a precipitate act. If even the liberal Grand-Duke of Weimar admitted the need for the reform of universities, who could blame the Austrian minister for following suit? And if the Assembly proved incapable of dealing with this urgent matter, was not Metternich merely expressing the consensus of Germany if he proposed an alternative procedure? Over the protests of the doctrinaire Gentz, Metternich therefore ordered the Austrian representative to go along with the Grand-Duke's proposal. "There is no point in treating this arch-Jacobin (the Grand-Duke) with contempt," he explained to Gentz. "He is used to that. It seems much wiser to interpret his designs favourably, to trap him on his own ground or to expose him as a liar."[2] It soon became apparent that the Assembly was not the proper organ for decisive action, as Metternich, who had designed it, well knew. While the Grand-Duke's proposal languished in committee, the hysteria of the German governments, which saw assassins lurking everywhere, hardly knew any bounds. With the Confederation discredited and Austrian indispensability sufficiently demonstrated, the moment for action had arrived. "There is no more time to be lost," wrote Metternich now. "Today the governments are afraid enough to act; soon their fear will have reached the stage of paralysis."

[1] N.P. III, p. 234f.
[2] N.P. III, p. 243f.

On 17 June, more than two months after he had learned of Kotzebue's assassination and while he was finally on the way north, Metternich transmitted a plan of action to Gentz.[1] He was going to Carlsbad for a rest, and he had arranged for the ministers of the German power to meet him there. His proposals to his colleagues would be based on the axioms that moral dangers could prove more dissolving than physical threats, that the common nationality made the isolation of even the most unimportant German state chimerical, and that only concerted and preventive measures could stem the revolutionary tide. The extent of the danger was sufficiently demonstrated by the fact that conspiracy had found a violent expression in Germany, the one country where it was traditionally confined to the pen. For this he blamed above all the universities and the license of the press. Only a tightened academic discipline and a system of censorship could reverse the trend. Little wonder that Gentz replied jubilantly: "My dark forebodings seem to evaporate when I see the one man in Germany, capable of free and decisive action, scale such heights. . . ."[2]

But Metternich wanted to leave nothing to chance. Although there was no real danger that Prussia would pursue a revolutionary policy, it was by no means certain how far she would go in supporting repressive measures. Nor did Metternich want to be placed in the position of imposing his will on the secondary powers. A repressive programme identified with Austria might strengthen Prussia, the state which so many patriots still considered as the exponent of a national mission. But by the same token, a repressive programme advanced by Prussia would undermine her last remaining advantage: the ability to appeal to the national movement. When Metternich visited the King of Prussia on 28 July at Teplitz, he therefore had two objectives: to develop a common programme for the Carlsbad conferences in order to separate Prussia from German nationalism; and to keep the King from implementing his promise to grant a constitution in order to paralyse the efforts of certain Prussian statesmen, such as Humboldt, to ally Prussia with German liberalism.

There ensued a strange and wonderful dialogue between Metternich and the Prussian king, in which Metternich, like a stern teacher, remonstrated about Prussia's sins, while the King, thoroughly

[1] N.P. III, p. 250f.
[2] N.P. III, p. 256.

chastened, desperately attempted to shift the blame on to his own ministers.[1] For to the panicky King, Metternich appeared on the scene as a prophet and a saviour. Had he not warned innumerable times, not least at Aix-la-Chapelle, against the dangers of a constitution? Had he not predicted the revolutionary danger? "Everything you foresaw has occurred," said the crestfallen King. But Metternich was severe. The revolution, he asserted, had merely been the demonstration which always follows the lesson. Its origin had been in Prussia, while Austria itself remained unaffected. Nevertheless, animated by its policy of friendship, Austria was willing to assist in stemming the revolutionary tide, but it would first have to determine which governments deserved that name. Should they be found wanting and indecisive, Austria would simply withdraw into its shell. Terrified by the prospect of being left alone in Germany with the Revolution, the King now blamed the associates of his Chancellor Hardenberg. In order to rectify his errors, and to demonstrate his good intentions, he suggested that Metternich, the minister of the power which had most to lose from a national policy, advise Hardenberg, the Chancellor of the state which had most to gain from it, on the constitutional structure suitable for Prussia. Metternich replied with a memorandum which explained that the promise of an assembly in Article XIII of the Act of Confederation did not necessarily imply representative institutions and to this, too, the Prussian King agreed. What could better illustrate Metternich's dominance than the King's plaintive advice as Metternich prepared to negotiate with the Prussian ministers: "Try, above all, to commit these people [the Prussian ministers] in writing"? Well might Metternich report triumphantly to his Emperor: "I found two negative elements engaged in a contest: the weakness of the King with the impotence of the Chancellor. . . . I conceived it my task so to strengthen the most active element in the King's soul, that tending towards paralysis, that he will hardly dare to take the boldest of all steps, that of introducing a constitution."[2]

The result was the Convention of Teplitz by which Austria and Prussia agreed on a common programme. Two conferences were to be held: in Carlsbad and in Vienna. The Carlsbad conference would deal with the immediate dangers and consider steps to restrain freedom of the press, to regulate the universities and to establish a Central Commission to investigate the revolutionary movement.

[1] N.P. III, p. 258f.; Stern, I, p. 568.
[2] N.P. III, p. 264f.

The conference in Vienna would deal with the organic institutions of the Confederation, particularly the interpretation of Article XIII. In addition, Hardenberg promised that no constitution would be introduced in Prussia until complete order was restored and then only with assemblies in the "literal", that is the Metternich, sense of deputations of provincial Estates.[1] In short, Austria's domestic legitimization had become the organizing principle of Germany.

With the ground thus carefully prepared the result of the Carlsbad Conference, which opened on 6 August, could not be in doubt. Its tone was set by the representative of Nassau, who expressed his warmest gratitude to Austria which "itself unaffected by the revolutionary current, has conceived the measures to arrest it". The Austro-Prussian proposals were accepted in their entirety. Each state undertook to submit publications of less than twenty pages to censorship and to suppress those found objectionable by any member of the Confederation. Thus every state, and Austria above all, had a complete veto over all publications within the territory of the Confederation. The universities were placed under the supervision of the governments by appointing a representative in each, charged with enforcing discipline and surveilling the spirit of the lectures. And a Central Commission with Headquarters in Mainz was to investigate revolutionary activities. So strong was Metternich's position that he could afford to appear as the advocate of moderation. It was Prussia which insisted on setting the number of pages subject to censorship at twenty, while Metternich would have been satisfied with fifteen. And when Prussia proposed the establishment of a special court not only to investigate but to try revolutionaries, Metternich insisted on the impossibility of trying individuals on the basis of ex-post-facto laws.[2]

Metternich had succeeded in a *tour de force*: Austria, the most vulnerable state, appeared as the repository of strength; the power which had most to gain from the Carlsbad decrees emerged as the most disinterested party. The deferential address with which the assembled diplomats thanked Metternich for having been permitted to do his bidding showed that conquest need not always take the form of arms: "If we may hope that this task, as difficult as it is honourable, for which you have assembled us, has been concluded in a manner not unacceptable to you, then we owe it to your . . . wise

[1] Stern, I, p. 573.
[2] N.P. III, p. 270f.; Stern, I, p. 577f.

leadership. . . . When, while still on the other side of the Alps, you heard the clamour of undisciplined scribes and the news of a monstrous crime, . . . you recognized the real cause of the evil . . . and that which we have accomplished here is no more than what you already conceived then."[1] The opprobrium heaped by posterity on Metternich's self-satisfied letters overlooked that much of the time they merely reflected the reality of extraordinary situations. So this missive from Carlsbad: "For the first time [in thirty years] there will appear a group of measures, anti-revolutionary, correct and peremptory. That which I have wanted to do since 1813 and which this terrible Emperor Alexander has always spoiled, I have accomplished now, because he was not present. . . . If the Emperor of Austria doubts that he is Emperor of Germany, he is mistaken." It was a paradoxical situation, dear to the whimsical streak in Metternich, that by giving up the Imperial Crown, Franz had become Emperor of Germany.

In this manner the Carlsbad Conferences ended with a spontaneous affirmation of Austrian predominance. Metternich was in effect the Prime Minister of Germany while protesting his disinterest. Prussia, with its own eager acquiescence, was diverted into a direction which kept it for over a generation from identifying itself with the national current; its more liberal ministers, such as Humboldt, were soon forced from office. And the German Confederation was reduced to a meeting place of subsidiary diplomats, while the really fundamental decisions were taken by direct negotiations among the Cabinets. The only organ which represented all of Germany had become a ratifying instrument. On 20 September, it approved unanimously and without debate the decisions taken at Carlsbad. So ended, for the time being, the dream of a unified Germany.

III

But Metternich's victory was not complete if what he called the revolutionary movement obtained foreign support. Should the foreign powers refuse to sanction the Carlsbad decrees, Austria would be put on the defensive not only within Germany but all over Europe. And as the Vienna conferences approached, the South German courts, particularly Württemberg, were becoming restive under the Austro-Prussian tutelage. Metternich, therefore, invited

[1] N.P. III, p. 284.

Britain and Russia to approve the Carlsbad decrees.[1] But this only brought to a head the difficulty of Castlereagh's position. It was impossible for any British statesman to express approval of a policy of domestic repression, however much he might sympathize with it. Nor could he countenance what was in effect a doctrine of general interference in the domestic affairs of other states. Despite his personal good will, Castlereagh had to confine himself to this reply to the Austrian ambassador: "We are always glad to see evil germs destroyed without the power to give our approval openly."[2]

Russia proved even more difficult. Capo d'Istria represented to the Tsar the danger of Austrian domination of Germany and did not fail to point out that the chief opponent of Alexander's *Alliance Solidaire* was now applying its maxims to his own advantage. The result was a Russian circular-note, testy and non-committal, which stated that if the Carlsbad decrees concerned German matters, Russia was not entitled to interfere, while if it was a European affair, Russia should have been invited to Carlsbad.[3] On 4 December, Capo d'Istria even sounded out Castlereagh regarding the possibility of a joint representation to the Vienna conference.

But if Castlereagh was unable to sanction Metternich's policy, he could at least prevent the Tsar from using it as an excuse to exploit the difficulties of Central Europe for Russian ends. If the principle of non-interference was a doctrine of self-limitation for Britain, it could also be used as a shield behind which Metternich could organize Central Europe. Castlereagh therefore returned a very skilful reply to the Russian proposition.[4] He admitted that the Acts of the Confederation were part of the Vienna settlement, and that foreign powers had the right to protest against their violation. But he denied that the Carlsbad decrees were anything other than a legitimate effort to insure domestic tranquillity, a goal he was certain Russia approved. Britain had not officially replied to the notification of the Carlsbad decrees, precisely because to give an opinion would have been to interfere in the domestic affairs of Germany. At the same time, Castlereagh sent a dispatch to his ambassador in Berlin making clear that Britain could do no more and that the German powers should not prolong the dispute: "Our

[1] N.P. III, p. 285.
[2] Webster, II, p. 192.
[3] Stern, I, p. 595.
[4] C.C. XII, p. 178f., 14 January, 1820.

Allies must recollect that we have a Parliament to meet and it is essential . . . not to have angry discussions on continental politics. . . ."[1]

The Carlsbad decrees marked the turning-point in European politics, the marginal case of Austro-British co-operation, the borderline where the doctrine of non-interference could be used to localize a social struggle. Because Austria was strong enough to defeat the revolution within Germany without the aid of non-German powers, the difference between Castlereagh and Metternich could still be obscured by utilizing *political* weapons to frustrate Russian intervention. On negative measures, on creating a framework of inaction, Metternich and Castlereagh were still agreed. But it was obvious that as soon as the social struggle took on a wider scope, a doctrine of inaction would not satisfy Metternich. Just as he had involved Prussia in his German policy, he was certain to attempt to involve Russia in his European efforts. This became all the more important as the experience of the Carlsbad decrees had shown that Russian approval might not be obtainable retroactively. The crucial test of Allied unity must come when the contest became explicitly social and on a European scale. And as the year 1820 progressed, revolutions breaking out in the most different parts of Europe announced that Alliances, no more than human beings, can live on the memory of the past and that the meaning of unity would have to be redefined in the light of the present.

[1] C.C. XII, p. 175, 15 January, 1820.

XIV

The Congress of Troppau and the Organization of Europe

I

By the end of 1819, Metternich had constructed one of his intricate combinations which obscured Austria's weakness by exploiting the legitimizing principles recognized by the various powers as a means to connect them to Austria. He had used the Quadruple Alliance as a bridge to Great Britain in order to be able to defeat Russian influence by political means. And he had appealed to the Holy Alliance in his relations to the Tsar in order to keep open the possibility of falling back on Russian support, should the social struggle get out of hand. Germany had been pacified with the assistance of Prussia and the German Confederation turned into an extension of Austrian policy with the eager acquiescence of the secondary powers, indeed at their request. The Vienna conferences had ended with a new definition of Article XIII, which was again so vague as to be meaningless and resolved itself into the truistic phrase that the promise of assemblies could not affect the sovereignty of the Princes. Italy was quiet.

All this had been achieved without opening unbridgeable schisms. Austria's central position had been transformed into a diplomatic asset by seeing to it that the differences of the major powers among each other were greater than their respective differences with Austria, so that in every international crisis Austria emerged as the pivotal state. Castlereagh considered Metternich the most "reasonable" of Continental statesmen, a little timid perhaps, but still the easiest to deal with, the most moderate, the least abstract. Alexander considered Metternich the most ideological of European statesmen, not quite ready, to be sure, to follow him to the heights, but still the only one capable of understanding the exalted flights of his imagination. And in foreign affairs Prussia was an Austrian satellite.

Metternich's policy thus depended on its ability to avoid major crises which would force an unequivocal commitment and on its capacity to create the illusion of intimacy with all major powers. It was finely spun, with sensitive feelers in all directions and so intricate that it obscured the fact that none of the fundamental problems had really been settled. For Alexander still clung to his idea of the *Alliance Solidaire* and its generalized right of interference, while Castlereagh was adamant in his insistence on the exclusively political purpose of the Alliance and the doctrine of non-interference. Only a dual illusion kept this conflict of conceptions from becoming apparent: while the Tsar had surrendered to Metternich's argument that the *Alliance Solidaire already existed*, Castlereagh believed that he had laid its ghost with his own interpretation of the treaty-structure at Aix-la-Chapelle. Because Alexander refrained from pressing his claims which he thought recognized *in principle*, Castlereagh was given no opportunity to make the schism within the Alliance explicit. But this illusion could be maintained only as long as no general problem occupied the attention of the Allies. As soon as a major power attempted to invoke the Alliance, it would become apparent that the differences of Aix-la-Chapelle still existed, that Allied unity was disintegrating because no agreement could be reached either on the nature or on the extent of the danger.

The year 1820 opened with the first of a number of upheavals which were fundamentally to transform international relationships. In January, a revolt broke out in Cadiz, Spain, among troops destined for duty in the rebellious South American colonies. Although it seemed unimportant at first, it soon spread, and by 7 March, the King felt obliged to proclaim the ultra-liberal Constitution of 1812. Here then was an accomplished revolution, not an isolated plot as in Germany; an overthrow of the existing order certain to lead to an attempt on the part of Russia to implement its interpretation of the Alliance. As early as 15 January, before he even knew of the events in Spain, Capo d'Istria had issued a circular dispatch which compared the new system of diplomacy founded on the exalted maxims of the Alliance with the old canons of selfishness and called on the monarchs to put their principles into practice.[1] No wonder that Capo d'Istria greeted the Spanish revolution almost as a godsend, as the final vindication of his point of view. He told the Austrian ambassador that, ever since the end of the occupation of France, the Alliance had been without the objective which alone

[1] Schwarz, p. 178f.

could give it unity. At a later interview, he argued, somewhat contradictorily, that the Quadruple Alliance had been superseded by the declaration of Aix-la-Chapelle, which he interpreted as a guarantee of the existing territorial arrangements and domestic institutions.[1] It was not surprising that a Russian note of 3 March invited the Allies to discuss common steps against Spain.

But Castlereagh's reaction could no longer be in doubt. Britain, which had been an ally of Spain for over a decade, would not permit France to intervene as the agent of the Quadruple Alliance, thus to achieve with the sanction of Europe what had eluded a conquering Napoleon. And the alternative that Russian troops might march across Europe to Spain was no more acceptable. Castlereagh therefore returned a very sharp reply, which drew a distinction between constitutional and autocratic states and once more affirmed the British view of the Alliance: "The alliance was made against France. It never was intended . . . as a union for the government of the world or for the superintendence of the affairs of other states." To be sure, it had been designed to guard Europe against the "revolutionary power"; but only against its military character, not against its principles. In any case, the difference in domestic structures between the constitutional states of the West and the autocratic Eastern powers made common action feasible only in case of an overriding danger.[2] Thus nothing that had happened since Aix-la-Chapelle had altered the fundamental difference which derived from a disagreement about the nature of the danger: the Continental statesmen, however they might differ in their choice of remedies, considered social unrest as the primary threat and attempted to deal with it as an international problem. But Castlereagh recognized only political threats, expressed in overt acts of aggression, and even then limited the British commitment to combating attacks on the European equilibrium.

This divergence was due less to a difference in constitutional principles, as Castlereagh believed, than to a difference in historical development and, above all, to the fact that in Great Britain the creation of the national state had been consummated. On the Continent, liberalism fought under the banners of the principles of the French Revolution, and doctrinal agreement superseded political

[1] Schmalz, p. 52f.

[2] Webster, II, p. 238f. Text, Harold Temperley and Lillian Penson, *Foundations of British Foreign Policy* (Cambridge, 1938), p. 48f.

loyalty. In Great Britain, where the French Revolution was identified with Napoleon, liberalism appeared as an indigenous growth in the shape of a utilitarian political economy. Attacks on the existing order, sometimes violent, occurred; but because the feeling of national cohesion superseded any domestic differences, they were considered internal problems by both the government and the reformers. On the Continent, a revolution had a *symbolic* significance as the application of universal principles. But for Great Britain, which denied the universality of these claims, a revolution had only a *practical* significance, whether it constituted a physical threat. On the Continent, where the twin movements of nationalism and liberalism could achieve their objectives only by the overthrow of the international order, both repression and reform were international problems to be dealt with by the maxims of foreign policy. In Great Britain, where the quest for reform was considered an internal problem, repression and reform remained in the sphere of domestic policy. When Castlereagh spoke of an overriding danger, he meant an attempt to achieve universal dominion. When Metternich invoked an overriding danger, he was referring to social upheaval. No amount of good intentions could bridge this gap in historical situations, which only Metternich's distrust of Russian intentions had hitherto obscured.

But the exchange between Castlereagh and Capo d'Istria placed Metternich in a difficult position. He was no more interested than Castlereagh in granting the Tsar the right to march his troops across Europe, yet he did not want to cause one of Alexander's sudden shifts of mood which might give the revolutionaries the support of a major power. He was aware of Britain's sensitivity with regard to Spain, but he also wished to take account of the Tsar's moral sensibilities. In short, he leaned towards Castlereagh's policy but towards Alexander's maxims. The result was the same compromise as at Aix-la-Chapelle; an agreement to the principle of Alexander's proposal, but a refusal of joint action because of its impracticability. And, as at Aix-la-Chapelle, Metternich utilized Castlereagh's intransigeance to demonstrate his moderation and goodwill. A conference which Britain refused to attend, he argued, would actually encourage the revolutionaries, and, in any case, foreign intervention would prove effective only against revolutions of localized importance.[1] But at the same time, Metternich attempted to turn the Tsar's frame of mind to

[1] Stern, II, p. 120.

his own account by proposing a point of moral contact in the form of an ambassadorial conference at Vienna, which he was certain to dominate. When Castlereagh rejected even this attempt to flatter the Russian craving for a symbol of solidarity, Metternich retreated to a proposal to send joint "Eventual Instructions" to the Allied ambassadors in Paris for the contingency of the death of Louis XVIII.[1] But to Castlereagh all these moves were merely short-sighted efforts to use the Alliance for selfish ends. "Eventual Instructions" were against every principle of an empirical foreign policy which dealt with dangers only as they arose. The Tsar had, therefore, to be satisfied with a joint step confined to Austria, Prussia, and Russia.

Nevertheless, an open break had been averted. For the final time Metternich was able to combine the principle of social solidarity with the doctrine of non-interference; to support Britain while demonstrating his loyalty to the Tsar. But on 2 July, an event occurred which put an end to all illusions. On that date, a revolution broke out in Naples, which led to the proclamation of the "Spanish constitution". Metternich could no longer avoid fighting his contest on a European scale.

II

Metternich could have no doubts about the seriousness of the new upheaval. This was not the act of a demented fanatic, as the assassination of Kotzebue; nor did it occur at the periphery of Europe in a country under British protection, as the revolution in Spain. Naples was the largest Italian state, tied to Austria by a treaty which prohibited it to change its institutions without consultation. Nor was the danger of this revolution merely its symbolic significance. For the first time the national and liberal movements joined hands, threatening one of the pillars of Metternich's policy: Austria's predominance in Italy. It was clear that he would not surrender it without a struggle.

To Castlereagh, contemplating events from behind the English Channel, the solution seemed obvious: since the revolution in Naples threatened Austria above all, it was up to Austria to defeat it. If military intervention became necessary, it should be based on the right of self-defence, not on a generalized right of intervention. He therefore spoke to the Austrian ambassador of the "very delicate and

[1] Webster, II, p. 211; Schwartz, p. 186.

honourable task" which lay before Austria, which Britain could approve but never join, and he urged a unilateral Austrian action against Naples.

But nothing in the complex policy of the Austrian minister ever worked so simply. To commit the main part of the Austrian strength in Italy, while leaving the Tsar free to pursue his own objects in Northern Europe, perhaps to appear as the apostle of nationalism; to fight the Neapolitan Bourbons without preventing their French cousins from restoring their position in Italy by appearing as their protectors, such a course would have been against every principle of Metternich's policy, always concerned with husbanding Austria's resources and fighting its battles with the widest moral and material base. But a joint action of the Continental powers might cause Britain to withdraw from the Alliance and leave Austria dependent on the goodwill of the Tsar. To complicate matters further, Austria had less than twenty thousand troops in Italy, and nothing could be done until they were reinforced. In the meantime, Metternich left no doubt about his determination. A circular note to the Italian courts declared that Austria meant to protect the tranquillity of Italy by force of arms if necessary. And a similar note to the German courts urged a policy of discipline while Austria was engaged in Italy.[1]

The reply of several Italian courts made the precariousness of Austria's Italian position evident. The Grand Duke of Toscana denied the necessity for Austrian assistance, while Consalvi, the Papal Secretary of State, expressed the fear that Austrian intransigeance might provoke a Neapolitan attack. And, on 9 August, a French note to the major powers placed the extent of Metternich's difficulties into sharp focus. It agreed to Austrian intervention in Naples but only for technical reasons, because Austria's geographical position made it the most suitable agent of a *European* action.[2] The revolutionary tide in Italy, the French note argued, could not be arrested except by a conference of the five major powers, because physical force without moral backing would only aggravate the evil. And it concluded with an ominous warning that a unilateral Austrian action might cause the Italian states to appeal to France, their traditional protector, which would find itself, albeit against its will, at the head of a constitutional movement.

[1] Stern, II, p. 121; N.P. III, p. 382.
[2] Schmalz, p. 61f.

In these circumstances, Metternich had no intention of rushing headlong into isolated action. British friendship was valuable, but British displeasure was less dangerous than that of Russia. A British withdrawal from the alliance would deprive Austrian policy of a great deal of its flexibility, but should Russia gain freedom of action she might use it to undermine Austria's European position. Metternich had not forgotten his experience of the previous year, when Capo d'Istria had attempted to play the role of spokesman for the secondary German powers. Never again was Metternich to risk his position by relying on retroactive Russian approval, or on the unsupported goodwill of the Tsar. He was determined, therefore, to take away Russia's options at almost any price. While Castlereagh was exhorting him to decisive action, as if Austrian intervention depended entirely on the balance of forces in the Peninsula, Metternich was much less concerned with the fact of action than its mode, less with defeating the revolution in Naples than with committing Russia to a joint course in Italy. He now reaped the fruits of his careful policy in the spring. While Castlereagh had rejected a five-power meeting on the Spanish question out of hand, Metternich had modified his rejection by a proposal for a meeting of the Emperor and the Tsar. He was therefore able to add the Neapolitan question to the agenda of the forthcoming conference, not as a plea for help, but as one other issue requiring the anxious attention of the monarchs. He drafted a flattering letter to Alexander for the signature of the Emperor, which included a reference to the "constitutional fetters" of Great Britain and compared them unfavourably with the exalted position of the monarchs of Austria and Russia, "the only Sovereigns who still possess freedom of action".[1]

But this subtle effort to lure the Tsar into giving his individual concurrence to Austrian intervention in Italy, while isolating France and keeping open the British connection, did not succeed. For Alexander, feeling finally vindicated, was not to be put off so easily. He wrote a warm personal letter to the Emperor agreeing to a meeting any time after the end of the session of the Polish Diet, to which Alexander was hastening;[2] but an accompanying note from Capo d'Istria suggested a five-power conference on the model of Aix-la-Chapelle to take place concurrently with the meeting of the mon-

[1] Gentz, Friedrich von, *Dépêches Inédites aux Hospodars de Valachie*, 3 Vols. (Paris 1876–7), Vol. 1, p. 75.

[2] Gentz, *Dépêches Inédites*, p. 76.

archs. It was becoming clear that Metternich would not be able to avoid an interpretation of the structure of the international order which must lead to British withdrawal from the Alliance.

All this time Castlereagh, who saw his life's work disintegrating, attempted to rescue the pretence of Allied unity by exhorting Metternich to immediate action, by counselling the wisdom of unilateral measures—all steps which Metternich was straining every effort to avoid. Castlereagh could see no other explanation for the incomprehensible vacillation of his Austrian colleague than fear of the physical strength of Naples, and he therefore sought to reassure him. "If Austria thinks fit to set her shoulders to the wheel," he wrote on 29 July, "there can be little doubt of her competence to overrun the Kingdom of Naples and dissolve the rebel army."[1] Another dispatch, on 6 September, attempted to elucidate the legal position with respect to the revolution in Naples, as if the dilemma imposed by Austria's central location could be removed by the patient reiteration of maxims of International Law.[2] The Alliance, insisted Castlereagh, could be operative only against an overt and overriding danger. While a revolution might well represent a threat, it affected the various powers in different ways. And as regards Naples, Britain was "not so . . . immediately menaced according to the doctrines . . . which have hitherto been sustained in the British Parliament [to] justify it in becoming party to an armed interference." And in a conversation with the Russian ambassador, Castlereagh repeated that British sympathy for its Allies could extend no further than benevolent neutrality: "We can give a much stronger moral support to a cause which is not strictly our own than to one to which we are an active party. The revolution should be treated as a *special* rather than as a *general* question, as an *Italian* question rather than as an *European*, and consequently as in the sphere of *Austria* rather than of the *Alliance*."[3] However great Castlereagh's devotion to the Alliance, no British statesman could conduct a policy totally at variance with the insular mentality. The fact of a revolution represented no threat to a country convinced of the uniqueness of its institutions and nobody could take seriously the danger of physical aggression from Naples.

Metternich was thus confronted with the situation that his most

[1] Webster, II, p. 262.
[2] C.C. XII, p. 311f.
[3] Webster, II, p. 271.

reliable ally announced the impossibility of assistance, while his most dangerous opponent was clamouring to extend aid. "Austria considers everything with reference to the *substance*," wrote Metternich. "Russia wants above all the *form*; Britain wants the *substance* without the form. . . . It will be our task to combine the *impossibilities* of Britain with the *modes* of Russia."[1] This led to a tenacious rearguard action, designed to keep Britain in the alliance as a counterweight to Russia without antagonizing the unstable Tsar. But if it should prove impossible to frame a policy acceptable to both Russia and Britain, Metternich decided to opt for the Tsar. He explained to Stewart, now British ambassador at Vienna, that although it was not in Austria's interest that Britain stand apart, it was *against* Austria's interest that Russia and France should act separately. If Austria had to quarrel with one of its Allies, it would prefer to do so with the power from which it had least to fear. And he was confirmed in this policy by a domestic crisis in Great Britain, which threatened daily to overturn the Liverpool Cabinet.[2]

Step by step, therefore, Metternich withdrew before Russian insistence. On 28 August, he appealed to the Tsar with the arguments which had proved so effective at Aix-la-Chapelle. The solidarity of the Alliance, he wrote, was so firm that it was unnecessary to demonstrate it by a formal congress. Instead, the Allies should break diplomatic relations with Naples, while constituting an ambassadors' conference at Vienna as a point of moral contact.[3] Metternich knew that such a conference would cause him no difficulty, because his domination of the ambassadors accredited in Vienna was so complete that cynics called them his harem. Perhaps if Alexander had not been in Poland in any case, he would have been content to agree to Metternich's proposal. Being so close to the scene, however, he could not bear the thought of great events taking shape without his participation. He replied that the evil could not be combated without demonstrating the moral unity of Europe and insisted on a five-power conference to meet at Troppau on 20 October. And Castlereagh removed the last prospects for Metternich's plan by flatly refusing to discuss the withdrawal of the British ambassador from Naples as an unwarranted interference in the domestic affairs of another state.

[1] Schmalz, p. 66.
[2] The King's divorce: Webster, II, pp. 214–15.
[3] Schmalz, p. 63.

By the end of September, Metternich yielded. He told Stewart that Austria could not act in Italy with a hostile Russia in its rear and that however eager he might be to take account of British susceptibilities, his pliability was limited by the requirements of Austrian security. In order to avoid worse embarrassments, Britain should send a representative to Troppau, if only as an observer. He had little difficulty convincing Stewart, who pleaded with Castlereagh to be permitted to go to Troppau "as a complete nonentity except as a channel of information for my government".[1]

But while Capo d'Istria was priding himself on his triumph and Castlereagh inveighed against Continental obtuseness, an almost imperceptible change had taken place in the situation which enabled Metternich to emerge once again as the Prime Minister of Europe. An Austrian demand for a conference in July would have been interpreted as a confession of weakness or of intransigeance. A reluctant surrender in September demonstrated Austria's self-confidence and moderation. Increasingly, Austria, which alone had a direct interest in intervention in Naples, found itself urged to do what it desperately desired. More and more the onus for the action was being shifted on the Tsar. Soon Alexander's invocations of lofty principles would be deprived of their ambiguity, and liberals and nationalists would despair of obtaining foreign support. Just as during the previous year at Teplitz, so now in the preparation for Troppau, Metternich paralysed the monarch he feared most by an ardent embrace.

From the moment a congress began to seem unavoidable, Metternich realized that his major problem was not Naples but the frame of mind of Alexander. A Franco-Russian entente would crush Central Europe; a reversion to the Tsar's liberal phase might unleash the revolution. But Russian support could prove equally dangerous, because Capo d'Istria's dogmatism might force Austria into a policy exceeding her resources. Metternich wanted to repress the revolution to symbolize the return to tranquillity; Capo d'Istria wished to overthrow it in order to bring about the new era envisaged in the Holy Alliance. Metternich desired a determinate measure of cabinet diplomacy; Capo d'Istria preferred to embark on a crusade to reform the governments of Europe. Capo d'Istria's correspondence during the period before the opening of Congress made his intentions only too evident. He wrote to Richelieu, the French Prime Minister, that Russia was preparing one more battle against egotism and he hoped

[1] Webster, II, p. 521f. (Appendix).

with more success than at Aix-la-Chapelle. And he told Anstett, his ambassador in Frankfurt, that Austria was deceiving itself if it sought to obtain Russian help to erect an Austrian satellite in Naples. The fault of revolutions lay, not with the people, but with the governments which had failed to give their people institutions which assured their tranquillity.[1] The fundamental problem at Troppau, then, was not the revolution in Naples but the future direction of Russian policy, whether the vague pronouncements of the Holy Alliance should sanctify Capo d'Istria's abstract notions of national constitutions or Metternich's policy of social repression. Until this issue was resolved, Russian policy would exhibit an extraordinary ambiguity, oscillating between pledges of reform and threats of intervention against all revolutions, depending on the Tsar's frame of mind and Capo d'Istria's momentary influence. To remove the source of this ambiguity was Metternich's primary goal: "Our task," wrote Gentz, "reduces itself to one word: Capo d'Istria."

In these circumstances, Metternich set out on a course which only his arrogance could make him even consider: he proposed not only to frustrate Capo d'Istria at the Congress, for that would still have provided the revolution with the symbol of a friendly major power; but to defeat Russia by no less a measure than supplanting its minister by himself, to conquer the revolution not only with Alexander's agreement but under his eager leadership. He therefore proceeded to have himself appointed High Priest of Alexander's religious exaltation, the officially recognized interpreter of the Holy Alliance, thus to achieve not only legitimacy for the social struggle but also sanctity.

The Austrian ambassador to Russia, Lebzeltern, was ordered not to leave the Tsar's side, and through him Metternich sent voluminous reports of a European conspiracy, with headquarters significantly in Paris, alleged to be attempting to undermine all thrones. The recalcitrance of the Polish Diet, strangely reluctant to accept the self-evidence of Alexander's beneficence, seemed designed to illustrate Metternich's homilies of the precedence of order over change and of stability over reform. The results were not long delayed. A Russian reply to the French circular note of 9 August warned of the danger of "outdated" diplomacy at a moment of such crisis. It reprimanded France for suspecting Austria's motives: "Let the [French] minister banish . . . any sentiment of jealousy towards

[1] Schwartz, p. 192.

Austria. The designs of that power cannot, must not excite [such feelings]."[1]

And Metternich's moderation had not been without effect on Castlereagh. To be sure, Castlereagh did not cease protesting against a five-power meeting. But at the same time, he could not bring himself to make the rupture in the Alliance evident, and he was afraid that his intransigeance might force Metternich into concessions which would leave no other choice. In this frame of mind, he was only too willing to use the golden bridge which Metternich had built for him and to permit Stewart's presence at Troppau as an observer.[2] To be sure, Stewart was ordered not to sign even a protocol and to restrict his observations to the *territorial* balance of Europe. But these were evasions for Parliamentary purposes. The symbolic effect of the presence of a British observer was none the less powerful and, more importantly, in case of a showdown he would add an important factor to Metternich's side. Moreover, while Castlereagh was reluctant to associate Britain in the overthrow of revolutions, he could at least prevent others from thwarting Austrian designs. Accordingly, he made clear to France that it could not count on British support in attempting any family compact with the Neapolitan Bourbons.[3] Rebuffed by Russia, under pressure from Britain, France had no choice but to forego her dream of emerging as the spokesman of the constitutional states at a European conference. In order to cover her retreat, France discovered an identity in constitutional principles among the Western Powers which forced her to follow the British example and confine her participation at Troppau to the role of an observer.

As the chief actors at the Congress of Troppau began to assemble, Capo d'Istria, as so many previous rivals of Metternich, suddenly found himself isolated through Metternich's dexterous utilization of his own proposals. Prussia was a diplomatic satellite of Austria. Britain was represented by Stewart, whose vanity made him an easy target for Metternich's wiles. France was represented by two observers, La Ferronay, the ambassador at Petersburg, and Caraman, the ambassador at Vienna. But Caraman was insanely jealous of his colleague and so dominated by Metternich that at crucial stages in the negotiations he showed him his confidential instructions. Capo

[1] Sbornick of the Imperial Russian Historical Society, Vol. CXXVII, p. 456f.
[2] Webster, II, p. 278.
[3] Webster, II, p. 281.

d'Istria had had his way. A congress was assembled, only to provide a forum for the manipulator from Vienna he so deplored. The five powers were gathered, but in practice it amounted to no more than a meeting of the Emperors of Austria and Russia, as Metternich had insisted all along, with the other participants in the role of Austrian reserves. Metternich had achieved this by first isolating France with the aid of Russia and then using this victory to isolate Russia with the aid of France. It is not surprising that Capo d'Istria began to feel uneasy. "I have pursued a bold policy," he said even before the Congress opened. "Perhaps I have been too bold."

Metternich was not interested in triumphs, however, but in obtaining a moral basis for action. Russia's isolation was a last resort, a psychological weapon all the more effective for never being put to explicit use. Just as he attempted to dominate the German Confederation with Prussian acquiescence instead of by outvoting it, so he sought to organize the concert of powers with Russia's assistance instead of through her isolation. For this purpose, he appeared in Troppau as the conscience of Europe, the custodian of its moral principles, to triumph in Naples by conquering the Tsar.

III

It was not for nothing, then, that Metternich's state of mind began to approach the sarcastic buoyancy of his great period of 1813. Once more he had made Austria appear as the pivotal state despite its vulnerability, and used its crisis to cement its international position. The King of Prussia, hastening to the Congress, asked his ministers to prepare a memorandum on Prussia's constitutional problems to be submitted for Metternich's approval. And Alexander increasingly lamented his unfortunate liberal phase. In these circumstances Metternich was confident that he would defeat that "fool" Capo d'Istria. He would have been even more sure of himself, had he known that Alexander had just put an end to an effort by Capo d'Istria for a concerted Franco-Russian policy at Troppau, because he considered the French domestic situation "too unstable".

Metternich arrived in Troppau on 19 October and the Tsar the following day. Their first meeting, shortly after the Tsar's arrival, lasted three hours and followed the pattern established at the interview with the King of Prussia at Teplitz during the previous year. Again a chastened monarch confessed his errors to a stern Austrian

Foreign Minister, who indicated that redemption lay in future unity. "Between 1813 and 1820, seven years have elapsed," said the penitent Tsar, "but they seem to me like a century. Under no circumstances would I do in 1820 what I did in 1812. You have not changed, but I. You have nothing to regret, but I."[1] Capo d'Istria might envision the Congress as the commencement of a new era; the restored tranquillity as the condition of fundamental reform leading to the introduction of constitutions, but if he wanted even to retain his own position, he had to flatter the Austrian minister: "I began our dialogue," reported Metternich after their first interview on 20 October, "by moving to my own ground, that of pure reason. He already was firmly established there. In order to test him I left it. He did not follow me. . . . 'This goes too far,' I said to myself, 'I will submit him to a real test.' I made an excursion into the apocalyptic; he suggested I burn . . . the gospel of the false John. . . . From this moment I thought: Now we can make progress. . ."[2]

At the first plenary session, on 23 October, Metternich therefore advanced the Austrian programme, which represented one more effort to satisfy the Russian quest for an expression of solidarity, without laying down principles which would force Britain into overt isolation.[3] Metternich asserted that no power had the right to interfere in the domestic affairs of other states unless these exerted an influence abroad. But, conversely, every state had the right to intervene when domestic transformations in other states threatened its own structure. Metternich was asking for nothing less than European sanction of a doctrine of non-interference, in the name of which he then proposed to overthrow the revolution in Naples. It was a dexterous effort to use Austrian intervention in Naples to commit the Tsar to a principle of self-limitation; to obtain a restrictive interpretation of the treaty structure while using the Alliance to repress social upheaval. Had Castlereagh been present he could hardly have made different proposals, for Metternich was proposing to legitimize his Italian policy by the "British" maxims.

But Capo d'Istria was not ready to surrender so easily. The Tsar might have abjured his earlier extravagances, but it was doubtful that even Metternich could induce him to return to pure cabinet

[1] N.P. III, p. 352.
[2] N.P. III, p. 351.
[2] Schmalz, p. 70f.

diplomacy. He had insisted on a Congress to demonstrate the moral unity of Europe, not to reiterate a right of self-defence which was unchallenged. Metternich might gain the substance of the victory, but only by clothing it in the forms which had become almost ritualistic with the Russians. There occurred a hiatus in the negotiations while Capo d'Istria prepared a formal reply and during which Metternich, in long private sessions with Alexander, conducted his battle for the Tsar's mind. On 29 October, at the second plenary session, Prussia produced a memorandum which so cravenly followed the Austrian lead that the Russians suspected it had been drafted by Metternich.

In the interval the Russian intentions were emerging. "Did the Emperor of Austria want 150,000 or 200,000 men to cut the throats of the carbonari?" Capo d'Istria asked Stewart. "They were at her disposal. But if they wanted an *appui moral* to overturn a government, it must be shown what was to be substituted in its place. The reconstruction of governments for the welfare of mankind was a subject worthy of the consideration of the great Association of Europe."[1] Nothing could have made the difference between the Austrian and Russian conception of the international order more evident: Metternich fought the revolution as a disturbance of the equilibrium; Capo d'Istria sought to defeat it because it prevented the lawful sovereigns from bestowing their beneficence on their peoples as philosopher-kings, often in the form of the very reforms the revolutionaries were advocating. A Russian memorandum of 2 November brought this difference into the open.[2] It based the proposed intervention, not on the right of self-defence, but on the treaties of 1814–15, which were said to represent a guarantee of the existing order. And it laid down three principles which justified the intervention of the Alliance: that a revolution automatically excluded the affected power from the Alliance; that the Allies had a right to take the requisite measures to prevent the epidemic from spreading and to restore the affected nations to the bosom of the Alliance; but that these measures could not affect the territorial arrangements of the treaties of 1814–15.

This was, of course, a repetition of the arguments of Aix-la-Chapelle; indeed an application of Metternich's own reasoning for rejecting the *Alliance Solidaire*, that the existing treaties were suffi-

[1] Webster, II, p. 290.
[2] Schmalz, p. 72f.

cient to accomplish all its objects. But Capo d'Istria's generalities gave Metternich less concern than their application to the problem of Naples. The purpose of Austrian intervention, argued the Russian minister, was to enable Naples freely to realize its national aspirations and to guarantee it a "dual freedom": political liberty and national independence. He therefore proposed that Austrian intervention be preceded by moral pressure on the part of the great powers or by the mediation of a neutral power, preferably the Pope. Even should this prove unavailing, Austria could obtain the sanction of the Alliance for intervention only by accounting for the institutions it proposed to establish in Naples. In short, Capo d'Istria meant to appoint himself as the constitutional arbiter of Europe. But no statesman is stronger than his domestic support, and by now Metternich had more influence with the Tsar than the Russian minister. "The only issue at Troppau," wrote Gentz, "is who is the stronger, Alexander or Capo d'Istria."[1]

The issue was soon resolved. On 5 November, Metternich rejected Capo d'Istria's interpretation of the treaties of 1814–15. Only the letter of treaties was binding, he argued, the interpretation of their spirit depended on circumstances. Nevertheless, Austria was ready, for the welfare of Europe, to accept a very liberal interpretation.[2] It was a characteristic Metternich manœuvre: it agreed to the principles advanced by Russia, but as an Austrian concession, not as a logical necessity. It accepted the Russian interpretation of the treaty structure, but only in order to establish a claim to a free hand in its application. It gave Alexander the symbol of European unity he had sought so long, but only to commit him irrevocably. Capo d'Istria soon found out that his victory was hollow. For Metternich proceeded to reject his proposal that the Allies agree on an alternative constitution for Naples in the name of the very principles that had just been laid down. The only task of the Alliance, argued Metternich, was to return the King to the concert of powers by restoring his freedom of action; any further interference would limit his sovereignty and thus negate the very purpose of the intervention. When, on 6 November, Capo d'Istria was obliged to admit that the sovereignty of the King of Naples could not be limited, it was clear that Metternich was becoming dominant. By 7 November, the Tsar

[1] Gentz, Friedrich von, *Briefe von Friedrich von Gentzan Pilat*, 2 Vols. (Leipzig, 1868), p. 436.

[2] Stern, II, p. 131; Schmalz, p. 76.

had forced Capo d'Istria to agree in principle to a compromise plan advanced by Metternich. "At last we are on solid ground," wrote Metternich to his ambassador in France. "Of course we will still encounter several obstacles, but we have occupied the heights, the battle will therefore be won. We have killed the expedients of the 'national wish' and of 'mediation'."[1]

Metternich's compromise plan agreed to the three principles which Capo d'Istria had laid down, modifying them only by adding a proviso, for British consumption, that intervention was to be used only as a last resort. But the substantive part of Metternich's plan revealed that this agreement was the means to put an end to any plans of reform. Nothing was said about the "dual freedoms" or about the reconstruction of the government. On the contrary, Metternich insisted that the measures to achieve domestic peace should be left to the wisdom of the legitimate ruler.[2] In this manner, the principles for which Capo d'Istria had fought so tenaciously emerged as a doctrine of self-denial on the part of Russia, as an admission that they were tools of repression but meaningless as instruments of reform. Metternich had won the struggle for the right to interpret the maxims of the Holy Alliance. Troppau thus marked not only the beginning of the end for the revolution in Naples, but, more importantly, for the revolutionary policy of Russia.

Capo d'Istria's proposal for mediation fared no better. What was designed as a means to rescue a modicum of constitutional rule became one of Metternich's subtle steps which isolated his opponents by confronting them with impossible alternatives. For Metternich proposed that the "good offices" should be tendered not by the Pope, nor yet by Bourbon France, which was another of Capo d'Istria's desperate suggestions, but by Europe assembled in Congress. The King of Naples was to appear before that body and plead his case. It was a diabolical proposal. If the King was refused permission to leave Naples, his lack of freedom would be demonstrated; if he appeared, he was certain to plead for Austrian intervention on the most extreme terms. The effort to remove the King from Naples was likely to lead to a violent dispute between the moderates and the extremists and thus weaken the country domestically before a shot was fired. And the Tsar would not miss an opportunity to demonstrate his beneficence before so imposing a tribunal. "I will gain

[1] Schmalz, p. 77.
[2] N.P. III, p. 391.

eighty-five per cent of the victory," reported Metternich. "With the remainder Capo d'Istria will rob the world of its tranquillity, reason of its respect and common sense of its honour."[1]

Metternich had every reason to be concerned about the use Capo d'Istria would make of his one achievement at Troppau: the right to draft the agreement. For while Metternich had deprived Capo d'Istria's principles of all meaning, their very enunciation might snap the tenuous thread by which Britain was still connected to the Alliance. No amount of hedging could obtain British approval of a generalized right of interference, and France would follow the British example. For this reason, Metternich had kept the representatives of the Western powers in complete ignorance of his negotiations. He had encouraged Stewart to absent himself twice to go to Vienna to visit his young wife, who was pregnant, assuring him that no decisions would be taken without him. And the split representation reduced France to impotence. When La Ferronay protested against the Austrian proposals of 23 October, Metternich asked him sarcastically whether he was expressing his own opinion, that of both French representatives, or that of France.[2] But the Tsar was outraged at what he took as a new demonstration of the French weakness for revolutions and threatened to keep France under military surveillance.

On 19 November, the Western representatives suddenly found themselves confronted by an accomplished fact. The unsuspecting Stewart, just returned from Vienna, was invited to a plenary session where he found an already signed document, the *Protocole Preliminaire*, which contained Metternich's compromise plan. It did not matter that Stewart protested violently and that both he and his French colleagues refused to sign. Metternich had isolated Capo d'Istria and committed the Tsar before the rupture in the Alliance had become evident. During the negotiations his British option had remained a bargaining device, and with the right of intervention assured and the Tsar under his domination, he could face the consequences of his duplicity. And so pronounced was Metternich's personal dominance that even now, after having been completely duped, Stewart still made excuses for him: ". . . The whole seemed an incomprehensible or at least an unkind proceeding. . . . [But Austria] fearing a change of government in Britain and a change of purpose in

[1] N.P. III, p. 356.
[2] Schmalz, p. 82

Russia, resorts to an intimate concert between the three great monarchist powers. . . . With Prince Metternich, however I may feel temporarily hurt . . . [it] will neither operate upon our confidential habits, nor for an instant weaken our friendship."[1]

But Castlereagh was not put off as easily as his brother. He knew the Tsar's mentality too well to expect Metternich to have obtained his objectives without some concessions which could not be defended in Parliament. As he saw his cherished conference system used for ends he had thought impossible, he grew increasingly testy: "I have never regretted as much as now," he told the Russian ambassador, "not being with the Emperor and able to submit my thoughts to him. . . . The Emperor has repeated on every occasion his unshaken determination not to contract new engagements, not to form new ties outside those already existing, not to seek new guarantees outside the General Alliance. This determination is in fact Europe's safety anchor. Why change it now?"[2] A dispatch to Stewart on 16 December reiterated the British position: To expel states from the Alliance and to reform their institutions by force was against International Law and against existing treaties. Moreover, if the Allies intended to apply this doctrine to themselves, the Act of Settlement would prevent British participation, and any attempt to do otherwise "would be so revolting to every class of the people that it might shake His Majesty's title to the throne if not expiated by the punishment of the minister by whom such advice had been given." This did not mean that Britain did not deplore secret societies and military revolutions. But, while admitting the right to intervene in self-defence, Britain would "not charge itself as a member of the Alliance with the moral responsibility of administering a general European police".[3]

Yet great dreams are not surrendered easily. Even now Castlereagh found it difficult to admit that the concert of Europe could not combine the insular concept of non-interference with the Continental policy of precaution. He still hoped that patience and goodwill might return the Alliance to the intimate relationship of wartime. His heart bled, he told the Russian ambassador, to have to send the dispatch of 16 December. He insisted that he was not opposing the aims of the Allies but the proclamation of an official document. And a private letter to Stewart, which accompanied the dispatch, testified once

[1] Webster, II, p. 528f. (Appendix).
[2] Webster, II, p. 302.
[3] Webster, II, p. 303f.

more to Castlereagh's reluctance to part with his vision of European government: "It is singular . . . that it should have occurred to the three Courts to reform an Alliance which has been found to adapt itself with great facility to all the exigencies of affairs upon the exploded doctrine of divine right and passive obedience. They might have foreseen that the House of Hanover could not well maintain the principles upon which the House of Stuart forfeited the throne. . . . It now rests with the three courts to decide whether to contend against the dangers . . . under separate banners. . . . They may contend about the case as we propose without laying down disputed principles. We cannot adhere to their principles and if they will be theorists, we must act in separation. . . ."[1]

But it was of no avail. Castlereagh saw the real achievement of the Alliance in inactivity, which would indicate the absence of political upheavals. The Continental powers, and Metternich above all, considered the Alliance a weapon against the current danger, whatever it might be. And since to Metternich the social struggle overshadowed all else, while Castlereagh refused to consider it an international problem, Metternich gradually separated himself from his British connection. Castlereagh's protest finished the *Protocole Preliminaire*, but it could not prevent an Allied circular dispatch on 8 December, drafted by Capo d'Istria, which in his apocalyptic manner again derived the justification for the intervention from the treaty structure of 1814–15 and, to make matters worse, even hinted at British approval.[2] The rupture in the Alliance was thus imminent. But before it occurred, Metternich had succeeded in so organizing the Continent that British aid was dispensable, and he had seen to it that the Allied measures should be blamed on the Tsar. Despite Britain's increasing separation from the Alliance, its relations with Austria remained closer than with any other power.

IV

The Congress of Troppau marks the high point of Metternich's diplomatic skill. Unwilling or unable to adapt Austria to the predominant trends of the period, confronted by the prospect of a battle against nationalism and liberalism, he succeeded in making it a European rather than an Austrian contest and thus avoided sym-

[1] Webster, II, p. 305.
[2] N.P. III, p. 392f.

bolizing the incongruity of Austria's domestic structure. Faced with the danger of a resurgent France restoring its Italian position by means of a family compact and an appeal to constitutionalism, he managed to isolate France and to reduce her to impotence. The role of the French representatives at Troppau could not have been more miserable. By appearing as the most conciliatory of the plenipotentiaries, Metternich lured them into one trap after another. When Caraman took up Capo d'Istria's suggestion of French mediation, Metternich obliquely encouraged him to advance the proposal at a plenary session, only to abandon him in the face of the Tsar's outraged protest against mediation between legitimate sovereigns and revolutionaries. And when the trusting Frenchman showed Metternich a confidential dispatch protesting against the *Protocole Preliminaire* and comparing the intervention in Naples with the yoke imposed on France, Metternich saw to it that Alexander should learn of the vacillation of his would-be ally.[1] France's final reaction to the *Protocole Preliminaire* only reflected its impotence: it refused to sign the Protocol but joined the invitation to the King of Naples and thus succeeded in antagonizing both Russia and Britain.

But outmanœuvring France would have availed Metternich little, had he not succeeded in neutralizing Russia. Two choices were available to him: the physical isolation of Russia or its moral domination. Although Metternich did not exclude the former and kept his British option open until the last moment for precisely this reason, he knew that it would ultimately force Austria into a policy beyond its resources. All his wiles were therefore employed to gain an ascendancy over the Tsar. He was aided by Alexander's disillusionment with his Polish experiment and increasing religiosity, but he completed the process himself by means of protracted conversations at Troppau. It was at Troppau that Metternich prepared his "profession of faith" for the Tsar's eyes, with its skilful criticism of the presumptuous man and its call for order before change.[2] His reference to the baneful impact of theoreticians clearly applied to Capo d'Istria, as did his identification of the advocacy of constitutions with the presumptuousness of the revolutionary. At Troppau, too, the Tsar learned of the mutiny of a regiment of the Russian Guards, caused by the brutality of its commander, but easily

[1] Stern, II, p. 135.
[2] See ante p. 201f.

explained by Metternich as a spread of the revolutionary virus and an attempt by radical elements to intimidate the Tsar.[1]

In this manner, the maxims of the Holy Alliance, which had hopefully envisaged a new order of society, became a means to restore Metternich's conception of the social equilibrium. Almost imperceptibly the Tsar's moral fervour was transformed from a revolutionary into a conservative, if not reactionary, force. If Alexander had a Prime Minister by the end of the conference of Troppau, it was Metternich, not Capo d'Istria. Alexander showed almost all of his dispatches to Metternich before sending them and could not repeat the catalogue of his sins often enough. The two courts prepared joint instructions for their ambassadors in London for the contingency of the fall of the Liverpool Cabinet, which was expected daily. And Metternich, never content with a simple measure, told this in confidence to Stewart, thereby furnishing a proof both of his goodwill and of the difficulty of his position.[2]

If Russia could have overthrown the European equilibrium by an independent policy, Prussia could have upset the balance within Germany by exploiting Austria's embarrassment in Italy. But Teplitz and Carlsbad had settled the problem of an independent Prussian foreign policy. The King of Prussia regarded the Congress of Troppau primarily as an opportunity to obtain Metternich's advice on Prussia's domestic structure. He did not arrive until 7 November, but was preceded by the Crown Prince, who soon fell under Metternich's spell and remained his life-long admirer. When the King joined his fellow monarchs, Metternich profited from the opportunity to submit his views on Prussia's internal administration with the result that the King once more delayed approving a communal reorganization.[3]

So strong was Metternich's position that at the end of the Congress he demonstrated his moderation by accepting Capo d'Istria's proposal for mediation by the Pope between the King of Naples and the revolutionaries. But while Capo d'Istria's note appealed to the Pope to assist in an act of conciliation, Metternich drafted a letter for the Emperor which simply asked for spiritual assistance in the chastisement of the revolution.[4] And just as Napoleon could have

[1] N.P. III, p. 355; Schmalz, p. 77.
[2] Webster, II, p. 296.
[3] Stern, II, p. 145.
[4] Stern, II, p. 137.

frustrated Metternich's designs in 1813 by accepting the Reichenbach basis; just as Prussia could have thwarted him at the Congress of Vienna by a refusal of joint action, so the revolutionaries in Naples could have made Metternich's course at Troppau very difficult by a policy of moderation. But in every case Metternich gambled on the tangibility of psychological factors—and in each instance he won. The conflict between the moderates and the extremists in Naples was brought to a head by the invitation to the King to attend the Congress of Laibach. The invitation could not be refused, but before his departure the King was forced to take another oath to the ultra-liberal "Spanish" constitution, a step which Alexander could only interpret as a direct provocation and which once and for all ended Capo d'Istria's quest both for a constitution and for mediation.

Metternich's policy, although essentially defensive in nature, had taken the only form by which a state, aware of its weakness, can preserve the status quo without exhausting its resources: the creation of a moral consensus. Where Castlereagh saw the problem of restraint of aggression in the assembly of superior force, Metternich sought it in a moral commitment which would make aggression inconceivable. It was a dexterous if not a constructive conception, this attempt to settle the problem of Alexander's instability and the social unrest of Europe at one blow by committing the Tsar to an anti-revolutionary crusade, thus embroiling him once and for all with all the movements he had heretofore encouraged by his ambiguities. Again diplomatic skill achieved what would have been impossible by physical pressure, the culmination of Metternich's campaign of a decade: On the continent of Europe, the domestic legitimization of Austria had become the organizing principle of the international order. And the Congress of Laibach, to which the King of Naples and the Allied monarchs were now hastening, symbolized the new nature of international relations. For Laibach was not, as previous congresses, a meeting of plenipotentiaries, but a stage on which the Austrian minister proposed to teach a moral lesson to the rest of Europe.

XV

The Congress of Laibach and the Government of Europe

I

IN the period between 1854 and 1859, the octogenarian Metternich wrote a series of memoranda for his successor, Buol, who, panicked by the vulnerability of Austria's position, sought a system of alliances, at almost any price. In his soberly oracular style, Metternich argued that the Central Empire could lean on no one, because it would soon discover that its neighbours were neither strong enough nor willing to serve as support. But neither was neutrality possible, because Austria's central position doomed it to become involved in every conflict and because neutrality would encourage the other powers to formulate demands incompatible with Austria's survival. The solution of this dilemma lay in relying on Austria's only real advantage: that it had no selfish desires in Europe, that all powers of repose must inevitably gravitate towards it. Austria was therefore never really isolated, and a blind commitment merely to have allies represented a weakening of Austria's position. Austria could commit itself only for specific goals; its real policy was to define, not passively to accept, the moral framework of coalitions by a policy of non-participation in the early stages of any conflict, in order to sell Austria's participation for the only object which interested this epitome of status quo powers: the conditions of repose. Isolation, Metternich insisted, was no cause for alarm as long as its purpose was clearly understood. The key to success in diplomacy was freedom of action, not formal relationships.[1]

This was the basis of Metternich's diplomacy throughout his life. Freedom of action, the consciousness of having a greater range of choices than any possible opponent, was a better protection than an alliance, because it kept open all options for the hour of need. But

[1] N.P. VIII, pp. 354–417.

while freedom of action for an insular power was assured by its geographic location, freedom of action for the Central Power had to depend on its moral position and by so arranging the commitments of the other powers that Austria's options were always greater than those of any potential rival. It was a policy which required cool nerves, because it sought to demonstrate Austria's indispensability by the calm acceptance of great risks, of isolation or sudden settlements at Austria's expense. Its success depended on the correct evaluation of the constellation of forces, above all on the fact that Austria's superior flexibility was not an illusion. Since its achievements could not emerge until the last moment, while its risks were immediately apparent, it was a policy that required for its execution the almost arrogant self-confidence which characterized Metternich. Because it depended on so many intangibles, it became increasingly difficult to carry out as Austria's position deteriorated throughout the nineteenth century, particularly after both Prussia and Russia came to consider Austria their primary rival, Prussia in Germany and Russia in the Balkans. And because Metternich's successors saw only the dangers and not the underlying conception, they substituted for his subtle manipulation a panicky vacillation between incompatible alternatives which sealed Austria's doom.

While he was still able to control events, however, one can discern two almost inevitable stages in Metternich's diplomacy during a crisis: A period of seeming hesitation during which the moral framework of the common effort was defined so imperceptibly that it appeared as the spontaneous expression of universal aspirations; followed by a symbolic act which committed Austria's allies to a policy of limited objectives through a public declaration. Thus, the tortuous negotiations of the spring of 1813 had been followed by the Congress of Prague, designed to illustrate the incompatibility of Napoleon's claims with a system of equilibrium; the Carlsbad Decrees had led to the Conference of Vienna demonstrating the moral unity of Germany; and the Congress of Troppau was followed by the Congress of Laibach symbolizing the moral unity of Europe—and in the process committing the Tsar irretrievably.

The Congress of Laibach was thus primarily an expression of the European government which Metternich had created at Troppau. It did not help Capo d'Istria that he appealed for British mediation; nor France that a third plenipotentiary, Blacas, appeared to supervise his colleagues and to prevent the King of Naples from behaving too cravenly. Metternich was in complete control, largely because of his domination of Alexander. "Nobody believes in the unanimity of the Emperor [Alexander] and myself and still it is true," he wrote. "The influence of the past four months is bearing fruit. The Russian Prime Minister is defeated. The stronger is carrying the weaker along according to the laws of mechanics, physics and morality."[1] The King of Prussia did not even appear and sent his Foreign Minister, Bernstorff, who was in effect an appendage of Metternich. Stewart, the British representative, was once more encouraged to repair to Vienna to visit his wife, not to return until the basic decisions had been taken and to repeat the scene of outraged innocence of Troppau. And the duplicity of the King of Naples was so extreme that Metternich could emerge once more as an advocate of moderation. For no sooner had this monarch left Naples behind him than he exorcised both his Parliament and the Constitution which he had just sworn to uphold with the dramatic phrase that lightning should strike him if he ever violated his oath.

In these circumstances, the decisions were taken rapidly. Alexander arrived on 8 January and by 10 January Metternich could report: "Today, unless the earth collapses or the sky falls down . . . we have won the game. Capo d'Istria twists and turns like the devil in holy water; but he *is* in holy water and can do nothing."[2] Metternich produced another member of his "harem", Ruffo, the Neapolitan ambassador at Vienna, and appointed him as the spokesman for Naples, while the constitutional Foreign Minister, Gallo, who had accompanied the King, had to cool his heels at Görz nearby. On 13 January, there ensued a scene which might have been drawn straight from the *opéra buffe*, which so delighted Metternich at Laibach. Ruffo appeared before a plenary session of the Congress and read a speech drafted by Gentz and Metternich, in which the King of Naples asked the Allies to invest him with the role of conciliator according "to the maxims of justice, wisdom and magnanimity". Metternich replied, equally exaltedly, that the Allies would be happy "to assist His Majesty to acquire one more claim to the affection of his people". But, unfortunately, it had been decided at Troppau, "not to recognize any upheaval brought about by criminal means and which could disturb the peace of the world from one moment to the next". In the face of such intransigeance, what was a

[1] N.P. III, p. 424.
[2] N.P. III, p. 424.

constitutional monarch to do? To make the supreme sacrifice, replied Metternich with the voice of Ruffo, and to give up the constitution about which the Allies refused to negotiate. Ruffo had come prepared with a letter to the Neapolitan people in which the King informed his subjects of the violation of his oath, "with perfect tranquillity before God and his conscience", as a means to spare them the horrors of war. But lest there be any opposition to this display of magnanimity, an accompanying confidential missive announced the arrival of an Austrian army of occupation as a "guarantee" for the fulfilment of the will of Europe.[1]

By the time Stewart returned to Laibach, the first act of the comedy was over, and he found Metternich busily engaged in writing the script for the second, in which the Duke of Gallo was to be notified of the decision of the Allies in the presence of the representatives of the other Italian courts. Again Stewart found the Allies preparing a declaration in the negotiation of which he had had no part and again he was asked simply to concur. Once more he rent the air with protestations of abused innocence, but he achieved no more than the permission to record on the Journals that "in spite of the presence of the British representative . . . he is not authorized to associate himself with the *Procès Verbal* of the Conferences. . . ."[2] And even this concession was soon proved illusory. When Stewart arrived, on 30 January, at the solemn occasion at which Europe in Congress was to announce its resolve to the Foreign Minister of Naples, he found that Metternich had substituted an entirely new declaration which made much of the solidarity of the Allies and which omitted Stewart's reservation altogether. While the delegates were already arriving, Stewart's indignation knew no bounds. He was finally persuaded to let the new declaration stand, while Metternich agreed to read his protest at the end. The Duke of Gallo was now called into the presence of the Congress, where Metternich with a lofty dignity, which belied the sharp practices preceding it, informed him of the Allied decisions and in a manner which nearly obscured Stewart's reservation. But the dénouement was an anti-climax, unworthy of the imposing array assembled. Instead of an outraged protest or a dignified affirmation of his principles, the minister of the Revolution listened to Metternich's severe lecture with a benevolent nod of the head which expressed his

[1] Stern, II, p. 150f.
[2] Webster, II, p. 316.

agreement. He thanked Metternich for his efforts and promised to support them to the best of his ability upon his return to Naples.[1] The revolution in Naples, which had led to two European congresses and kept the chancelleries of Europe in a turmoil for nearly a year, provided a demonstration of its fatuousness in defeat, which all of Metternich's stage management had been unable to achieve in seven months of tortuous diplomacy.

Only now, after Austria could act as the agent of Europe and more than half a year since the outbreak of the Revolution, did an Austrian army cross the Po. But more important even than being able to intervene in Naples with the sanction of Europe, was Metternich's influence over the Tsar, which caused a British diplomat to report that Metternich could not act more confidently if Russia were an Austrian province. For despite his protestations of eternal Austro-Russian friendship which succeeded each other in effusive eloquence, Metternich, in a conversation with Stewart, left no doubt about whom he considered his real adversary. "He told me," reported Stewart, "that he has at last been able to commit the Emperor of Russia with all the *Liberaux*, not only of Italy, but of all of Europe. . . . The sequel of these conferences would show that he had not been deceived in any of his calculations, and that he had conducted the Austrian monarchy, under the greatest peril with which it has ever been threatened, to a secure and creditable triumph."[2]

II

Before these beneficial consequences could occur, however, Britain had to be heard from once more. Stewart had played at Laibach the same almost ridiculous role as at Troppau. But with a Parliamentary session approaching and the Opposition inveighing against foreign interference with independent powers, Castlereagh could not rest content with Stewart's ineffectual protests. The result was the circular dispatch of 19 January, which was ostensibly a reply to the Allied declaration of Troppau on 8 December and which once more summarized the British position.[3] In its tone of studied reasonableness, in its pedantic repetition of all the arguments which had proved unavailing in the previous year, the note revealed that it was really

[1] Stern, II, p. 154f.; Webster, II, p. 318f.
[2] Webster, II, p. 315.
[3] Webster, II, p. 321f.

written for submission to Parliament and that Castlereagh desired nothing less than to produce a rupture in the Alliance. All the arguments of insular policy were repeated: a right of general interference was contrary to the fundamental law of Great Britain; but even if this objection did not exist, Great Britain could not become part of such an engagement, because in the hands of "less beneficent monarchs" it might lead to universal tyranny. Interference was not rejected in principle, indeed the British Cabinet had often admitted its necessity in self-defence. But it could not be founded on a generalized right and certainly not on an interpretation of the treaties of 1815 which Great Britain had consistently rejected. Interference was an exception, never a rule of international conduct.

And even this dispatch, which contained nothing new, ended on a note which indicated that the Alliance of Europe was Castlereagh's only foreign policy. It concluded by asserting that Britain paid "full justice to the purity of intentions of the Eastern powers" and that the "differences in sentiment" could not affect "the cordiality and harmony of the Alliance on any other subject, or abate their common zeal in giving the most complete effect to all their existing engagements". Castlereagh's was a tragic obtuseness which refused to recognize that common action was no longer possible, not through anyone's fault, but because the insular and the Continental conceptions of danger had become incompatible. Castlereagh could not admit this, however, without denying himself. To him the disagreements were not inherent in the effort to construct a system of collective security, but in its abuse; not in the nature of the Alliance, but in the effort to give it a direction for which it was never designed. He therefore saw his task in vindicating the Alliance rather than in announcing a rupture and a covering letter to the circular note revealed the inward reserve with which it was drafted: ". . . You will avoid any discussion," it read, "which might give occasion to a suspicion that the different modes in which the question has been viewed by the Allied governments might possibly produce some abatement in the cordiality of their union, which upon all points really embraced by the treaty you will always regard and declare to subsist in full harmony and vigour."[1] Not without justice could the Austrian ambassador in London report to Metternich: "Castlereagh is like a great lover of music who is at Church; he wishes to applaud but he dares not."

[1] Webster, II, p. 323f.

It was only appropriate, therefore, that Castlereagh's last foreign policy speech before the House of Commons should be a powerful defence of the Alliance, whose mistakes he admitted while arguing its continued efficacy. He painted a picture of Carbonari activity that not even Metternich could have improved upon. And he defended Austria's motives, whose purity, he argued, had been sufficiently demonstrated by Austria's ability to obtain the agreement of Europe assembled in Congress. Not the fact of Austrian intervention was at issue, therefore, only its justification. Nevertheless, this difference did not call for a rupture of the Alliance, much less for a policy of isolation. The Alliance continued in undiminished force: "With regard to the Alliance of the Continental sovereigns of which so much has been said, I am far from being disposed to shrink from its defence. It is not surprising that the gentlemen opposite should feel a little sore at an alliance which has so much disappointed their dismal forebodings. It is perhaps too much to expect of human nature to behold with patience . . . what, so long as it endures, must be a monument to their folly. This Alliance, which I hope will long continue to cement the peace of Europe, has proved . . . the absurdity of those prophecies in which the honourable gentlemen opposite have indulged, and the schemes of policy which they have recommended."[1]

Here in the customary ponderous phrases, delivered with the usual glacial calm, was a vision of European unity doomed to failure, because it remained forever incomprehensible to the British public, to whom an alliance to cement the peace was a contradiction in terms. Alliances had specific objects, and they were directed *against* someone. In the absence of an overriding danger, a common policy with the Continent could simply not be legitimized domestically. Castlereagh's vision of the unity of Europe achieved by good faith, of the government of Europe through the mere fact of Allied harmony, was a mirage which doomed its advocate to destruction and none the less tragic for appearing in the guise of sober pedantry.

III

In the meantime, while the Austrian army was advancing towards the south, Metternich insisted that the comedy be played to the end, that the audience be not dismissed until every possible moral had been

[1] Hansard (Commons), 21 February, 1821.

exhibited. Never one to give a defeated opponent a chance to recover, Metternich now set about to remove Capo d'Istria's last possible excuse for interference: the promise of Troppau to give Naples organic institutions which would assure its repose. And just as at Carlsbad Metternich had moderated the panicky German powers, so now at Laibach he ameliorated the insistence of the craven King of Naples to be restored as absolute ruler. In protracted negotiations Metternich persuaded him to accept a "Draft of a Fundamental Law for the Kingdom of Naples" which was submitted confidentially to the Tsar and approved by him. It was an exact reflection of Metternich's governmental maxims: while it provided for a decentralized administration, it strengthened the authority of the monarch, which was limited only by a Council of State with purely advisory functions and a Consulta, an assembly of deputations of the Estates, in both Naples and Sicily.[1] It was in vain that Capo d'Istria appealed to the Tsar to save at least a modicum of representative institutions. The legitimizing principle of the European order invested a "legitimate" ruler, even so ludicrous a figure as the King of Naples, with a *character indelibilis,* and no appeal from his decisions was possible. In any case, Metternich was now strong enough openly to go over Capo d'Istria's head and to induce Alexander to silence his Prime Minister. "The gulf between Capo d'Istria and the Emperor is becoming ever greater," reported Metternich. ". . . [But] the Emperor is the stronger and for obvious reasons."[2]

Indeed, Metternich's greatest problem now was to put a rein on the Tsar's exuberance. "We are engaged in a combat with the realm of Satan," wrote Alexander, proving how well he had studied Metternich's "profession of faith". "Ambassadors do not suffice for this task. Only those whom the Lord has placed at the head of their peoples may, if He gives His blessings, survive the contest . . . with this diabolic force. . . ." Ever since the Cabinets had met on the basis of the maxims of the Holy Alliance, he wrote another time, all enemies of Christianity, all revolutionaries, Carbonari and radical equalizers had sworn vengeance.[3] In this mood, it was not difficult to recur to the idea of a crusade, not, to be sure, to reform humanity, but to defeat the revolution; not to begin a new era, but to

[1] Stern, II, p. 155f.
[2] N.P. III, p. 429.
[3] Schwarz, p. 224.

restore tranquillity. "Do you think," said the Tsar to the French representative, "that the only purpose of this meeting is the punishment of a few Carbonari? . . . Naples, swept along by the example of Spain, should in turn serve as the example for the latter. . . . If we have created a just order in Naples, perhaps the moment will come for France to play the role towards Spain which Austria has assumed with respect to Naples."[1]

But Metternich had no intention of permitting France to profit from his laborious negotiations. And he knew that in Spain Britain would not limit itself to benevolent protests. An Allied intervention on the Iberian Peninsula would result not merely in essentially academic discussions about the legitimization of a step to the substance of which Britain readily agreed, but must lead to an open, final and irrevocable rupture with the Alliance. And while Metternich was ready to conduct an independent policy, he was not prepared to drive Britain into open opposition. He was well aware that it was his British option which had enabled him to pursue a policy of cold-blooded effrontery, by which he granted the Tsar the principle of each measure while so completely retaining control of the substance that not one specifically "Russian" objective was achieved. For Castlereagh's friendship limited Metternich's risks. As long as the line to Britain was open, nothing worse could happen than a purely political struggle between Austria and Russia, which, however baneful, would be ameliorated by the certainty of British support. But if Britain were driven into irrevocable opposition, Metternich's policy would lose its flexibility, and he would have to hedge his risks by flattering the Tsar's prejudices. Metternich dealt with this problem with the by now well-tried tactics of Aix-la-Chapelle. He convinced Alexander that, in view of the unstable conditions in France, an intervention in Spain was premature; but he sweetened his refusal with the prospect of another opportunity to demonstrate the moral solidarity of Europe by proposing to defer the Spanish question to another congress to meet in Florence the following year. "My greatest merit," reported Metternich, "is to have so used my influence as to prevent [Alexander] from exceeding the bounds of what is good or correct. For the evil begins at the border of the good, and so imperceptibly that reason cannot discover this borderline without a powerful aid which is called tact."[2]

[1] Stern, II, p. 152.
[2] N.P. III, p. 438.

On 28 February, the congress was formally closed with a final address by Metternich. On 7 March, the Austrian troops destroyed the Neapolitan army at Rieti. On 24 March, the Austrian army, which had suffered almost no casualties, entered Naples with olive twigs on its bayonets. Nothing could have expressed better the ultimate meaning of Metternich's policy of peace as a weapon, moderation as an instrument and a moral consensus as a basis.

IV

But at the very moment when Austrian troops were advancing unopposed towards Naples, the plenipotentiaries still assembled at Laibach were surprised by the news of an event which seemed to demonstrate the validity of the homilies of the Austrian minister about the interconnection of all revolutions. On 12 March, it was learned that a revolution had broken out in Piedmont, the only Italian state not under Austrian influence, and had led to the abdication of the King. But with the experience of the past year, Metternich could deal with this outbreak almost mechanically and with the same tactics that had proved so successful against Naples and in Germany. It was not necessary to convince Alexander of the reality of the new threat, but, if anything, to restrain his eagerness. "Now I understand," exclaimed the Tsar, "why the Lord has kept me here until this moment. How much gratitude do I owe Him, for so arranging things that I was still together with my Allies. . . . If we save Europe it is because He has desired it."[1] Ninety thousand Russian troops were set in motion to form a reserve for an Austrian army hastening towards Italy and to discourage any temptation to intervene on the part of France. In the meantime, the Russian ambassador in Turin was authorized by Metternich to attempt to negotiate for the surrender of the revolutionaries to the new King, the brother of the abdicated monarch, in return for an amnesty—a certain means to bring dissension into the revolutionary camp. On 8 April, an Austrian army completely defeated the Piedmontese.

One would have thought that Metternich was certain of obtaining general acclaim within Austria for a policy which, in two campaigns of less than two weeks, had overthrown two revolutions and cemented Austria's predominance in Italy without exhausting the moral and material resources of the Empire. But the wisdom of a

[1] Schwarz, pp. 211, 225.

policy becomes apparent only in retrospect, while the risks are evident immediately. This was particularly the case with a policy as finely spun as Metternich's, always ready to surrender the form if it could achieve the substance. From the vantage point of crushing victories, the statesmen of the "Austrian school", with Metternich's predecessor, Stadion, at their head, took Metternich's achievements as a matter of course, while criticizing the risks as unwarranted. Because they had not understood the extent of the danger, they could not comprehend the nature of the success. Russian participation in the campaign against Piedmont seemed to them a dangerous surrender of Austrian sovereignty. Indeed, they questioned the very necessity of the campaign in view of the already heavy financial burden and accused Metternich of having needlessly transformed Austria from a British ally into a satellite of Russia. It was a tribute to Metternich's skilful self-effacement that even his colleagues took at face value the play so carefully arranged at Laibach. But it was an ironical twist of fate that Metternich, at the moment of his greatest triumph, should have had more difficulty with the Cabinet at Vienna, than with that of Russia.

Metternich replied in two long dispatches to Stadion, dated 22 April, which recalled the great statements of policy of 1813.[1] Their tone was set by an aphorism and a query: "I have courage, but no illusions. . . . If I were not master of making [the Russian troops] retreat just as I made them advance do you think I should ever have set them in motion?" This proud assertion was preliminary to a summary of Metternich's motivations. He admitted that it had not been necessary to develop such a display of power to defeat the Piedmontese and Neapolitan revolutions. But isolated upheavals in Piedmont or Naples had never been his concern. The real danger lay elsewhere and not in Italy: "I [thought it] my duty to kill Russian liberalism and to demonstrate to Europe that the radicals were opposed by the *two* powers still freest in their actions. . . . Only facts speak in 1821. All the promises, all the phrases of the Emperor of Russia were without value; the movement of a hundred thousand troops . . . the expenditure of twelve million for their mobilization—this is a fact. The order to halt—this is another, no less important, fact. One hundred and twenty thousand troops placed near our borders, to advance only at our request . . . this is a third fact." And Stadion should have no illusion about what had been achieved

[1] N.P. III, p. 467f.

or about the dispensability of Russia: "An immense good has been brought about; but it does no more than barely give us the possibility to continue to live. We must not delude ourselves; we have taken only one single step in the direction of this possibility. . . . The evil has reached prodigious heights. . . . Rest assured that [in all the capitals of Europe] our triumphs will be judged as crimes, our conceptions as errors and our views as criminal folly."

No more complete admission of sterility could have been made. At the height of his triumph, while Europe looked to him almost as its Prime Minister and three monarchs would not take a step without him; after two crushing victories, Metternich was aware not of power, nor of glory, but of weakness, of danger, of impending disaster. Nothing could have made clearer that the Central Empire was doomed than the pessimism of its Foreign Minister at the apogee of his career. Unwilling to adapt its domestic structure, unable to survive with it in a century of nationalism, even Austria's most successful policies amounted to no more than a reprieve, to a desperate grasping to commit allies, not to a work of construction, but to deflect part of the inevitable holocaust. For this reason Metternich's policy was diplomacy in its purest sense, a virtuoso performance of an essentially instrumental kind, whose very skill testified to its ultimate futility, to the fact that the Central Empire, which required stability above all, could survive only through a *tour de force*.

But, in April, 1821, a *tour de force* had been brought off; and while it supplied no final solution for the Austrian dilemma, it had prevented disaster. If Metternich had misgivings, he had given no indication of them to the outside world. In his task of obscuring the weakness of the state he represented, Metternich had succeeded so well that Austria's leadership on the Continent was unchallenged and, as Metternich correctly judged, without alienating Great Britain. "Russia does not lead us," concluded Metternich, "it is we who lead the Emperor Alexander and for several very simple reasons. He needs advice, but he has lost all his advisers. He considers Capo d'Istria a Carbonari chief; he distrusts his army, his ministers, his nobility, his people. In such a situation, one does not lead. . . . And England is completely on our side." This was the real achievement of Metternich's policy, that it had killed Russian liberalism and achieved a measure of domination over Austria's most dangerous rival in the guise of submitting to him.

In May, the reunion of European powers finally broke up. But before he permitted the Tsar to expose himself to the influence of his court, Metternich submitted another memorandum to tide Alexander over until their meeting the following year. In its outline it followed the "profession of faith" of Troppau,[1] with its analysis of the cause of revolutions and the danger of presumption, with its reference to revolution masquerading behind the demand for a constitution—an unmistakable attack on Capo d'Istria—and its reiterated insistence on order before change.[2] But where the memorandum of Troppau was written with the eloquence of a proselytizer, that of Laibach spoke with the measured self-confidence of accomplished mastery. It extended the homage, not only of Austria but of society at large, to the Tsar for having recognized the social malady and also the remedy which lay in the unity of Europe. Alexander, added Metternich, would find his recompense in his conscience—an oblique hint that Russian assistance in Italy had been a duty and constituted no claim on Austria. Metternich concluded with a summary of the means by which Austria and Russia could jointly arrest the spread of the revolutionary disease. They included a continuation of the most intimate relations between the two courts, joint instructions to their ambassadors in the major capitals on important issues, an ambassadors' conference in Vienna as a point of contact and the *precise application* of the principles of Laibach. What Metternich meant by this ambiguous phrase was to become apparent in the next few months.

A circular dispatch by Metternich and a declaration by the monarchs concluded the Congress which for the space of five months had constituted in effect the government of Europe.[3] The circular dispatch contrasted the spirit of justice, conservatism and moderation of the Allied monarchs with the dark intentions of the revolutionaries, eager to destroy everything that rose above a chimerical equality. Faced with such a threat, the governments had no choice but to conserve everything legally established. This did not mean that necessary reforms should be avoided, only that changes had to emanate "from the free decision, from the enlightened views of those on whom God had conferred the responsibility . . . lest upheaval usurp a degree of power which would become a general scourge".

[1] See ante p. 201f.
[2] N.P. III, p. 480 f.
[3] N.p. III, p. 486f.

And this was declared, not as the opinion of the Austrian minister, nor yet of the assembled monarchs, but as an "eternal truth".

V

It is in the nature of successful policies that posterity forgets how easily things might have been otherwise. A Hitler overthrown in 1936 would appear as a rather ridiculous revolutionary chieftain; just as the flight of the Neapolitan army at Rieti makes their effort appear pathetic, rather than dangerous. But had all the revolutions of 1819–1820 occurred simultaneously, there is no doubt that the Austrian Empire would have collapsed a century before its ultimate demise. Instead, Metternich managed to pacify Germany by using the British doctrine of non-interference as a shield. And when Capo d'Istria's dogmatism and the weakness of the Liverpool Cabinet made this a risky course with regard to Naples, he outmanœuvred the Russian minister by achieving a complete personal dominance over the Tsar. He defeated the revolution in Naples before the outbreak in Piedmont. And he had pacified Piedmont when the Alliance was put to its severest test by the revolutions in the Danube Principalities and in Greece—all this as the agent of Europe and without exhausting the moral and material resources of his Empire. He had remained firm against Castlereagh's protests while moderating the Tsar's eagerness to conduct a crusade against Spain. And he had resisted the criticism of the narrow "Austrian school" of diplomats.[1] So it happened that the government of Europe became a reality, if only for an instant and for a sterile cause. It was symbolic that on 5 May, a week before the end of the Congress of Laibach, Napoleon died on St. Helena. The political unification of the Continent, which he had been unable to achieve by conquest, had come about through a voluntary submission to a legitimizing principle.

In the process of making Europe conform to the Austrian version of legitimacy, the incompatibility of the Continental and the insular conception of foreign policy had become increasingly apparent. However great his sympathies for Metternich's objectives, the

[1] "I am back in my good city," he wrote sarcastically after his return to Vienna. "Of course everybody has known everything and predicted it all along. Nobody admits that the course of events might ever have been different; everything having been so simple and clear. . . . Everything went so easily, and everybody has always wanted it this way. . . . After a success, discussion is impossible. . . ." N.P. III, p. 442.

realities of the British domestic scene forced Castlereagh into ever greater isolation. When the Austrian ambassador implied that his increasing reserve was caused by the difficulties of the Liverpool Cabinet, Castlereagh replied in exasperation: "They idly persevere in attributing the line we have taken *and must steadily continue to take* to the temporary difficulties in which the government has been placed, instead of imputing them to those principles *which in our system must be immutable* and which, if the three courts persevere much longer in the *open* [my italics] proclamation of their Ultra doctrines, they will ere long work a separation which it is the wish of all of us to avoid."[1] In this manner the outline of the constellation which posterity has identified with the whole post-Vienna period began to emerge; the three Eastern powers assuming the right to police Europe, not only against political, but against social upheaval; confronted by an increasingly hostile Britain pursuing an independent foreign policy, with France conducting its vacillating measures of expediency between these forces.

But after Laibach this was delayed, not only by Castlereagh's reluctance to surrender his ideal of diplomacy by conference, but also by an event which for a time seemed to demonstrate that the whole dispute between Castlereagh and Metternich had been a quibble about words. For the uprisings in the Danube Principalities and Greece suddenly confronted Metternich and Castlereagh with the danger of the expansion of Russian political influence to the Mediterranean. And as Castlereagh observed the dexterous use made by Metternich of the Laibach basis, he came to realize that a doctrine of common intervention can furnish a more useful tool to frustrate action than the doctrine of non-interference. Not for nothing had Metternich insisted, in his final memorandum to the Tsar, on joint instructions on important measures and on the precise application of their common principles. The news of the rebellion in the Danube Principalities had reached Laibach while the congress was still in session; and while the Tsar had given Austria a blank cheque in Italy, Metternich was far from ready to do the same for Alexander in the Balkans. The firm Metternich represented had a policy against writing blank cheques, all the more so because it realized that the requirement for joint action would keep activity at the level of the least enterprising member of the Alliance. And Austria's only interest in the Balkans was that everything remain unchanged.

[1] Alison, III, p. 223.

And the policy of Castlereagh in the Greek crisis revealed that the doctrine of non-interference did not reflect a superior morality, nor even entirely a difference in domestic structures, but primarily the consciousness of safety conferred by an insular position. For in Greece, where Austrian and British interests were about equally involved—where, in other words, Britain felt as vulnerable as Austria—it suddenly appeared that the insular power, too, could appeal to the Alliance, and, by implication, even to the Holy Alliance. Here, surprisingly, even Castlereagh emerged with a doctrine of the wickedness of revolution and of the danger of an international conspiracy, no less eloquent, if more ponderous, than that of Metternich. When it was again a question of frustrating the Tsar, the old concert between Metternich and Castlereagh was re-established in full force, and it was strange to read the protestations of friendship of a Castlereagh eager to thwart Alexander, which were exceeded in fervour only by those of Metternich, who had the advantage of a year's experience.

XVI

The Greek Insurrection

I

"I FEEL as if I were in the middle of a web," wrote Metternich in the early summer of 1821, "like my friends the spiders whom I love because I have so often admired them. . . . I have brought to bear my moral means in all directions . . . but this state of things forces the poor spider to remain in the centre of its fine web. These webs are beautiful to behold, artfully spun and capable of resisting light attacks; but not a gust of wind."[1] This ironically whimsical aphorism reflects the essence of the "Metternich system"; the policy of enmeshing the opponent by his own moves, of frustrating him with invisible bonds, and dependent on the myth that the "rules of the game" prevented the adversary from sweeping the web away in a moment of impatience. By these tactics Metternich had achieved extraordinary successes. But at the precise moment of his greatest triumph, when he had pacified Germany and Italy and the long-sought tranquillity seemed finally at hand, the "gust of wind" came and from a totally unexpected quarter, the Balkans. And although it did not immediately rend the web, it forced its artful construction to undergo its severest test. Even before the Congress of Laibach ended, news arrived of an uprising in the Danube Principalities against the Turks.

The crisis in the Balkans raised problems, both moral and physical, totally different from recent events in Central Europe. Only by the widest construction could the Ottoman Empire, the militant theocracy against which Europe had been struggling for five hundred years, be considered a "legitimate" government; nor did the fraternal association of monarchs imbued with the maxims of Christianity include the Sultan, who had refused to join the Holy Alliance and whose membership would in any case have constituted an incongruity. But should the analogy to recent events hold, it would only

[1] N.P. III, p. 444.

raise new problems. For Russia, not Austria, would reap the fruits of an intervention in the Balkans. Ever since Peter the Great, Russia had expanded at the expense of the Ottoman Empire, a tradition followed by Alexander in the early years of his reign when he had used the freedom of action conferred on him by the Treaty of Tilsit to invade the Danube Principalities. Only the threat of Napoleon's invasion had forced him, in 1812, to conclude the Treaty of Bucharest, by which Russia obtained a kind of protectorate over the Danube Principalities. Under its terms, the Turkish Satraps, the Hospodars, in Jassy and in Bucharest, were appointed by the Porte but approved by Russia and were drawn from the ranks of the Greek nobility. It was for this reason that the "Greek" rebellion first broke out in an area which was no more Greek than Russia itself, and that it was led by two Greeks who had been officers in the Russian army, one of whom, Ypsilanti, had been a favourite of Alexander's during his campaign against Turkey. In February, 1821, Ypsilanti boldly proclaimed that a great power was ready to support him, and he appealed to the Tsar in the name of Christianity: "Save us, Your Majesty, save our religion from its persecutors, return to us our temples and our altars from which the divine light radiated to the great nation you govern."[1]

What was the founder of the Holy Alliance to respond? This was not a revolution of middle-class origin to achieve political liberty, but a national movement with a religious basis against a power with which even then the Russian ambassador at Constantinople was negotiating about repeated and cynical breaches of the Treaty of Bucharest. Nor was Turkey part of the treaty structure of 1814–15; it was therefore not protected by the Russian interpretation of the Alliance. Moreover, Capo d'Istria, eager to realize his ideals of Greek independence, had known about Ypsilanti's plans and had secretly encouraged him to hope for Russian support. Ypsilanti's letters reached Laibach on 17 March, only three days after the news of the revolution in Piedmont. Should Russia then play in the Balkans the role Austria had reserved for itself in Italy? Was this to be the final result of Metternich's careful manipulation, that he had created a doctrine which would enable Alexander to realize the dreams of Peter the Great?

But Metternich was not ready to sacrifice his conception of the

[1] Text, Prokesch-Osten, Anton von, *Geschichte des Abfalls der Griechen*, 5 Vols. (Vienna, 1867), Vol. III, p. 61f.

requirements of repose to a doctrinaire application of formal analogies. As early as 1808 he had declared the preservation of the Ottoman Empire a fundamental Austrian interest, for the characteristic reason that it secured the tranquillity of Austria's southern borders, while any change in this situation could only bring about prolonged turmoil.[1] He was not prepared now to let Alexander achieve under Austrian aegis what had eluded him as a result of his understanding with Napoleon at Tilsit. But preventing a Russian descent on Turkey was not as easy as the desire for it. The main part of Austria's strength was in Italy, and it was in any case unthinkable that Austria should make war with the very power which had just placed a hundred thousand troops at its disposal.

Thus, the last contest between Alexander and Metternich came to be joined on a plane which the Tsar had come to consider his own, that of absolute moral claims. For Metternich proceeded to prove that Alexander, although master of his actions, was not master of his will; that the same maxims which had supplied a principle of intervention in Italy could also furnish a doctrine of non-intervention in the Balkans. However sincere Alexander's religious exaltation, it became to Metternich a political "fact" on whose correct exploitation depended survival. Metternich accordingly dealt with Alexander by admitting his moral claim while reserving the right to interpret its application to concrete instances. He proceeded to prove that the analogy between the Balkans and Italy was an illusion, fostered by cunning revolutionaries to reverse the tide running so strongly against them: "This explosion is without doubt the result of a careful plan," read a memorandum submitted by Metternich to Alexander, "directed against the power most terrible for these conspirators: the union of the two monarchs in a system of conservation. . . . This is a torch thrown between Austria and Russia, . . . and by creating discord between the most powerful monarch of the Greek-Orthodox profession and his people . . . to force him to withdraw from the West and to keep him completely occupied in the East."[2] In short, the same Alliance which had enabled Metternich to act in Italy was to be used to prevent Russian action in the Balkans. For the privilege of assisting Austria in the West, Alexander was asked to reverse a century of Russian policy in the East. Friendship was to provide the fetter which force could not have supplied.

[1] N.P. II, p. 164f.
[2] Schwarz, p. 216.

The results were not long delayed. Alexander told Metternich that "the revolution in the Danube-Duchies was nothing but a new conflagration, brought about by the hope of frustrating the application of the Christian principles proclaimed by the Holy Alliance". Ypsilanti was discharged from the Russian army; his associate, Wladimerescu, was deprived of his Russian decoration. And Capo d'Istria, whose only real passion was the independence of Greece, was instructed to send a reply to Ypsilanti, which lectured him that liberty could not be obtained by conspiracies and advised him to repent and cease in his endeavour.[1] In these circumstances it was not difficult for the Turks to defeat the revolt. Ypsilanti fled to Hungary, where he disappeared into a prison for six years.

The Congress of Laibach had thus crushed three revolutions, two by a doctrine of intervention and the third by a doctrine of non-intervention; and both doctrines had been legitimized as the application of the maxims of the Holy Alliance. But Metternich wanted to leave nothing to chance. A week before they separated, he obtained Alexander's promise to take no steps in the Balkans without his Allies. And his final memorandum declared Austro-Russian co-operation and joint instructions to their ambassadors the foundation of European tranquillity. Metternich had succeeded in preventing the gust of wind from tearing his web. But the Turkish problem was not to be settled so easily or by Metternich alone. For the unsuccessful revolt in the Danube Duchies provided the signal for the "real" Greeks in the Morea to assert their claim to independence. In less than three months the Turks were expelled from the Peninsula, and the Eastern question became the central problem of European diplomacy.

II

The Ottoman Empire had long ceased to be the powerful state which had kept Central Europe in a state of terror as late as the seventeenth century. Extending over three continents, it represented a strange mixture of military dictatorship and feudal relationships, its components ruled by satraps, in various states of independence from the Sultan in Constantinople. But if the Bei of Tunis, the Emir of Egypt, the Pasha of Morea and Hospodars of the Danube Principalities enjoyed differing degrees of authority, they were all subject to the

[1] Text, Prokesch-Osten, III, p. 65f.

treacherous attacks by which the Central Government attempted to obscure its increasing weakness and to assert its supremacy. Among the European vassals of the Sultan, the Greeks occupied a favoured position, dominating the Balkan peninsula culturally, economically and administratively. The Turkish navy was largely manned by Greek sailors. The university of Jassy carried a Greek impress, and the Hospodars in the Danube Principalities were customarily drawn from the ranks of the Greek nobility. The Greek rebellion was therefore a mortal attack on the very structure of the Ottoman Empire. If it succeeded and the control of the Aegean was lost, how could the Porte retain its more distant provinces? It is not surprising that the reaction of the Turks to the loss of the Morea was hysterical and that it was transformed into frenzy by the appeal of the Greeks to their co-religionists. The early spirit of religious fanaticism returned and led to a slaughter of the Greeks in the Turkish capital. On Easter Sunday, 1821, the Greek Patriarch of Constantinople, together with several of his Bishops, was hanged at the door of his cathedral.

This was a direct challenge to Russia, the traditional protector of the Greek-Orthodox faith, doubly provocative to a monarch of Alexander's religious mania and already ill at ease about the tales of Turkish brutality in repressing the rebellion in the Danube Principalities. Above all, Alexander was now removed from the influence of Metternich and exposed to Capo d'Istria's interpretation of his moral duty, which proved all the more persuasive for being supported from two unexpected quarters. In June, a memorandum by Ancillon, the tutor of the Prussian Crown-Prince, denied that the Ottoman Empire was a "legitimate" government and proposed the appointment of Russia as the agent of the Holy Alliance in restoring order. And his proposal was seconded by a voice from the past. Baroness Kruedener, long since fallen from favour, re-emerged with a vision of a new crusade and wrote ecstatically to her former disciple that she was certain he would celebrate the Christmas Mass in Jerusalem. "It requires a strong soul to resist the influence of one's environment, an even greater one to break it," wrote Metternich. "The Emperor [Alexander] still holds fast, but he stands alone. . . ."[1]

So it happened that throughout the summer Alexander withdrew into his characteristic pose of indecision masquerading as fortitude, of vacillation in the guise of intransigeance. He wanted to retain

[1] N.P. III, p. 444.

Metternich's friendship without exposing himself to the strictures of his minister. He desired Allied unity, but he also wished to appear as the Saviour of the Greek-Orthodox religion. Alexander's communications throughout July reflected this ambiguity. While he protested his allegiance to the spirit of Laibach, he appealed to the Austrian Emperor on 11 July with the query whether Europe could expect him to stand idly by in the face of Turkish atrocities. While recriminating against the slaughter of his co-religionists, he assured Metternich on 17 July that he would act only in unison with his allies.[1] But Metternich, a past master at the exploitation of the term "unity", could have no doubt that it would prove next to impossible to put a limit on the heir of Catherine the Great once hostilities had broken out. And events transpiring in Constantinople made war appear unavoidable.

All this time, the Russian ambassador in Turkey, Stroganov, had been negotiating with the Porte, partly about infractions of the Treaty of Bucharest, partly in his self-appointed capacity as the protector of the Greek-Orthodox faith in the Ottoman Empire. Stroganov was a diplomat of the old "Russian school", which considered Russia the heir of the Byzantine Empire and Constantinople the natural goal of Russian policy. Since he received his instructions directly from Capo d'Istria, Stroganov's behaviour did nothing to ameliorate the tension, while the Porte, for its part, treated the Russian minister with more than its customary insolence. For if Alexander's measures proved ambiguous for the West, they were all too clear to the suspicious Turks, to whom the Holy Alliance seemed a call for a new crusade and the Tsar's beneficent maxims a subterfuge for a descent on the Straits. So tense did relations become that Stroganov withdrew from Constantinople to a port on the Black Sea from which, on 5 June, he sent a long account of Turkish atrocities.

Capo d'Istria's reply was peremptory.[2] It spoke of the outrage committed against the Christian religion and invoked the consensus of Europe on behalf of Russia. It demanded the immediate reconstruction of the destroyed churches, guarantees for the inviolability of worship, a distinction between the innocent and guilty and assurance of a peaceful existence for those who had not participated in the revolution. A refusal would prove that the Ottoman Empire was

[1] Text, N.P. III, p. 416 (Letter to Metternich); Prokesch-Osten, III, p. 124f. (Letter to the Emperor.)

[2] Stern, II, p. 217; Webster, II, p. 355.

unfit to associate with Christian states, and Russia, together with the rest of Christianity, would protect its co-religionists. The Porte's reply was demanded within eight days. As Capo d'Istria undoubtedly expected, the frenzied Sultan refused even to consider an ultimatum, and only the intercession of the British ambassador, Lord Strangford, saved Stroganov from assassination at the hands of the incensed Turks. When the Russian ambassador sailed for Odessa on 10 August, a declaration of war seemed the inevitable next step.

But Metternich was not to be swept off his feet. He knew that Alexander was seeking not political but moral conquests and that, therefore, philosophical ties might more than counterbalance political relationships. It was thus the same struggle as at Laibach, and as then, the contest resolved itself into an exegesis of the maxims of the Holy Alliance. Capo d'Istria argued that the Tsar's moral duty impelled him to an active policy in the East. Metternich maintained that the appeal to the Tsar's religion was a proof of the cunning wickedness of evil. But since Alexander had promised at Laibach not to separate himself from his allies, Metternich's negotiating position was stronger than it appeared, despite the traditions of Russian policy and the intransigeance of the Turks. For an alliance furnishes a wider moral and material base for action only if there is an identity of wills. Because Metternich had succeeded in dominating Alexander in 1821, Austria had reduced Russia to a diplomatic satellite during its pacification of Italy. Because Alexander could not obtain a similar acquiescence from Austria, the Alliance frustrated Capo d'Istria in his Greek projects. The issue between Metternich and Capo d'Istria thus resolved itself into a contest whether the maxims of a legitimizing principle could defeat the claims of national interest.

All of Capo d'Istria's impetuosity could not hide the fact that, in Metternich's words, "two factions are opposing each other all over the world: the Capo d'Istrias and the Metternichs. Since the Tsar is a Metternich, his opponents will be left to their fate". As his brilliant "portrait" of the Tsar was to prove, Metternich understood Alexander's character, whose indecisiveness took the form of stubborn persistence in whatever course of action he had adopted, usually after long hesitation. Because he conducted policy in a mood of exaltation, Alexander tended to invest unavoidable decisions with a single-minded fanaticism which he identified with the dictates of morality. Thus, in 1807, after the defeat at Friedland, his hatred of Napoleon had changed almost overnight into enthusiastic admiration; so after he was forced into war in 1812, he had persisted with a stubbornness which he considered as the moral vindication of the burning of Moscow; similarly after 1815, his frustration at Vienna had given rise to his mood of religious mysticism. Metternich therefore sought to prevent a Russian change of course at any cost, for he knew that once embarked on war Alexander would soon transform it into a crusade. "If one cannon is fired, *Alexander will escape us at the head of his retinue* [my italics] and then there will be no limit any longer to what he will consider his divinely ordained laws."[1]

In this situation, Metternich arranged for a veritable flood of police reports to descend on the impressionable Tsar, dispatching so many messengers that at one point he had none left at his disposal in Vienna. And all these appeals culminated in one proposition: The fundamental Russian interest in Europe was to suppress the social revolution, not to avenge the cruelties of the Turkish Empire, however painful these might prove to Alexander personally. The diabolical Central Revolutionary Committee in Paris was, in some undetermined manner, inciting the outbreaks in the Morea in order to undermine the Alliance which doomed it to futility. "The evil we have to combat," replied Emperor Franz to the Tsar's letter of 11 July, "is situated in Europe, rather than in Turkey. . . . In order to lose any illusion about the real nature of their aims, it is only necessary to look at those who now wax so enthusiastically about the so-called Christian interests: . . . They are the very people who do not believe in any God and who respect neither His laws nor those of man. . . . In the unity of the Allied courts, resides the last hope to avert the threatening evil."[2] This was an appeal to the Tsar of Laibach to sanctify his work through persistence in adversity, to resist the temptation wrought by the malicious cunning of the Central Committee, which had attempted to create a conflict between Alexander's moral duty and his humanitarian precepts. But where at Troppau and in the early stages at Laibach Allied unity had been invoked to justify common action, it was now used to develop a doctrine of inaction. And on this basis, unexpectedly, Castlereagh rejoined the Alliance as if he had never really been away.

For Turkey and the control of the Straits was not a remote, "abstract" problem like the mode of suppressing the revolution in

[1] Schwartz, p. 234.
[2] Text, Prokesch-Osten, III, p. 156f., 22 August, 1821.

Naples. Here it was not a case of insular security dictating a policy of self-righteous aloofness. The destruction of the Ottoman Empire might involve the loss of the control of the Mediterranean and almost certainly of the Near East. Here for the first time was an issue which offered as great a threat to Great Britain as to Austria. And suddenly nothing was heard any longer of Metternich's timidity and policy of precaution. If anything, Castlereagh now criticized Metternich for not being precautionary enough; in fact, he suspected him of being in league with the Tsar for the dismemberment of the Ottoman Empire.[1] He therefore remained cool during June to Metternich's pleas for joint action in Constantinople. But on 16 July, without any prearrangement with Metternich, Castlereagh made an overture to the Tsar which revealed that where basic British interests were concerned, Castlereagh, too, could appeal to the Alliance, even in its widest interpretation. For what emerged in a private letter to Alexander in a, for Castlereagh, rare burst of eloquence was an appeal to the Tsar of Troppau and Laibach, the guardian of the Alliance, the magnanimous ruler whose beneficence would assure European repose. Forgotten were the strictures of the previous year about the unwarranted extension of the Alliance. Ignored were the criticisms of only a few months ago of the Tsar's futile vision of a European government. Even the principle of non-interference in the domestic affairs of other states was violated, for the dispatch contained a scarcely veiled attack on Capo d'Istria.

Castlereagh's pretext for writing to the Tsar was a remark Alexander had made at the end of the Congress of Aix-la-Chapelle three years previously, that Castlereagh should feel free to appeal to him directly in case of an overriding crisis. The letter began with an oblique reference to the Tsar's domestic difficulties, coupled with an affirmation of British-Russian unity and of the controlling nature of the Alliance, only recently so anxiously limited. He had no hesitation to write Alexander, affirmed Castlereagh, "as I feel an intimate conviction, however your Imperial Majesty may be pressed . . . *by local considerations and by the peculiar temper of your people*, [my italics] that Your Majesty's views of the complicated evils will correspond with that of the British government; and I entertain a no less sanguine persuasion that Your Imperial Majesty, *triumphing over every local impediment* [my italics] . . . will afford another, but not unexpected, proof of Your Majesty's determination to main-

[1] Webster, II, p. 361.

tain inviolably the European system, as consolidated by the late treaties of peace." It was a strange doctrine to enunciate, in view of all that had gone before. Turkey was to be afforded the protection of treaties she had refused to join, while their applicability to Naples, which had been a signatory, had been steadfastly rejected. No less remarkable was Castlereagh's interpretation of the real issue in the Greek rebellion. He denied that it represented an isolated phenomenon. Rather it formed "a brand of that organized spirit of insurrection which is systematically propagating itself throughout Europe, and which explodes wherever the hand of the governing power, from whatever cause, is enfeebled." Not nine months had passed since Castlereagh had branded the Tsar's efforts to combat *the* revolution "a beautiful phantom which Britain, above all, cannot pursue".

Castlereagh did not deny that the atrocities committed by the Turks "made humanity shudder". But, like Metternich, he insisted that humanitarian considerations were subordinate to maintaining "the consecrated structure" of Europe which would be jarred to the core by any radical innovation. He therefore appealed to Alexander "to afford posterity a proud manifestation of your Imperial Majesty's principles . . . by exercising towards this . . . semi-barbarous state that degree of magnanimity which a religious . . . respect for the system which your Imperial Majesty has so powerfully contributed to raise in Europe could alone dictate under such provocations". And the letter concluded with an assertion that the recent disagreements within the Alliance had been minor disputes about common objectives and that Britain's attachment to the Tsar had remained unabated: "I feel . . . convinced that each state . . . adhering to its peculiar habits of action, will nevertheless remain unalterably true to the fundamental obligations of the Alliance, and that the present European system . . . will long continue to subsist for the safety and the repose of Europe."[1]

In the light of the recent past, this letter would have constituted an unparalleled effrontery were its matter-of-factness not so disarming an illustration of Castlereagh's mentality. Now that British interests were threatened, he was no more able to understand that the danger might not prove self-evident, than in the previous year he had been ready to admit that the Alliance might be capable of various interpretations. Here was the "overriding danger" so often invoked, and it was only natural that Castlereagh should

[1] C.C. XII, p. 403f., 16 July, 1821.

see the Alliance again in all its pristine glory as the guardian of the peace.

Although Alexander's first reaction to Castlereagh's letter was not very encouraging, he was unable to resist the onslaught of his two great allies. That which he had sought in vain for nearly a decade, the approbation of a grateful Europe, was his now for the asking. For the first time no petty considerations limited the universal application of his maxims and if the appeal to his ideals amounted in practice to a call for unlimited self-restraint, it was still a final, if belated, vindication. In the meantime, Metternich had induced Prussia's Foreign Minister to declare Ancillon's memorandum his "private opinion", so that all protestations of friendship barely obscured the fact that Russia was isolated again. All this combined to make Alexander draw back. When in early August Capo d'Istria argued that a war in the Balkans would restore its former unity to the Alliance, Alexander replied in the language of Metternich: "If we reply to the Turks by making war, the Revolutionary Committee in Paris will triumph and no government will remain standing." And he forbade Capo d'Istria to mention the prospect of war in any of his dispatches. When Stroganov presented himself after his return from Constantinople, he was informed of Alexander's decision and ordered to comply with it. On 29 August, Alexander replied to Castlereagh, if somewhat ambiguously: "I shall carry my forbearance as far as possible."[1] With justice might Metternich write on 3 September: "Daily, I receive new proofs that the Emperor Alexander takes increasing roots in my 'school' . . . Capo d'Istria wants action, but not the Emperor."[2]

But while much was gained by averting the immediate outbreak of the war, the factors that had produced the tension still existed. The Greek rebellion continued with countless atrocities by both sides. Capo d'Istria remained Russian minister and was joined in his entreaties for decisive action by almost all the Russian diplomats. And as the travail of his soul increased, Alexander took refuge in a mystifying ambiguity which sought to compensate for each act of conciliation with a warlike pronouncement. Alexander's decision had thus given Castlereagh and Metternich a breathing space, but no more. Alexander told the British Ambassador that they had the whole winter to attempt to avoid the calamity of war, but that it might be wise for the Allies to consider their course of action should war be

[1] Text, Prokesch-Osten, III, p. 191f.
[2] N.P. III, p. 448.

forced on him.[1] Metternich's solution was to recur to his old stand-by, the ambassadors' conference in Vienna, which would supply Alexander with a symbol of solidarity and Metternich with a means to thwart Russia's ambitions. But Castlereagh was afraid that Metternich might prove too accommodating, and he thought the question in any case too complicated to be entrusted to ambassadors.[2] Metternich next proposed a personal meeting with Castlereagh for which the British King's impending visit to his subjects in Hanover might provide a pretext.

When Metternich broached this subject to Gordon, the British *chargé d'affaires* in Vienna, it was coldly received. Still steeped in Castlereagh's policy of cautious aloofness of the previous year, Gordon insisted that separate negotiations would lead to "false interpretation and jealousies and evil reports in other quarters".[3] But he was lagging behind events. His view of the Alliance was that of Troppau and Laibach, where no immediate British interest had been involved, or of Aix-la-Chapelle, where France was considered the only threat. But the case of Turkey was different, and it was characteristic that to Castlereagh the difference appeared as between a practical problem and an issue over abstract theory, a view of the Neapolitan revolution which would certainly have startled Metternich: "Were the question chiefly pressing upon our attention one of *ordinary* character, and involving immediately the particular form of government under which any portion of Europe was to subsist (as that of Naples lately did), I should feel as you have done about an interview with Prince Metternich. . . . But the question of Turkey is of a totally different character and one which in England we regard not as a *theoretical* but a *practical* consideration. . . ."[4] [My italics.] In this manner, the two great statesmen of repose met for the final time at the end of October, 1821, to work out, as so often before, a common plan of action to preserve the equilibrium of Europe.

III

Metternich's procession across Germany was a triumphal tour. At every court he was greeted as the man who had vanquished the revolution, and he reported that the German Cabinets were asking

[1] Webster, II, p. 373.
[2] Webster, II, p. 365.
[3] C.C. XII, p. 439, 3 October, 1821.
[4] Webster, II, p. 366.

for commands rather than advice.[1] Nor was his reception by the King of England of a nature to diminish his self-confidence. It was expressive of Metternich's position as the conservative conscience of Europe, that at his first interview with George IV the conversation dealt at considerably greater length with the domestic affairs of Great Britain than with the Greek insurrection. George was determined to force Liverpool's resignation, and he sought the advice of the "doctor of revolutions" on the best means to accomplish it with the least turmoil. For his part, Metternich, although he did not care for Liverpool, wanted to be sure that the change in government would not lead to a withdrawal of Castlereagh from office. He therefore attempted to persuade Castlereagh to arrange for Liverpool's resignation and to form a new cabinet himself. Castlereagh consented on condition that Liverpool resign voluntarily; otherwise he would go out with him.[2]

When Castlereagh and Metternich at last turned to a consideration of the Greek insurrection, they found themselves in substantial agreement. Metternich had brought with him a memorandum which dealt with the Russo-Turkish dispute in three parts. It asserted that, in order to obtain a basis for negotiation, the Alliance should be "considered as actually existing in full force"—a thinly veiled hint to Castlereagh not to repeat his self-righteous strictures of the previous year; that Capo d'Istria was the chief obstacle to a settlement and that the Austrian and British representatives at Constantinople should attempt to obtain some concessions from the Porte in order to remove all pretexts for war.[3] Castlereagh concurred, and the two ministers agreed to concert their efforts towards maintaining the peace, to evade Russian requests for a clarification of the British and Austrian attitude in case of war and to send parallel instructions to the Austrian and British ambassadors in Russia. But each minister was to use the arguments appropriate to his particular situation in order to avoid the appearance of an Austro-British understanding against Russia.[4] Lord Strangford, the British ambassador in Turkey, was to conduct the negotiations with the Porte. Thus, by the end of October, Metternich's spider-web was stronger than ever. At Laibach he had obtained the Tsar's promise to take no

[1] N.P. III, p. 492.
[2] N.P. III, p. 494; Webster, II, p. 356f.
[3] Schwarz, p. 239; Phillips, W. A., *The Confederation of Europe* (London, 1913), p. 225.
[4] N.P. III, p. 492f.; Webster, II, p. 375f.

separate diplomatic action; at Hanover, he had arranged for co-ordinated measures with Britain. As in the crucial spring of 1813, Metternich represented the bridge between the protagonists, because he possessed a legitimizing principle recognized by both sides, the appeal to the political equilibrium for Castlereagh and to the social equilibrium for Alexander.

Castlereagh was the first to appeal to Alexander, although he took the latitude to use peculiarly British arguments somewhat too literally. Instead of appealing to the exalted principles of the Alliance, he attempted to dissuade the Tsar from rash steps by demonstrating their "unreasonableness". Instead of interpreting Alexander's moral maxims to support his own arguments, he denied their applicability altogether. As agreed at Hanover, Castlereagh refused to discuss the Russian inquiries about the British attitude in case of war, because "no power could predict its attitude in case of so portentous a contest". Even should a war prove inevitable, he could not agree that its goal should be the establishment of a Greek state, "originating in a system of revolt so much reproved by the Emperor". If a Russian minister recommended such a scheme, added Castlereagh, let him formulate it in some clear and intelligible manner and not expect to receive any advice from Russia's allies, who must on the contrary protest against it. But this direct attack on Capo d'Istria proved unfortunate, because the Tsar did not understand the British fiction of ministerial responsibility and considered it aimed at himself. Nor did the remainder of Castlereagh's dispatch help matters. For while it admitted that atrocities had in fact been committed by the Turks, it delivered a lecture on the relation between sentiment and statesmanship which Alexander could only interpret as a challenge to all the maxims he was so profuse in professing: ". . . If a statesman were permitted to regulate his conduct by the counsels of his heart instead of the dictates of his understanding, I really see no limits which might be given to his impulse. . . . But we must always recollect that his is the grave task of providing for the peace and security of those interests immediately committed to his care, that he must not endanger the fate of the present generation in a speculative endeavour to improve the lot of that which is to come. . . ."[1]

But to the extent that Castlereagh disdained using the sacramental language of the Tsar, he lost the ability to persuade; and throughout the autumn relations deteriorated. This was due in large part to Capo

[1] Webster, II, p. 376f., 28 October, 1821.

d'Istria, who was still writing the dispatches and gave the Tsar's intentions the sharpest possible formulation, in the hope that he might lure Castlereagh or Metternich into an incautious reply. But Alexander was becoming restive himself. He pointed out that his troops had always been at the disposal of Europe, and he promised ominously that even in the middle of his army he would act as if the representatives of Austria, France, Great Britain, and Prussia were assembled around him. This was one promise, however, which Metternich was determined not to put to test. On 5 December, he therefore appealed to Alexander in a language the Tsar found more comprehensible than the ponderous logic of Castlereagh. The Oriental crisis, asserted Metternich, was the last onslaught of the evil principle before its final defeat. He told Alexander of his journey across a Germany very different from 1818, whose tranquillity was due largely to the Tsar's attitude at Laibach. Although this was a slight exaggeration, it gave Alexander a reputation to sustain and served as the proper introduction to Metternich's concluding passage which attempted to resolve the doubts of his unstable opponent by elevating constancy into a moral act: "Let nothing deroute or distract us. A renown awaits the monarchs worthy of their constancy and their noble efforts. It is nothing less than to have saved civilization from the general conflagration which perverse spirits . . . have for a long time dared to foment. . . . History, Sire, gives a much different account of moral conquests than of those which have no other goal but the conquest of provinces or the fall of Empires."[1]

And to put into sharp focus the moral conquests awaiting Alexander, the performance of the previous summer was repeated. Messengers followed each other in rapid succession with voluminous reports of revolutionary conspiracies in Germany and Italy. Even Castlereagh weighed in with a dispatch which in laboured phrases spoke of a revolutionary gulf stream flowing from the shores of South America to those of the Aegean.[2] Although these reports produced no immediate amelioration of the tension, they increased the Tsar's indecisiveness. "Everything inspires him with distrust and suspicion," reported Lebzeltern, and soon intelligence reached the West that Alexander was instituting a secret police on the Austrian model.

[1] Stern, II, p. 561f. (text).

[2] C.C. XII, p. 443, 14 December, 1821. This was actually never delivered because the British ambassador was afraid that certain threatening passages would produce an effect contrary to that intended.

Metternich next turned his barrage on another chink in Alexander's armour, the ambiguous position of his Prime Minister. "Capo d'Istria wants a war and yet he does not want it," wrote Metternich. "He wants Russian assistance to bring Greek affairs to a conclusion, but not . . . for Russian ends. He sees himself confronted with a tremendous responsibility and has the embarrassment peculiar to such a situation: to serve two causes and only one master. . . . And there is nothing more contradictory than these two causes; erect a Greek state and you will see that it will consider Russia the only enemy it need fear."[1] To expose this contradiction, Metternich, on 28 January, finally replied to Capo d'Istria's threatening missives. In a dispatch of artful subtlety he rejected the charge that Austria had not lived up to the spirit of Laibach.[2] On the contrary, by refusing to let itself be drawn into Turkish affairs, Austria had prevented the outbreak of another round of revolutions in the West. But together with the ritualistic condemnation of the revolution and its atheistic advocates, Metternich advanced a proposal for the resolution of the dilemma by distinguishing between the issues raised by Turkish infractions of existing treaties with Russia, on whose fulfilment Russia had a right to insist unilaterally, and those brought on by the Greek insurrection, which were a general European concern and the proper topic of a European congress. Metternich promised to prove Austria's friendship by supporting the purely "Russian" grievances, which he grouped under four headings: (a) the restoration of the Greek churches, (b) the protection of the Greek religion, (c) the recognition of a distinction between guilty and innocent Greeks, (d) the evacuation of the Danube Principalities. By his offer of support for the "Russian" demands, Metternich attempted to demonstrate the "Greek" motivation of Alexander's minister and to lure Alexander into what would amount to a surrender of any *special* right to interfere in the Greek insurrection.

But throughout February, the Tsar continued to envelop himself in silence; and if Capo d'Istria's bitter dispatches were any indication of his frame of mind, war was unavoidable. When Lord Strangford's negotiations at Constantinople collapsed in the face of Turkish intransigeance, Capo d'Istria seemed to have triumphed. He replied

[1] Schwarz, p. 246.

[2] Text, N.P. III, p. 531f.; see also Webster, II, p. 379. Even Webster, for all his reservations about Metternich, praises the "adroitness" of this dispatch.

to Metternich's note with such sharpness that the Austrian ambassador thought it a prelude to the rupture of relations. But Capo d'Istria's note was to prove his last fling at Metternich. Only three days after it was sent, Alexander, as during the previous August, recoiled before the prospect of isolated action. The vision of a reconciled humanity was not easily given up, even for the traditional goal of Russian policy, the control of the Straits. And characteristically, Alexander escaped his dilemma by a flight into Allied unity. He told Lebzeltern that he was tired of the exchange of notes and that he was sending a plenipotentiary to Vienna to negotiate with Metternich. His choice was hardly fortunate, because Taticheff, the former ambassador in Madrid, had distinguished himself by his intrigues against Britain in 1817. But while the Tsar might flatter himself that all options were still open to him, Metternich could not doubt that he had won the fundamental point: to transform the dispute from a moral into a political issue, to be resolved by the methods of cabinet diplomacy in which he was master. "The bomb has exploded," he wrote sarcastically, "and it was filled—with cotton. . . . Since one does not know what to *say*, having exhausted the reserve of idiocies, one now wishes to *discuss*. One has chosen the man who happened to be available, for the simple reason that nothing is so rare in Russia as a man. . . . Now things will get moving."[1]

Things did not get moving, however, for Taticheff's behaviour was as ambiguous as the motivations of his Court. He arrived with a note drafted by Capo d'Istria, which insisted on Russian protection over the Christians in the Ottoman Empire and the transformation of Turkish sovereignty over Greece into suzerainty. But Taticheff also admitted that Capo d'Istria's note did not exhaust his instructions, that, in addition, Alexander had told him to stress Russia's determination to act only in unison with its allies. This was more to Metternich's liking, because the requirement of unity gave Austria a veto over Russia's actions. It was dangerous to send a subordinate plenipotentiary to negotiate with Metternich, it was doubly dangerous to hold the negotiations in Vienna; it was fatal to send the plenipotentiary with a dual set of instructions which amounted to no more than a resolve to achieve agreement.[2] In addition, Taticheff's

[1] N.P. III, p. 505.

[2] For the negotiations Metternich-Taticheff, see Prokesch-Osten, III, p. 303f.; also N.P. III, p. 549f. Metternich's account is contained in dispatches written to his ambassadors, particularly in Turkey. No motive would seem to exist for colouring them; every motive to render them accurate.

extraordinary vanity made him believe that he could dupe Metternich, and Metternich had always known how to exploit opponents who underestimated him. "Few people understand," he said regarding Taticheff, "how advantageously one can use people who fancy themselves shrewd. . . . Only the entirely honest opponent is difficult to vanquish."

Thus, Metternich was given an opportunity for another virtuoso performance of pure cabinet diplomacy; of exhibiting his mastery of a negotiation in which the goal was given and everything depended on the correct exploitation of the opponent's psychology. It was his last such performance, for never again would he be able to conduct himself with the effrontery conferred by the certainty of his British option. Taticheff soon joined the distinguished company of Narbonne, Aberdeen, Caraman, Hardenberg, and Stewart, who had negotiated with Metternich only to find themselves completely outmanœuvred or, as happened equally frequently, transformed into spokesmen of the wily Austrian minister. At their next meeting, Metternich persuaded Taticheff to negotiate on the basis of the Tsar's instructions rather than Capo d'Istria's. With the requirement for unity thus firmly established, Metternich next asked Taticheff to formulate Russia's maximum demands for submission first to the Austrian Cabinet and then to the Allies; but, in the end, Taticheff's draft never got beyond Metternich. Metternich eliminated one after another of Taticheff's demands; he would not agree to a Russian "protectorate" over the Greeks; nor to Turkish suzerainty; nor to Allied military action, so that Taticheff was confronted with a void. When Taticheff plaintively asked Metternich to formulate an alternative programme, he merely made evident his dilemma: unity is not an end but a series of conditions. When it becomes an end, it leads to an abdication of statesmanship and to the domination of an alliance by its most determined member, the member who knows his goals. "Only two alternatives are possible," wrote Metternich. "Either they want to deceive me or they do not know what they want or what they can do. The former is too ridiculous for consideration, the latter so in conformity with my knowledge of their country that without hesitation I assume it to be the correct explanation."[1]

At this point Metternich's finely-spun performance was nearly upset by an intransigeant note from the Porte, which not only rejected the Russian demands but accused Russia of fomenting the

[1] N.P. III, p. 506.

Greek Revolution in a tone seemingly made to order to furnish Capo d'Istria with a pretext to sever relations.[1] But Metternich was not yet at the end of his resources, and he escaped his dilemma by a demonstration of solidarity with Russia: he read the Turkish note to Taticheff together with the Austrian reply that it was below Austria's dignity to transmit such a communication to Russia. Thus Metternich's first act of partisanship was a measure which removed an excuse for a declaration of war. And Taticheff accepted Metternich's evasion; indeed, he expressed his conviction that Turkish insolence could not affect Russia's calm resolution. The negotiations at Vienna, therefore, degenerated into a cat-and-mouse game, not in order to achieve Russia's goals, but to discover the reason for Taticheff's foolish pliability. Finally, on 27 March, Taticheff revealed that Metternich had in fact succeeded in driving a wedge between Alexander and Capo d'Istria. It appeared now that Taticheff had been instructed to report directly to Alexander, by-passing Capo d'Istria. And Alexander's sole desire, reported Taticheff, was to find an honourable way to get through the summer, so that he could appear at the Congress in the fall without having his hands tied. "The whole affair begins only today," wrote Metternich. "After having robbed the world of a few months of peace, the Emperor Alexander takes his head in his hands and presents himself before me with the request that I explain its content to him. . . . [He] wants to find his way in a labyrinth and asks his old Ariadne for yarn."[2]

And yarn was to be supplied to him in profusion. Metternich now took charge of both sides of the negotiation. He first of all drafted Taticheff's official report to Capo d'Istria explaining the impossibility of obtaining Austria's acquiescence to Capo d'Istria's instructions. This was supplemented by an official note by Metternich, still designed for Capo d'Istria, restating the Austrian position along the lines of the memorandum of 28 January and retaining its distinction between Russo-Turkish disputes and the Greek insurrection. Next came a semi-official letter for the Tsar, which, in order to moderate his impatience, urged that the date of the European Congress be advanced to August. Finally, Taticheff was given a confidential letter to Alexander via Nesselrode in which Metternich asked for confidence, above all, and disingenuously pleaded guilty to conducting a purely Austrian policy, if by that term was meant his extreme

[1] Text, Prokesch-Osten, III, p. 278f.
[2] N.P. III, p. 507, 3 April, 1822.

desire to become a pillar of strength for his friends.[1] And since Alexander had to be given some proof of the value of Austria's friendship, a letter from Emperor Franz, drafted by Metternich, announced Austria's decision to break relations with Turkey, if it persisted in its refusal to satisfy Russian demands growing out of existing treaties—*provided all the Allies agreed*, a safe enough promise in view of Castlereagh's intransigeance. And to determine the sense of the Allies, ministerial conferences were to be held in Vienna starting in June. To while away the campaigning season Alexander was to be fed a diet of European solidarity.

IV

Capo d'Istria was defeated. The Greek was separated from the Turkish question, Russian ambition thwarted in the name of the very Alliance Capo d'Istria had striven for seven years to give the widest possible interpretation. It was in vain that Capo d'Istria attempted to demonstrate the duplicity of this interpretation of the Alliance, invoked grandiloquently only to obtain Alexander's consent to a doctrine of self-limitation. It was futile that, in order to separate Britain and Austria, he called for the formation of a European army against the revolution in Spain. Metternich merely added this proposal to the agenda of the ministerial conference and thus gave Alexander another motive for attendance. Metternich's major concern was no longer Capo d'Istria but Castlereagh's pedantic intransigeance: "Castlereagh will never understand the core of the issue," wrote Metternich, "which is that the Emperor Alexander does not desire the Turkish involvement, while Capo d'Istria . . . sees in the Spanish question a means to force matters to a head in Turkey. . . . This is again a case where Castlereagh and I will proceed completely differently. . . . Castlereagh will write a memorandum to demonstrate that the absurd can never be reasonable; I, on the other hand, have confined myself to sending a little invitation complete even with R.S.V.P. . . . But if something can save Alexander and the cause of reason, it will be the invitation and not the memorandum."[2]

This was indeed the difference between Castlereagh and Metter-

[1] N.P. III, p. 539f. All communications are dated 19 April, 1822. Also Prokesch-Osten, III, p. 363f.

[2] N.P. III, p. 512.

nich, between the conception of the self-evidence of dangers and courses of policy, on the one hand, and the effort constantly to create a framework of continuing relationships, on the other. Castlereagh's policy was empirical because the insular outlook of Great Britain involved a conviction of invulnerability. Britain could therefore act jointly with its Allies only on its own terms; only against threats it reserved the right to define. And since the consciousness of the need for joint action was brought about by specific issues of determinate scope, British policy tended to concentrate all its energy on the task at hand with little regard for future consequences. But such an *ad hoc* approach was too dangerous for a Continental power whose foreign policy problem was not a temporary threat but a continuing vulnerability. Metternich was unable to choose his point of commitment or to fight only his own battles. His continuing need for support forced him into conducting a policy of establishing "claims", of creating a framework in which there were no basic antagonisms or at least a maximum number of potential allies. Britain's risk was isolation; Austria's was disintegration. To Castlereagh the substance of a settlement was everything; to Metternich its mode was almost as important. Because Castlereagh could withdraw across the Channel after a conference, he considered a settlement the end of a diplomatic campaign. Because Metternich had to remain in close contact with the protagonists, he considered a settlement the definition of continuing relationship. For this reason the main tendency of Castlereagh's policy was to demonstrate the "unreasonableness" of Russia's claims and to marshal a superior force should this fail. By the same token, the predominant tendency of Metternich's policy was to build golden bridges for his mercurial opponent, so that the resolution of the conflict would appear as a gesture of volition, not of surrender. So it came about that the last dispute between Castlereagh and Metternich, as usual, concerned the *form* of a measure about whose substance they were in complete agreement.

For however much Castlereagh might sympathize personally with Metternich's dexterous use of the Alliance, the British domestic structure prohibited him from committing himself too directly. Even at this moment when, for the first time since Aix-la-Chapelle, the Alliance had an objective with which Britain could agree, Castlereagh had to take pains to present his policy as a British and not a European action. "I begin to foresee a crisis approaching . . ." he wrote to Metternich, "which may possibly compel both Austria and

Great Britain in pursuit *of their common purpose* to place themselves, as they did at Laibach, somewhat in a different attitude, consonant to the nature and resources of their respective governments. The distinctive character of the Turkish question . . . has enabled us to employ our first offices with much more activity, but when the final question arrives for decision ours must be a policy . . . which will . . . not so implicate us as to render it necessary . . . to bring the whole negotiation before Parliament."

All this was only leading up to an admission that Britain could not co-operate in the measure with which Metternich had hoped to lure Russia to the ministerial conferences: the promise to *discuss* the withdrawal of ambassadors from Constantinople. Just as in 1813 Britain had refused to discuss a peace plan whose significance resided in its seeming moderation, so now it could not participate in a manœuvre designed merely to save the Tsar's face. The strength of an empirical foreign policy, that it imparts a great singleness of purpose, involves a corresponding weakness, that it must take all measures at face value. Metternich had offered to break relations with Turkey to demonstrate his attachment to Russia, to provide an inducement for a conference and, above all, to gain time. But Castlereagh, faced with Parliamentary difficulties, could not agree even *to discuss* this step. Metternich had wanted to let British opposition to his proposal emerge at the ministerial conference; but Castlereagh had no margin for dissimulation, and he was loth to let a British plenipotentiary participate in a conference which Parliament might construe as a violation of the doctrine of non-interference. He therefore could offer Metternich no more than the continued good offices of Lord Strangford at Constantinople, to furnish Metternich "with a fulcrum on which you may bring your lever to act".[1]

This phrase marked the basis of the co-operation between Castlereagh and Metternich: the Austro-British understanding gave Britain an advocate on the Continent defending its policy in Continental terms; while it furnished Metternich with an option which was the condition for the flexibility of his policy. Metternich acknowledged this in his reply. He postulated the identity of interests of the two courts as a fundamental principle of policy, even if in pursuance of their aims they sometimes chose different routes. But his reaction to Castlereagh's hesitations about British participation in a ministerial conference indicated that, for all his shrewdness,

[1] Text, Webster, II, p. 537f. (Appendix), 30 April, 1822.

Metternich had not yet understood the root fact of the British domestic situation, that the *fact* of participation in *any* European Congress was becoming increasingly difficult to legitimize. He therefore ascribed Castlereagh's reluctance to a fear of the *consequences* of a meeting, and he sought to allay it by explaining that a conference would strengthen the Tsar's reluctance to utter the fateful word "war". To be sure, the "Greek party" at the Russian court would hope to make the negotiations serve its own ends; but, added Metternich, "there will be two of us playing the game, and I did not see that the Russian Cabinet won in 1821. The day that I see the Emperor Alexander accept our proposition, I, for one, will have the feeling that things will go in 1822, as they did in 1821; that is to say that they will go well."[1]

And Alexander accepted the proposition. After weeks of disquieting silence came the news that the Russian army would not cross the Pruth, that instead another negotiator, the fated Taticheff was being sent to Vienna. Alexander's indecisiveness was ended by the first conciliatory step of the Turks, and the alacrity with which he grasped it demonstrated his eagerness to accede to the appeals of his allies. When, at the beginning of May, the Porte finally accepted the "Four Points" in principle, Strangford transmitted this gesture directly to St. Petersburg, despite the fact that the Turks remained studiously silent about the timing of their implementation. And the Tsar, eager to escape his dilemma, professed to see in it a sufficient reason to re-establish diplomatic relations. It was not clear whether the invitation or the memorandum had produced the Tsar's decision, but there could be no doubt which had provided the *mode* of its accomplishment: "I could have permitted myself to be swept along by the enthusiasm for the Greeks," said Alexander to the Prussian envoy, "but I have never forgotten the impure origin of the rebellion or the danger of my intervention for my allies. Egotism is no longer the basis of policy. The principles of our truly Holy Alliance are pure."[2] On 25 June, Capo d'Istria went on an extended leave of absence from which he never returned.

And what was Metternich's reaction to this victory? A feeling of exulting triumph, a boastful reaffirmation of the correctness of his maxims, the satisfaction of a technician certain of his skill. "These maxims have now been proved true," he wrote, "[Policy is based]

[1] Text, Webster, II, p. 538f., 16 May, 1822.
[2] Stern, II, p. 250.

not on novels but on history, not on faith but on knowledge."[1] "I am not more stubborn than others, but more tenacious." "The Emperor Alexander claims that he trusts only me. Do you want to know what impression that makes on me? A smile and nothing else."[2] Not for Metternich were discussions about abstract theories; nor an immersion in the vision of a reconciled humanity. An eighteenth century product, he considered policy a science, not an act of sentiment. The Tsar had been frustrated—this was not a moral but a political fact. Russia, with its own acquiescence, had been deflected from a measure dictated by its whole tradition—this was not an ethical but a historical event. "The great work of Peter the Great has been disintegrated," he reported to the Emperor. "Everything is now on a new basis."[3] The sober manipulator in Vienna did not propose to repeat the mistake of Alexander at Laibach. The Congress soon to assemble was not to become a forum to demonstrate solidarity for its own sake, but a means to commit the Tsar irretrievably. While the British Cabinet considered the Turkish problem solved for the time being and the Tsar looked forward to appearing as the Saviour of Europe, Metternich set about to arrange one of the congresses he knew so well how to transform into moral symbols, in the process to put an end once and for all to Russian designs in the Balkans. Unlike the previous year, however, the Congress was not to illustrate Austro-Russian agreement, but to elevate a paradox into a general principle: to thwart the Tsar in the East, while still retaining him as an eager member of the Alliance. And for this end it was necessary to demonstrate the widest possible moral consensus, so that Austria would not have to carry the brunt of the opposition to Alexander.

All of Metternich's wiles were therefore exerted to induce Castlereagh to appear at the Congress slated for Verona. "Russia has suffered a decisive set-back," he wrote to Castlereagh. "But the Emperor Alexander will not consider himself defeated. The great mistakes committed by his Cabinet will be interpreted by him as so many sacrifices brought to the interests of Europe. What force Russian policy has lost in the East, it will attempt to replace by a great activity in the West. . . . [But] the risks which the Cabinets run are nevertheless much diminished, since [the issues] are now on a plane not suited to material action. For the strongest laws governing

[1] N.P. III, p. 542.
[2] N.P. III, p. 520.
[3] N.P. III, p. 554.

states are those of geography. . . . The four [Western] powers are thus masters of their action; but in order to remain so they must understand each other." Everything therefore depended on Castlereagh's participation in the forthcoming Congress, where there was nothing to do but much to avoid. And the letter ended with an admission that for all its intricate subtlety Metternich's policy was as fragile as a spider's web, as ephemeral as a house of cards: "If you fail me, I shall be alone . . . and the battle will become unequal. God has blessed me with enough courage not to refuse the contest; but the issues will not be well placed, if I must alone sustain what should be contested by the two Cabinets which understand each other best, given the uniformity of their political views."[1]

But the gods do not like hybris, the spiritual pride of Metternich in his moment of greatest triumph. Castlereagh decided to come to Verona, but the decision only served to make plain the incongruity of his position. An alliance which could prevent action in one quarter of Europe only by the prospect of intervention in another; a concert of Europe feeding on repression and constant turmoil, these were a far cry indeed from the conference system envisaged so hopefully at Paris. Each meeting became increasingly a jockeying for position and instead of exhibiting the beneficent advantages of harmony, each succeeding Congress resolved itself into a test of manipulative skill. And at home, Castlereagh stood more and more alone. He was the only member of the Cabinet who had participated in the great days of wartime Coalition, when for a fragile moment Europe seemed so at one that it was forgotten that common danger had provided the bond. Singly he had called into being the conference system. But seven years had now elapsed, and the stability of his creation made it impossible for his country to understand Castlereagh's vision of Europe. The prospect of a Congress, instead of vindicating his policy, only served to point up his dilemma: that his achievements were becoming taken for granted, but by the same token that which he considered their real meaning was growing increasingly incomprehensible. For what could Castlereagh achieve at Verona? All of Metternich's diplomacy was predicated on granting Alexander the form while denying him the substance. But the basic fact of British public feeling in 1822 was the impossibility of considering the concert of Europe a sufficient British concern to make to it *any* concession, however formal. Britain could still co-operate with the Continent, but not for

[1] Text, Webster, II, p. 541f. (Appendix).

the sake of co-operation, only on specific issues of finite scope; in short, only by returning to that insular outlook which Castlereagh had striven so mightily to transcend. To Castlereagh the Congress still was designed to demonstrate the unity of Europe; but to the British Cabinet it implied a dangerous involvement in European affairs. The gulf between these conceptions had become unbridgeable. "Sir," said Castlereagh at his last interview with the King, "it is necessary to say good-bye to Europe; you and I alone know it and have saved it; no one after me understands the affairs of the Continent."

Four days later he committed suicide.

XVII

The Nature of Statesmanship

I

THE death of Castlereagh marked a turning-point in European politics. With Castlereagh disappeared Great Britain's last link with the Alliance, the memory of the wartime coalition. Henceforth, no motive existed for maintaining the gap between foreign policy and the possibility of its domestic legitimization, and British policy became as insular as the mentality of the people. "[Castlereagh's death] is a great misfortune," wrote Metternich. "The man is irreplaceable, above all for me. An intelligent man can make up the lack of everything except experience. Castlereagh was the only man in his country who had experience in foreign affairs. He had learned to understand me. Now several years will have to elapse until somebody else acquires a similar degree of confidence."[1] At the moment that he had defeated his most dangerous adversary, Metternich lost his only reliable friend.

And events soon proved that Metternich's masterful manipulation had ultimately depended on his British option. To be sure, his great successes had been achieved by a remarkable diplomatic skill which had enabled him to control events by defining their moral framework. But the boldness of its measures was made possible by the certainty that in a showdown Britain would be found on Austria's side. This had enabled Metternich to persist in every negotiation until he had achieved all the Austrian objectives while thwarting Alexander, now by deferring the consideration of the Russian proposals to another congress, now by a doctrine of self-limitation. It is doubtful, to be sure, whether this performance could have continued indefinitely, whether Alexander would have been prepared over a long period of time to make concessions to a mirage of European unity whose fulfilment seemed always to lie in the future. The intricate combination by which Britain and Russia remained members of the same

[1] N.P. III, p. 522.

Alliance, while interpreting its obligations in a diametrically opposite manner, could probably not have been maintained much longer even with Metternich's resourcefulness in devising formulae which made the incompatible seem complementary. But the death of Castlereagh made the latent schism explicit and at one blow swept away the illusion of Allied unity, which was the condition of Metternich's policy. With Canning as Foreign Secretary, friendship with Russia was transformed for Austria from an act of policy into a condition of survival. No longer could Metternich count on Castlereagh's benevolent neutrality, which exerted its influence to prevent other powers from profiting from Austria's embarrassments. On the contrary, an isolationist, suspicious Britain, eager to play its traditional role of balancer of the equilibrium, was more likely to encourage divisions on the Continent than to ameliorate them.

With his margin of safety thus reduced, Metternich was forced into an increasingly rigid policy of hedging his risks. Because everything now depended on retaining Russia in the Alliance, the requirement of Allied unity became for Metternich an end and not a negotiating weapon. Henceforth it was he whose bargaining position was undermined by Russia's knowledge that Austria could not afford a rupture. It is thus that the gods revenge themselves by fulfilling our wishes too completely. Metternich had now achieved all he sought. He was in effect Prime Minister of Russia, as Wellington reported from Verona; he was the key figure of Europe. But he was also a prisoner of his myth, for he no longer dared to destroy Alexander's faith. Confronted by a suspicious Britain, he was obliged to flatter the Tsar's craving for crusades—and in the process to transform British reserve into hostility. Gone was the brilliant manipulation which had sought Austria's safety in the dexterity of its manœuvres in a fluid situation. It was replaced by an increasing exaltation of legitimacy, by drawing the lines as rigidly as possible, so that the very inflexibility of relationships symbolized the impossibility of change. What posterity has associated with the entire post-Vienna period, the doctrinaire adherence to the status quo almost at any price, really dates from the death of Castlereagh. From this moment, Metternich sought refuge in an alliance of the three "Eastern powers", held together by the fear of social upheaval and confronted by a Britain pursuing a policy of limited objectives in more or less open opposition to the maxims of what was now called the Holy Alliance of Austria, Prussia, and Russia.

It was paradoxical that Canning, who sought to dissociate Britain from Continental involvements, should thereby bring about the full implementation of the maxims he so deplored; whereas Castlereagh's reluctance to cause an open rupture, which earned him the opprobrium of posterity, was a means, if unintended, of ameliorating social repression. To be sure, the difference between Castlereagh and Canning was primarily a question of emphasis. Castlereagh, who considered the Alliance his own creation, was more ready to retain its form even after it engaged in measures to which no British statesman could agree; while Canning, who opposed not only its measures but its principle, used every opportunity to make the gulf explicit. But on this precise nuance depended Metternich's policy. Nobody has better summed up the meaning of Castlereagh's death than Chateaubriand: "I believe that Europe will gain by the death of the first minister of Great Britain. I have often spoken to you of his anti-Continental policy. Lord Londonderry [Castlereagh] would have done much harm at Vienna. His connections with Metternich were obscure and disquieting; Austria, deprived of a dangerous support, will be forced to come near to us."[1] It was the final irony of Castlereagh's life that his quest for the unity of Europe should have been interpreted—and correctly—as an anti-Continental policy.

In this manner the Congress of Verona, which Metternich had hopefully envisaged as opening a new era of Austro-British cooperation,[2] marked its end. To be sure, Wellington appeared as the British plenipotentiary with the instructions drafted by Castlereagh for his own use. But instructions are not self-implementing; and if Wellington did not lack ability, he was without domestic support. It was clearly understood that he would attend merely because the suddenness of Castlereagh's death made it impossible to change his dispositions completely, but he was not to commit Great Britain to any concerted measures. Wellington's role at Verona was therefore hardly different from Stewart's at Troppau, only that now the schism was to be permanent. Thus Metternich was forced into a position for which he was not well suited either by temperament or by conviction: to contest openly and alone with the Tsar about the implementation of the Alliance. As Metternich had foreseen, Alexander attempted to substitute common action in the West for his self-restraint in the East. And Metternich, for whom everything now

[1] Webster, II, p. 488; d'Antioche, Chateaubriand, pp. 342, 348.
[2] Webster, II, p. 541 (Appendix).

depended on retaining Russia in the Alliance, was obliged step by step into sanctioning measures which led France to play the role in the Iberian Peninsula which Austria had assumed in Italy during the previous year. But, equally inevitably, the intervention in Spain caused Great Britain to break openly with the Alliance.

So ended Castlereagh's vision of a Europe united by the self-evident requirements of harmony. But it had lasted long enough to enable the European order to be taken for granted, the most difficult step in achieving permanence. Perhaps never again has European unity been so much a reality as between 1815 and 1821, so much so that it came to be forgotten with what forebodings the Vienna settlement had been greeted by Gentz, who predicted a major war within five years, and by Castlereagh himself, who thought it would do well if it prevented another conflict for a decade. Not for a century was Europe to know a major war, however, because in the interval the myth of a united Europe had been reduced to political terms, which enabled Metternich first to dominate Europe morally and then to construct a grouping of powers which made a major conflict impossible physically. By the time Britain withdrew from the Alliance, the elements of the equilibrium had been established: the legitimizing principle defined at Laibach served as the bond for the three Eastern powers, Prussia, Russia, and Austria, which confronted a France unable to conduct a Continental policy against their united opposition and a Britain increasingly aware of its extra-European role. Because the moral framework of the Eastern bloc was defined by Austria, the policy of the dominant group of powers was conservative and status quo and did not for this reason lead to the active hostility of Great Britain. To be sure, for a brief interval after the death of Alexander, Russia pursued an independent policy in the Balkans, allied with Great Britain. But the revolutions in Western Europe in 1830 served to demonstrate to the new Tsar the correctness of Metternich's maxims of the danger of social upheaval, and the constellation of powers remained for over a generation with the "Holy Alliance" predominant on the Continent and Great Britain across the seas.

II

Few periods present such a dramatic contrast of personalities or illustrate so well the problems of organizing a legitimate order as the interval between the defeat of Napoleon in Russia and the Congress

Verona. While Napoleon dominated Europe, policy based on a conception of national strategy was impossible. The fate of states depended on the will of the conqueror, and safety could be found only in adaptation to the French system. But Napoleon's defeat in Russia made clear that Europe could no longer be governed by force, that the man of will would have to find safety in a recognition of limits. And the disintegration of the Grande Armée obliged the European nations to define anew their place in the international order, to create a balance of forces to discourage future aggression, and to wrest out of the chaos of the disintegrated structure of the eighteenth century some principle of organization which would ensure stability.

It is fortunate for the lessons posterity may draw from this period that its chief protagonists were men of marked individuality, each in his way symbolizing an answer to the problem of order: Napoleon of the claims of power; Alexander of the indeterminacy of a policy of absolute moral claims; Castlereagh of the conception of an equilibrium maintained by the recognition of the self-evident advantages of peace; Metternich of an equilibrium maintained by an agreement on a legitimizing principle. Napoleon and Alexander were revolutionaries, because both strove to identify the organization of Europe with their will. To be sure, Napoleon sought order in universal dominion and Alexander in a reconciled humanity. But the claims of the prophet are sometimes as dissolving as those of the conqueror. For the claims of the prophet are a counsel of perfection, and perfection implies uniformity. Utopias are not achieved except by a process of levelling and dislocation which must erode all patterns of obligation. These are the two great symbols of the attacks on the legitimate order: the Conqueror and the Prophet, the quest for universality and for eternity, for the peace of impotence and the peace of bliss.

But the statesman must remain forever suspicious of these efforts, not because he enjoys the pettiness of manipulation, but because he must be prepared for the worst contingency. To be dependent on the continued goodwill of another sovereign state is demoralizing, because it is a confession of impotence, an invitation to the irresponsibility induced by the conviction that events cannot be affected by one's will. And to rely entirely on the moral purity of an individual is to abandon the possibility of restraint, because moral claims involve a quest for absolutes, a denial of nuance, a rejection of history. This in its fundamental sense is the issue between the conqueror or the prophet on the one side and the statesman on the other; between the identification of conception and possibility and the insistence on the contingency of the individual will; between the effort to escape time and the need to survive in it. It is a tragic and necessarily inconclusive contest. For the statesman will treat the prophet as a political manifestation, and the prophet will judge the statesman by transcendental standards. The prophet, however pure his motives, pays the penalty for the "false" prophets who have preceded him, and it is the latter for which statesmanship attempts to provide. And the statesman is confronted with what must always upset his calculations; that it is not balance which inspires men but universality, not security but immortality.

It is the inextricable element of history, this conflict between inspiration and organization. Inspiration implies the identification of the self with the meaning of events. Organization requires discipline, the submission to the will of the group. Inspiration is timeless; its validity is inherent in its conception. Organization is historical, depending on the material available at a given period. Inspiration is a call for greatness; organization a recognition that mediocrity is the usual pattern of leadership. To be effective politically one requires organization, and for this reason the translation into political terms of prophetic visions always falsifies the intentions of their proponents. It is no accident that the greatest spiritual achievements of religious or prophetic movements tend to occur when they are still in opposition, when their conception is their *only* reality. Nor is it strange that established religions or prophetic movements should exhibit a longing for their vanished period of "true" inwardness. It is the origin of mass frenzy, of crusades, of "reformations", of purges, this realization that the spontaneity of individual reflection cannot be institutionalized.

While the conqueror attempts to equate his will with the structure of obligations and the prophet seeks to dissolve organization in a moment of transcendence, the statesman strives to keep latent the tension between organization and inspiration; to create a pattern of obligations sufficiently spontaneous to reduce to a minimum the necessity for the application of force, but, at the same time, of sufficient firmness not to require the legitimization of a moment of exaltation. It is not surprising that Castlereagh and Metternich were statesmen of the equilibrium, seeking security in a balance of forces. Their goal was stability, not perfection, and the balance of power is the classic expression of the lesson of history that no order is safe without physical safeguards against aggression. Thus the new international order came to be created with a sufficient awareness of the connection between power and morality; between security and legitimacy. No attempt was made to found it entirely on submission to a legitimizing principle; this is the quest of the prophet and dangerous because it presupposes the self-restraint of sanctity. But neither was power considered self-limiting; the experience of the conqueror had proved the opposite. Rather, there was created a balance of forces which, because it conferred a relative security, came to be generally accepted, and whose relationships grew increasingly spontaneous as its legitimacy came to be taken for granted.

To be sure, the international order had been founded on a misunderstanding and a misconception; a misunderstanding because the conference system which Castlereagh created as a symbol of harmony was used by Metternich as a diplomatic weapon to isolate his opponents. And a misconception because Castlereagh equated stability with a *consciousness* of reconciliation. But the belief that *all* threats, not only those of universal dominion, would be interpreted in the same manner by every power proved a tragic mistake. It is the essence of a revolutionary period that the attack on the "legitimate" order obliterates all differences within it; but by the same token it is the nature of a stable period that the acceptance of its legitimacy makes it safe to contest on local or peripheral issues. Because after Napoleon's overthrow the international order no longer contained a revolutionary power, no real motive for Britain's continued participation in the conference system existed, all the less so since the chief threat to the international order, the twin movements of liberalism and nationalism were not considered dangerous in Great Britain. Thus the conference system led either to a dispute on peripheral issues, which seemed petty and distasteful to Castlereagh, or it exhibited a unanimity over a threat that Britain could not admit as an international problem. When the unity of Europe came to pass, it was not because of the self-evidence of its necessity, as Castlereagh had imagined, but through a cynical use of the conference machinery to define a legitimizing principle of social repression; not through Castlereagh's good faith, but through Metternich's manipulation.

But even with these qualifications, it remains to be asked how it was possible to create an approximation to a European government, however tenuous, and with Britain as an observer on the sidelines.

What enabled Metternich to emerge as the Prime Minister of Europe? It was Metternich's misfortune that history in the latter half of the nineteenth century was written by his opponents, to whom he was anathema both by principle and policy and who ascribed his achievements to a contradictory combination of cunning and good fortune, of mediocrity and incompetent adversaries, without explaining how such a man managed to place his stamp on his period. For the documents of his period leave no doubt that for over a generation nothing occurred in Europe which was not shaped by Metternich either directly or through his opposition. To be sure, Metternich was aided by the instability of the Tsar and the indecisiveness of the Prussian King. But the Tsar's mercurial temper might also have resulted in a new crusade; and although Alexander's instability was there for everyone to exploit, only Metternich managed to achieve a personal domination. On the other hand, Metternich's own interpretation of the superiority of his philosophical maxims is refuted by their conventionality, while mere deviousness could not have duped all of Europe for over a decade. Rather, Metternich's successes were due to two factors: that the unity of Europe was not Metternich's invention, but the common conviction of *all* statesmen; and because Metternich was the last diplomat of the great tradition of the eighteenth century, a "scientist" of politics, coolly and unemotionally arranging his combinations in an age increasingly conducting policy by "causes". The maxims on which he so prided himself had therefore a psychological, but not a philosophical, significance: because he was convinced, indeed cocksure, of his rectitude, he could soberly and cynically evaluate the maxims of others as forces to be exploited. Because he considered policy a science, he permitted no sentimental attachments to interfere with his measures. There was not found in Metternich's diplomacy the rigid dogmatism which characterized his choice of objectives nor the undisciplined sentimentality of Alexander's conduct. And because, despite his vanity, he was always ready to sacrifice the form of a settlement for the substance, his victories became, not wounds, but definitions of a continuing relationship.

Metternich was aided by an extraordinary ability to grasp the fundamentals of a situation and a profound psychological insight which enabled him to dominate his adversaries. In 1805, he was almost alone in pointing out that Prussia was no longer the state of Frederick the Great; in 1812, he was one of the first to realize the essential transformation brought about by Napoleon's defeat; after

1815, he understood better than anyone the nature of the social transformation preparing itself in Europe, and that he decided to defy the tide may be a reflection on his statesmanship but not on his insight. He therefore had the great advantage over his adversaries that he knew what he wanted; and if his goals were sterile, they were fixed. "Everybody wants something," wrote Metternich at the height of the Greek crisis, "without having any idea how to obtain it and the really intriguing aspect of the situation is that nobody quite knows how to achieve what he desires. But because I know what I want and what the others *are capable of* [Metternich's italics] I am completely prepared."[1] That this statement was boastful, vain, and smug does not detract from its truth.

But all his diplomatic skill would have availed Metternich nothing, had he not operated in a framework in which his invocation of the unity of Europe could appear as something other than a euphemism for Austrian national interest. The early nineteenth century was a transition period, and, as in all such periods, the emergence of a new pattern of obligation for a time served only to throw into sharp relief the values being supplanted. The political structure of the eighteenth century had collapsed, but its ideals were still familiar. And because those ideals were derived from a rationalistic philosophy validated by its truth, they claimed a universal applicability. To Metternich's contemporaries the unity of Europe was a reality, the very ritualism of whose invocation testified to its hold on the general consciousness. Regional differences were recognized, but they were considered local variations of a greater whole. Unity was not yet equated with identity, nor the claims of the nation with the dictates of morality. All of Metternich's colleagues were therefore products of essentially the same culture, professing the same ideals, sharing similar tastes. They understood each other, not only because they could converse with facility in French, but because in a deeper sense they were conscious that the things they shared were much more fundamental than the issues separating them. When Metternich introduced the Italian opera in Vienna, or Alexander brought German philosophy to Russia, they were not being consciously tolerant or even aware that they were importing something "foreign". The ideal of "excellence" still was more important than that of origin. Thus the Russian Prime Minister, Capo d'Istria, was a Greek, the Russian ambassador in Paris, Pozzo di Borgo, was a Corsican, while Richelieu, the French

[1] N.P. III, p. 511

Prime Minister, had been governor of Odessa. Wellington gave military advice to Austria in its campaign against Murat, and in 1815 both Prussia and Austria asked Stein to serve as their ambassador with the Assembly of the Confederation. And Metternich with his cosmopolitan education and rationalist philosophy, Austrian only by the accident of feudal relationships, could be imagined equally easily as the minister of any other state. If he had any special ties to Austria, they derived from a philosophical not a national identification, because the principles Austria represented were closest to his own maxims, because Austria, the polyglot Empire, was a macrocosm of his cosmopolitan values. "For a long time now," he wrote to Wellington in 1824, "Europe has had for me the quality of a fatherland [*patrie*]."

For these reasons, Metternich was effective not only because he was persuasive but, above all, because he was plausible. Of all his colleagues he was best able to appeal to the maxims of the eighteenth century, partly because they corresponded to his own beliefs, but, more importantly, because Austria's interests were identical with those of European repose. And because the end-result of Metternich's policy was stability and Austria's gain was always intangible, his extraordinary cynicism, his cold-blooded exploitation of the beliefs of his adversaries did not lead to a disintegration of all restraint, as the same tactics were to do later in the hands of Bismarck. Metternich's policy was thus one of status quo *par excellence*, and conducted, not by marshalling a superior force, but by obtaining a voluntary submission to his version of legitimacy. Its achievement was a period of peace lasting for over a generation without armament races or even the threat of a major war. And when the change came after 1848, it could be integrated into the existing structure without leading to the disintegration of Austria or to permanent revolution.

But its failure was the reverse side of this success. The identification of stability with the status quo in the middle of a revolutionary period reinforced the tendency towards rigidity of Austria's domestic structure and led eventually to its petrifaction. The very dexterity of Metternich's diplomacy obscured the real nature of his achievements, that he was merely hiding the increasing anachronism of Austria in a century of nationalism and liberalism; that he was but delaying the inevitable day of reckoning. To be sure, a truly successful policy for a polyglot Empire may have been impossible in a century of nationalism. And the Emperor would certainly have opposed any serious effort of domestic reform with his characteristic obtuse stubbornness. Nevertheless, the end of the Napoleonic war marked the last moment for Austria to attempt to brave the coming storm by adaptation, to wrench itself loose from the past, however painful the process. But Metternich's marvellous diplomatic skill enabled Austria to avoid the hard choice between domestic reform and revolutionary struggle; to survive with an essentially unaltered domestic structure in a century of rationalized administration; to continue a multi-national Empire in a period of nationalism. So agile was Metternich's performance that it was forgotten that its basis was diplomatic skill and that it left the fundamental problems unsolved, that it was manipulation and not creation. For diplomacy can achieve a great deal through the proper evaluation of the factors of international relations and by their skilful utilization. But it is not a substitute for conception; its achievements ultimately will depend on its objectives, which are defined outside the sphere of diplomacy and which diplomacy must treat as given. So resourceful was Metternich that for a time he could make a performance of juggling appear as the natural pattern of international relations; so dexterous were his combinations that during a decade they obscured the fact that what seemed the application of universal principles was in reality the *tour de force* of a solitary figure.

Only a shallow historicism would maintain that successful policies are always possible. There existed no easy solution for Austria's tragic dilemma; that it could adapt itself by giving up its soul or that it could defend its values and in the process bring about their petrifaction. Any real criticism of Metternich must therefore attack, not his ultimate failure, but his reaction to it. It is Metternich's smug self-satisfaction with an essentially technical virtuosity which prevented him from achieving the tragic stature he might have, given the process in which he was involved. Lacking in Metternich is the attribute which has enabled the spirit to transcend an impasse at so many crises of history: the ability to contemplate an abyss, not with the detachment of a scientist, but as a challenge to overcome—or to perish in the process. Instead one finds a bitter-sweet resignation which was not without its own grandeur, but which doomed the statesman of the anachronistic Empire in his primary ambition: to become a symbol of conservatism for posterity. For men become myths, not by what they know, nor even by what they achieve, but by the tasks they set for themselves.

Metternich had learned the lessons of the eighteenth-century cabinet diplomacy too well. Its skilful sense of proportion was appropriate for a period whose structure was unchallenged and whose components were animated by a consciousness of their safety; but it was sterile in an era of constant flux. Whenever Metternich operated within a fixed framework, when an alliance had to be constructed or a settlement negotiated, his conduct was masterly. Whenever he was forced to create his own objectives, there was about him an aura of futility. Because he sought tranquillity in the manipulation of factors he treated as given, the statesman of repose became the prisoner of events. Because he never fought a battle he was not certain of winning, he failed in becoming a symbol. He understood the forces at work better than most of his contemporaries, but this knowledge proved of little avail, because he used it almost exclusively to deflect their inexorable march, instead of placing it into his service for a task of construction. Thus the last vestige of the eighteenth century had to prove the fallacy of one of the maxims of the Enlightenment, that knowledge was power. And for this reason, too, the final result of Metternich's policies had the quality of a series of ironies: that the policy of the statesman who most prided himself on the universality of his maxims lost its flexibility with the death of one man; that its structure was disintegrated by Prussia, the power he had conceived as one of its pillars, and that its legitimacy collapsed through the efforts, not of a representative of the social revolution or the middle class, but of the most traditionalist segment of Prussian society: Otto von Bismarck, whose ancestry antedated even that of the Prussian monarchs and who nevertheless completed the work of the futile revolutions which Metternich had mastered.

The two statesmen of repose were therefore both defeated in the end by their domestic structure: Castlereagh by ignoring it, Metternich by being too conscious of its vulnerability. But their achievements remain, not only in the long period of peace they brought about, but also in their impact on their time. The concert of Europe which emerged out of the Napoleonic wars was almost identical with their notion of the equilibrium, and the conference system which maintained it was Castlereagh's personal creation. It was he who mediated the differences of the Coalition and who, throughout his life, remained the conscience of the Alliance, even after he was forced into an increasingly passive role. Almost singlehandedly, he identified British security with Continental stability; and while in time the realities of an insular mentality reasserted themselves, British participation had lasted long enough to launch the new order without catastrophe. And Metternich, however he might struggle against the term "Metternich system", summed up the meaning of a generation of struggle. Between 1809 and 1848, it was possible to disagree with him, to detest him, but never to escape him. He was the High Priest of the Holy Alliance, the recognized interpreter of its maxims. He was the manipulator of the conference system, where his opponents suddenly found themselves isolated through the dexterous utilization of their own proposals. The very bitterness of the attacks on him testified to his central role. Anonymously, obliquely, indirectly, he demonstrated that policy may be based on knowledge, but that its conduct is an art.

III

What then is the role of statesmanship? A scholarship of social determinism has reduced the statesman to a lever on a machine called "history", to the agent of a fate which he may dimly discern but which he accomplishes regardless of his will. And this belief in the pervasiveness of circumstance and the impotence of the individual extends to the notion of policy-making. One hears a great deal about the contingency of planning because of the unavailability of fact, about the difficulty of action because of the limitation of knowledge. It cannot be denied, of course, that policy does not occur in a void, that the statesman is confronted with material he must treat as given. Not only geography and the availability of resources trace the limits of statesmanship, but also the character of the people and the nature of its historical experience. But to say that policy does not create its own substance is not the same as saying that the substance is self-implementing. The realization that the Napoleonic Empire was tottering was the *condition* of policy in 1813, but it was not *itself* a policy. That the period of revolution should be replaced by an order of equilibrium, that the assertion of the will give way to an insistence on legitimacy may have been "in the air". But one has only to study the vacillating measures of most powers to appreciate that neither the nature of this equilibrium nor the measures to attain it were immediately apparent. However "self-evident" the national interest may appear in retrospect, contemporaries were oppressed by the multiplicity of available policies, counselling contradictory courses of action: in 1813, most Austrian statesmen who did not advocate unconditional neutrality argued either for a continued alliance with France to solidify Austria's relations with the invincible Conqueror or for an immediate change of sides in deference to the national passion sweeping across Europe. Almost alone Metternich held firm, because he was convinced that the incompatibility of Napoleon's Empire with a system of equilibrium did not necessarily imply the compatibility of a polyglot Empire with an era of nationalism. At the same moment, the British Cabinet only reflected public opinion when it urged Napoleon's overthrow and, later on, a harsh peace. It was Castlereagh who brought about a peace of equilibrium and not of vengeance, a reconciled and not an impotent France. The choice between these policies did not reside in the "facts", but in their interpretation.[1] It involved what was essentially a moral act: an *estimate* which depended for its validity on a conception of goals as much as on an understanding of the available material, which was based on knowledge but not identical with it.

The test of a statesman, then, is his ability to recognize the real relationship of forces and to make this knowledge serve his ends. That Austria should seek stability was inherent in its geographic position and domestic structure. But that it would succeed, if only temporarily and however unwisely, in identifying its domestic legitimizing principle with that of the international order was the work of its Foreign Minister. That Great Britain should attempt to find security in a balance of power was the consequence of twenty-three years of intermittent warfare. But that it should emerge as a part of the concert of Europe was due to the efforts of a solitary individual. No policy is better, therefore, than the goals it sets itself. It was the measure of Castlereagh's statesmanship that he recognized the precedence of integration over retribution in the construction of a legitimate order, as of Metternich's that he never confused the form and the substance of his achievements, that he understood that the Central Empire could survive, not on its triumphs, but only on its reconciliations. It was their failure that they set themselves tasks

[1] The argument that policy is "objective" because it reflects the requirements of security amounts to a truism which assigns a motivation to completed action. For the crucial problem of statesmanship is not to find a formal definition for accomplished policy, but to understand its *content* at any given period. Disputes over policy never concern a disagreement over the wisdom of safety but over its nature, nor about the desirability of security but about the best means to accomplish it.

beyond the capacity of their material: Castlereagh through a vision beyond the conception of his domestic structure, Metternich through an effort unattainable in a century of nationalism.

But it is not sufficient to judge the statesman by his conceptions alone, for unlike the philosopher he must implement his vision. And the statesman is inevitably confronted by the inertia of his material, by the fact that other powers are not factors to be manipulated but forces to be reconciled; that the requirements of security differ with the geographic location and the domestic structure of the powers. His instrument is diplomacy, the art of relating states to each other by agreement rather than by the exercise of force, by the representation of a ground of action which reconciles particular aspirations with a general consensus. Because diplomacy depends on persuasion and not imposition, it presupposes a determinate framework, either through an agreement on a legitimizing principle or, theoretically, through an identical interpretation of power-relationships, although the latter is in practice the most difficult to attain. The achievements of Castlereagh and Metternich were due in no small measure to their extraordinary ability as diplomats. Both dominated every negotiation in which they participated: Castlereagh by the ability to reconcile conflicting points of view and by the single-mindedness conferred by an empirical policy; Metternich through an almost uncanny faculty of achieving a personal dominance over his adversaries and the art of defining a moral framework which made concessions appear, not as surrenders, but as sacrifices to a common cause.

The acid test of a policy, however, is its ability to obtain domestic support. This has two aspects: the problem of legitimizing a policy *within* the governmental apparatus, which is a problem of bureaucratic rationality; and that of harmonizing it with the national experience, which is a problem of historical development. It was no accident, even if it was paradoxical, that in 1821 Metternich had greater difficulty with the Austrian than with the Russian ministers, or that in every negotiation Castlereagh had to fight a more desperate battle with his Cabinet than with his foreign colleagues. For the spirit of policy and that of bureaucracy are diametrically opposed. The essence of policy is its contingency; its success depends on the correctness of an estimate which is in part conjectural. The essence of bureaucracy is its quest for safety; its success is calculability. Profound policy thrives on perpetual creation, on a constant redefinition of goals. Good administration thrives on routine, the definition of relationships which can survive mediocrity. Policy involves an adjustment of risks; administration an avoidance of deviation. Policy justifies itself by the relationship of its measures and its sense of proportion; administration by the rationality of each action in terms of a given goal. The attempt to conduct policy bureaucratically leads to a quest for calculability which tends to become a prisoner of events. The effort to administer politically leads to total irresponsibility, because bureaucracies are designed to execute, not to conceive.

The temptation to conduct policy administratively is ever present, because most governments are organized primarily for the conduct of domestic policy, whose chief problem is the implementation of social decisions, a task which is limited only by its technical feasibility. But the concern with technical problems in foreign affairs leads to a standard which evaluates by mistakes avoided rather than by goals achieved, and to a belief that ability is more likely to be judged by the pre-vision of catastrophes than the discovery of opportunities. It is not surprising that, at the height of the dispute at Vienna in 1814, Vansittart simply denied the reality of the Russian threat, or that Stadion in 1821 protested against the drain on the Austrian treasury of a campaign against Piedmont. In each instance the risks were immediately apparent, while the dangers were either symbolic or deferred; in each case the quest for determinacy took the form of denying the reality of the danger.

For this reason, too, it is dangerous to separate planning from the responsibility of execution. For responsibility involves a standard of judgment, a legitimacy. But the standard of a bureaucracy is different from that of the social effort. Social goals are justified by the legitimizing principle of the domestic structure, which may be rationality, tradition or charisma, but which is in any case considered an *ultimate* value. Bureaucratic measures are justified by an essentially *instrumental* standard, the suitability of certain actions for achieving ends conceived as given. A society is capable of only a limited range of decisions, because its values are relatively fixed; an ideal bureaucracy should be able to carry out *any* decision which is administratively feasible. The attempt to define social goals bureaucratically will, therefore, always lead to the distortion inherent in applying a rationality of means to the development of ends. It was in large part the identification of conception and responsibility which gave Castlereagh's policy such flexibility and which allowed Metternich to conduct himself with such subtle pliability. Because they were legitimized by the goals of the social effort and not an administrative routine, Castlereagh and Metternich were able to plan policy as long-range national strategy. Because their tenure in office was prolonged, they could execute their conception with due regard to the relation of their measures to each other and not only their individual rationality.

In addition to the obstacle of bureaucratic inertia, a statesman will tend to have great difficulty legitimizing his policy domestically, because of the incommensurability between a nation's domestic and its international experience. The whole domestic effort of a people exhibits an effort to transform force into obligation by means of a consensus on the nature of justice. The more spontaneous the pattern of obligation, the more "natural" and "universal" will social values appear. But the international experience of a people is a challenge to the universality of its notion of justice, for the stability of an international order depends on self-limitation, on the reconciliation of different versions of legitimacy. A nation will evaluate a policy in terms of its domestic legitimization, because it has no other standard of judgment. But the effort to identify the legitimizing principle of the international order with a parochial version of justice must lead to a revolutionary situation, particularly if the domestic legitimizing principles are sufficiently incommensurable. If a society legitimizes itself by a principle which claims both universality and exclusiveness, if its concept of "justice", in short, does not include the existence of different principles of legitimacy, relations between it and other societies will come to be based on force. For this reason competing systems of legitimacy find it extremely difficult to come to an understanding, not only because they will not be able to agree on the nature of "just" demands, but, perhaps more importantly, because they will not be able to legitimize the attainable international consensus domestically.

But even when there exists no fundamental ideological gulf, a nation's domestic experience will tend to inhibit its comprehension of foreign affairs. Domestically, the most difficult problem is an agreement on the nature of "justice". But internationally, the domestic consensus inherent in the definition of a policy must often be compromised with a similar domestic consensus of other powers. It is no accident that the tool of policy domestically is bureaucracy, which symbolizes the unity of will and execution, while its tool internationally is diplomacy, which symbolizes the contingency of application. Not for nothing do so many nations exhibit a powerful if subconscious, rebellion against foreign policy, which leaves the travail of the soul inherent in arriving at decisions unrewarded, against this double standard which considers what is defined as "justice" domestically, merely an object for negotiation internationally. Nor is it an accident that the vision of itself of so many societies exhibits a picture of rectitude deprived of its birthright by the sharp practices of foreigners. For the impetus of domestic policy is a direct social experience; but that of foreign policy is not actual, but potential experience—the threat of war—which statesmanship attempts to avoid being made explicit.

The statesman is therefore like one of the heroes in classical drama who has had a vision of the future but who cannot transmit it directly to his fellow-men and who cannot validate its "truth". Nations learn only by experience; they "know" only when it is too late to act. But statesmen must act *as if* their intuition were already experience, as if their aspiration were truth. It is for this reason that statesmen often share the fate of prophets, that they are without honour in their own country, that they always have a difficult task in legitimizing their programmes domestically, and that their greatness is usually apparent only in retrospect when their intuition has become experience. The statesman must therefore be an educator; he must bridge the gap between a people's experience and his vision, between a nation's tradition and its future. In this task his possibilities are limited. A statesman who too far outruns the experience of his people will fail in achieving a domestic consensus, however wise his policies; witness Castlereagh. A statesman who limits his policy to the experience of his people will doom himself to sterility; witness Metternich.

It is for this reason that most great statesmen have been either representatives of essentially conservative social structures or revolutionaries: the conservative is effective because of his understanding of the experience of his people and of the essence of a continuing relationship, which is the key to a stable international organization. And the revolutionary, because he transcends experience and identifies the just with the possible. The conservative (particularly if he represents an essentially conservative social structure) is legitimized by a consensus on the basic goals of the social effort and on the nature of the social experience. There is, therefore, no need to justify every step along the way. The revolutionary is legitimized by his charismatic quality, by an agreement on the legitimacy of his person or of his principle. His means are therefore considered incidental; his ends or his person legitimize the means. A conservative structure produces a notion of *quality*, which provides the framework of great conception; a revolutionary order produces a notion of *exaltation*, which dissolves technical limitations. Both thus deal with the fundamental problem of statesmanship: how to produce an understanding of the *complexity* of policy when it is impossible to produce a comprehension of its *substance*.

This book has dealt with conservative statesmen of countries with traditionalist social structures, of societies with sufficient cohesion so that policy could be conducted with the certainty conferred by the conviction that domestic disputes were essentially technical and confined to achieving an agreed goal. This enabled Metternich to pursue a policy of "collaboration" between 1809 and 1812 without being accused of treason and Castlereagh to negotiate with Napoleon without being charged with "selling his country". Statesmanship thus involves not only a problem of conception but also of implementation, an appreciation of the attainable as much as a vision of the desirable. The description of the efforts of Castlereagh and Metternich to harmonize the just with the possible and the international with the domestic legitimization was their story as statesmen. Their failure to achieve permanence for that which they held most dear was their story as men.

IV

There remains the question of the validity of conclusions drawn from historical experience, expressed in the assertion that historical events are essentially unique. It can be admitted that events do not recur precisely, that in this sense history does not "repeat" itself. But this is true of even the coarsest physical experience. A man seeing an elephant for the first time would not know what he was confronting. (Unless he had seen a picture or description which is a substitute for experience.) When he saw a second elephant, he might be able to name it by abstracting from its individual appearance in time and by establishing a standard of correspondence. A concept, therefore, never says "everything" about an object nor a "law" about a class. It is no indictment of Newton's Law that it fails to say anything significant about apples, because its significance resides precisely in the fact that it abstracted from the apples both their "uniqueness", their individual appearance in time, and their "appleness", their appearance as members of a class, through the recognition of a formal relationship of "falling bodies". Similarly, it is no objection to a study of international relations in terms of history to point out that Napoleon is not exactly equivalent to Hitler or Castlereagh to Churchill. Whatever relationship exists depends, not on a precise correspondence, but on a similarity of the problems confronted. And the conclusions will reflect—just as with any other generalization—the ability to abstract from the uniqueness of individual experience.

A physical law is an explanation and not a description, and history teaches by analogy, not identity. This means that the lessons of history are never automatic, that they can be apprehended only by a standard which admits the significance of a range of experience, that the answers we obtain will never be better than the questions we pose. No profound conclusions were drawn in the natural sciences before the *significance* of sensory experience was admitted by what was essentially a moral act. No significant conclusions are possible in the study of foreign affairs—the study of states acting as units—without an awareness of the historical context. For societies exist in time more than in space. At any given moment a state is but a collection of individuals, as positivist scholars have never wearied of pointing out. But it achieves identity through the consciousness of a common history. This is the only "experience" nations have, their only possibility of learning from themselves. History is the memory of states.

To be sure, states tend to be forgetful. It is not often that nations learn from the past, even rarer that they draw the correct conclusions from it. For the lessons of historical experience, as of personal experience, are contingent. They teach the consequences of certain actions, but they cannot force a recognition of comparable situations. An individual may have experienced that a hot stove burns but, when confronted with a metallic object of a certain size, he must decide from case to case whether it is in fact a stove before his knowledge will prove useful. A people may be aware of the probable consequences of a revolutionary situation. But its knowledge will be empty if it cannot *recognize* a revolutionary situation. There is this difference between physical and historical knowledge, however: each generation is permitted only one effort of abstraction; it can attempt only one interpretation and a single experiment, for it is its own subject. This is the challenge of history and its tragedy; it is the shape "destiny" assumes on the earth. And its solution, even its recognition, is perhaps the most difficult task of statesmanship.

Bibliography

I. DOCUMENTARY SOURCES

A. British Sources

CASTLEREAGH, Viscount, *Correspondence, Dispatches and Other Papers* (12 vols.) Edited by his brother, the Marquess of Londonderry. (London, 1848–52) *Referred to in footnotes as* C.C.

The collection is as miscellaneous as the title. Volumes 8–12 deal with Castlereagh's foreign policy. A useful supplement to secondary sources, but it is impossible to reconstruct events from the documents, particularly after 1815.

British and Foreign State Papers. Edited by the Librarian of the Foreign Office. (London, 1841) *Referred to as* B.F.S.P.

Official documents which had been published by 1841. To be used with caution because Castlereagh was something less than frank in his dealings with Parliament. Volumes 1–9 deal with the period in question.

Parliamentary Debates. Referred to as Hansard.

Useful primarily to indicate the difficulty Castlereagh confronted in legitimizing his policy domestically. Volumes 20–41 of the 1st Series and Volumes 1–7 of the New Series deal with the period in question.

TEMPERLEY, Harold, and Lillian PENSON, *Foundations of British Foreign Policy*. (Cambridge, 1938)

A collection of key illustrative documents. The documents dealing with the period of this thesis are few but well chosen.

WEBSTER, Charles, *British Diplomacy, 1813–15*. (London, 1921) *Referred to as* B.D.

A collection of Foreign Office documents, supplemented by excerpts from Castlereagh's correspondence, giving an excellent picture of the period covered.

WELLINGTON, Duke of, *Dispatches* (13 vols.) Edited by Gurwood. (London, 1837) *Referred to as* Gurwood.

Since both as a soldier and diplomat Wellington was intimately associated with the events of this period, his dispatches provide useful background material. Vols. 8–13 cover the period in question.

——, *Supplementary Dispatches, Correspondence and Memoranda* (15 vols.) Edited by his son. (London, 1858–76) *Referred to as* W.S.D.

Volumes 6–14 cover the period in question. A collection of documents of other key figures with whom the Duke of Wellington was associated either directly or indirectly. It includes many dispatches and memoranda by Castlereagh. A miscellaneous, but invaluable, source. In many respects more useful than Castlereagh's correspondence.

B. Austrian Sources

GONSALVI AND METTERNICH, *Correspondance 1815–23 du Cardinal Gonsalvi avec le Prince de Metternich.* Edited by Charles Van Duerm. (Louvain, 1899)

Metternich's correspondence with the Papal Secretary of State. Useful for Metternich's Italian policy and his sober attitude toward the Church.

GENTZ, Friedrich von, *Depêches Inédites aux Hospodars de Valachie* (3 vols.) Edited by Anton Prokesch-Osten. (Paris, 1876–77) *Referred to as Depêches Inédites.*

——, *Briefe von Friedrich von Gentz an Pilat* (2 vols.) Edited by Karl Mendelson-Bartholdy. (Leipzig, 1868)

———, *Tagebuecher, aus dem Nachlass Varnhagen von Ense* (4 vols.). (Leipzig, 1873–74)

Documents by one of Metternich's closest associates, including some memoranda by Metternich. Although Gentz tends to exaggerate his own role, they give a useful picture of events, particularly after 1815.

HANOTEAU, Jean, *Lettres du Prince de Metternich à la Comtesse de Lieven.* (Paris, 1909)

Metternich's love letters to the wife of the Russian ambassador in London. Interesting for Metternich's picture of himself and, above all, his rationalist philosophy.

KLINKOWSTROEM, Alfons, *Oesterreich's Theilname an den Befreiungskriegen.* (Vienna, 1887)

Gentz's history of Austria's participation in the war of 1813. Particularly useful for an appendix containing an exchange of letters between Metternich and Schwarzenberg.

KUEBECK, Max, *Metternich und Kuebeck, Ein Briefwechsel.* (Vienna, 1910)

An exchange of letters from 1849–50 between Metternich and the Austrian diplomat dealing with German problems. Particularly useful for Metternich's views on the question of German unity.

METTERNICH, Clemens, *Aus Metternich's Nachgelassenen Papieren,* (8 vols.) Edited by Alfons v. Klinkowstroem. (Vienna, 1880) *Referred to as* N.P.

Documents left by Metternich in lieu of an autobiography. The first volume contains Metternich's self-satisfied and frequently inaccurate biographical fragment and his splendid "portraits" of Napoleon and Alexander. The remainder is a collection of diplomatic documents, private letters, and notes. Some doubt has been cast on the accuracy of the documents, but the deviations are all trivial and the documents are consistent with Metternich's other writings which have since come to light. (See Baillieu, Section III D.) Also available in French as *Mémoires*, and the first five volumes in English. But only the above edition brings the documents in their original form, containing manuscripts in both French and German.

——, *Briefe des Staatskanzlers Fuerst Metternich-Winneburg an den Oesterreichischen Minister des Aüsseren Graf Buol-Schauenstein aus den Jahren, 1852–59*. Edited by Carl J. Burckhardt. (Munich, 1934)

Letters by Metternich to his successor as Foreign Minister, advising him on Austrian policy. An excellent source for an understanding of Metternich's basic foreign policy doctrine.

——, *Metternich-Hartig, ein Briefwechsel.* (Vienna, 1923)

Correspondence from 1848 to 1851 between Metternich and the former Austrian Governor of Lombardy. Interesting for Metternich's views on the nature of statesmanship and administration.

ONCKEN, Wilhelm, *Oesterreich und Preussen im Befreiungskriege* (2 vols.) (Berlin, 1880)

A narrative of Austria's and Prussia's policy in the first six months of 1813 with a very full appendix of major diplomatic dispatches and the German translation of others in the text. The narrative is disorganized, but the documents are invaluable.

PROKESCH-OSTEN, Anton von, *Geschichte des Abfalls der Griechen* (5 vols.) (Vienna, 1867)

A history of the achievement of Greek independence by the Austrian diplomat best acquainted with the Ottoman Empire. Volumes 1 and 2 are a narrative, the remainder documents. The latter are invaluable for the intricate diplomacy of 1821–22.

——, *Aus dem Nachlass Prokesch-Osten's* (2 vols.) (Vienna, 1881)

Volume 2 contains correspondence between Metternich and the author, who was Metternich's expert on the Eastern question. Particularly good for the period after 1848.

C. Other Sources

ANGEBERG, Comte d', *Le Congrès de Vienne et les Traités de 1815* (2 vols.) (Paris, 1863–64)

A basic source for the Congress of Vienna with additional

documents on the Congress of Chatillon and the Congress of Aix-la-Chapelle.

Acte du Congrès de Vienne. (Vienna, 1815)
The official Final Act of the Congress of Vienna.

CAULAINCOURT, *Mémoires.* Edited by J. Hanoteau. (Paris, 1933)
The memoirs of Napoleon's ambassador to Russia and last Foreign Minister. Not very profound but a well-written, fine account of the final stages of the Empire.

KLÜBER, Johann, *Acten des Wiener Congresses* (9 vols.) (Erlangen, 1815)
A very full, but miscellaneous, collection of documents beginning with the Treaty of Chaumont and extensive protocols of the Congress of Vienna.

MARTENS, G. F., *Nouveau Récueil de Traités* (16 vols.) (Göttingen, 1817–1842) *Referred to as* Recueil.
A practically complete collection of major treaties between 1808 and 1839 in which Russia was a party, supplemented by a miscellaneous collection of other key documents. Volumes 3–10 cover the period in question.

MUENSTER, Ernst, Count von, *Political Sketches of the State of Europe, 1814–1867.* (Edinburgh, 1868)
Dispatches by the envoy of Hanover to the Allied armies and the Congress of Vienna during 1814–15; written for the then Prince Regent of Britain in his capacity as King of Hanover. Primarily useful for German problems.

NESSELRODE, Graf von, *Lettres et Papiers* (11 vols.) Edited by A. von Nesselrode. (Paris, 1904)
Papers left by the long-time Russian Foreign Minister. Volumes 3–7 deal with the period in question.

PASQUIER, Duc du, *Mémoires du Chancellier Pasquier* (6 vols.) Edited by d'Audiffret-Pasquier. (Paris, 1893–94)
By the French Foreign Minister of the time of Laibach and Troppau. A useful, if one-sided, source for this period.

Sbornik of the Imperial Russian Historical Society (vols. xxxi, civ, cxii, cxix, cxxvii) (St. Petersburg, 1880–1904)
An overpoweringly comprehensive Russian publication of documents of 148 volumes. Only moderately useful because of its random arrangement.

TALLEYRAND, C. M. de, *Mémoires de Talleyrand* (5 vols.) Edited by the Duke of Broglie. (Paris, 1891–92)
The memoirs of the great French diplomat, most similar to Metternich of all his contemporaries. Like Metternich's autobiography, Volume 1 and part of Volume 2 of Talleyrand's *Mémoires* is a fragmentary narrative; the remainder consists of official correspondence. An invaluable source particularly for the period of the Congress of Vienna. Talleyrand's reports to the King

must nevertheless be taken with a grain of salt, since the former Foreign Minister of Napoleon was eager to demonstrate his indispensability.

——, *Correspondance Inédite pendant le Congrès de Vienne*. Edited by G. Pallain. (Paris, 1905)

Rather self-explanatory.

NOTE: Some of the secondary works, such as Webster, Fournier, or Luckwaldt, have appendices containing much primary material. Indications will be found with the appropriate listing.

II. BIOGRAPHIES OR BIOGRAPHICAL MONOGRAPHS

A. On Castlereagh

ALISON, Sir Archibald, *The Lives of Lord Castlereagh and Sir Charles Stewart* (3 vols.) (London, 1861)

The first attempt to rehabilitate Castlereagh, commissioned by his half-brother, Sir Charles Stewart. Based primarily on the *Castlereagh Correspondence* and contemporary sources, it suffers from inadequate documentation and a fatuous analysis. The insight of the author is revealed by the fact that he treats Castlereagh and Stewart as of equal importance. Superseded by Webster's classic, which uses all of Alison's material with a few minor exceptions from the Londonderry archives.

HYDE, H. M., *The Rise of Castlereagh*. (London, 1933)

A very useful account of Castlereagh's career in Ireland and his part in suppressing the Irish rebellion. Very sympathetic to Castlereagh.

LEIGH, Jane, *Castlereagh*. (London, 1951)

A fairly superficial biography. Useless for diplomatic events. Of moderate use for Castlereagh's personality and of the events leading up to his suicide.

MARRIOTT, Sir J. A. R., *Castlereagh, The Political Life of Robert, Second Marquess of Londonderry*. (London, 1936)

A belated vindication by a historian who in his youth had violently attacked Castlereagh. Scant on diplomatic history, but an excellent description of Castlereagh's personality and also of his difficulties domestically.

SALISBURY, Marquess of, *Biographical Essays*. (London, 1905)

The classic defence of Castlereagh by a later Foreign Secretary in the *Quarterly Review* (January 1862). Based on insufficient information, the appropriate volume of Wellington's *Supplementary Dispatches* not having yet appeared, the essay has a certain polemical quality; but it has the merit of being the first substantial recognition of Castlereagh's European vision.

WEBSTER, Sir Charles, *The Foreign Policy of Castlereagh* (2 vols.) Vol. I, 1812–15 (London, 1931); Vol. II, 1815–22 (London, 1925)

The standard work on Castlereagh's foreign policy, drawn primarily from the Foreign Office archives, supplemented by researches in other archives. The material is utilized with an almost pedantic objectivity which eschews analysis to such a degree that the work is more useful as a primary source for the very full quotations than as an account of events. The description of Castlereagh is very fair, although perhaps the British point of view is somewhat overdone. The constant invocation of Metternich's obtuse timidity as a foil to Castlereagh's superior wisdom is quite misleading, as is Webster's account of Continental motivations in general. Excellent appendices contain much otherwise unavailable primary material.

B. On Metternich

NOTE: Because of the wealth of Metternich literature, much of it purely polemical, only the most representative works have been listed.

AUERNHEIMER, Raoul, *Metternich, Statesman and Lover*. (New York, 1940)

An adulatory biography. A silly psychological effort which attempts to relate Metternich's love life to his diplomacy.

BIBL, Victor, *Metternich, der Dämon Österreich's*. (Leipzig, 1936)

As the title implies, a polemical tract by an eminent historian. Since his tool is a textual exegesis of individual phrases, and since he insists on taking Metternich's every manœuvre at face value, Bibl has no difficulty demonstrating that Metternich was a liar, a traitor, a coward, and a fool. A good latter-day illustration of the reaction of the Liberal school of historiography to Metternich.

——, *Metternich in Neuer Beleuchtung*. (Wien, 1928)

Another contribution in Bibl's never-ending war on the conservative statesman. In this volume, Bibl deals with the correspondence between Metternich and the Bavarian minister, Wrede, from 1831 to 1834. In Bibl's skilful hands, it demonstrates that Metternich was a liar, a traitor, a coward, and a fool.

CECIL, Alger, *Metternich*. (London, 1933)

A short, sympathetic biography. Weak on diplomatic history and Austria's domestic policy, but an adequate account of Metternich's motivations.

DU COUDRAY, Helen, *Metternich*. (New Haven, 1936)

Another biography inspired by Srbik's monumental work.

Somewhat emotional, but sensitive characterization of Metternich.

MALLESON, C. B., *Life of Prince Metternich.* (London, 188–)
The first Metternich biography in English. Typical of the reaction of Liberal historiography, it describes Metternich as the intriguer who overthrew the soldier, as the Jesuit who followed Attila, only to enslave Europe for over a generation.

MAZADE, Ch. de, *Un Chancellier d'Ancien Régime. Le Règne Diplomatique de Metternich.* (Paris, 1889)
A French attempt to contrast Metternich with Bismarck to the latter's disadvantage. Rather skimpy, but good in its analysis of Metternich's eighteenth-century roots.

PALEOLOGUE, Maurice, *Romantisme et Diplomatie.* (Paris, 1924)
A study of Talleyrand, Metternich, and Chateaubriand. A particularly rewarding section on Metternich.

SANDEMANS, G. A. C., *Metternich.* (London, 1911)
The first relatively sympathetic Metternich biography in English. Written when not too much material was available, it nevertheless remains perhaps the most balanced effort by an English historian.

SOREL, Albert, *Essais d'Histoire et de Critique.* (Paris, 1883)
A splendid chapter on Metternich, particularly good in its emphasis on Metternich's diplomatic skill. French historians have in general proved kinder to Metternich than their German counterparts, for in order to exalt Napoleon they had to respect his chief antagonist.

SRBIK, Heinrich von, *Metternich der Staatsmann und der Mensch* (2 vols.) (Munich, 1925)
A monumental work exhibiting an extraordinary erudition and power of analysis. In many respects the definitive biography. Unfortunately Srbik slights Metternich's diplomatic skill by exalting his philosophic insights, so that the picture which emerges is almost exactly Metternich's vision of himself as the eighteenth-century philosopher-king. The work contains also an excellent analysis of Austria's domestic difficulties.

——, *Meister der Politik* (Vol. 3). Edited by Erich Marcks. (Stuttgart, 1924)
Sbrik's long chapter on Metternich in this series is a synopsis of his major work and in every respect admirable.

WOODWARD, E. L., *Three Studies in European Conservatism.* (London, 1929)
A useful, brief description of Metternich's thought drawn almost entirely from the "Profession of Faith" in the N.P. Not very profound, but an adequate introduction.

III. SPECIAL STUDIES AND MONOGRAPHS

NOTE: There exists a vast Napoleon literature describing the Coalition of 1814 from the French point of view, such as the works of Thiers, Bignon, Houssaye, Fain, etc, but since their approach is quite parochial they are not listed here.

A. The Period 1812-15

BRYANT, Arthur, *Years of Victory*. (London, 1944)

A rather trivial account of Britain's war with Napoleon between 1802 and 1812, obviously written under the impact of Britain's experience in World War II.

BUCKLAND, C. S. B., *Metternich and the British Government*. (London, 1932)

An extremely interesting account of Metternich's careful policy *vis-à-vis* Britain's between 1809 and 1813 and his skilful handling of a succession of British emissaries of more or less official status. An excellent source for Austria's precarious and intricate domestic situation in the crucial period leading up to the formation of the Fourth Coalition.

DEMELITSCH, Fedor von, *Metternich und Seine Auswaertige Politik*. (Stuttgart, 1898)

Intended as a definitive study of Metternich's foreign policy, but only the first volume was completed before the author's death. A splendid analysis of Metternich's foreign policy between 1809 and 1812. Based primarily on the Vienna archives.

FOURNIER, August, *Der Congress von Chatillon*. (Vienna, 1900)

A pedantic, careful study of Metternich's diplomacy between the Treaty of Teplitz and the fall of Napoleon. Very useful appendices contain Metternich's correspondence with Hudelist; the military deliberations of the Allies; the documents relating to the crisis at Troyes; Hardenberg's diary; and reports from Muenster to the Prince Regent.

LUCKWALDT, Friedrich, *Oesterreich und die Anfänge des Befreiungskrieges von 1813*. (Berlin, 1898)

An extremely well-written and acute study of Metternich's subtle policy leading to Austria's entry into the Coalition. Based primarily on documents in the archives at Vienna. A small but useful appendix of diplomatic documents.

MACUNN, F. J., *The Contemporary English View of Napoleon*. (London, 1914)

OMAN, Carola, *Napoleon at the Channel*. (New York, 1942)

Another trivial wartime effort, drawing the obvious comparisons between Britain's experiences with Hitler and with Napoleon.

ONCKEN, Wilhelm, *Oesterreich und Preussen im Befreiungskriege* (2 vols.) (Berlin, 1880) See IB of Bibliography above.

——, *Die Krisis der letzten Friedensverhandlungen mit Napoleon.* Raumer's Historisches Taschenbuch VI, 5. (Leipzig, 1886)

A useful monograph about the final peace negotiations with Napoleon. Not nearly as full as Fournier, however.

——, *Aus den letzten Monaten des Jahres 1813.* Raumer's Historisches Taschenbuch VI, 2. (Leipzig, 1883)

An excellent monograph on Metternich's diplomacy in the last three months of 1813.

ROSE, John Holland, *Napoleonic Studies.* (London, 1904)

Essays on several aspects of the Napoleonic period including a useful, but not very detailed, chapter on Metternich's policy in 1813.

——, *The Revolutionary and Napoleonic Era, 1789–1815.* (Cambridge, 1894)

A useful account of the survey type. Relatively fuller for the period 1812–15 than for the remainder.

SOREL, Albert, *L'Europe et la Revolution Française.* (Paris, 1904)

Volume 8 of this eminent work deals with the Fourth Coalition. It paints a somewhat exaggerated picture of the Machiavellian Metternich destroying the hero through deviousness and finesse, but is in most respects an admirable study. It contains, also, a sympathetic and generally excellent appraisal of Castlereagh.

B. The Congress of Vienna

FERRERO, Gugliemo, *The Reconstruction of Europe.* (New York, 1941)

A well-written account of the Congress of Vienna. It is based almost entirely on Talleyrand's *Mémoires*, which are taken at face value. The approach is somewhat too moralizing and the relationship to the modern period drawn too patly. Through it all, Talleyrand appears as of almost superhuman quality.

FOURNIER, August, *Die Geheimpolizei auf dem Wiener Kongress.* (Vienna, 1913)

An interesting account of the operations of the very efficient Austrian secret police during the Congress of Vienna, together with a publication of confidential documents intercepted by it. Primarily useful as a demonstration that most secret documents are not worth stealing.

LA GARDE-CHAMBONAS, Comte A. de, *Souvenirs du Congrès de Vienne.* (Paris, 1901)

Spirited reminiscences of the social life at Vienna by a member of the French delegation. In the tradition of the literature of the "dancing" Congress. An amusing description of some of the social lions, such as the old Prince de Ligne. Also available in English and German.

NICOLSON, Harold, *The Congress of Vienna.* (London, 1945)
A study of the diplomacy of the Fourth Coalition and the Congress. Urbanely written, but entirely from the point of view of the professional diplomat, ascribing to negotiating skill what may have been due to a great many other factors. Another paean of praise for Talleyrand.

WEBSTER, Sir Charles, *The Congress of Vienna.* (London, 1934)
Written at the request of the Foreign Office in preparation for the Versailles conference to draw the lessons from the other great peace-making effort. A straightforward, pedantic account, which somewhat over-emphasizes Castlereagh's role. Useful also as an illustration that the lessons of history are not as simple as an arithmetical example and that success is not necessarily defined by the exact opposite of failure. Webster's conclusion that it was one of the errors of Vienna to permit France to negotiate and the acceptance of his advice not to repeat this mistake with respect to Germany turned out to be one of the banes of the treaty of Versailles.

WEIL, Commandant M-H, *Les Dessous du Congrès de Vienne* (2 vols.) (Paris, 1917)
Another publication of confidential documents intercepted by the Austrian secret police. Same general comment applies as to Fournier's work above.

C. The Period after the Congress of Vienna to 1822

NOTE: No first-rate study of either the Congress of Vienna or its aftermath exists. By the time the documents became available, historians were engaged in a self-righteous condemnation of the period.

BRYANT, Arthur, *The Age of Elegance.* (London, 1950)
A well-written, useful account of life in Britain between 1812 and 1822. Not very serious, but useful as background material.

CRESSON, W. P., *The Holy Alliance.* (New York, 1922)
A study of the relations of the Holy Alliance with the New World, leading to the promulgation of the Monroe Doctrine. Not very useful for an understanding of the major events in Europe.

MARRIOTT, Sir J. A. R., *The Eastern Question.* (Oxford, 1925)
A useful survey of the Eastern question, but very scant on the period of this book. Good background material.

MOLDEN, Ernst, *Zur Geschichte des Osterreichisch-Russischen Gegensatzes.* (Vienna, 1916)

A useful account of Austro-Russian tensions between 1815 and 1818, somewhat affected by the wartime atmosphere of its origin. Based on the Vienna archives.

MUEHLENBECK, E., *Etude sur les Origines de la Sainte Alliance.* (Paris, 1887)
An interesting study, well told, of Alexander's increasing religious exaltation and his relations with Baroness Kruedener.

NAEF, Werner, *Zur Geschichte der Heiligen Allianz.* (Bern, 1928)
An excellent monograph discussing the origin of the Holy Alliance. A very good analysis of the nature and the import of the textual changes of Metternich in Alexander's drafts.

PHILLIPS, W. A., *The Confederation of Europe.* (London, 1913)
The first systematic attempt to rehabilitate Castlereagh. Based on Foreign Office documents, it is not nearly so complete as Webster's work, but its analysis is perhaps more lucid.

RIEBEN, Hans, *Prinzipiengrundlage und Diplomatie in Metternich's Europapolitik, 1815–48.* (Bern, 1942)
A very good account of the conceptual basis of Metternich's policy; an adequate summary of his diplomacy.

SCHENK, H. G., *The Aftermath of the Napoleonic Wars.* (London, 1947)
A neo-Marxist account of the social struggle following the Congress of Vienna. A good, if one-sided, Ph.D. thesis. Useless for diplomatic history.

SCHMALZ, Hans, *Versuche einer Gesamteuropäischen Organisation, 1815–20.* (Bern, 1940)
A usefully documented monograph of Metternich's policy of intervention with special emphasis on the Congress of Troppau. Based primarily on the Vienna archives.

SCHWARZ, Wilhelm, *Die Heilige Allianz.* (Stuttgart, 1935)
An extremely well-written account of the post-Vienna period, which suffers from the fact that it never distinguishes between the Holy and the Quadruple Alliance and from a tendency to sacrifice accuracy to journalistic effect.

WARD, Sir A. W., *The Period of the Congresses.* (New York, 1919)

D. Miscellaneous Sources

BAILLIEU, Paul, *Die Memoiren Metternich's.* Historische Zeitschrift, 1880.
A devastating attack on the autobiographical fragment of Metternich in N.P. I on the basis of documents printed in the remaining volumes. It demolishes the value of Metternich's autobiography as a historical, although not as a psychological, source; but the remainder of the N.P. remains invaluable for its documents.

BRINTON, Crane, *The Lives of Talleyrand.* (New York, 1936)
A well-written, occasionally brilliant, book, but too thin for serious research.

COOPER, Duff, *Talleyrand.* (London, 1932)
A good biography of Talleyrand, although very one-sided and accepting Talleyrand's evaluation of himself at face value.

CROWE, Eyre Evans, *History of the Reigns of Louis XVIII and Charles X*, (2 vols.) (London, 1854)
Particularly useful for its account of the two Restorations in Volume 1. Small, but useful appendices.

HALL, John R., *The Bourbon Restoration.* (London, 1909)
A well-written, usefully documented account.

LOCKHARDT, J. G., *The Peacemakers.* (London, 1932)
A collection of essays on Talleyrand, Metternich, Alexander, Pitt, Castlereagh, Canning, and Wilberforce. Mediocre and superficial.

MEINECKE, Friedrich, *Weltbuergertum und Nationalstaat.* (Munich, 1928)
An extraordinary study by an eminent historian of the conflict between the cosmopolitan and the nationalist values of the nineteenth century.

MIKHAILOVITCH, Le Grand Duc Nicolas, *L'Empereur Alexander* I (2 vols.) (St. Petersbnrg, 1912)
The most comprehensive biography of a strange man. The analysis rarely goes very deep, but the documents are valuable.

——, *Les Rapports Diplomatiques du Lebzeltern.* (St. Petersburg, 1913)
An extremely interesting discussion and compilation of the reports of Austria's ambassador at St. Petersburg, although its analysis of Metternich's policy is weak.

ONCKEN, Wilhelm, *Das Zeitalter der Revolution, der Kaiserreiches und der Befreiungskriege* (2 vols.) (Berlin, 1886)
An excellent account of the period of revolutionary wars. Volume 2 deals with the period between 1800 and 1815. Particularly good in its analysis of Austria's policy.

SCHIEMANN, Theodor, *Geschichte Russlands unter Nikolaus I* (4 vols.) (Berlin, 1904)
Volume 1 is a very good biography of Alexander with a useful appendix of primary sources.

SCHMIDT-PHISELDEK, *Die Politik nach den Grundsätzen der Heiligen Allianz.* (Kopenhagen, 1822)
A contemporary apologia for the Holy Alliance. Interesting for this reason.

SRBIK, Heinrich von, *Deutsche Einheit* (4 vols.) (Munich, 1936)
A profound study of the quest for German unity and the

struggle between Austria and Prussia. Volume 1 deals with the Metternich period.

TEMPERLEY, Harold, *The Foreign Policy of Canning*. (London, 1925)

VIERECK, Peter, *Conservatism Revisited.* (New York, 1949)
A polemical treatise on Metternich, Emperor Franz, and various contemporaries, all of whom emerge as representative types of the author's special demonology. An interesting effort, but in the tradition of the French essay, not of serious historical research.

IV. BASIC REFERENCE WORKS

Cambridge History of British Foreign Policy (5 vols.). Edited by A. W. Ward. (Cambridge, 1907)
Volume 2 deals with the period in question. The chapter on the period 1816–22 was written by W. A. Phillips and formed the basis of his *Confederation of Europe*. Contains a useful bibliography.

Cambridge Modern History. Edited by Sir A. W. Ward and G. P. Gooch. (New York, 1922–23)
Volumes 9 and 10 deal with the period covered by this treatise. In many respects a better account than the C.H.B.F.P., it also has a much fuller bibliography.

SCHNABEL, F., *Deutsche Geschichte im Neunzehnten Jahrhundert* (3 vols.) (Freiburg, 1929–37)
An excellent survey of German nineteenth-century history. Very skimpy on diplomatic history; but extremely useful for an analysis of domestic institutions and intellectual development.

SPRINGER, Anton, *Geschichte Oesterreich's seit dem Wiener Frieden von 1809* (2 vols.) (Leipzig, 1863)
An excellent account, particularly good on Austria's domestic problems. Its analysis of Metternich and the Empire is balanced and sane.

STÄHLIN, Karl, *Geschichte Russlands von den Anfängen bis zum Gegenwart*, (4 vols.) (Berlin, 1935)
Volume 3 deals with the period in question.

STERN, Alfred, *Geschichte Europas seit den Vertraegen von 1815 bis zum Frankfurter Frieden von 1871* (10 vols.) (Munich–Berlin, 1913–24)
A major work of the survey type, but with an excellent blending of documentary material. Small but useful appendices contain illustrative documentary material. Volumes 1 and 2 cover the period of this treatise.

TREITSCHKE, Heinrich von, *Deutsche Geschichte in Neunzehnten Jahrhundert* (5 vols.) (Leipzig, 1880)
The classic nationalist history of Germany. Needless to say, Metternich's cosmopolitan values were anathema to the author and

his description of Metternich's policy is poisonous. Volumes 1 and 2 deal with the period in question.

V. OTHER REFERENCES

BRINTON, Crane, *Anatomy of Revolution.* (New York, 1938)

FERRERO, Gugliemo, *The Principles of Power.* (New York, 1942)

JOUVENEL, Bertrand de, *On Power.* (New York, 1949)

MORGENTHAU, Hans, *Politics among Nations.* (New York, 1950)

PETTEE, George, *Process of Revolution.* (New York, 1938)

Index

SENTRY EDITIONS

1. A Week on the Concord and Merrimack Rivers *by Henry David Thoreau*
2. A Diary from Dixie *by Mary Boykin Chesnut, edited by Ben Ames Williams*
3. The Education of Henry Adams: An Autobiography
4. J.B. *by Archibald MacLeish*
5. John C. Calhoun *by Margaret L. Coit*
6. The Maritime History of Massachusetts: 1783–1860 *by Samuel Eliot Morison*
7. My Antonia *by Willa Cather*
8. Patterns of Culture *by Ruth Benedict*
9. Sam Clemens of Hannibal *by Dixon Wecter*
10. The Great Crash, 1929 *by John Kenneth Galbraith*
11. The Year of Decision: 1846 *by Bernard DeVoto*
12. Young Man with a Horn *by Dorothy Baker*
13. Mein Kampf *by Adolf Hitler*
14. The Vital Center *by Arthur M. Schlesinger, Jr.*
15. The Course of Empire *by Bernard DeVoto*
16. O Pioneers! *by Willa Cather*
17. The Armada *by Garrett Mattingly*
18. American Capitalism *by John Kenneth Galbraith*
19. The Emancipation of Massachusetts *by Brooks Adams*
20. Beyond the Hundredth Meridian *by Wallace Stegner*
21. Paul Revere and the World He Lived In *by Esther Forbes*
22. Chosen Country *by John Dos Passos*
23. The Tragic Era *by Claude G. Bowers*
24. Parkinson's Law *by C. Northcote Parkinson*
25. Across the Wide Missouri *by Bernard DeVoto*
26. Manhattan Transfer *by John Dos Passos*
27. A Cartoon History of Architecture *by Osbert Lancaster*
28. The Song of the Lark *by Willa Cather*
29. A Mirror for Witches *by Esther Forbes*
30. The Collected Poems of Archibald MacLeish
31. The Journals of Lewis and Clark *edited by Bernard DeVoto*
32. Builders of the Bay Colony *by Samuel Eliot Morison*
33. Mont-Saint-Michel and Chartres *by Henry Adams*
34. Laughing Boy *by Oliver La Farge*
35. Wild America *by Roger Tory Peterson and James Fisher*
36. Paths to the Present *by Arthur M. Schlesinger*
37. U.S.A. *by John Dos Passos*
38. Economic Development *by John Kenneth Galbraith*
39. The Crisis of the Old Order *by Arthur M. Schlesinger, Jr.*
40. Three Soldiers *by John Dos Passos*
41. The Road to Xanadu *by John Livingston Lowes*

(continued on next page)

42. More in Sorrow *by Wolcott Gibbs*
43. The Coming of the New Deal *by Arthur M. Schlesinger, Jr.*
44. The Big Sky *by A. B. Guthrie, Jr.*
45. The Dartmouth Bible *edited by Roy B. Chamberlin and Herman Feldman*
46. The Far Side of Paradise *by Arthur Mizener*
47. The Politics of Upheaval *by Arthur M. Schlesinger, Jr.*
48. Jefferson and Hamilton *by Claude G. Bowers*
49. The Price of Union *by Herbert Agar*
50. Mark Twain's America *and* Mark Twain at Work *by Bernard DeVoto*
51. Jefferson in Power *by Claude G. Bowers*
52. Fifty Best American Short Stories 1915–1965 *edited by Martha Foley*
53. Names on the Land *by George R. Stewart*
54. Two Kinds of Time *by Graham Peck*
55. The Young Jefferson 1743–1789 *by Claude G. Bowers*
56. The Promised Land *by Mary Antin*
57. Personal History *by Vincent Sheean*
58. The New Industrial State *by John Kenneth Galbraith*
59. The Battle of Gettysburg *by Frank A. Haskell, edited by Bruce Catton*
60. On Becoming a Person *by Carl R. Rogers*
61. A History of Mexico *by Henry Bamford Parkes*
62. Flaubert and Madame Bovary *by Francis Steegmuller*
63. Paths of American Thought *edited by Arthur M. Schlesinger, Jr., and Morton White*
64. The South Since the War *by Sidney Andrews*
65. The Elizabethan World *by Lacey Baldwin Smith*
66. Literature and the Sixth Sense *by Philip Rahv*
67. Turbulent Years *by Irving Bernstein*
68. Renaissance Diplomacy *by Garrett Mattingly*
69. The Death of the Past *by J. H. Plumb*
70. The Affluent Society *by John Kenneth Galbraith*
71. The Way We Go to War *by Merlo J. Pusey*
72. Roosevelt and Morgenthau *by John Morton Blum*
73. The Lean Years *by Irving Bernstein*
74. Henry VIII *by Lacey Baldwin Smith*
75. Presidential Government *by James MacGregor Burns*
76. Silent Spring *by Rachel Carson*
77. The Book of Family Therapy *by Andrew Ferber, Marilyn Mendelsohn, and Augustus Napier*
78. The Beginnings of Modern American Psychiatry *by Patrick Mullahy*
79. A World Restored *by Henry A. Kissinger*

SE 15